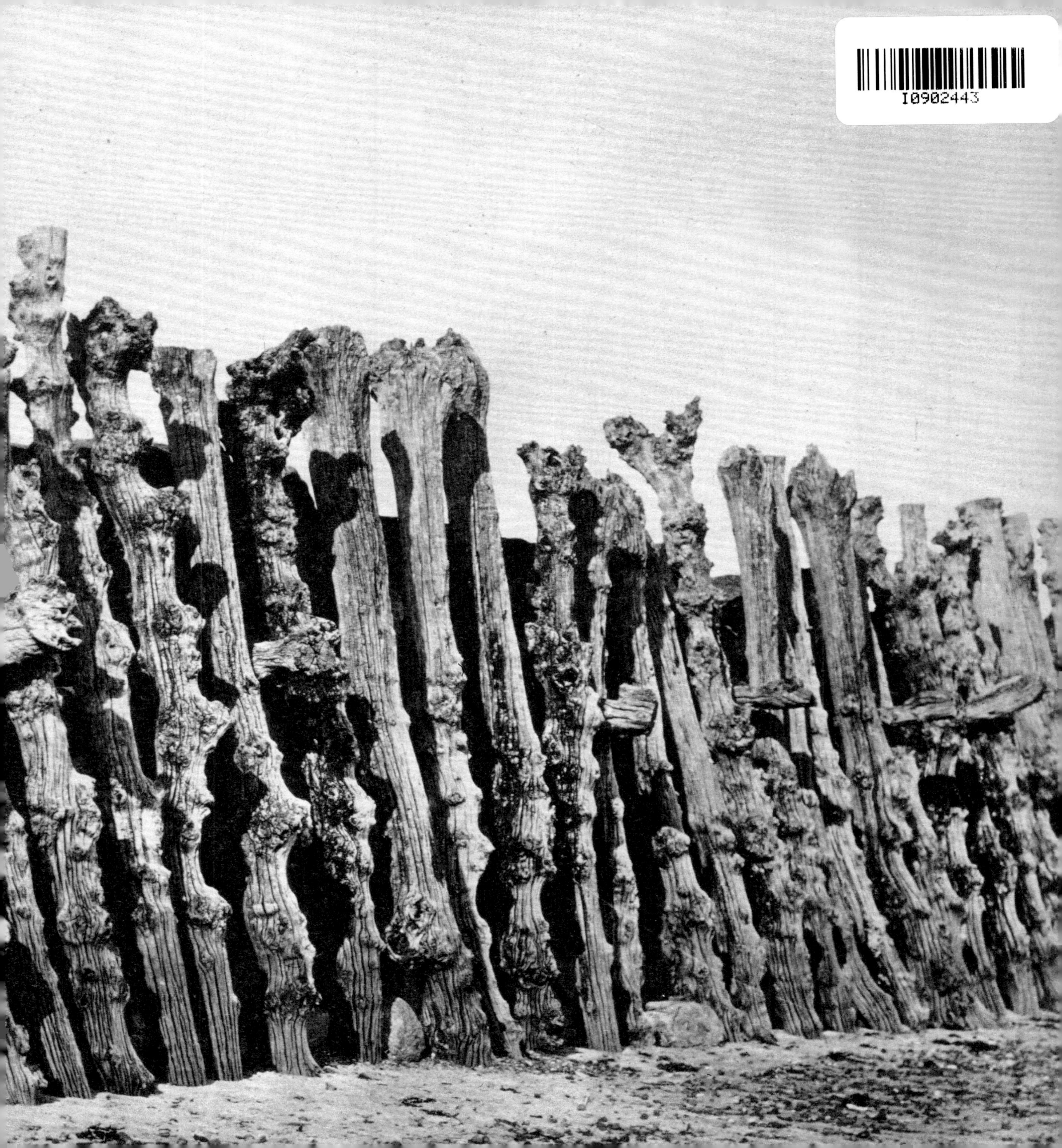

# STONES TO STAINS

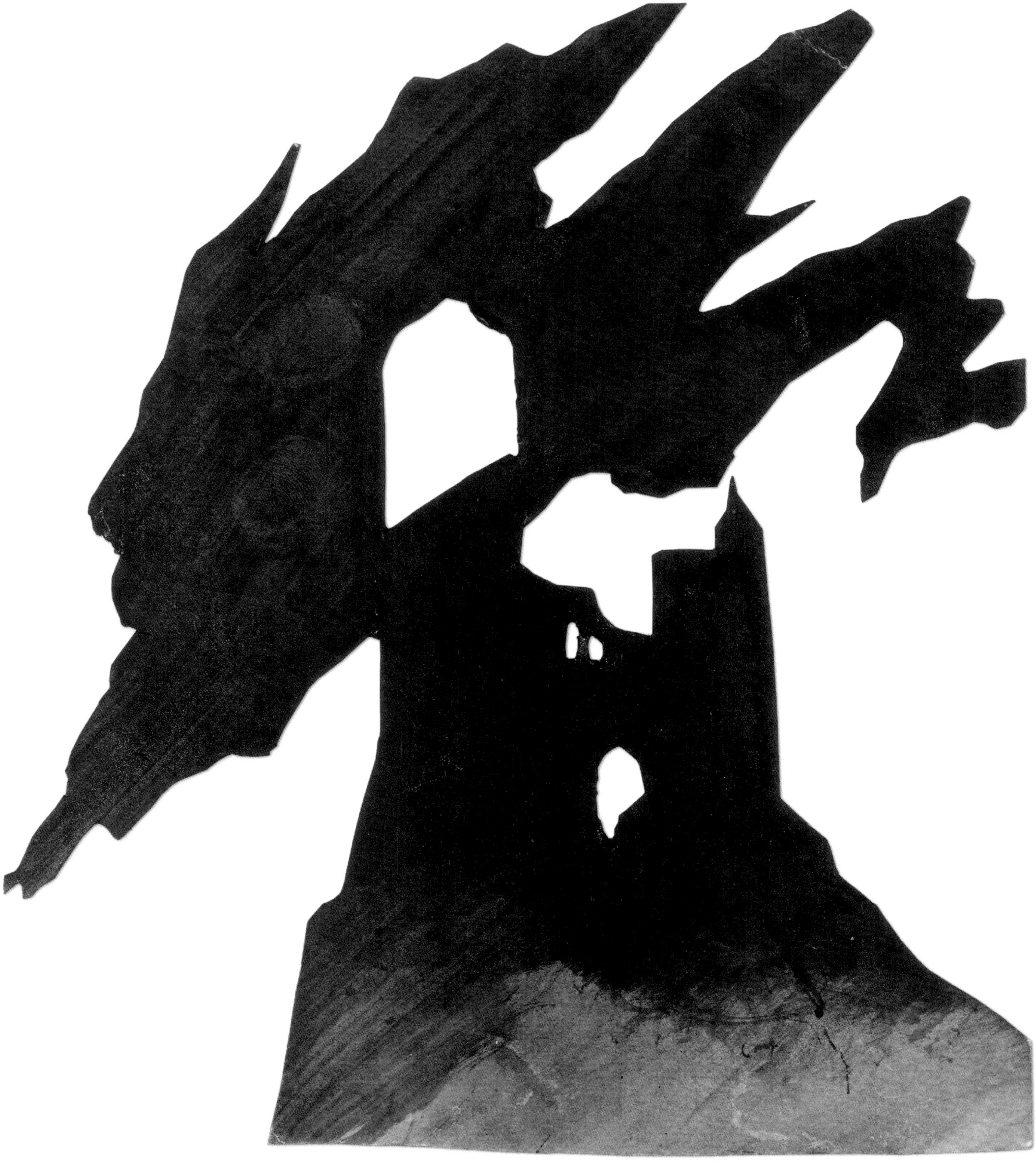

# STONES TO STAINS

## THE DRAWINGS OF VICTOR HUGO

Cynthia Burlingham and Allegra Pesenti

With essays by Cynthia Burlingham,
Allegra Pesenti, and Florian Rodari

Hammer Museum
University of California, Los Angeles

DelMonico Books•Prestel
Munich London New York

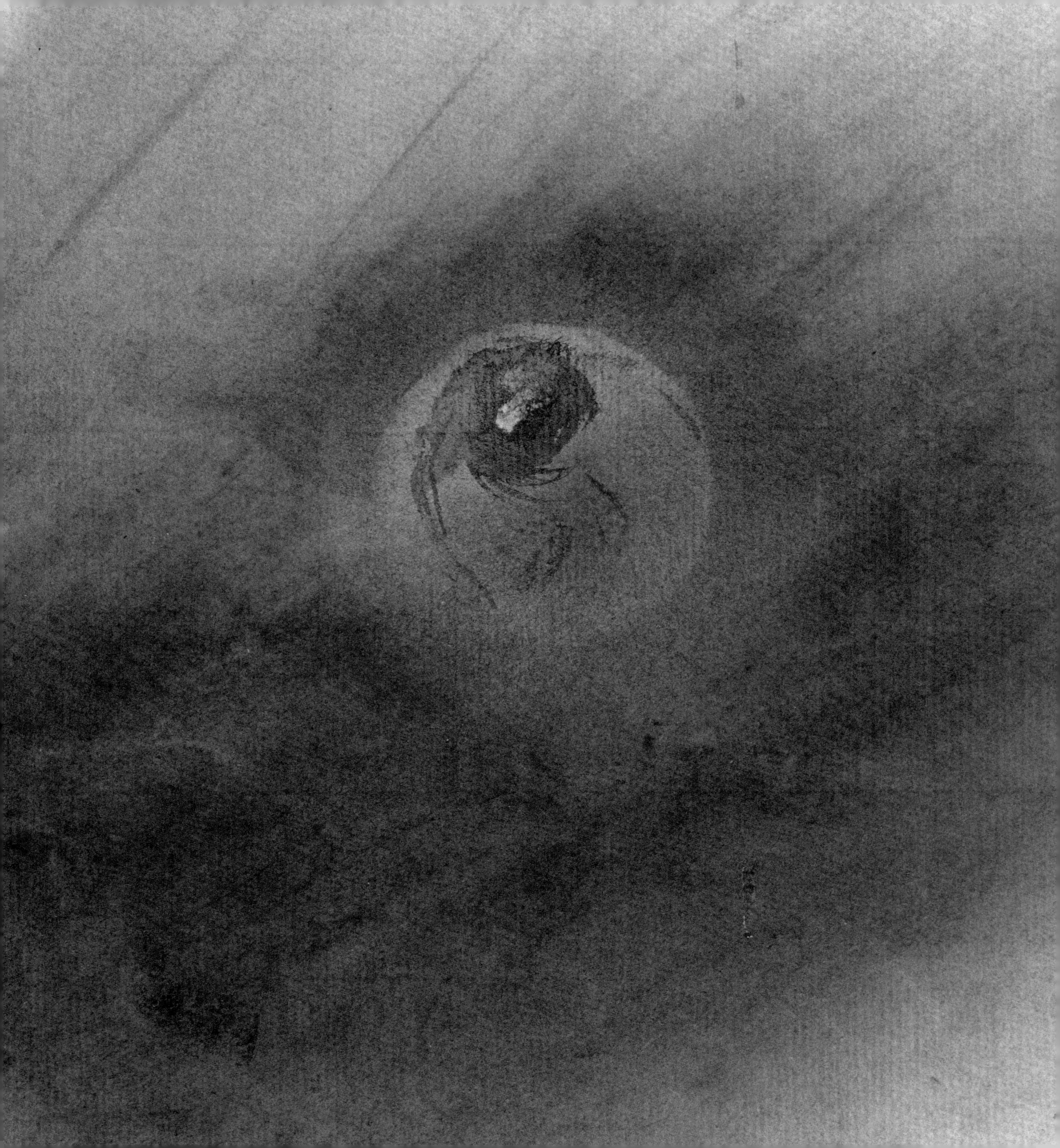

In memory of Debbie Snyder

**Published on the occasion of the exhibition *Stones to Stains: The Drawings of Victor Hugo*, organized and presented by the Hammer Museum, Los Angeles, September 27–December 30, 2018.**

**The exhibition is curated by Cynthia Burlingham, deputy director, curatorial affairs, and Allegra Pesenti, associate director and senior curator, Grunwald Center for the Graphic Arts, Hammer Museum, in collaboration with independent scholar Florian Rodari.**

***Stones to Stains: The Drawings of Victor Hugo* is made possible by lead support from Alice and Nahum Lainer. Major support is provided by the LLWW Foundation. Generous funding is also provided by Frances F. L. Beatty and Allen Adler, Catherine Benkaim and Barbara Timmer, the John R. Eckel Jr. Foundation, Nancy Lainer, Margo Leavin, Lee Ramer, Anne-Marie and Alex Spataru, Susan Steinhauser and Dan Greenberg, and Karen and Gary Winnick, with additional support from Clare Casademont and Michael Metz.**

**This exhibition has benefited from exceptional loans from the Bibliothèque nationale de France and the Maisons de Victor Hugo, Paris / Guernesey.**

Published in 2018 by the Hammer Museum and DelMonico Books•Prestel



Hammer Museum
10899 Wilshire Boulevard
Los Angeles, CA 90024-4201
www.hammer.ucla.edu

The Hammer Museum is operated and partially funded by the University of California, Los Angeles. Occidental Petroleum Corporation built the museum's building and established its endowment.

DelMonico Books, an imprint of Prestel, a member of Verlagsgruppe Random House GmbH

Prestel Verlag
Neumarkter Strasse 28
81673 Munich

Prestel Publishing Ltd.
14–17 Wells Street
London W1T 3PD

Prestel Publishing
900 Broadway, Suite 603
New York, NY 10003

www.prestel.com

Designers: Miko McGinty and Rita Jules, Miko McGinty Inc.
Editor: Karen Jacobson
Proofreader: Dianne Woo
Indexer: Kathleen Preciado
Director of publication management: Melanie Crader
Project manager: Courtney Smith
Color separations: Professional Graphics, Inc., Rockford, Illinois
Printer: Conti Tipocolor S.p.A., Florence, Italy

The book is typeset in Fakt and printed on Gardapat Kiara paper.

ISBN: 978-3-7913-5764-5

Library of Congress Cataloging-in-Publication Data

Names: Burlingham, Cynthia, 1955– | Pesenti, Allegra. | Rodari, Florian. | Hammer Museum, organizer, host institution.
Title: Stones to stains : the drawings of Victor Hugo / Cynthia Burlingham and Allegra Pesenti ; with essays by Cynthia Burlingham, Allegra Pesenti, and Florian Rodari.
Description: Los Angeles, CA : Hammer Museum, University of California, Los Angeles ; Munich ; New York : DelMonico Books-Prestel, 2018. | Includes bibliographical references and index.
Identifiers: LCCN 2018020070 | ISBN 9783791357645 (hardback)
Subjects: LCSH: Hugo, Victor, 1802–1885—Exhibitions. | BISAC: ART / Individual Artists / Monographs. | ART / History / Baroque & Rococo. | ART / History / Modern (late 19th Century to 1945).
Classification: LCC NC248.H86 A4 2018 | DDC 741—dc23 LC record available at https://lccn.loc.gov/2018020070

A CIP catalogue record for this book is available from the British Library.

# CONTENTS

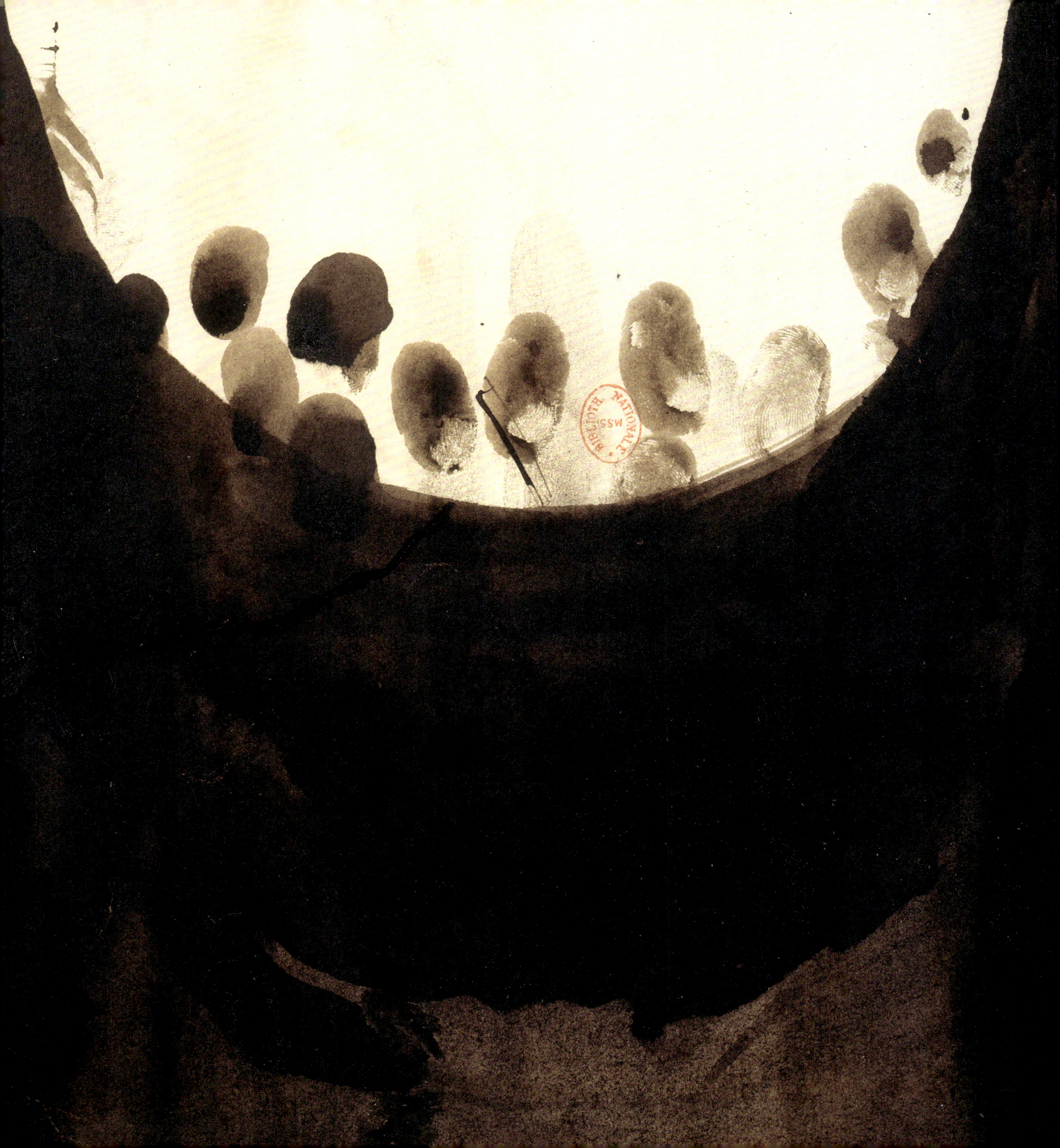
BIBLIOTH. NATIONALE

## FOREWORD

The Hammer Museum is pleased to be organizing the first US exhibition in two decades of the drawings of the nineteenth-century French poet, novelist, playwright, and critic Victor Hugo. One of the greatest writers of all time, Hugo was also an accomplished draftsman and produced a lesser-known but remarkable body of works on paper. His drawing practice was largely a private endeavor, and although more than three thousand sheets by him survive today, they were rarely seen in public during his lifetime. The sole American museum exhibition devoted to his graphic work to date was organized by the Drawing Center in New York in 1998, when I was director there, and I am thrilled that the Hammer is introducing Hugo's experimental and enigmatic practice to a new generation in the United States. *Stones to Stains: The Drawings of Victor Hugo*, beautifully conceived and curated by Cynthia Burlingham and Allegra Pesenti, includes a major selection of drawings and photographs that were not seen in New York and are thus being presented to American audiences for the first time. The Hammer has long been committed to showing a wide spectrum of historical and contemporary works on paper through exhibitions such as *Tea and Morphine: Women in Paris, 1880–1914*, *Rachel Whiteread Drawings*, and *Zarina: Paper Like Skin* and through the acquisition of works on paper by the Grunwald Center for the Graphic Arts and the Hammer Contemporary Collection. We are pleased to add the remarkable drawings of Victor Hugo to this list.

My deepest gratitude goes to the institutional and private lenders to the exhibition who entrusted us with their rare and fragile drawings. We are unusually fortunate to have an exceptional number of loans from both the Bibliothèque nationale de France and the Maison de Victor Hugo in Paris, and I extend my thanks to Laurence Engel, president, and Thierry Grillet, director of cultural affairs, Bibliothèque nationale de France, and to Gérard Audinet, director, and Claire Lecourt-Aubry, registrar, Maison de Victor Hugo. I am delighted that this project has provided the opportunity for a renewed partnership with our great friend and colleague Florian Rodari, who was my collaborator on the 1998 exhibition. I would also like to extend special thanks to Christophe Girard for his help in ensuring the success of the exhibition as well as to Christophe Lemoine, consul general of France in Los Angeles.

An ambitious exhibition such as this can be realized only with the important contributions of our supporters. We are deeply indebted to Alice and Nahum Lainer for their major support and enduring friendship. We express our sincere gratitude to the LLWW Foundation and acknowledge Frances F. L. Beatty and Allen Adler, Catherine Benkaim and Barbara Timmer, Clare Casademont and Michael Metz, the John R. Eckel Jr. Foundation, Nancy Lainer, Margo Leavin, Lee Ramer, Anne-Marie and Alex Spataru, Susan Steinhauser and Dan Greenberg, and Karen and Gary Winnick for their generous contributions to this exhibition.

Ann Philbin
Director, Hammer Museum

## ACKNOWLEDGMENTS

*Stones to Stains: The Drawings of Victor Hugo* is the result of an extended period of research on our part and has come to fruition with the support of many people across Europe and the United States. Our first words of thanks go to the Hammer Museum's director, Ann Philbin, who encouraged us to revisit the drawings of Victor Hugo almost twenty years after her own exhibition on the subject at the Drawing Center in New York. We have endeavored to shed new light on the work and to propose a different though no less important presentation of it. To date, these are the only two public surveys of Hugo's visual oeuvre in the United States, and although the drawings are still little known, they remain fundamentally vital in subject, medium, and composition. We are dearly grateful to our friend and collaborator Florian Rodari for his insight and the beautiful elucidation of our theme in his essay. The exhibition was expertly administered in its early stages by Leslie Cozzi, former curatorial associate, and more recently by Matthieu Vahanian, curatorial assistant at the Grunwald Center for the Graphic Arts. We also thank Matthieu for lending his knowledge and acumen to the making of this book and for contributing the chronology.

The exhibition could not have been realized without the commitment of two primary lenders, the Bibliothèque nationale de France and the Maison de Victor Hugo in Paris. We are deeply indebted to our colleagues at each of these institutions for appreciating the importance of this survey and for validating it with their loans. We thank the president of the Bibliothèque nationale, Laurence Engel, and Thierry Grillet, director of cultural affairs, along with their exceptional curatorial team, in particular Thomas Cazentre, curator, Modern and Contemporary Manuscripts; Guillaume Fau, head, Modern and Contemporary Manuscripts; Isabelle le Masne de Chermont, director, Department of Manuscripts; Charlotte Servat, registrar; Valérie Sueur-Hermel, curator in charge of nineteenth-century prints, Prints and Photography Department; Anne Verdure-Mary, curator, Department of Manuscripts; and Charles-Eloi Vial, curator, Modern and Contemporary Manuscripts. Gérard Audinet, director of the Maisons de Victor Hugo, Paris / Guernesey, has been a gracious ally throughout this project, and we are greatly appreciative of his support and of the unfailing assistance of registrar Claire Lecourt-Aubry, who was crucial to the success of this project. We also thank Alexandrine Achille in the Department of Photographs and Stéphanie Duluc, researcher at Hauteville House. At the Musée d'Orsay, we were kindly assisted by Thomas Galifot, curator of photographs, and Fabrice Golec, print room superintendent, as well as registrar Candice Brunerie, and we thank them and the museum's president, Laurence des Cars, for the loan of photographs by the Hugo circle. For other loans from France, we thank Marie-Jean Mazurier, director of the Maison Vacquerie–Musée Victor Hugo, and Christine Martin, head of cultural affairs, City of Dijon, and the staff of the Musée des Beaux-Arts de Dijon, including curator Sandrine Balan, archivist Anne Camuset, chief curator David Liot, and registrar Éléonore Markus.

The exhibition received generous loans from the Nationalmuseum Stockholm, and for these we extend our thanks to Berndt Arell, director general; Brigitta Castenfors, acting director general; Per Hedström, director of exhibitions; and Carl-Johan Olsson, curator, as well as to Karin Sandstedt, Marina Strouzer-Rodov, and Jonas Burvall. We are equally indebted to our institutional colleagues in the United States for agreeing to lend their rare holdings of works by Hugo. At the Art Institute of Chicago, we are grateful to James Rondeau, president and Eloise W. Martin Director; Kevin Salatino, Anne Vogt Fuller and Marion Titus Searle Chair and Curator of Prints and Drawings; Victoria Sancho Lobis, Prince Trust Curator; Natasha Derrickson; Toni Owen; Aimee Marshall; and Emily Ziemba. At the Metropolitan Museum of Art, we thank Nadine Orenstein, Drue Heinz Curator in Charge of the Department of Drawings and Prints, and her colleagues Ashley Dunn, Allison Rudnick, Jillian Pfifferling, and Mary Zuber. At the Morgan Library, New York, we thank director Colin B. Bailey, together with John Bidwell, Astor Curator and Department Head, Printed Books and Bindings; Isabelle Dervaux, Acquavella Curator of Modern and Contemporary Drawings; Jennifer Tonkovich, Eugene and Clare Thaw Curator; John D. Alexander; Eva Soos; and Sophie Worley. At Yale University Art Gallery, we thank director Stephanie Wiles, together with Suzanne Boorsch, Robert L. Solley Curator of Prints and Drawings; Elisabeth Hodermarsky, Sutphin Family Senior Associate Curator of Prints and Drawings; and Lynne Addison.

A number of individuals granted access to their collections during the course of our research and agreed to part with their drawings for the duration of the exhibition. We thank Almine and Bernard Ruiz-Picasso and the Fundación Almine y Bernard Ruiz-Picasso para el Arte, and we are especially indebted to curator and secretary François Bellet for his time and counsel and to Iro Biehler, Thomas Chaineux, Anne-Claire Duperrier, and Gwenvael Launay for their kind support. For the loan of outstanding examples of Hugo's draftsmanship, we thank David Lachenmann, with the assistance of Julia Lachenmann; Louis-Antoine and Véronique Prat, with the assistance of Philippe Cros and Laurence Lhinares; Frances Beatty and Allen Adler, Alexander Adler, with the assistance of Rachel Graham; and Gordon VeneKlasen, with the assistance of Colleen Cunningham, John McGill, and Jeff Alford.

We pay tribute to Pierre Georgel, author of the forthcoming catalogue raisonné of drawings by Victor Hugo, for laying the groundwork for all current research and scholarship in the field and for his guidance throughout this project. We were very fortunate to have met Laurence Devinat, and we extend our gratitude to her and her family for our enlightening visits and conversations. A special word of thanks goes to Christophe Girard, former mayor, 4th arrondissement of Paris, for his interest and encouragement. For the informative exchanges we held on the subject of this exhibition, we thank Henri Zerner, professor emeritus of history of art and architecture, Harvard University; Prof. Dr. Raphael Rosenberg, Department of Art History, University of Vienna; and Prof. Dr. Hermann Mildenberger, head of the Abteilung Graphische Sammlungen, Klassik Stiftung Weimar. During the course of our work on Hugo, we sought the help of numerous colleagues and collectors, and we acknowledge them all for their invaluable support: Dr. Szilvia Bodnár, Museum of Fine Arts, Budapest; Hugo Chapman, British Museum; Line Clausen Pedersen, Ny Carlsberg Glyptotek, Copenhagen; James Cuno, president and CEO, J. Paul Getty Trust; George Goldner, formerly at the Metropolitan Museum of Art; Mazie Harris, J. Paul Getty Museum; Virginia Heckert, J. Paul Getty Museum; Lee Hendrix, formerly at the J. Paul Getty Museum; John and Paul Herring; Max Hollein, formerly at the Fine Arts Museums of San Francisco and now at the Metropolitan Museum of Art; Marie Hugo; Miriam Y. Katz, J. Paul Getty Museum; Bernd and Verena Klüser, Munich; Edouard Kopp, Harvard Art Museums; Hans P. Kraus; Paul LeClerc, former president and CEO, New York Public Library; Rachel Matta, J. Paul Getty Museum; David Rade, Swan Isle Press; Angela Roche, British Museum; David Rodes, director emeritus of the Grunwald Center for the Graphic Arts; Marie-Pierre Salé and Xavier Salmon, Musée du Louvre; Jacob Samuel, UCLA Department of Art; Hinrich Sieveking; Victoria Steele; Naoko Takahatake, Los Angeles County Museum of Art; Martha Tedeschi, Harvard Art Museums; and Benjamin Weiss, Museum of Fine Arts, Boston.

We attribute the success of *Stones to Stains* to the outstanding staff of the Hammer Museum and thank our colleagues for their contributions to its making. Connie Butler and our curatorial colleagues Erin Christovale, Anne Ellegood, Aram Moshayedi, Ikechukwu Onyewuenyi, MacKenzie Stevens, and Vanessa Arizmendi have stood by us through the intricacies of its planning. Melanie Crader and Courtney Smith ensured the smooth management of the exhibition and this publication. Portland McCormick, Haley Di Pressi, Susan Hersey, Jean-ha Park, and former assistant registrar Alex Bancroft expertly handled the registrarial responsibilities. Justin Glasson, Veridiana Pontes, Curt Shepard, Hannah Howe, Julia Howe, Sara Friedman, and the development team rallied financial support for the exhibition. Scott Tennent, Mitch Marr, Susan Edwards, Chisa Hughes, Nancy Lee, Arielle Feldman, and the communications team, as well as designers Patrick O'Rourke and Tara Morris, mastered the promotional side and digital presence of the exhibition. Claudia Bestor, Janani Subramanian, Alison Lambert, Theresa Sotto, Zoe Silverman, and Olivia Fales engage our public through their dynamic cultural and educational programs. Sara Beattie and Brooke Berlin accompanied the exhibition with a selection of items available at the museum's store. For the production and installation of the exhibition, we rely on the expertise of

Jason Pugh, Michael Terzanc, Luke Whitlatch, and Peter Gould. We are, as ever, grateful to our paper conservator, Mo McGee, for her involvement. We also acknowledge the participation of Henry Clancy, Hilary Fahlsing, Peter Fox, Hanna Girma, Sarah Gnirs, Michael Harrison, Alec Moore, Daniel Munoz, Kirk Nickel, Michael Nock, and Margot Stokol. For her sincere passion and knowledge of Victor Hugo, we thank Laure Murat, director, Center for European and Russian Studies, UCLA.

Book designers Miko McGinty and Rita Jules, together with Claire Bidwell, approached this publication with characteristic talent and sensitivity to the subject. We thank them and editor Karen Jacobson for our ongoing collaboration. We are also grateful to Deke Dusinberre for his exemplary work on the translations, to Dianne Woo for proofreading, and to Kathleen Preciado for indexing. The team at Professional Graphics met the challenge of reproducing these shadowy works on paper, as did Dr. Roberto Conti, Marta Conti, Laura Cuccoli, and their colleagues at Conti Tipocolor. We entrusted Johnson Marklee with the installation design and thank Sharon Johnston, Mark Lee, Andri Luescher, and Toshiki Niimi for lending their vision to the project.

We are, as ever, thankful for the major and enduring support of Alice and Nahum Lainer. We join our director in conveying our sincere appreciation to the LLWW Foundation, Frances F. L. Beatty and Allen Adler, Catherine Benkaim and Barbara Timmer, the John R. Eckel Jr. Foundation, Nancy Lainer, Margo Leavin, Lee Ramer, Anne-Marie and Alex Spataru, Susan Steinhauser and Dan Greenberg, Karen and Gary Winnick, and Clare Casademont and Michael Metz. Finally we are dearly grateful to Roland Augustine, Carolyne Aycager, Evgenia Citkowitz, Lucy Gale, Konstantin Kakanias, Leon Kenyon, and Kate Kornberg for their spirited support of our extensive forays into the visionary realm of Victor Hugo.

Cynthia Burlingham
Deputy Director of Curatorial Affairs, Hammer Museum
Director, Grunwald Center for the Graphic Arts, Hammer Museum

Allegra Pesenti
Associate Director and Senior Curator, Grunwald Center for the Graphic Arts, Hammer Museum

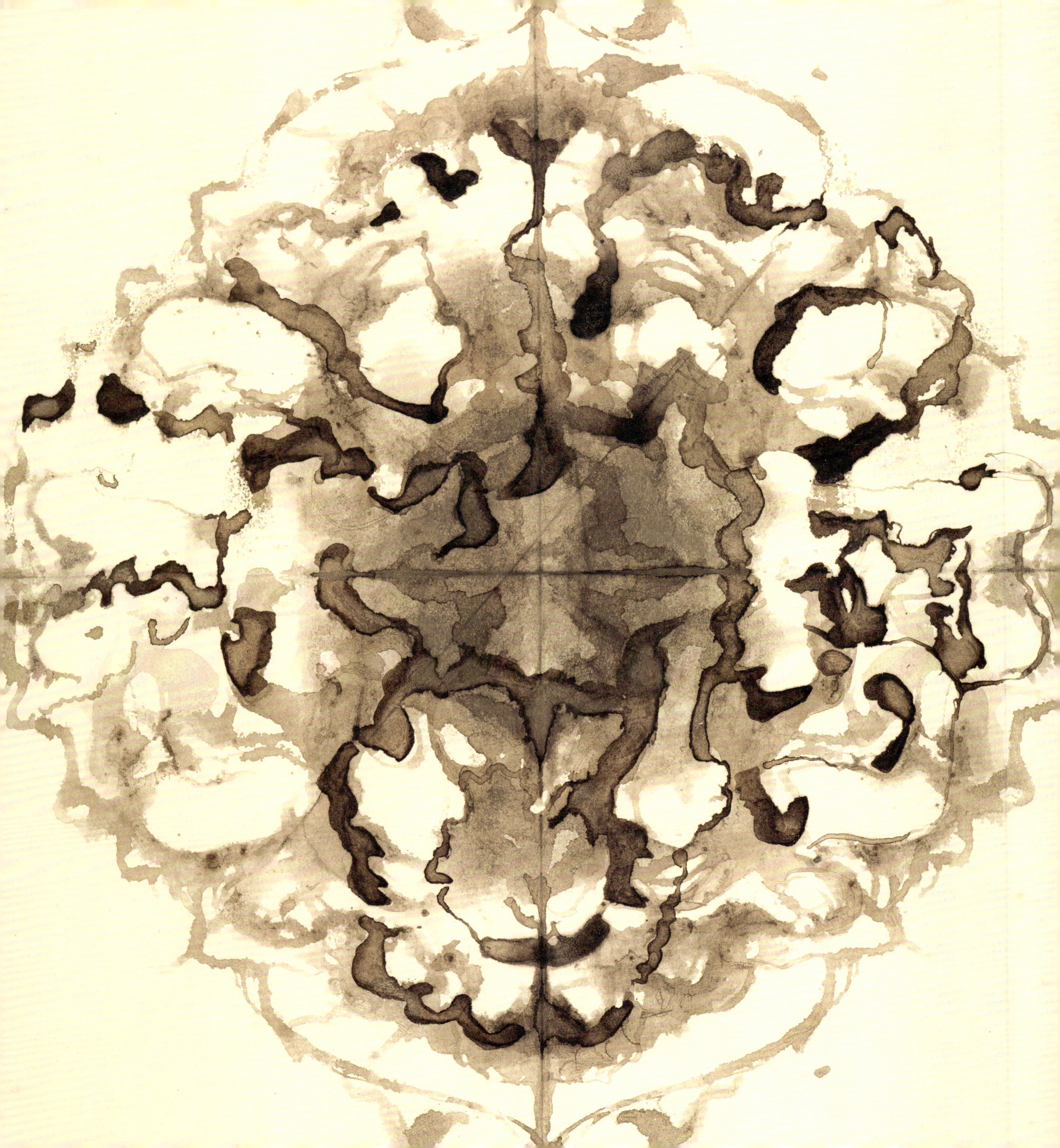

# From Stones to Stains

Florian Rodari

The barely disguised self-portrait of Victor Hugo, who had his son Charles take a photograph of him on top of the Rocher des Proscrits (exiles' rock) on the island of Jersey in 1853, is misleading (p. 127). Contrary to appearances, there is in fact no guarantee of solidity in the enormous mass of stone on which the poet proudly sits, defying France, glimpsed in the distance. Hugo himself asserted as much in his introduction to *Les travailleurs de la mer* (*The Toilers of the Sea*): "Nothing changes shape like clouds, except rocks."[1] Hence the impression of power conveyed by this boulder, firmly anchored to the ground, is immediately linked to a sense of impermanence and illusion. Just as in Hugo's writings darkness inevitably accompanies light, casting a shadow over the least—and even the most magnificent—manifestation of light, so a dreadful precariousness exists within all things visible, even the most stable: in the mind of the poet haunted by dereliction and death, the ability of things to withstand the wear of time is merely apparent.

The fascination exerted by the mineral kingdom on Hugo's sensibility was fundamental to much of his poetic vision. Indeed, architecture—whether the product of natural accident, or long pondered by humankind, or suffering the ravages of time—occupied a prime place in his meditations throughout his written oeuvre of novels, poetry, and travel accounts.

Thus it is hardly surprising to find the concept of stone at the heart of Hugo's entire oeuvre. It is ubiquitous, sometimes welcoming and protective, sometimes destructive and overwhelming—stone is tomb, stone is book. It is the wall of the dungeon where the convict hastily scribbles his final hopes, just as it is the wall of the cell on which the scholar etches a lapidary phrase, carving the dreadful letters that evoke the inevitable fate to which all humans are subject: 'ΑΝΑΓΚΗ.[2] And it is the facade of

Opposite: Victor Hugo, *Rosace* (Rosette), ca. 1859 (detail; see p. 175).

Notre-Dame Cathedral in Paris, source of one of Hugo's finest meditations on the construction of a language based on erecting and assembling stones (fig. 1):

> Architecture began like any other form of writing. It was first of all an alphabet. A stone was set upright and it was a letter, and each letter was a hieroglyph, and on each hieroglyph a group of ideas rested, like the capital on a column. . . . Later on, they formed words. Stone was superimposed on stone, and these granite syllables were coupled together, the word tried out a few combinations. The Celtic dolmen and cromlech, the Etruscan tumulus, the Hebrew *galgal*, are words. Some of them, the tumulus especially, are proper nouns. Sometimes even, when they had plenty of stone and an extensive site, they wrote a sentence. The massive accumulation of Carnac is a complete formula in itself.[3]

In Hugo's novel *Les misérables*, a dark, stony landscape is evoked in turn by the streets of Paris, the walls of the convent, the peeling hovels, the fortifications, the incredible heaps of barricades, and the maze of the city's sewers; that is where consciences must struggle between appearance and reality, truth and lie, sordid schemes and shining behavior. Finally there are the Douvres rocks, rising like a capital *H*, which Hugo described in *The Toilers of the Sea* as "some Titanic cromlech, planted there in mid-ocean by an imperious whim, and built up by hands accustomed to proportion their labors" to the vastness of the abyss.[4]

We should not forget that, for this writer, who towered over his times, the marriage of the sublime and the abyss was often assimilated—in what may even have been the unconscious mark of his entire poetics—to a kind of binary system. No other pair reappears so frequently in his oeuvre. Sublime and abyss are two sides of a single reality that is simultaneously enigmatic and constantly evolving. The slope leading downward is basically the same as the one that once soared—or will soon soar—upward. So in the incessant whirlwind that sweeps up individuals, peoples, and periods, every fall is accompanied by potential redemption. The angel of evil will encounter the angel of good, stars will collapse and vanish (as do empires, families, and consciences) even as others are born. Oxymoron being the foundation on which Hugo's entire philosophy rests—if I may use that expression—the yoking of high and low, beautiful and ugly, great and small, strong and weak is ubiquitous in his writing. Opposing extremes exist in every being, every object. Quasimodo is perhaps the emblematic figure of Hugo's conception of duality, for the two terms merge in him. His ugly appearance, full of bumps and twists, contains a pure heart. He is hunchbacked yet upright. Jean Valjean, the protagonist of *Les misérables*, is persecuted throughout the novel as a vile habitual criminal yet is in fact generosity itself, indeed the human incarnation of integrity. Gilliatt, meanwhile, is a simultaneously wild and dreamy giant who emerges victorious from an extraordinary battle with the storm in *The Toilers of the Sea* yet is undone by a young woman's heedlessness.

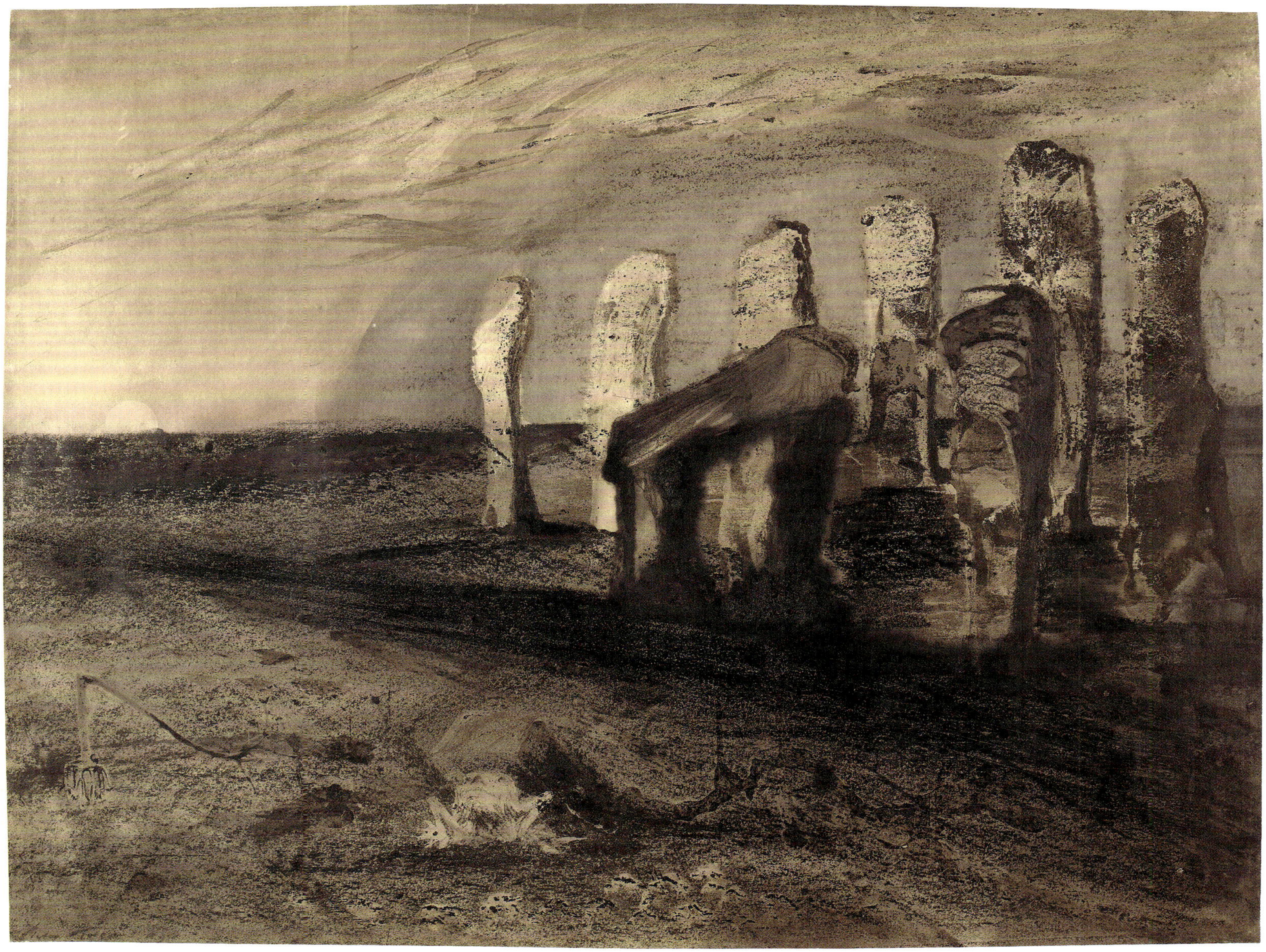

Hugo's vision, however, was not restricted to the human temperament. The major forces of nature are caught up in the same web of contradictions—sometimes beneficial, sometimes harmful—which can alter their appearance in a flash. Without warning, calm weather as far as the eye can see may erupt into a cyclone; the light may fail and the horizon vanish, even though just an hour earlier everything was bright and peaceful. Hugo, haunted by darkness and dereliction, no longer trusted apparent stability. Even in the presence of granite giants, his obsession with nothingness led him to

Fig. 1. Victor Hugo, *Dolmens et menhirs* (Dolmens and menhirs), ca. 1850. Brown ink and wash on paper. 18 7/16 × 24 3/16 in. (46.9 × 61.4 cm). Maisons de Victor Hugo, Paris / Guernesey, MVHP.D.130.

meditate on ruin. Thus he could describe an artless drop of water as a "tremendous toiler" able to bring "vast mountains" low by stubbornly hollowing them.[5]

Right from an early age Hugo displayed a strong visual bent. He was both incredibly curious and a highly skilled draftsman. It is said that, from the top of the tower of Notre-Dame, he was able to make out the color of the dress worn by Charles Nodier's daughter, lost among the crowd on the square below. When sitting as a member of the legislature, he blithely sketched the faces made by his fellow representatives. Not long after, during his travels, in addition to writing letters, he jotted down memories with a sketching pencil, drawing architectural details, the outlines of plants, and the plans and outlines of medieval fortifications. His voracious eye noticed and took an interest in everything, including the writing scribbled on walls by children. Whenever he could, he championed the beauty of old cities, with their mazes of streets conducive to encounters and to mischief; he railed against the rectilinear avenues that modern town planners proclaimed to be more practical. Everywhere he constantly defended disorder, proliferation, improvisation, irregularity—in short, the commotion of life. In *Les misérables*, the barricade in Faubourg Saint-Antoine was nothing less than an extraordinary "composite of paving-stones and rubble, timbers, iron bars, broken window-panes, seatless chairs, rags, odds and ends of every kind—and curses. It was great and it was trivial, a chaotic parody of [the abyss], a mingling of the debris. Sisyphus had cast his rock upon it and Job his potsherd."[6] In short, it was tremendous.

---

Hugo traveled a great deal from 1830 to 1840. He went several times to Belgium, Germany, and Switzerland. He traversed the Alps and the Pyrenees. He crossed mountains, beheld passes, entered gorges, leaned over precipices. He observed erosion, marveled at cascades spurting from rocks, wondered at summits and at the rockfalls that regularly scarred them. And yet these vast ranges were not what primarily inspired him. He didn't have the panoramic inclination that might have prompted him, for example, to set one of his novels in sublime alpine valleys or rugged ice fields.

Right to the end of his life, however, stone and its various incarnations continued to inspire Hugo. His last novel, *Quatrevingt-treize* (*Ninety-Three*), was set in La Tourgue, the proud castle of the Lantenac family, a bastion of reaction against the changes overtaking the world. One of Hugo's final manuscripts, containing scattered thoughts, is titled "Pierres" (Stones). So it seems fairly normal that as soon as he began to draw, Hugo was fascinated by the mineral kingdom. At first he seemed interested mainly in human constructions, notably Gothic architecture, though in doing so was merely adopting the habit of most aesthetes of his day. Very soon, however, he displayed a special penchant for the excessive details and dense disorder of medieval cities. His letters to his family and his early sketches often describe some old town standing on the banks of the Meuse or the Rhine. He was captivated by castles with their towers rising above the houses; he liked their sharp, irregular outlines. His eye was drawn to

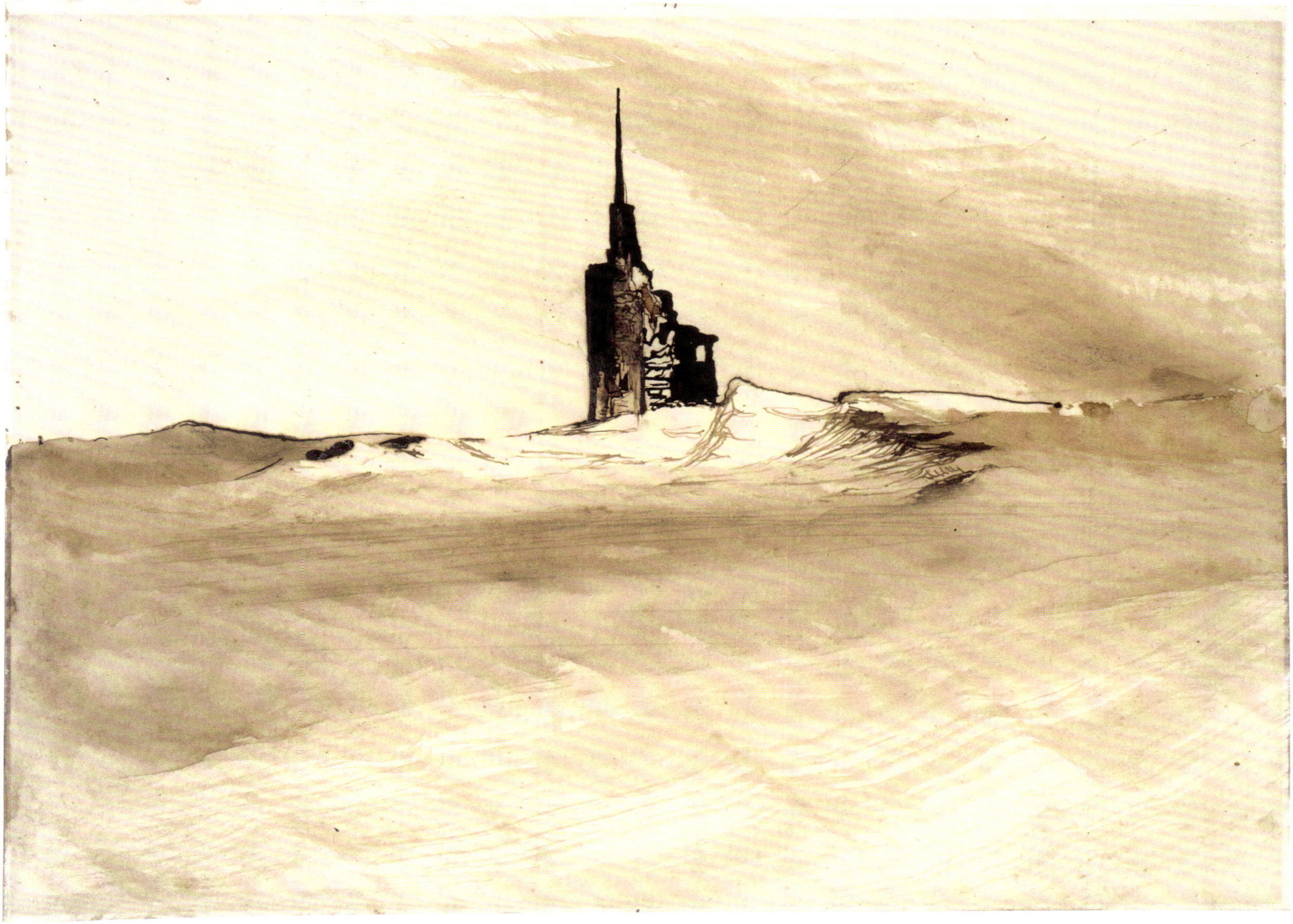

a solitary cathedral or to a ruin on a plain (fig. 2). At other times he delighted in trees whose shadows traced fleeting, grotesque figures along the path. Once exiled to the Channel Islands, he made many sketches of lighthouses (fig. 3), abandoned towers, keeps, and sentinels looming above the waves. Photographs taken by his fellow refugees show his figure mingling among stone buildings. Better still, he did not scorn geologic curiosities: he would pick up pebbles on the beach, writing his name and the date on them, in the perhaps unavowed hope of gathering the entire earth unto himself (p. 119).

Fig. 2. Victor Hugo, *Le clocher dans la dune* (Bell tower in a dune), ca. 1870(?). Brown ink and wash on paper. $10\frac{1}{16} \times 13\frac{3}{4}$ in. (25.6 × 34.9 cm). Maisons de Victor Hugo, Paris / Guernesey, MVHP.D.158.

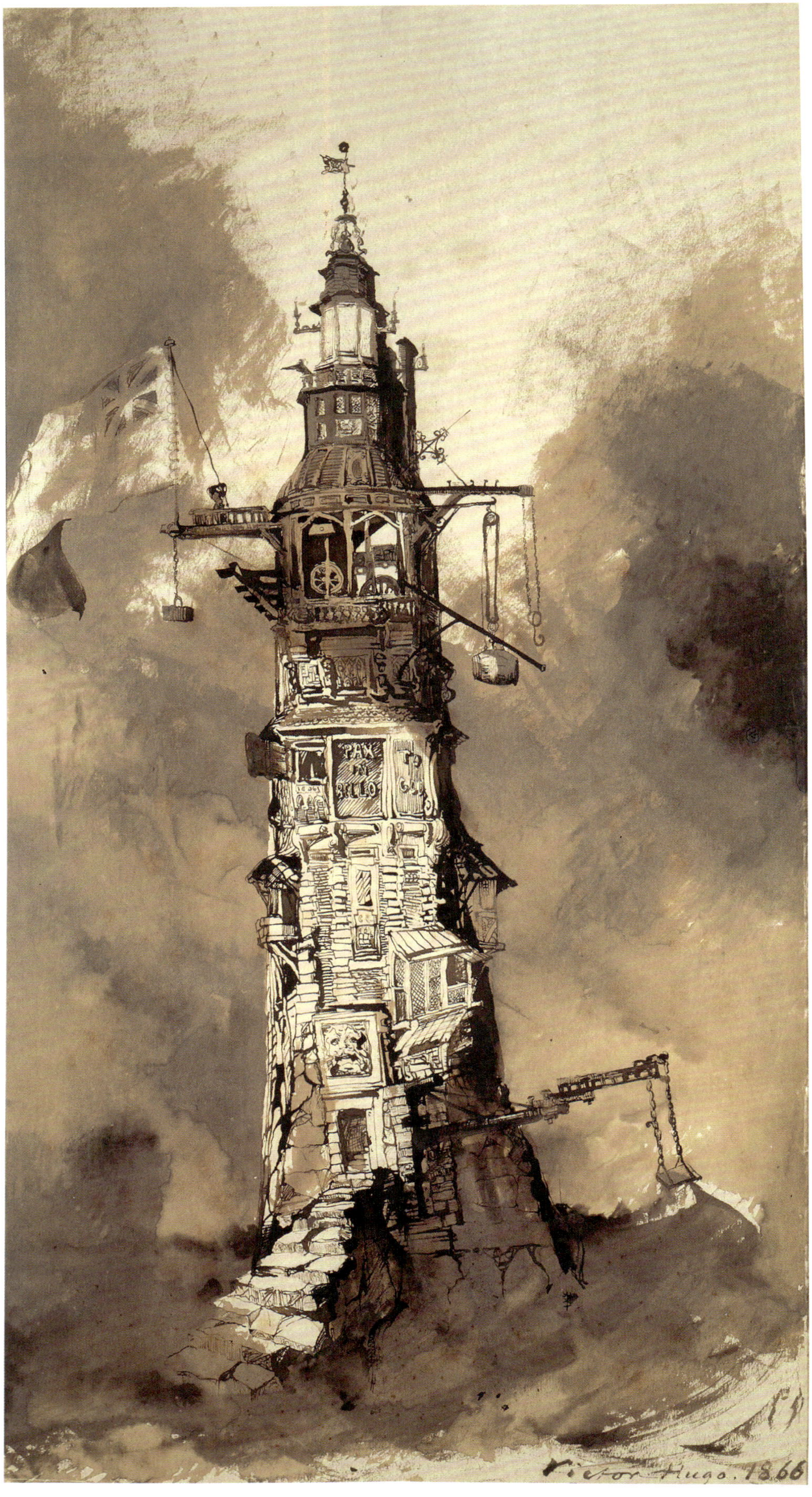


Fig. 3. Victor Hugo, *Le phare d'Eddystone* (The Eddystone lighthouse), 1866. Brown ink and wash on paper. 35¼ × 18¾ in. (89.5 × 47.7 cm). Maisons de Victor Hugo, Paris / Guernesey, MVHP.D.181.

There was a reason for that. The romantic artist, governed by the principle of analogy, viewed nature as a book whose alphabet needs spelling out. Everything was coded, had a meaning. Stone constructions, like the rocks testifying to primal catastrophes, had something to say. The shapes that arose from transformations were signs of the secret desire of the unknown to communicate with us. It was up to artists to uncover meanings. For Hugo, the least projection raised a question—every belfry, tower, or lighthouse had a story to tell. And a reef looming in the open sea spelled tragedy.

---

What remains of those grandiose verbal constructions, thousands of pages long, in which Hugo sought to rehearse the history of language (from primitive alignments in nature to skillful assemblages indebted to the human mind and ingeniousness), once the writer gives way to the artist? What becomes of those verbose descriptions (the endlessly resumed sentences in which Hugo established the settings of his novels, placing the dark fates of human souls in intricate buildings) once words give way to drawing? What happens to all the novelist's long passages of darkness, to all those shafts of light he slips into the gaps, to all those pitfalls avoided by his protagonists (not to mention all those porches, columns, breached walls, and enormous historiated forms, all those macabre, bloody descriptions of stone that slow the flow of straightforward perception, sometimes even strangling it), once the artist's pen, freed from the weight of too many words, throws them directly onto paper? The change in means of expression condenses them.

In fact, applying ink to a blank sheet by pen or brush accelerates expressiveness incredibly. A line's accents—its breaks and pauses—reconstruct a heap of houses and streets; through a repetition of forms it restates complicated assemblages and diverse accumulations. A shadow line, sometimes flowing, sometimes jerky, accompanies every inflection, movement, or gap. Thanks notably to the use of stencils, which carve a reserve into the mass of ink, the strong outlines of all those porches, towers, belfries, and gables orchestrate the space, imparting rhythm to the drawing. The traveler's fascinated vision of towns along the Rhine takes, on paper, the form of emerging peaks, furrows, and cracks that sketch a kind of visual dance in which the voids create lively space for the solids (fig. 4). Imagistic needles weave a lacy web throughout—everywhere there are towers, keeps, battlements, pinnacles, spires, chimneys, lanterns, and finials. Space is riddled with holes; niches lodge everywhere; crevices rise and sink (fig. 5). The line that separates day from night thereby effects a transmutation of stone's oppressive compactness into a pure, refined play of silhouettes. This is perhaps a way of expressing ruin, intrusion and fall, cracks and erosion. Henceforth it is the sharp edge of a line that will reveal the invisible.

---

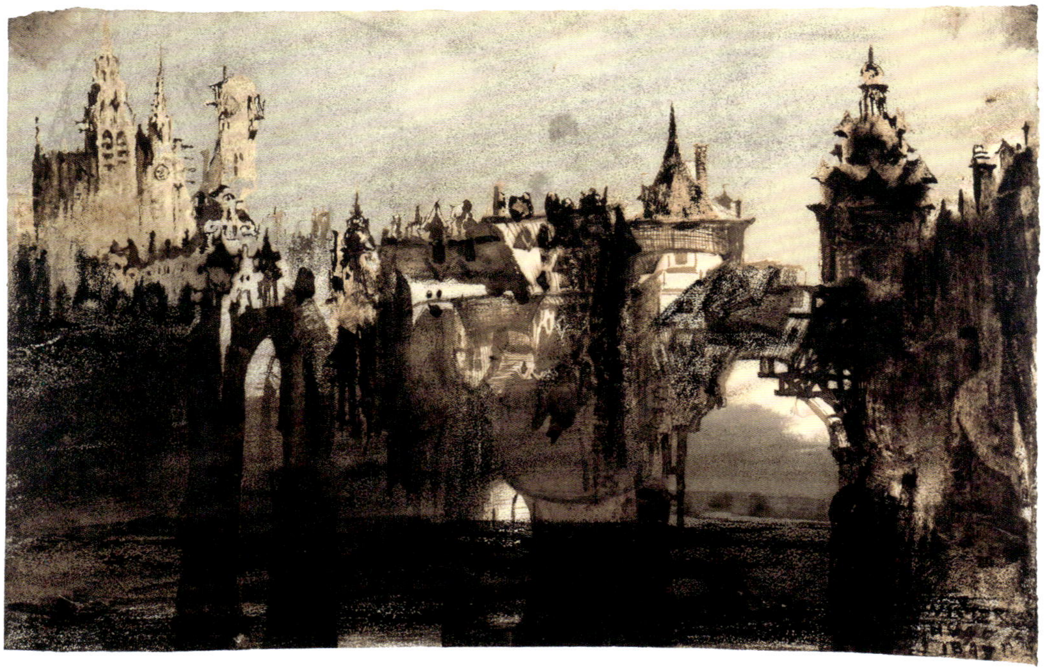

Fig. 4. Victor Hugo, *Ville au pont rompu* (Town with broken bridge), 1847. Brown ink and wash, charcoal, and watercolor on paper. 5⅜ × 8¼ in. (13.7 × 20.9 cm). Maisons de Victor Hugo, Paris / Guernesey, MVHP.D.51.

As a contemplator of nature, Hugo would refresh and refine his ideas during those years of exile. A new spectacle unfolded before his eyes, composed of a constantly changing landscape and the diluting effect of water, sky, and clouds. Before the vastness of the ocean and the incessant flux of waves, the compass of Hugo's gaze would widen, his clock of contemplation would extend into infinity. Enigma was henceforth everywhere, as boundless as natural phenomena. In 1856, when composing "Dieu" (God), a poem not published during his lifetime, he recalled the miracle of the Cirque de Gavarnie: that megalithic colossus stirred a vision of "a world which is not man and which is no longer thing," in which the impossible rises up.[7] From this moment onward, the poet was no longer content with Notre-Dame or even with all of Paris: he wanted to take the vastness of the Douvres rocks and the endless scope of the ocean for his framework. Alone, with a tempest outdoors and "a tempest in [his] skull," Hugo ran up against the wall of darkness; he confronted the unfathomable mystery of ocean depths and tides.[8] His gaze changed in scope: gaps widened; all distance was merely illusion. A grain of sand contained the stars, a tear reflected the entire sky, eternity ruled at every instant. The shadows thickened in and around him. They clung unceasingly to daylight, merging with it.

In the Channel Islands' shifting landscape—which vanished only to reemerge, ever different—everything was a sign yet was simultaneously oxymoronic. Wind, sand, and surf built even as they destroyed. The writer could no longer be content with appearances; it was no longer enough to blissfully contemplate grandeur and admire beauty. Henceforth every spectacle, every moment, was endowed with new eloquence:

the unknown constantly surfaced; nature was no longer content to construct reality but introduced troubling dreams into it. Hugo's visual bent turned visionary. The rocks lining the landscape of the Channel Islands were petrified water. Wind and sea-foam left sketches on the stone—sometimes skillful lace, sometimes frightening masks or, worse, traps that could fatally ensnare. Cliffs effaced by mists rose all the more formidable. From the breaking waves there emerged bizarre hybrid creatures. A kind of secret complicity united the rhythm of the tides and the slow wearing away of the waves; the howl of storms was related to the design of the enormous facades on which the ocean left its mark. Water was not a well-behaved element; stone was not

Fig. 5. Victor Hugo, *Ruines d'un aqueduc* (Ruined aqueduct), ca. 1850. Brown ink and wash on paper. 9¹³⁄₁₆ × 12¹⁵⁄₁₆ in. (24.9 × 32.9 cm). Maisons de Victor Hugo, Paris / Guernesey, MVHP.D.820.

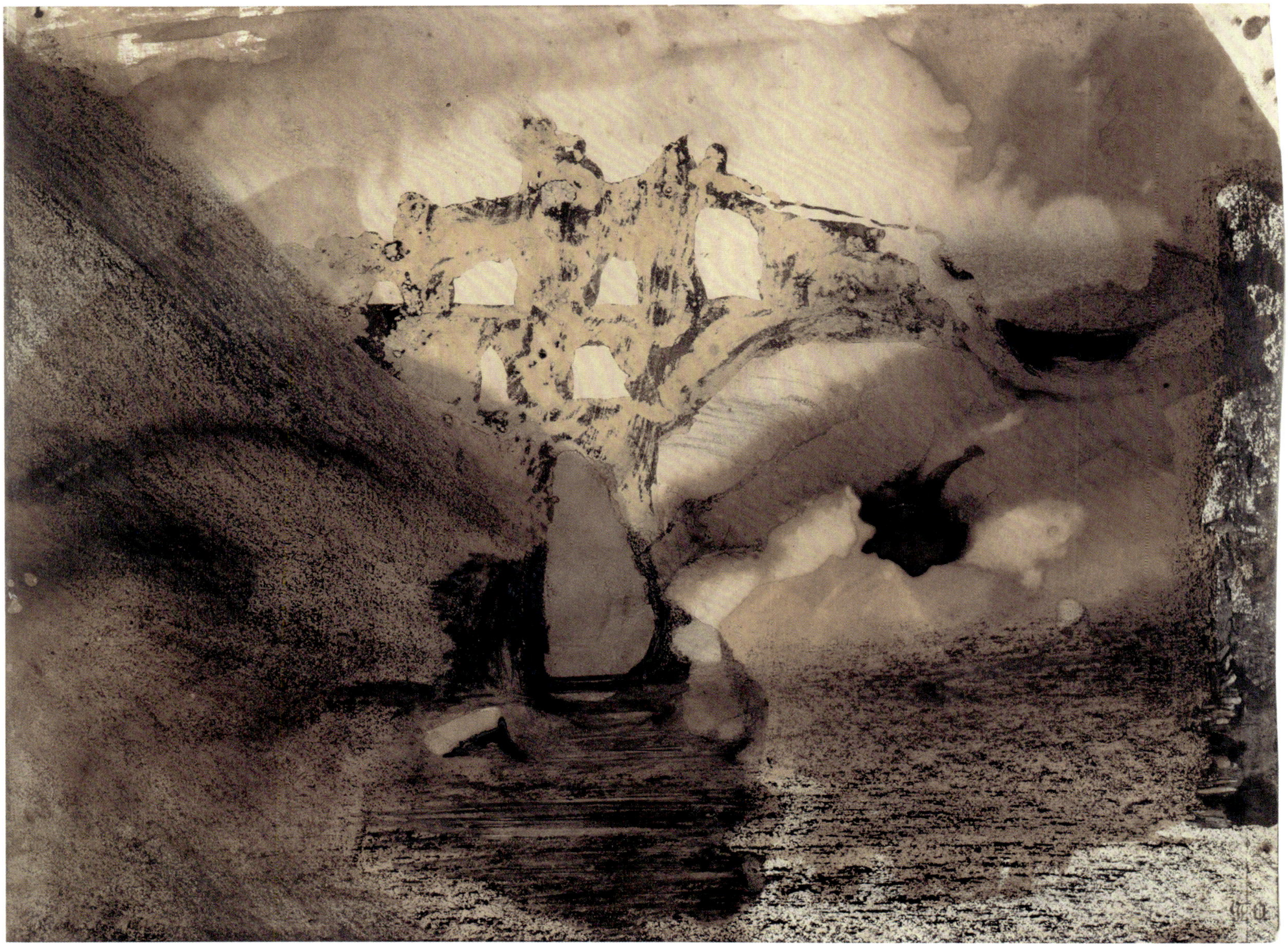

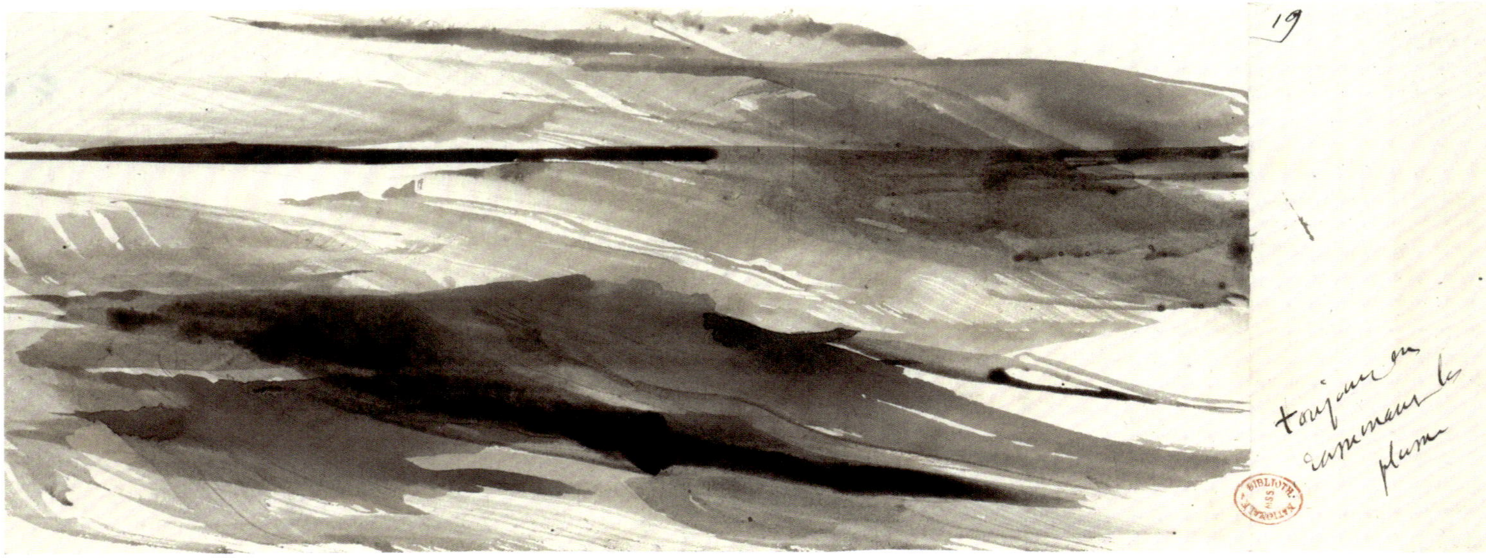


Fig. 6. Victor Hugo, *"Toujours en ramenant la plume"* (Ever drawing back the quill), ca. 1856. Brown ink and wash on paper. $4\frac{1}{8}$ x 11 in. (10.5 x 28 cm). Bibliothèque nationale de France, NAF 13351, fol. 19.

enduring. A drop of water—whether a "tear falling from the eyelash of a cloud" or a "quivering bead at the tip of a rustling blade of grass"—would stubbornly, steadily bore into granite, sliding between two slits, hollowing the stone, sculpting it, and thereby "creating an abyss in the vast edifice."[9]

Humans envision such metamorphoses. Artists embrace them. On Guernsey the poet's imagination was swamped by water. He sank into it. The many pen-and-wash drawings Hugo did, alongside his writing, followed new cadences. The ink on paper would henceforth run and spread—its fluid motion engulfed every projection. It diluted shapes: castles with their crenellated towers were soon floating, foundationless, like ghosts in boundless space. And soon every stroke delineating an outline would fade in order to leave room, on the paper, for moistenings, stumpings, frottage, spurts, ebbs and flows, vague blotches in the night, fleeting figures in the mist. The rock retreated; all identification became lost in the upheaval. Only pale accents could still be made out, and even then they remain jumbled, uncertain, similar to the lapping of waves. "Toujours en ramenant la plume" (Ever drawing back the quill) is the inscription at the bottom of one of Hugo's washes of around 1856 (fig. 6), evoking the relentless rhythm of the waves. The vastness seems to dissolve all boundaries. The sea gnaws, breaks up, rubs out. Beneath it, all is just a sunken dream. Victor Hugo's very name—those large initials composing it, of which he was ordinarily so proud—clings desperately to the ruin, sometimes sinking beneath the sand and the flowers of foam. And the poet would go so far as to identify his fate with a boat overturned by the wave that sweeps away all in its path.

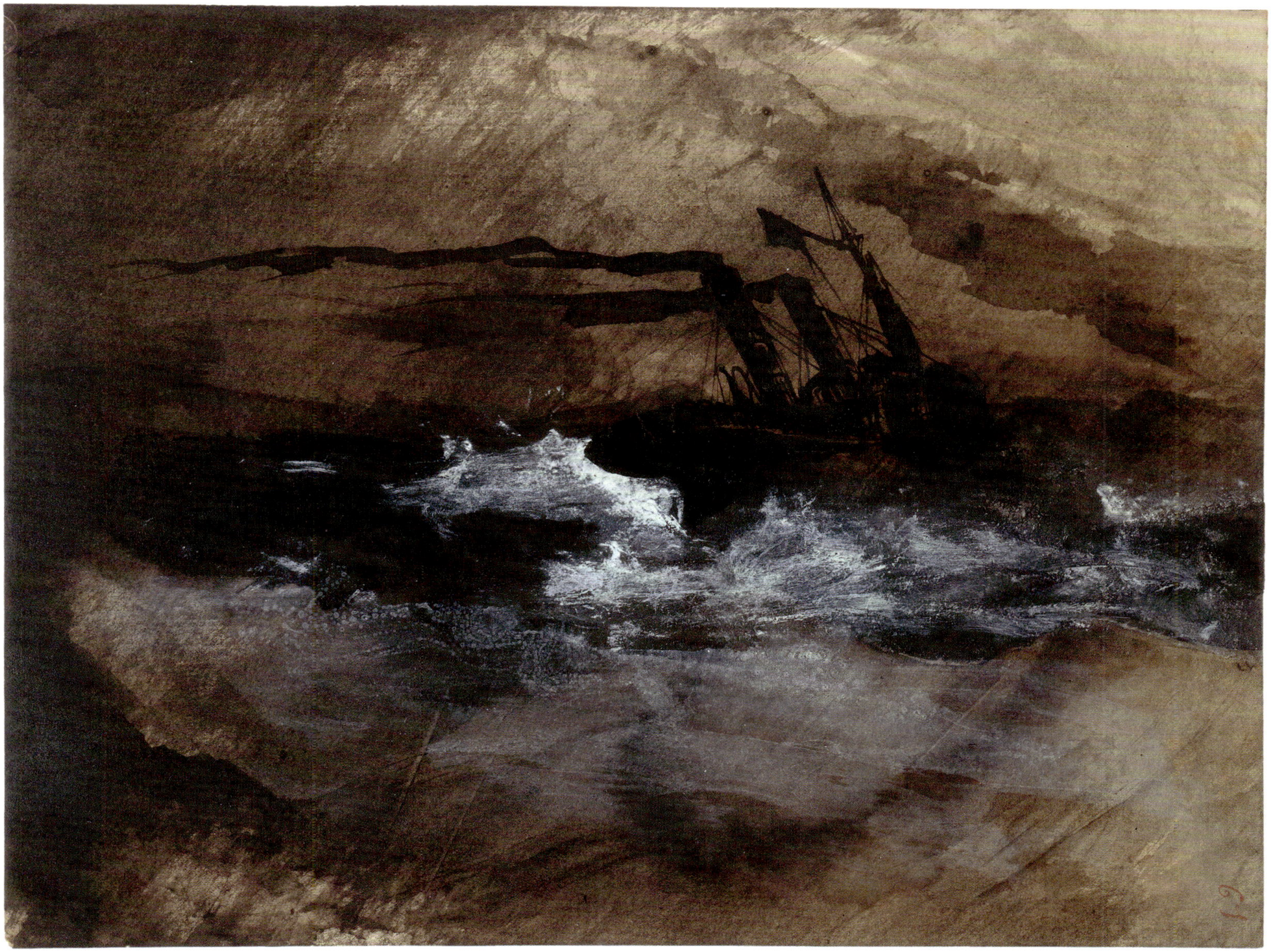

Thus, in many of the drawings done in exile, the implement in the poet's hand would traverse the surface of the paper, sweeping over it in successive waves. Those waves run across the entire space of the sheet, in some cases racing in bursts (fig. 7), in others undulating inexorably. Hugo adopted multiple approaches, inventing all kinds of movements for the hand holding the pen, varying its effects. For example, giving free rein to his imagination, he let the ink run along the sheet, then immediately reworked it, sometimes by frottage (using improvised tools such as sticks, matches, or pen handles), sometimes by folding (thus transferring, by pressing, a reflected pattern), or

Fig. 7. Victor Hugo, *Gros temps, la Durande* (Heavy weather, the *Durande*), ca. 1864–65. Brown ink and wash and white gouache on paper. 7$\frac{9}{16}$ × 9$\frac{7}{8}$ in. (19.2 × 25.1 cm). Bibliothèque nationale de France, NAF 24745, fol. 85.

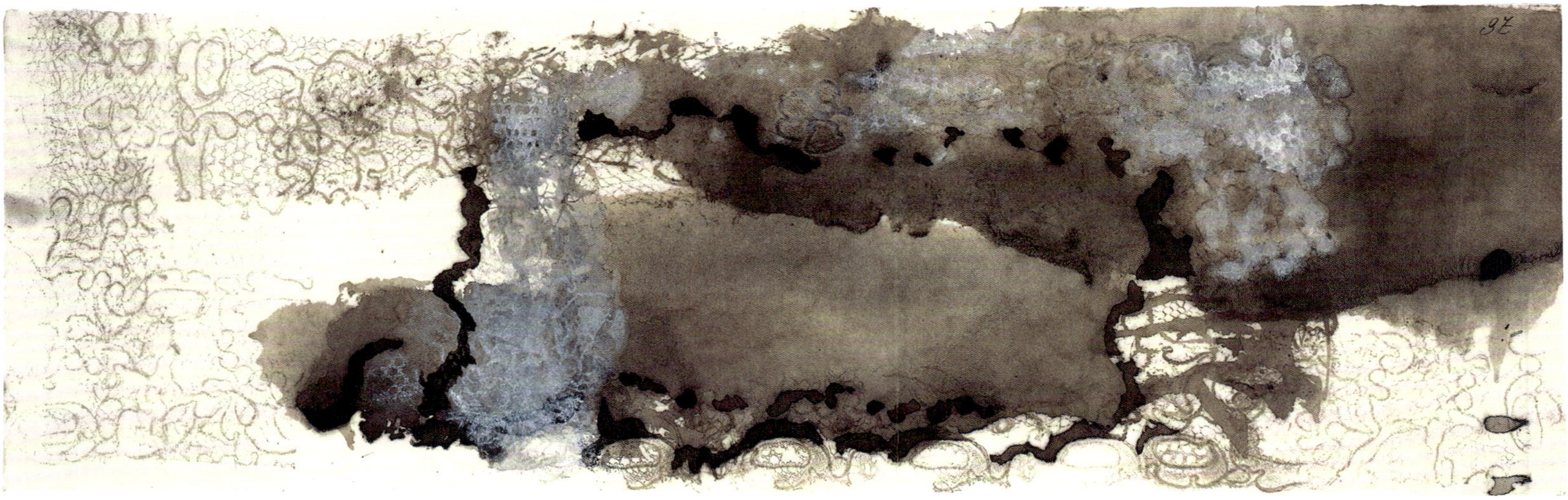

Fig. 8. Victor Hugo, *Empreinte de dentelles* (Impression of lace), ca. 1855. Brown ink and wash, white gouache, and lace impressions on paper. 4¾ × 14⅞ in. (12 × 37.8 cm). Bibliothèque nationale de France, NAF 13351, fol. 37.

finally by dabbing, using a rag or his fingers (which leave their veined prints on the edge of the sheet). Sometimes he would even feminize the flow, weaving it into a web of fine lace (fig. 8). Tiny, infinitely varied touches would convey the progression and retreat of the water, expressing the uncertain, mottled, fluctuating realm—sometimes diaphanous, sometimes dark—of the ocean.

The fruit of stubborn contemplation, these shifting drawings—increasingly agile, imaginative, steeped in a liquid element that drenches the entire landscape—attempt to reflect the incessant battle between two implacables: rock and water. Their struggle—also recounted in the great novel that Hugo wrote in those years, *The Toilers of the Sea*—henceforth insistently fueled the melancholy of Hugo the exile, the remorseful father, the philosopher-poet. We should not forget that scarcely ten years earlier his daughter Léopoldine had drowned in the Seine and that Hugo had been unable to pull her out of the fatal chasm—from whence, in contrast, the convict Jean Valjean, having overcome entrapment himself, resurfaces with the young Marius on his shoulders. The tragedy haunted Hugo; an obscure guilt overwhelmed him. He still experienced the ordeal when confronting the empty ocean. After that dramatic day, not a single text failed to evoke being engulfed by water, or being buried beneath the earth, or consigning souls to stone. A profound doubt plagued Hugo, reducing reality and its most concrete features to slim possibilities, uncertain hypotheses. Thereafter his writing oscillated in an undulating movement similar to the ebb and flow that guided his washes. On the islands Hugo discovered a spectacle to his measure, and from exile he drew the strength to express his vision.

Thus, going from stone to stain and from the jagged outline of rocks to the indistinctness of the sea, the artist allowed water to wash over the lines of his figures; as years went by, its waves finally carried off the little of them that the eye could still discern. At the same time his novels abounded in scenes of drowning: the unexpected one of a man sinking inexorably into the quicksand on a beach, prompting a singular digression between two chapters of *Les misérables*; a collective drowning in *L'homme qui rit* (*The Man Who Laughs*) when the group of Comprachicos sink beneath the waves in the tragic silence of the calm that follows a storm, echoed later—at the end of the same novel—by the suicide of the protagonist, Gwynplaine, who throws himself into the Thames; then, in *The Toilers of the Sea*, it is the turn of Sieur Clubin, captain of the *Durande*, to be pulled to the deep in the arms of an octopus. Hugo concluded that same tale with a final, moving scene in which the mineral and the liquid are bound more tightly than ever: Gilliatt, the unfortunate protagonist, having curled up in the hollow of Gild-Holm'-Ur, a seat cut by the sea into the rocky cliff, watches enraptured as his love disappears in the distance. As the tide rises, covering him little by little, his "deep gaze" looks one last time upon the world before sinking beneath the waters forever:

> The "Cashmere," now scarcely perceptible, had become a mere spot in the thin haze. Gradually, this spot, which was but a stain, grew paler.
>
> Then it dwindled, and finally disappeared.
>
> At the moment when the vessel vanished on the line of the horizon, the head of Gilliatt disappeared. Nothing was visible now but the sea.[10]

Translated from the French by Deke Dusinberre

## Notes

1. Victor Hugo, "L'archipel de la Manche," introduction to French editions of *Les travailleurs de la mer* (Paris: Émile Testard, 1891), 1:22.
2. In a prefatory note to *Notre-Dame de Paris* (*The Hunchback of Notre-Dame*) dated 1831, Hugo wrote, "A few years ago, when the author of this book was visiting, or rather exploring, Notre-Dame, he found, carved by hand on the wall in a dark recess of one of the towers, the word: 'ΑΝΑΓΚΗ [fatality]. The Greek capitals, black with age and cut quite deep into the stone, the forms and attitudes of their calligraphy, which had something peculiarly Gothic about it, as if to show that the hand which had inscribed them there was a medieval one, and above all their grim and fatal import, made a keen impression on the author." Victor Hugo, *Notre-Dame of Paris*, trans. John Sturrock (London: Penguin, 2004), 25.
3. Ibid., 189–90.
4. Victor Hugo, *The Toilers of the Sea*, trans. W. Moy Thomas (London: Sampson, Low & Son, 1866), 2:140.
5. Victor Hugo, "Dieu" (God, 1855–62), XII. Appended to this essay is an excerpt from the poem.
6. Victor Hugo, *Les Misérables*, trans. Norman Denny (London: Penguin, 1982), 988–89.
7. Hugo, "Dieu," XII.
8. This is the title of chapter 3 of part 7 of *Les misérables*.
9. Hugo, "Dieu," XII.
10. Hugo, *Toilers of the Sea*, 3:286 (translation slightly modified here).

# Excerpts from "Dieu" (God)

Victor Hugo

*Voici que sur le haut du mur géant, il pleut.*
*La pluie erre et s'en va, par le vent emportée ;*
*Mais une goutte d'eau sur le faîte est restée.*
*Le lendemain, la brume, humide et blanc rideau,*
*Revient ; il pleut encore ; une autre goutte d'eau*
*S'ajoute à la première ;*
*. . .*
*Il pleut, il pleut, il pleut ; janvier lugubre et mort*
*Passe avec l'ombre, il pleut ; la goutte tombe, mord,*
*Et creuse ; avril arrive et rapporte la nue,*
*Il pleut ; la goutte d'eau, féroce, continue ;*
*. . .*
*revient, revient, revient encore,*
*Et tombe opiniâtre, et se fait dès l'aurore*
*Rapporter par le vent qui, la nuit, l'enleva,*
*Et fait ses volontés dans la montagne, et va,*
*Vient, soumettant le marbre à ses lois triomphantes,*
*Et passe entre deux plans, et glisse entre deux fentes,*
*Et démolit et sculpte, infatigable main.*
*. . .*
*Hydre, outil, vilebrequin, pioche, trompe, suçoir,*
*Commençant le matin, recommençant le soir,*
*Descendant l'escalier de l'épaisseur des couches,*
*Polissant leurs largeurs en murailles farouches,*
*Élargissant le haut, baissant l'âpre fond noir,*
*Évasant et fouillant sans cesse l'entonnoir,*
*Cognant partout, toujours, hiver, printemps, automne,*
*Son petit marteau sombre, effrayant, monotone,*
*Usant le mont, coupant le roc, sciant le grès,*
*Complétant sa ruine et faisant son progrès,*
*Et profitant d'un creux pour creuser davantage,*
*Et d'une argile à l'autre, et d'étage en étage,*
*Du haut en bas, de bloc en bloc, de banc en banc,*
*Errant, roulant, brisant, sapant, taillant, courbant,*
*La goutte d'eau travaille, et, terrible ouvrière,*
*Tord en cercles profonds l'énorme fondrière.*
*Le vaste mont, battu des aquilons sifflants,*
*Frémit de voir creuser dans ses ténébreux flancs*
*Ce puits prodigieux par cette vrille infime,*
*Et de sentir l'atome en lui créer l'abîme.*

Behold, on top of the giant wall, it is raining.
The rain meanders and then departs, swept away
By the wind; but on the summit, a droplet remains.
The next day, the fog, a moist white curtain,
Returns; it is raining again. Another drop of water
Is added to the first
. . .
It is raining, raining, raining; pale, dead January passes with
The darkness, and it rains still; the raindrops fall, biting
And hollowing; April arrives and brings back the clouds,
And it continues to rain. The fierce droplets persist
. . .
Again and yet again the droplet returns, unflagging
And at dawn, makes the wind, which at night had
Carried it off, carry it back. It acts according to its fancy
In the mountain, coming and going, subjecting the
Marble to its triumphant laws, passing between two
Planes here, and slipping between two fissures there.
It demolishes and sculpts, a tireless hand.
. . .
Monster, implement, drill, pickaxe, trunk, proboscis,
Beginning in the morning, resuming again at night,
Descending the staircase of thick layers,
Burnishing the breadth of fierce high walls,
Enlarging the top, lowering the bitter, black bedrock,
Widening and searching ceaselessly the funnel,
Banging everywhere, always, winter, spring, autumn,
Its small, dark, terrible, monotonous hammer,
Corroding the mountain, cutting the rock, sawing the sandstone,
Progressing through its act of destruction,
And taking advantage of a hollow in order to hollow out more,
From one clay and one level to another,
From top to bottom, block after block, stratum after stratum,
Wandering, tumbling, breaking, undermining, cutting, bending,
The droplet works, and, terrible worker,
Cuts in deep circles the enormous rut.
The vast mountain, beaten by the whistling north winds,
Trembles while it views, on its dark sides, the digging
Of this prodigious well by this tiny tendril,
Feeling the atom, within, creating the abyss.

Translated from the French by R. G. Skinner. Originally published in Victor Hugo, *God and the End of Satan* (Chicago: Swan Isle Press, 2014); reprinted by permission.

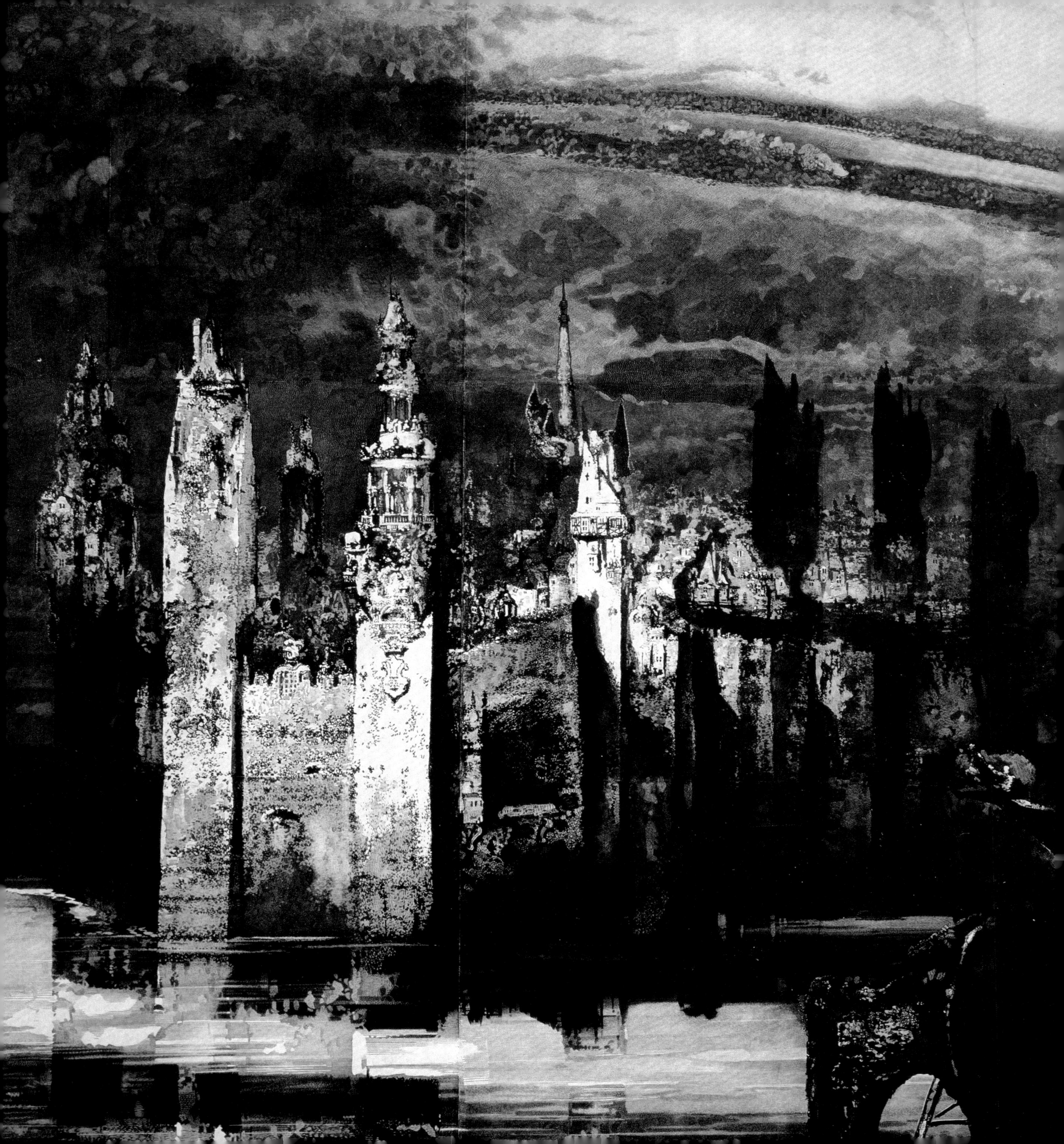

# "Nothing but Shadow and Light"

## Hugo's Drawings in Print

Cynthia Burlingham

The drawings of Victor Hugo are celebrated for their radical conception and experimental techniques and are more often acclaimed as visionary precursors of later artistic movements than seen as representative of the art of their own time. Although Hugo is now considered one of the most revolutionary artists of the nineteenth century, relatively little was known of his drawings during his lifetime. In contrast to the professional artists who exhibited in the annual Salons and whose finished drawings were widely available for sale, he was an amateur draftsman who produced his most innovative works in exile far from the artistic center of Paris. Moreover, as the most illustrious writer of the age, he was mindful of the primacy of his literary reputation and often downplayed the importance of the drawings. He had mixed views about promoting them, claiming that they were merely personal experiments "to amuse me between verses," and resisted repeated entreaties from his wide circle of friends and supporters to make them better known.[1] As a result, Hugo's drawings were not exhibited publicly until 1888, three years after his death. The drawings were nevertheless mentioned frequently in the critical writings of the day, and they drew accolades from a small but influential circle of admirers, mostly writers and critics, who included them in larger discussions of the visual arts.[2]

Many of Hugo's supporters encouraged him to engage a broader audience for his drawings by disseminating them through reproductive prints. Though these ventures often resulted in relatively uninspired prints that failed to capture the remarkable qualities of the drawings, they provided the most public venue for his art during his lifetime. Hugo did not engage in printmaking directly, though he was repeatedly urged to do so. Instead he permitted a small number of printmakers to make prints after his drawings, some of whom succeeded in capturing the subtle and sublime qualities of

Opposite: Fortuné-Louis Méaulle (French, 1844–1901), after Victor Hugo, *Le burg à la croix* (The castle with the cross), ca. 1880 (detail; see p. 43).

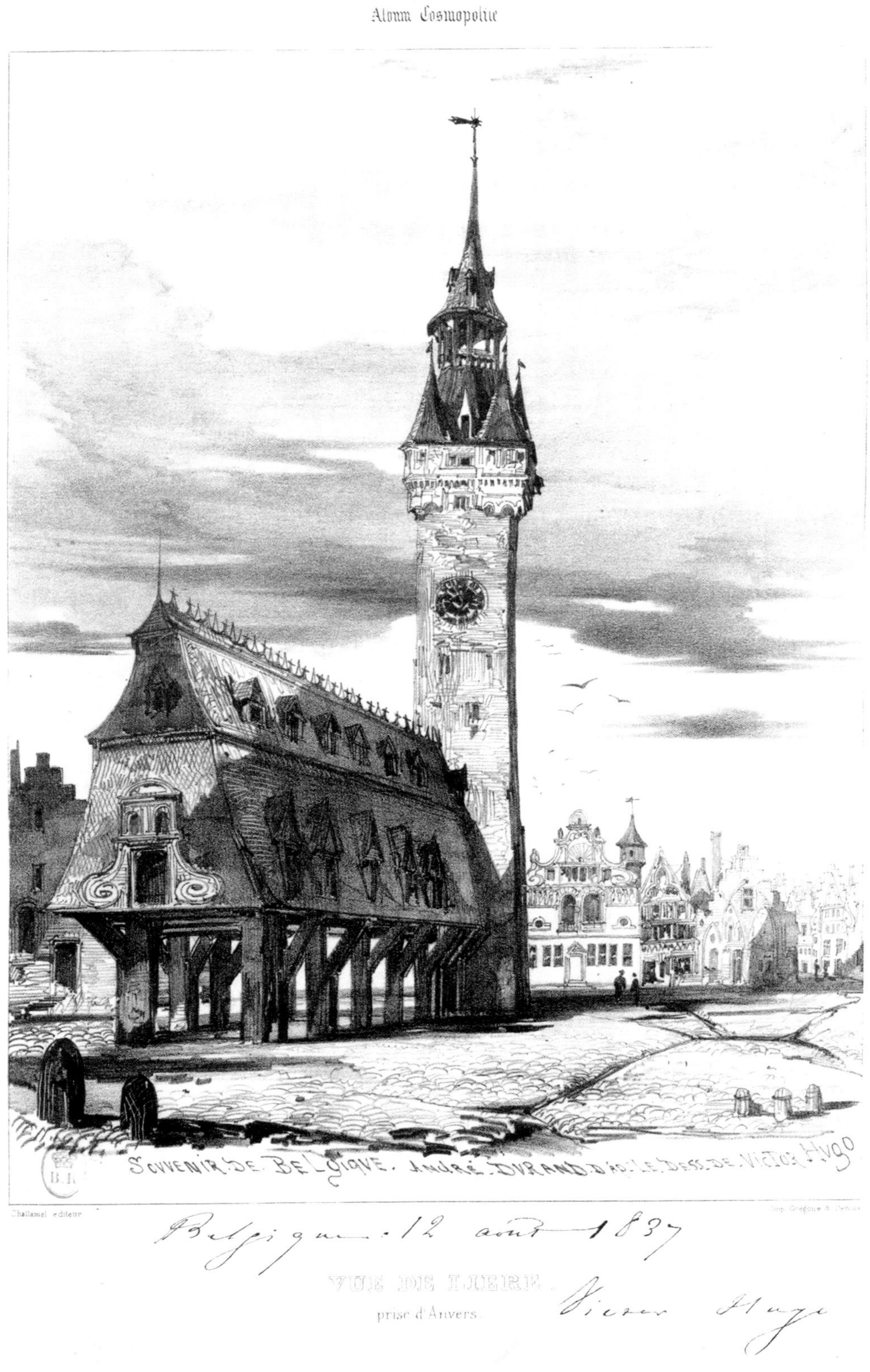


Fig. 9. André Durand (French, 1807–1867), after Victor Hugo, *Vue de Lierre* (View of Lier), ca. 1838. Lithograph. Sheet: 9½ × 7 in. (24.1 × 17.8 cm). Published in Alexandre Vattemare's *Album cosmopolite*, 2nd ed. (Paris: Impr. de Béthune & Plon, 1848).

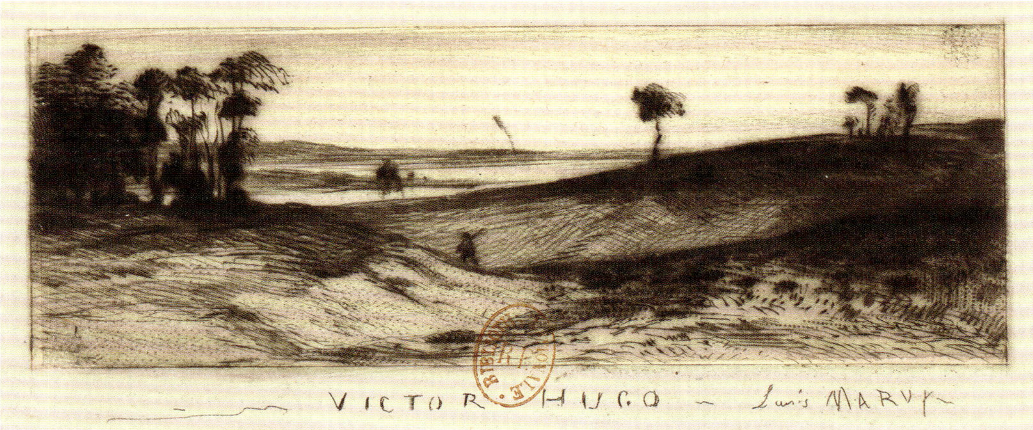


Fig. 10. Louis Marvy (French, 1815–1850), after Victor Hugo, *Paysage de campagne vallonnée* (Country landscape with hills), 1847. Drypoint. Plate: $4\frac{1}{2} \times 4\frac{15}{16}$ in. (11.5 × 12.5 cm). Sheet: $9\frac{13}{16} \times 10\frac{1}{2}$ in. (24.9 × 26.7 cm). Bibliothèque nationale de France, EF-331 [A]-PET FOL.

his art. But his interest in the medium—its different techniques and its capacity for reproduction and dissemination—is suggested repeatedly in exchanges with his wide circle of friends, colleagues, and collaborators, and his attitudes toward printmaking are important to consider in discussions of his larger artistic practice.[3]

"Fac-similes" of Hugo's drawings were published in various popular journals, as single-sheet prints, and in deluxe-edition portfolios that were targeted toward a limited circle of collectors and connoisseurs. From the late 1830s through his exile, beginning in 1851, and his return in 1870, the drawings that were reproduced in print form were most often landscape etchings. They were generally modest works, relatively conventional in style and aligned with prints by other contemporary landscape artists. After Hugo's return to Paris, printers specializing in wood engraving reproduced some of his grander and more inventive compositions, most published in connection with his literary works rather than as completely independent works of art. Whereas Hugo had controlled the choice of images and their contexts in his earlier ventures with printmakers, the numerous prints produced toward the end of his life may have been guided primarily by others. And his most unconventional abstract imagery was never represented in printed form during his lifetime.

The earliest Hugo drawing to be reproduced in a journal was a lithograph (fig. 9) made after his drawing *Le beffroi de Lierre* (The belfry of Lier, August 1837; p. 73), one of many drawings of the castles, rivers, and landscapes that appeared alongside his letters and in his journals recording his travels to northern France, Belgium, the Rhine, and the Pyrenees. It was published in *Album cosmopolite* in 1838, with comments by the prominent art and literary critic, poet, and novelist Théophile Gautier. Gautier, who reprinted his article that year in the widely read *La Presse*, was the first critic to identify the writer as "Monsieur Hugo dessinateur" and remained an enthusiastic supporter of his drawings.[4] The drawing sits firmly within the contemporary picturesque tradition of architecture and landscape prints.[5] A decade later, in 1847, Hugo allowed several small landscape drawings to be etched by the landscape draftsman and printmaker Louis

Marvy and used as prizes in a lottery (fig. 10). Hugo praised Marvy as "an admirable translator," and the etching, soft-ground etching, and drypoint mediums ably captured the delicate lines and washes of Hugo's vignette-style landscapes, which recall the works of his contemporaries of the Barbizon school, such as Charles-Émile Jacques and Théodore Rousseau, whose works were also engraved by Marvy.[6]

Certainly Hugo's long exile to the islands of Jersey and Guernsey precluded a larger audience for his drawings. But during his exile he remained connected to the world of art and art criticism in Paris through frequent correspondence and visits from friends and admirers. The importance of his drawings was acknowledged by several prominent writers and critics in addition to Gautier. The poet and critic Charles Baudelaire mentioned Hugo's drawings in his review of the Salon of 1859, declaring, "our poet is the king of landscape painters."[7] Philippe Burty, a prominent critic in Paris from the 1860s onward, remained an ardent supporter, as both a critic and a collector.

After Hugo left Paris, several important drawings remained there, including a number that were included in an 1852 sale of the furnishings from his apartment on the rue de la Tour d'Auvergne. Friends who staged the sale pledged that they would hold the works for safekeeping and give them back to Hugo upon his return to Paris. Auguste Vacquerie and Paul Meurice, future executors of Hugo's estate, purchased a number of the drawings. Among the most revelatory was the monumental and elaborately detailed *Le burg à la croix* (The castle with the cross, 1850; fig. 11), purchased by Meurice. The drawing was framed and remained in Meurice's apartment until Hugo's return in 1870, suggesting that it and other drawings would have been available for invited visitors to view in Paris during the author's exile.[8]

In an article about the sale published in *La Presse* in 1852, Gautier enthusiastically praised Hugo's drawings: "He excels at combining, in his somber and fierce fantasies, the effects of the chiaroscuro of Goya and the terrifying architecture of Piranesi."[9] In evoking Hugo's name alongside those of Francisco de Goya and Giovanni Battista Piranesi, Gautier was comparing Hugo's drawings with those of the master printmakers whose works were archetypes for the European etching revival that would begin around 1860. Proponents of the revival in Paris, led by the founding of the Société des Aquafortistes in 1862, promoted etching as an original and accessible print medium for artists through critical writings and the publishing of print albums in regular and deluxe editions.[10] Championed by critics such as Gautier, Baudelaire, and, overwhelmingly, Burty, the movement was at its height during the years of Hugo's exile. Hugo appreciated the works of the *peintres-graveurs*, or artist-printmakers, and intermediaries like Baudelaire, Burty, and the painter Jules Laurens kept him abreast of developments in Paris, often sending him gifts of prints by Félix Bracquemond, Rodolphe Bresdin, François Chifflart, Auguste Delâtre, Charles Meryon, and others. Writing from his island, Hugo engaged in the critical dialogue about the merits of the original etching, noting in a letter to Baudelaire in reference to Meryon, "Without color, nothing but shadow and light, the chiaroscuro completely alone and left to itself, this is the challenge of etching."[11]

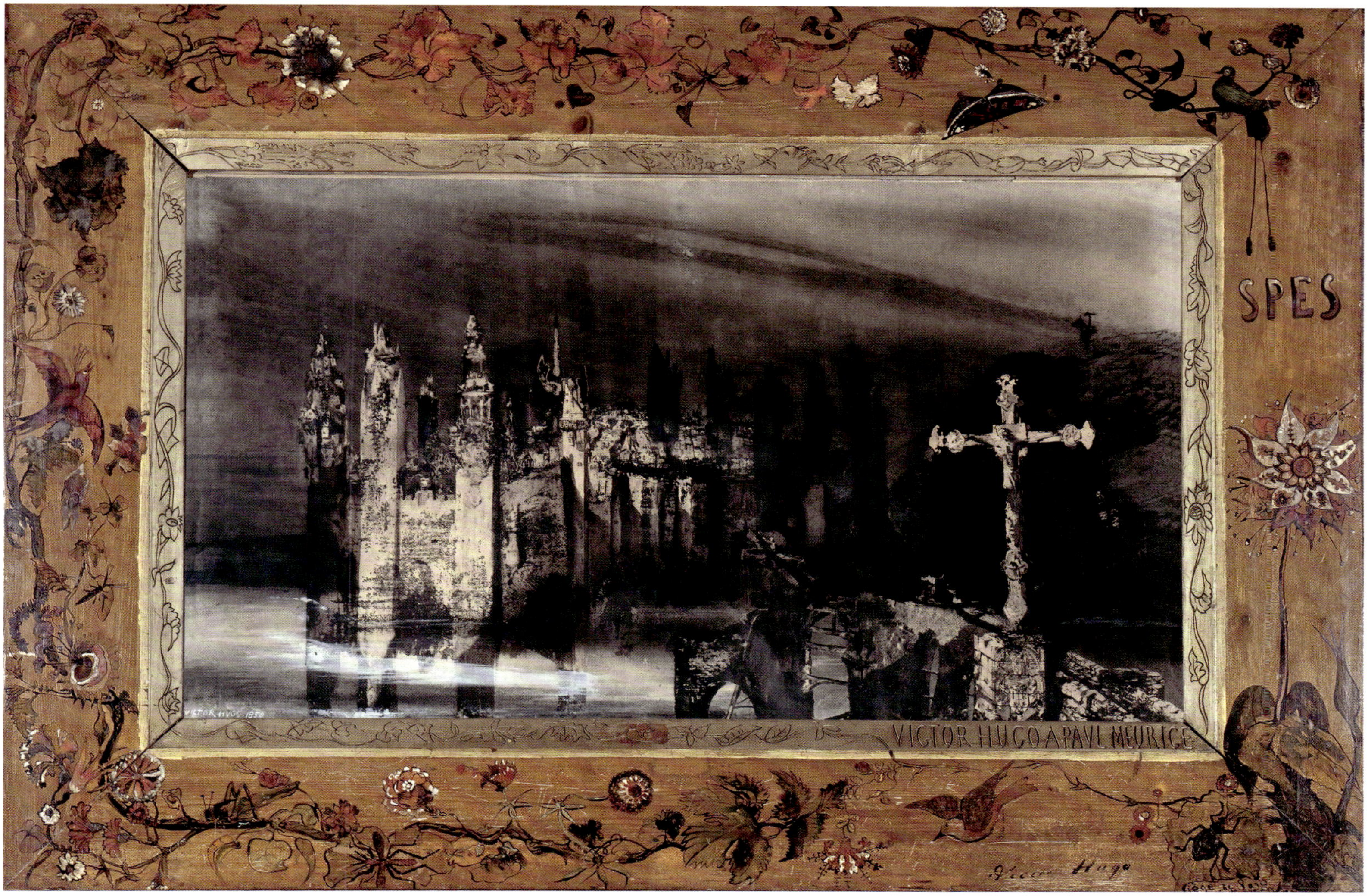


Fig. 11. Victor Hugo, *Le burg à la croix* (The castle with the cross), 1850. Brown ink, brown wash, and charcoal on paper. 28 × 49 7/16 in. (71.1 × 125.6 cm). Maisons de Victor Hugo, Paris / Guernesey, MVHP.D.40.

One might expect Hugo to have shown interest in making his own etchings, given the promotion of the medium within his circle of literati, its semblance to the immediacy of drawing, and its potential to convey both dynamic chiaroscuro and the subtlety of ink washes. Some of his friends reached out to try to engage him in the practice, but he resolved to keep drawing only with his pen.[12] For Hugo, who worked alone in his small studio, the technical demands of copperplates and acid, likely requiring an experienced collaborator, must have seemed far too complicated when compared to the directness of pen, ink, and paper. Perhaps if Hugo had remained in Paris, the creative hub of the original etching movement, he would have been more easily lured into experimenting with copperplates, instead of remaining "a latent etcher."[13]

In 1860, driven more by political motivations than artistic ones, Hugo allowed his brother-in-law Paul Chenay to produce an aquatint of an 1854 drawing originally made

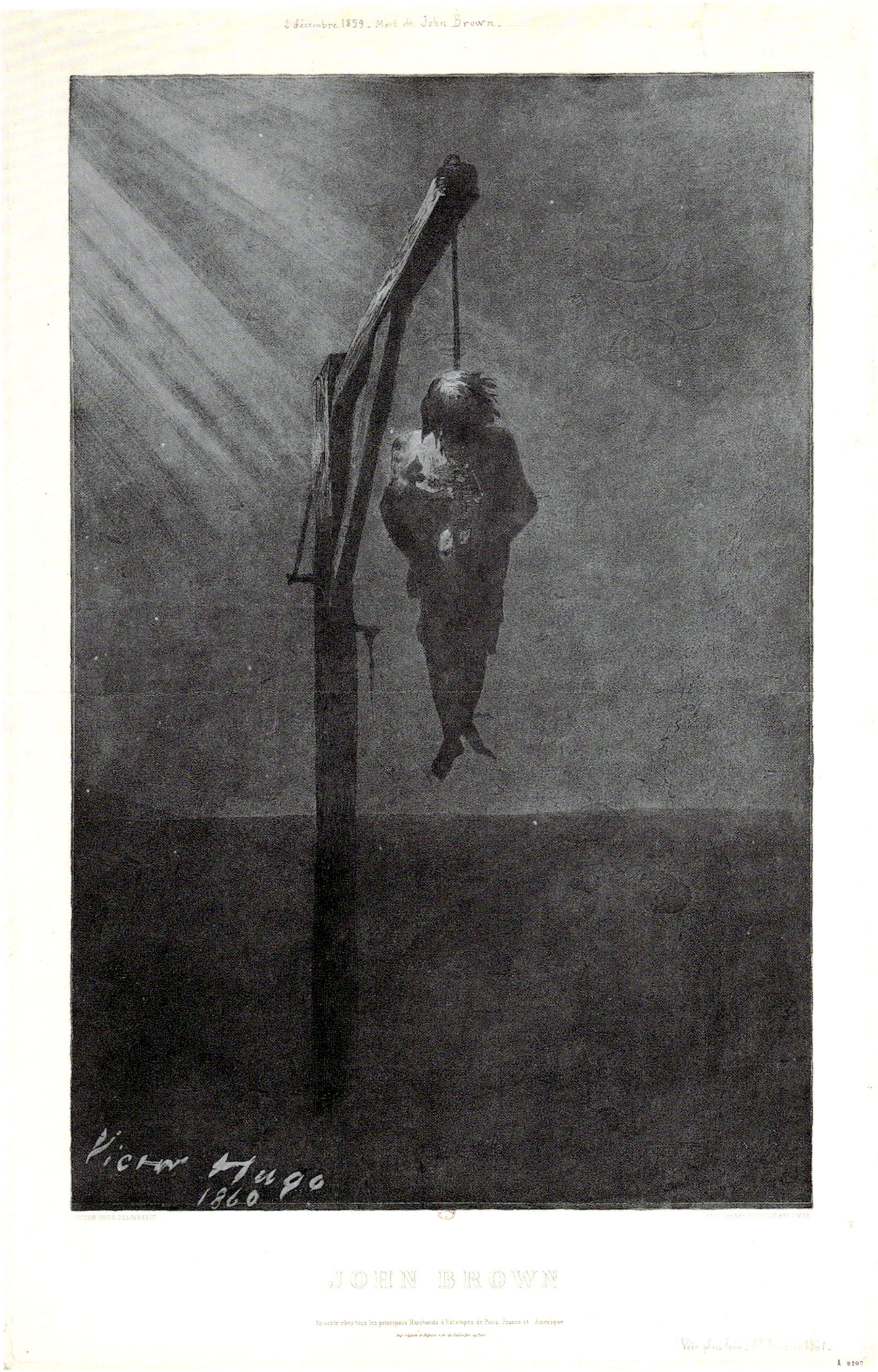

Fig. 12. Paul Chenay (French, 1818–1906), after Victor Hugo, *John Brown*, 1861. Heliogravure. Plate: 20⅝ × 13³⁄₁₆ in. (52.4 × 33.5 cm). Sheet: 24¹³⁄₁₆ × 15⅝ in. (63 × 39.7 cm). Bibliothèque nationale de France, QF-1 (1846–1901)-FOL.

in response to the hanging of a local criminal on Guernsey (p. 154, 155). Engraved with a new date and title, *John Brown* (fig. 12), the drawing was repurposed by Chenay and circulated as a protest against the execution of the American abolitionist in 1859. Chenay's aquatint successfully invoked the somber and nuanced tonalities of the drawing, one of Hugo's most haunting and powerful works. For Hugo, who noted that his drawing was reproduced "with gripping fidelity," thanks to Chenay's "great talent," the print medium provided an effective means of reproduction and dissemination of an important political statement.[14] Credited to both its creator (*Victor Hugo delineavit*) and its interpreter (*Paul Chenay sculpsit fac-simile*), it was widely distributed and became Hugo's best-known printed work.[15]

The success of the John Brown print led to a more ambitious venture between Hugo and his brother-in-law to produce a portfolio of etchings after Hugo's drawings. Published in Paris in 1863, the large-format album, titled *Dessins de Victor Hugo*, featured twelve etchings and aquatints by Chenay after Hugo's drawings. The size and scope of the publication were characteristic of such print portfolios during the latter half of the century. Its title page prominently featured Hugo's name, followed by those of the engraver Chenay and the critic Gautier. A promotional announcement emphasized both the artistic and the literary gravitas of the project: "at once a book and an album; a book by the colorful and original text of Théophile Gautier and an album by the original drawings of the great poet."[16] Gautier's preface noted that Hugo's drawings were "engraved by M. Paul Chenay, with such expert accuracy that nothing is lost of the naïveté of the original," emphasizing the importance of faithfully reproducing the unique character of the drawings.[17] Gautier's preface was interspersed with ten rather stilted vignette-style wood engravings after Hugo landscapes by Alphonse Gérard.[18] The book also contained a long letter to the editor from Hugo himself, in which he declares that the proceeds from the sale of the book would benefit poor families on the island, perhaps providing a hedge to the book's artistic purpose by suggesting a more philanthropic justification. At the end of all of these preambles were Hugo's twelve landscapes, printed in etching and aquatint to capture the tonal and atmospheric qualities of his washes. They were treated as independent works of art, printed on separate pages with only titles beneath and blank on the verso. The drawings Hugo selected for the album were primarily small-scale landscapes from the 1840s and 1850s, dominated by castles and châteaux, that recalled early picturesque and Barbizon landscapes.[19]

Hugo was clearly invested in the success of the project, noting in a letter to Chenay that "it is important that the album remain absolutely serious."[20] There was substantial correspondence between the two regarding the publication, including an early proof of one of the prints (fig. 13; see also p. 87). A note from Hugo praises the print as an excellent facsimile but requests the addition of highlights on the tower's summit or on the curve of the tower, which he also indicated by gouache additions on the proof, suggesting that he was engaged with the process and approved the translation of the drawings into print.

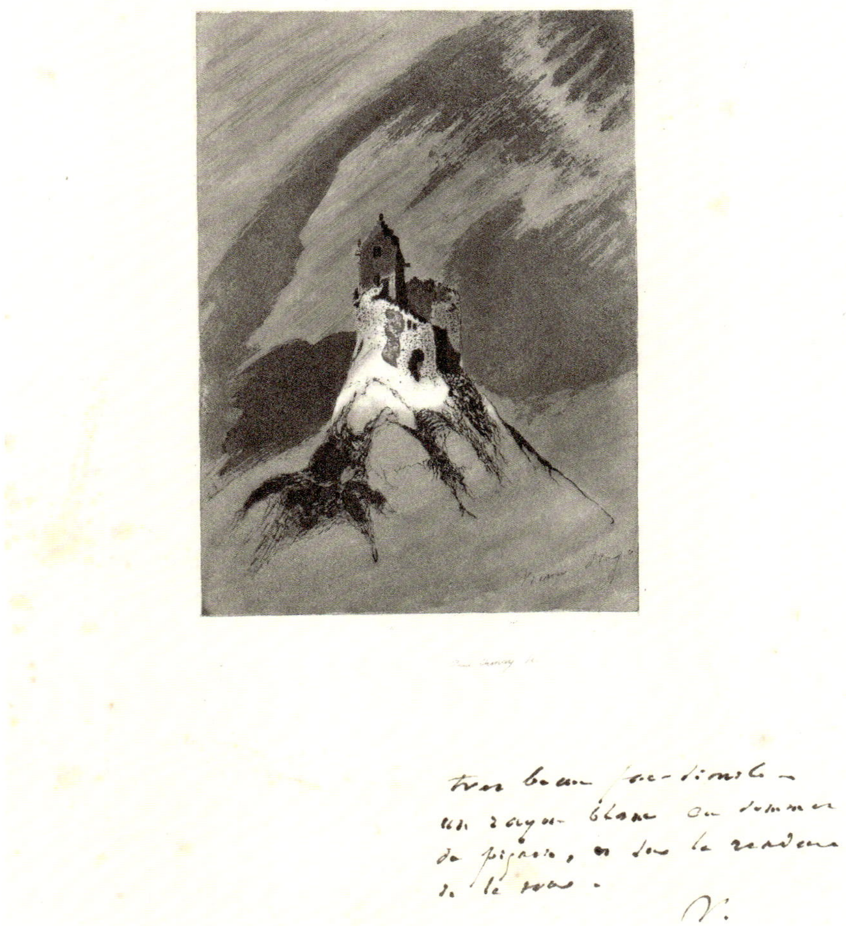

Fig. 13. Paul Chenay (French, 1818–1906), after Victor Hugo, *Le burg* (The castle). Etching and aquatint with gouache additions. Plate: $10\frac{7}{8}$ × $7\frac{5}{16}$ in. (27.7 × 18.5 cm). Sheet: $13\frac{5}{16}$ × $9\frac{3}{4}$ in. (33.8 × 24.8 cm). Inscribed and signed by Victor Hugo "très beau fac-simile – / un rayon blanc au sommet du / pignon, ou dans la rondeur / de la tour V." [very beautiful facsimile—a white ray at the top of the gable or in the curve of the tower V.]. Maisons de Victor Hugo, Paris / Guernesey, MVHP.L.2015.0.31FOL32.

The portfolio, produced in an edition of four thousand, was presumably intended to create a larger audience for the drawings than Hugo's small circle. But the commercial response was less than hoped for, and only four hundred copies were sold. There was wide discussion in the press, with predictably positive reception from Hugo's supporters, but his disappointment with its reception led to a strained relationship with his brother-in-law. The whole experience discouraged Hugo from any major effort to make further prints from his drawings, and there were only scant publications of the drawings during the last years of his exile.[21]

A modest exception was occasioned by Burty, who continued to hold fast to the idea of connecting artists and writers through the medium of etching, repeatedly

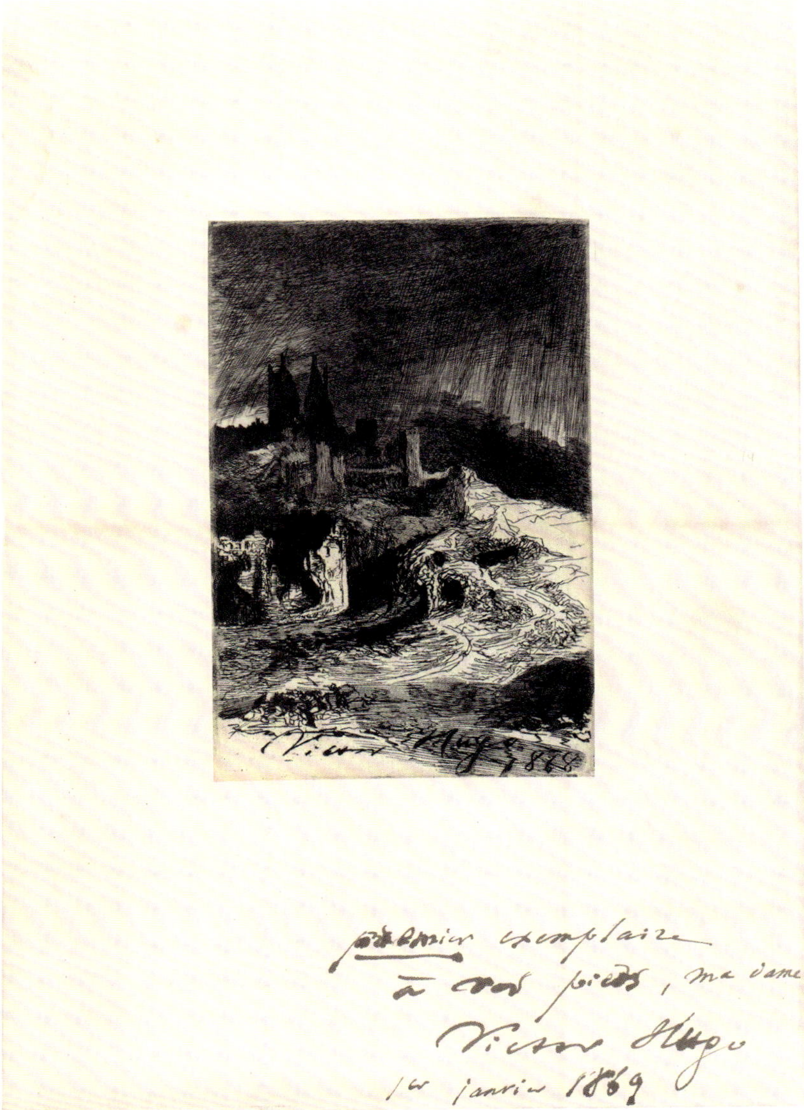

Fig. 14. Charles Courtry (French, 1846–1897), after Victor Hugo, *L'éclair* (Lightning), 1869. Etching. Plate: $8\frac{7}{16} \times 5\frac{1}{2}$ in. (21.5 × 14 cm). Sheet: $16\frac{3}{4} \times 11\frac{15}{16}$ in. (42.5 × 30.3 cm). Inscribed, dated, and signed by Victor Hugo "premier exemplaire / à vos pieds, ma dame. / Victor Hugo 1er / Janvier 1869" [first impression at your feet my lady. Victor Hugo January 1, 1869]. Maisons de Victor Hugo, Paris / Guernesey, MVHP.E.622.1.

trying to convince Hugo to make etchings himself or to allow others to make them. Hugo persistently declined, recalling in a letter to Burty the failure of the Chenay album and the damage to the reputation of his "pauvres dessins" and lamenting the absence of Marvy, whom he clearly considered a more successful imitator.[22] Burty again pleaded with Hugo to make an etching for his 1869 publication *Sonnets et eaux-fortes* (notably asking him for a drawing rather than a poem). For the album Burty commissioned forty-two artists to produce etchings in response to selected poems, demonstrating the sympathetic relationship between etching and literature. In the end Hugo relented and provided a drawing that was etched by Charles Courtry and paired with a poem by Hugo's great friend Paul Meurice (fig. 14). In comparison to the more tonal approach of the Chenay prints, Courtry's composition is rendered entirely through the expressive line of the etching medium. Clearly pleased with the result, Hugo called the work a "beautiful facsimile" and the book "a superb struggle" between poets and painters.[23]

Soon after Hugo's return to Paris in 1870, he was introduced to the wood engraver Fortuné-Louis Méaulle. Méaulle was several decades younger than Hugo and ran an active and successful studio, engraving book illustrations after drawings by a number of artists, most notably the prolific illustrator Gustave Doré and the painter, printmaker, and illustrator François Chifflart. Chifflart, whose work Hugo admired, was invited by Hugo to visit him in exile on Guernsey in 1868, the year that Chifflart was selected to provide seventy drawings for an edition of Hugo's novel *Les travailleurs de la mer* (*The Toilers of the Sea*), more than half of which were to be engraved by Méaulle. Hugo showed him the drawings that he had bound into his manuscript for *Les travailleurs*, creating in effect his own artist's book and directly associating his literary work with his drawings.[24] Many of Chifflart's own illustrations for *Les travailleurs* were informed by the expressive nature of Hugo's drawings, and some quite closely imitated them. Hugo and Chifflart even jointly signed three of the illustrations with their initials.

For decades Hugo's books had featured illustrations by dozens of artists, reproduced in a variety of mediums by printmakers, who were generally engaged by the publishers. The collaboration with Chifflart was unusual in Hugo's level of engagement with the illustrator and because his own drawings were connected with illustrations for a published work. Given their trusting relationship, it seems likely that Chifflart would have facilitated Hugo's introduction to Méaulle upon the writer's return to Paris.[25]

Until his collaborations with Méaulle, Hugo's main experience with wood engravings after his own drawings had been limited to the vignettes in the prologue for the ill-fated Chenay album. Wood engraving had been the preferred medium for large-edition book illustrations from the 1820s onward.[26] The end blocks of wood were dense and could be intricately carved with a graver, allowing for a wide range of tones and great detail and could be easily and cheaply printed alongside text. In contrast, printing text in combination with etchings was technically challenging, and thus it was limited to smaller deluxe editions.

Méaulle became the sole translator of Hugo's drawings, ultimately producing almost two hundred wood engravings, most associated primarily with Hugo's literary works, a connection that Hugo had rarely made previously.[27] Méaulle's first efforts included an 1874 wood engraving of the famous John Brown drawing, one of a group of illustrations by Hugo and other artists included in an edition of Hugo's novel *L'année terrible*, and three wood engravings after Hugo for an article about Hugo's drawings by Burty in 1875.[28] The most extensive of Hugo's projects with Méaulle was a large portfolio devoted solely to Méaulle's prints after Hugo's drawings for *Les travailleurs de la mer*, published in a limited edition on different papers without the text in 1882. The portfolio featured sixty-four wood engravings, of which fifty-two were related to drawings for *Les travailleurs* and the rest were engraved after other marine drawings by

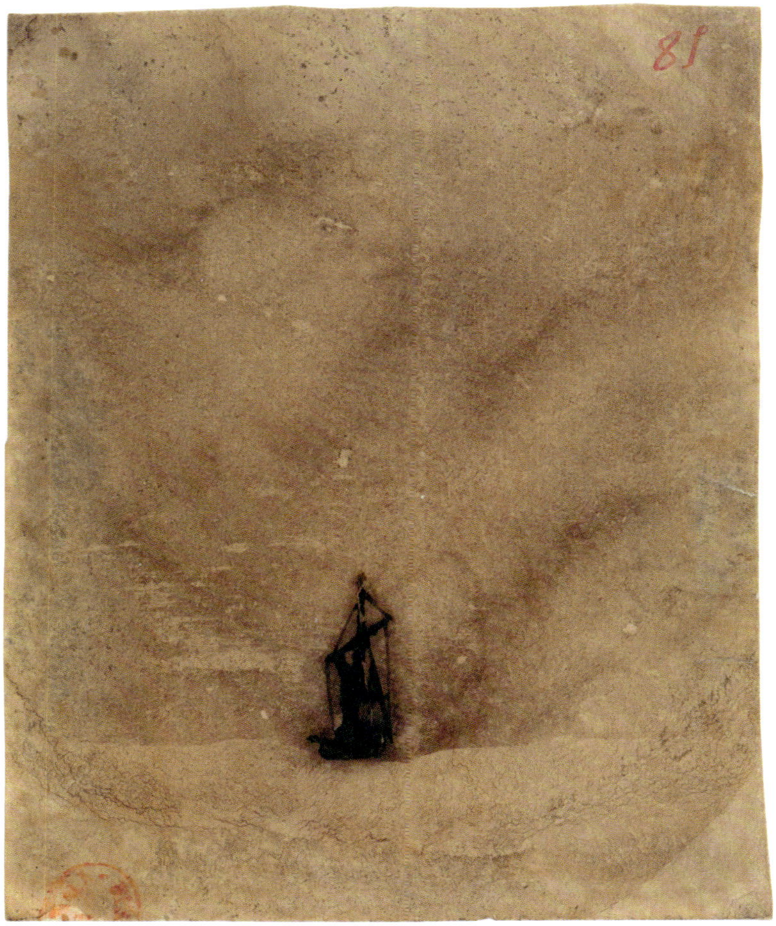

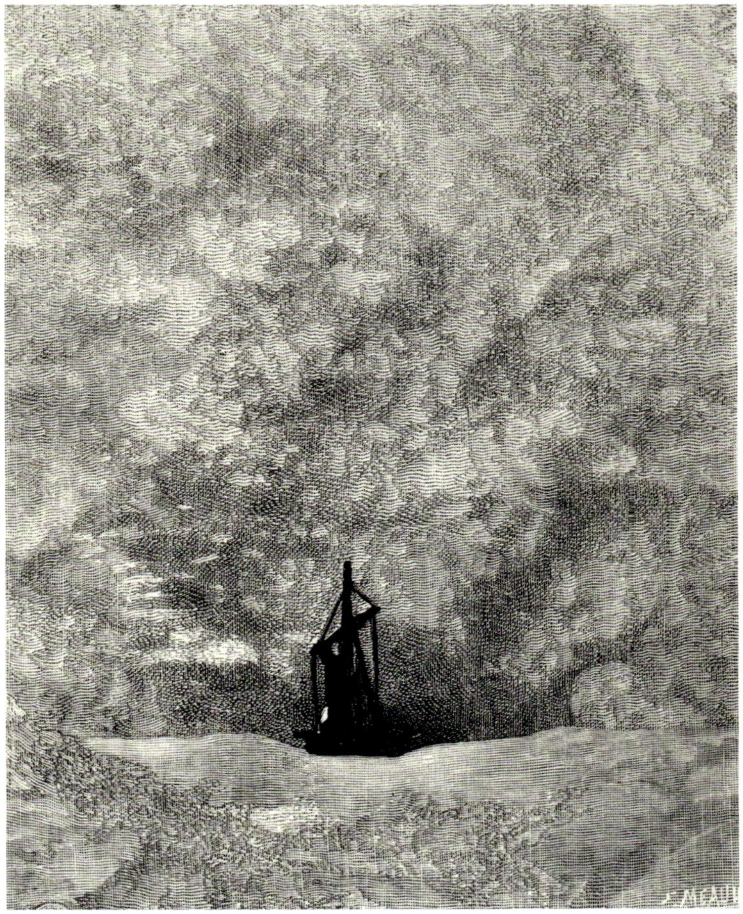

Hugo. The preface, presumably written by Meurice, declared that the portfolio's intended audience was Hugo's "friends and some amateurs."[29] The preface also noted that the additional marines were added to the portfolio in order to include "all the sketches for which the ocean, friend of his exile, had posed during its eighteen years in front of him." The portfolio edition seems to have drawn its inspiration from Hugo's original inclusion of his drawings with the manuscript that he had assembled years before in Guernsey, which was not intended to be published.

The medium of wood engraving relies solely on the use of line, as opposed to etching and aquatint, which can produce tonal effects. Thus Méaulle's intricate networks of lines translated, rather than imitated, the nuances of the delicate washes and dramatic chiaroscuro of clouds, mist, sky, and water in Hugo's drawing (see figs. 15, 16).[30] As has been noted, Hugo himself had used the term *translation* in reference to Doré's wood engravings for an 1866 edition of *Les travailleurs de la mer*.[31] Perhaps Hugo was convinced that Méaulle's interpretive wood engravings translated his drawings in a way that the earlier Chenay etchings had failed to achieve. But though Hugo

Fig. 15. Victor Hugo, *Dans la brume* (In the fog). Brown ink and wash. 3¾ × 3$\frac{1}{16}$ in. (9.5 × 7.7 cm). Bibliothèque nationale de France, NAF 24745, fol. 102.

Fig. 16. Fortuné-Louis Méaulle (French, 1844–1901), after Victor Hugo, *Dans la brume* (In the fog). Wood engraving. Sheet: 14⅛ × 10⅞ in. (35.8 × 27.7 cm). Maisons de Victor Hugo, Paris / Guernesey, MVHPEREC.1319.8.

purportedly had a close relationship with Méaulle, the extent of his role in the development of the edition is unknown. It seems plausible that Hugo's entourage, particularly Meurice, played a larger role in these endeavors late in the writer's life and that Hugo was not as directly engaged in the oversight of the productions as he had been with the Chenay album.[32] A persuasive example is the popular edition of *Les travailleurs de la mer*, published the same year as the limited-edition album, with full text and the addition of a substantial number of plates from two earlier editions illustrated by Chifflart in 1869 and Daniel Urrabieta Vierge in 1876 in addition to Méaulle's prints after Hugo's drawings. The result was a disappointing mélange, combining Vierge's more traditional illustrative style with Hugo's meditative and nuanced images. Given the disconnections between images by the three different artists as well as other liberties taken with the text and the placement of images, it is hard to imagine that Hugo had much involvement with the publication.

Two monumental engravings produced by Méaulle after drawings from Meurice's collection, *Le burg à la croix* of 1850 and *Le phare à la cloche* (Lighthouse with bell) of around 1866, perhaps represent the most successful translation of Hugo's drawings in printed form (figs. 17, 18).[33] Thought to date to around 1880, the prints were produced at the scale of the original drawings. *Le burg à la croix*, more than four feet wide, was the largest sheet in Hugo's oeuvre, attaining the scale of a large painting. Méaulle's wood engraving, intricately carved and printed from eighteen blocks, must be considered the fullest expression of his talent as an engraver. The rigorous networks of lines delineate a wide variety of textures, from the flickering light on the architectural elements to the glassy reflections on the water to the darkest shadows, and give a vibrant surface quality to the entire composition. The original drawing, purchased by Meurice in the Paris sale of Hugo's belongings in 1852 and exhibited in his home during Hugo's exile, was given back to the author on his return to Paris. Hugo in turn made an elaborate frame for it and returned it to his friend in gratitude (see fig. 11). For Meurice, whose collection later formed the core of the Maison de Victor Hugo, the grand drawing, created decades earlier, remained the pinnacle of Hugo's achievement as an artist.[34]

These two drawings and many others from Meurice's large collection were among the most prominent of those presented in the first exhibition of Hugo's drawings, at the Galerie Georges Petit in Paris in 1888, three years after Hugo's death, which presented astonishing examples of his work to great acclaim. Still emphasizing Hugo's stature as a literary giant, the exhibition also included several important manuscripts that the author had bequeathed to the Bibliothèque nationale de France, including those for *Les misérables* and *Les travailleurs de la mer*. Their accomplishment and importance notwithstanding, the drawings featured in that exhibition were masterworks of his traditional practice rather than his more abstract drawings. The daring inkblots, silhouettes, and abstractions that Hugo had left to his family and the Bibliothèque nationale along with his manuscripts would have to wait until a succession of exhibitions revealed them to the public during the course of the next century.

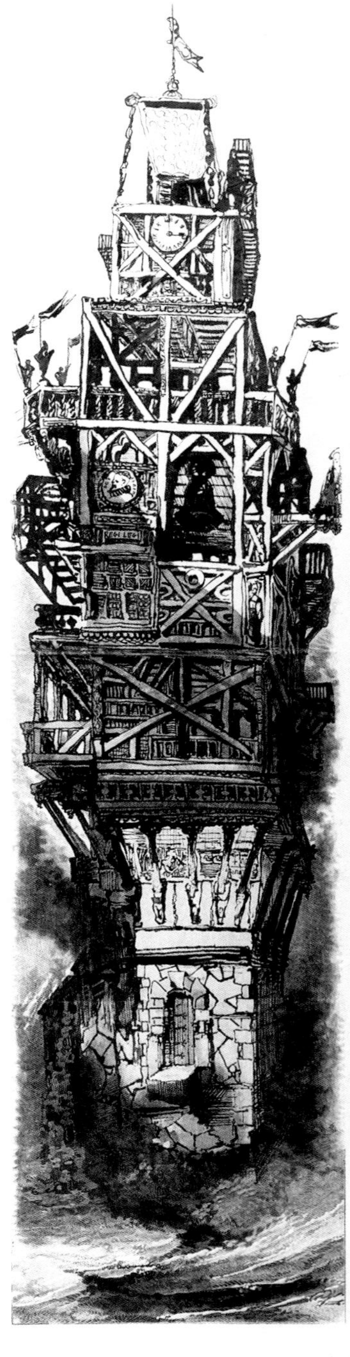

Fig. 17. Fortuné-Louis Méaulle (French, 1844–1901), after Victor Hugo, *Le phare à la cloche* (Lighthouse with bell), ca. 1880. Wood engraving. Sheet: 35 13/16 × 11½ in. (91 × 29.2 cm). Bibliothèque nationale de France, AA-5 (MEAULLE, LOUIS FORTUNE).

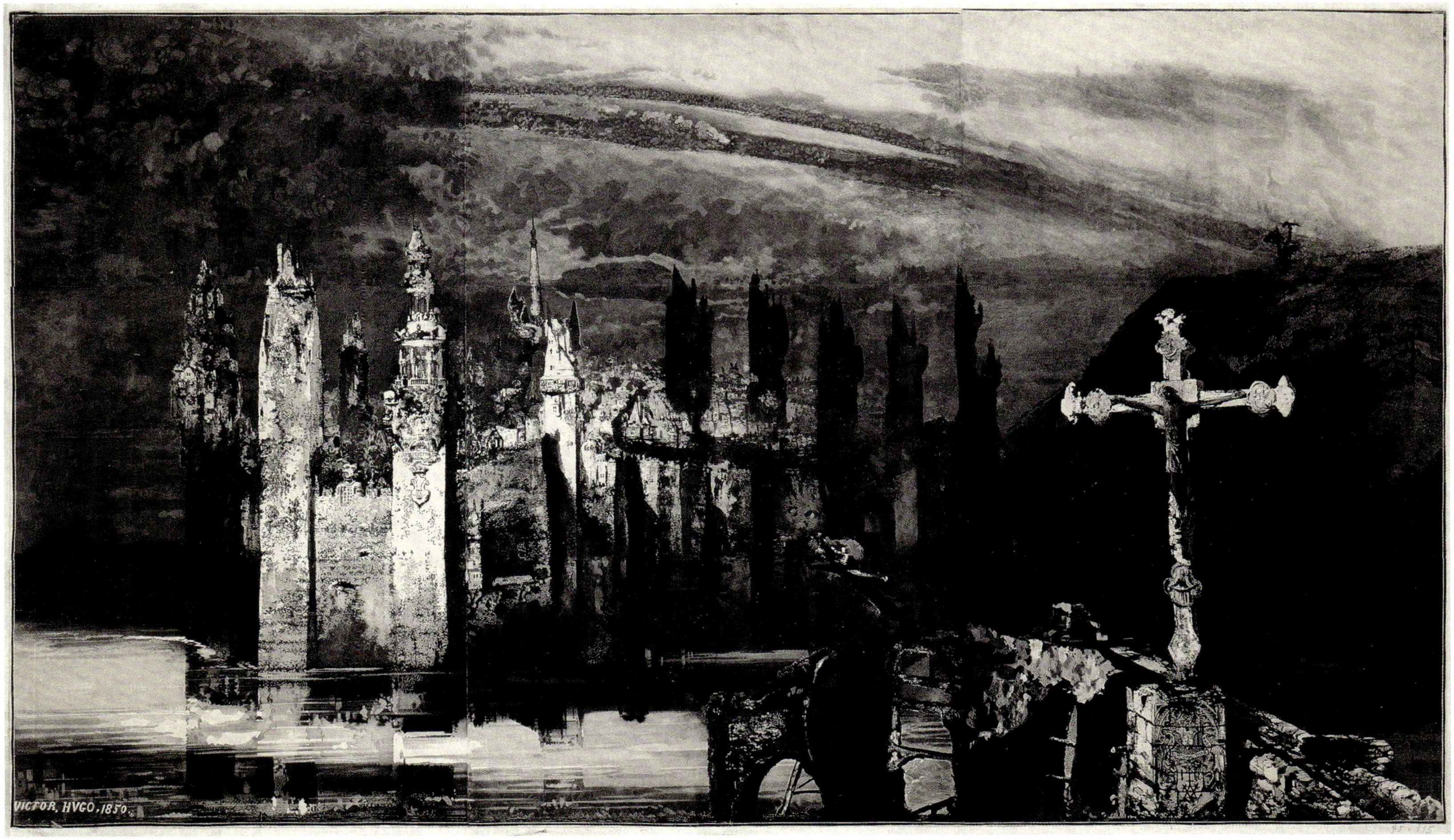


Fig. 18. Fortuné-Louis Méaulle (French, 1844–1901), after Victor Hugo, *Le burg à la croix* (The castle with the cross), ca. 1880. Wood engraving. Sheet: 39⅜ × 53⅛ in. (100 × 135 cm). Bibliothèque nationale de France, AA-7 (MEAULLE, LOUIS FORTUNE).

## Notes

1. Victor Hugo to Charles Baudelaire, April 29, 1860, in *Correspondance*, vol. 2, *1849–1866*, vol. 12 of *Œuvres complètes de Victor Hugo* (Paris: Albin Michel, 1950), 334.
2. For the legacy of Hugo's drawings, see Pierre Georgel, "Les avatars du peintre malgré lui," in *La gloire de Victor Hugo*, exh. cat. (Paris: Réunion des musées nationaux, 1985), 482–95. See also Georgel, "The Artist in Spite of Himself," and Florian Rodari, "Victor Hugo, a Precursor *a Posteriori*," in *Shadows of a Hand: The Drawings of Victor Hugo*, exh. cat. (New York: Drawing Center, 1998), 13–20, 21–28.
3. Jean Adhémar included Hugo as an engraver and illustrator in his major inventory of French prints, despite his acknowledgment that Hugo had never actually made prints. See Adhémar, *Inventaire du fonds français après 1800* (Paris: Bibliothèque nationale, 1949), 526–28. For Hugo's relationships with printmakers of the period, see Pierre Georgel, "Le romantisme des années 1860: Correspondance Victor Hugo–Philippe Burty," *Revue de l'art*, no. 20 (1973): 58–64. See also Gérard Blanchard, "Victor Hugo et les graveurs de son temps," *Communication et langages*, no. 62 (1984): 65–85, and *Victor Hugo (1802–1885): Photographies et dessins gravés*, exh. cat. (Bordeaux: Conseil général de la Gironde, 2002). See Valérie Sueur-Hermel, "Fortuné Méaulle, interprète de Victor Hugo, ou la gravure sur bois au service du 'choc des rayons et des ombres,'" *Nouvelles de l'estampe*, no. 185–86 (December 2002–February 2003): 34n12.
4. Théophile Gautier, "Monsieur Victor Hugo dessinateur," *La Presse*, June 27, 1838.
5. The drawing recalls the many that appeared in series such as *Voyages pittoresques et romantiques dans l'ancienne France*, a multivolume endeavor published from 1820 to 1878 that documented the monuments of various regions of France.
6. In an 1863 letter to Philippe Burty, Hugo notes that Marvy had engraved sixteen of his drawings. See Georgel, "Romantisme des années 1860," 39. The Bibliothèque nationale has four landscapes by Marvy (cote Ef-331a, pet. Fol.), and the others are unknown. Hugo's drawing for the drypoint illustrated in fig. 10 is dated 1842 and was formerly in the collection of Ian Woodner. See http://www.libson-yarker.com/pictures/landscape.
7. See Jonathan Mayne, ed., *Art in Paris, 1845–1862: Salons and Other Exhibitions Reviewed by Charles Baudelaire* (Ithaca, NY: Cornell University Press, 1981), 202.
8. See Paul Meurice, "Victor Hugo, Artist," pt. 2, *Harper's Monthly*, February 1901, 448. Pierre Georgel notes that Baudelaire saw Hugo's drawings in Mme Meurice's salon. Georgel, "Romantisme des années 1860," 15. For a discussion of *Le burg à la croix*, see Pierre Georgel, *1850, Le burg à la croix: Victor Hugo* (Paris: Paris musées and Maison de Victor Hugo, 2007).
9. "Il excelle à mêler, dans les fantaisies sombres et farouches, les effets de clair-obscur de Goya à la terreur architecturale de Piranesi." Théophile Gautier, "Vente du mobilier de Victor Hugo en 1852," *La Presse*, June 7, 1852.
10. See Janine Bailly-Herzberg, *L'eau forte de peintre au dix-neuvième siècle: La Société des Aquafortistes, 1862–1867*, 2 vols. (Paris: L. Laget, 1972).
11. "Sans la couleur, rien qu'avec l'ombre et la lumière, le clair-obscur tout seul et livré à lui-même, voilà le problème de l'eau forte." Quoted in Georgel, "Romantisme des années 1860," 32.
12. In 1864, at Burty's request, the etcher Léopold Flameng sent prepared etching plates to Hugo on the island. See Burty to Hugo, ibid., 43.
13. "On est aquafortiste d'une façon latent et sans s'en douter." Richard Lesclide, untitled article in *Paris à l'Eau-forte: Actualité, Curiosité, Fantaisie* 4 (November 12, 1876): 4; see also Georgel, "Romantisme des années 1860," 36n150.
14. "Beau talent avec une fidélité saisissante." For a discussion of the drawings, see Jean-Luc Mercié, *Victor Hugo et Julie Chenay: Documents inédits* (Paris: Lettres modernes, 1967), 95–110. See also Pierre Georgel, *Dessins de Victor Hugo*, exh. cat. (Paris: Maison de Victor Hugo; Villequier: Musée Victor Hugo, 1971), 119.
15. The heliogravure after the Chenay print in the collection of the Bibliothèque nationale (fig. 12) bears the inscription: "En vente chez tous les principaux marchands d'estampes de Paris, France et Amérique." Impressions of the Chenay aquatint can be found in the collection of the Maison de Victor Hugo (MVHP.E.3204, MVHP.E.3203). The print was also reproduced in an 1861 pamphlet published by Dentu and Dusacq, which included transcriptions of two letters by Hugo (MVHH JOH 1861).
16. "À la fois un livre et un album; un livre par le texte coloré et original de Théophile Gautier et un album par les dessins originaux du grande poète." See Maurice Clouard, "Notes sur les dessins de Victor Hugo accompagnées de lettres inédites," *Revue d'Histoire Littéraire de la France* 5, no. 3 (1898): 355.
17. "Elle est du reste gravée par M. Paul Chenay avec une science fidèle qui n'enlève rien à la naïveté de l'original." Théophile Gautier, preface to *Dessins de Victor Hugo* (Paris, 1863), 20. Gautier's preface was written the same year as his preface for the first portfolio of original etchings by the Société des Aquafortistes, in which he lauded Rembrandt as the paragon of etchers.
18. Contemporary journals such as the *Gazette des Beaux-Arts* followed similar formats, combining wood engravings with text but prominently featuring etchings as single-sheet prints. See Antony Griffiths, *The Print before Photography: An Introduction to European Printmaking, 1550–1820* (London: British Museum, 2016), 497.
19. See Georgel, "Romantisme des années 1860," 14, 18. Two drawings for the Chenay album are included in this exhibition (see pp. 82, 87).

20. "Je ne veux *d'aucune caricature*; il importe que l'album reste absolument sérieux." Clouard, "Notes sur les dessins," 348. A copy of the book in the collection of the Maison de Victor Hugo includes this and other letters from Hugo to Chenay, pasted in the volume, presumably by Chenay himself. While the title page is the same as that in the regular edition, it includes impressions of the prints before the addition of titles.
21. For a discussion of the critical response to the album, see Georgel, "Romantisme des années 1860," 16.
22. Hugo to Burty, April 18, 1864, ibid., 41. Marvy had died in 1850 at a young age, a short time after making etchings based on Hugo's drawings. For further discussion of Burty as a critic, see also Gabriel P. Weisberg, *The Independent Critic: Philippe Burty and the Visual Arts of Mid-Nineteenth Century France* (New York: Peter Lang, 1993), and Michael R. Orwicz, *Art Criticism and Its Institutions in Nineteenth-Century France* (Manchester: Manchester University Press, 1994).
23. Hugo to Burty, January 20, 1869, in Georgel, "Romantisme des années 1860," 54.
24. For a discussion of the relationship between Hugo and Chifflart, see Marie-Laure Prévost and Valérie Sueur-Hermel, "Autour des *Travailleurs de la mer*: Le dialogue de Victor Hugo et François-Nicolas Chifflart à propos de l'édition illustrée de 1869," *Revue de la Bibliothèque nationale de France*, no. 33 (2009): 42–55. See also Pierre Georgel, *Les dessins de Victor Hugo pour "Les travailleurs de la mer" de la Bibliothèque nationale* (Paris: Herscher, 1985), and Marie-Laure Prévost, *Victor Hugo: L'homme océan* (Paris: Bibliothèque nationale and Seuil, 2002).
25. See Prévost and Sueur-Hermel, "Autour des *Travailleurs*," 43ff.
26. See Griffiths, *Print before Photography*, 489, and Stephen Bann, *Distinguished Images: Prints in the Visual Economy of Nineteenth-Century France* (New Haven, CT: Yale University Press, 2013), esp. 16ff. Whereas illustrators such as Doré drew directly on the blocks, Hugo's wood engravings were made from his preexisting drawings.
27. For an extensive discussion of Méaulle and his prints after Hugo's drawings, see Valérie Sueur-Hermel, "Fortuné Méaulle, interprète de Victor Hugo, ou la gravure sur bois au service du 'choc des rayons et des ombres,'" *Nouvelles de l'estampe*, no. 185–86 (December 2002–February 2003): 32–45. The popular edition *Victor Hugo illustré*, begun in 1876 and not finished until 1897, combined engravings after Hugo's drawings with illustrations by an eclectic group of artists, including Gustave Brion, François Chifflart, Daniel Urrabieta Vierge, Léopold Flameng, and Jules Laurens. An 1876 edition of *Quatrevingt-treize* included illustrations of drawings by Hugo engraved by Méaulle combined with those of artists such as Émile-Antoine Bayard, Karl Bodmer, and Daniel Urrabieta Vierge. See also Ségolène Le Men, "L'édition illustrée, un musée pour lire," in *Gloire de Victor Hugo*, 527–68.
28. Philippe Burty, "Les dessins de Victor Hugo," *L'Art*, no. 37 (1875): 32–38. Méaulle also engraved a number of drawings owned by Paul Meurice, including *Château de Sylva*, shown in the Salon of 1876 and illustrated the following year in the magazine *Le Monde Illustré* under the title *Châteaux en Espagne*.
29. Edition of 100 on vellum paper, 80 on Whatman, and 70 on japan paper.
30. As noted in Sueur-Hermel, "Fortuné Méaulle," 40.
31. See ibid., 39, 40, for a discussion of the *bois de teinte* or *bois d'interprétation* in comparison with the *bois de trait* or *en fac-similé*.
32. See Georgel, *Dessins de Victor Hugo*, 27, and Sueur-Hermel, "Fortuné Méaulle," 39.
33. Impressions of *Le burg à la croix* are in the Département des estampes et de la photographie at the Bibliothèque nationale (AA7 MEAULLE) and at the Maison de Victor Hugo in Paris (inv. MVHP.E.1498). A proof impression of *Le phare à la cloche* is in the Département des estampes et de la photographie at the Bibliothèque nationale (AA5 MEAULLE), and the blocks are in the Maison de Victor Hugo in Paris (inv. MVHP.E.3544). On the drawing for *Le phare à la cloche*, see *Gloire de Victor Hugo*, 808, no. 873, illustrated on 55 and 609.
34. Meurice discussed *Le burg à la croix* in his article about Hugo's drawings, but his role in the creation of the wood engraving is unknown. See Meurice, "Victor Hugo, Artist," 448.

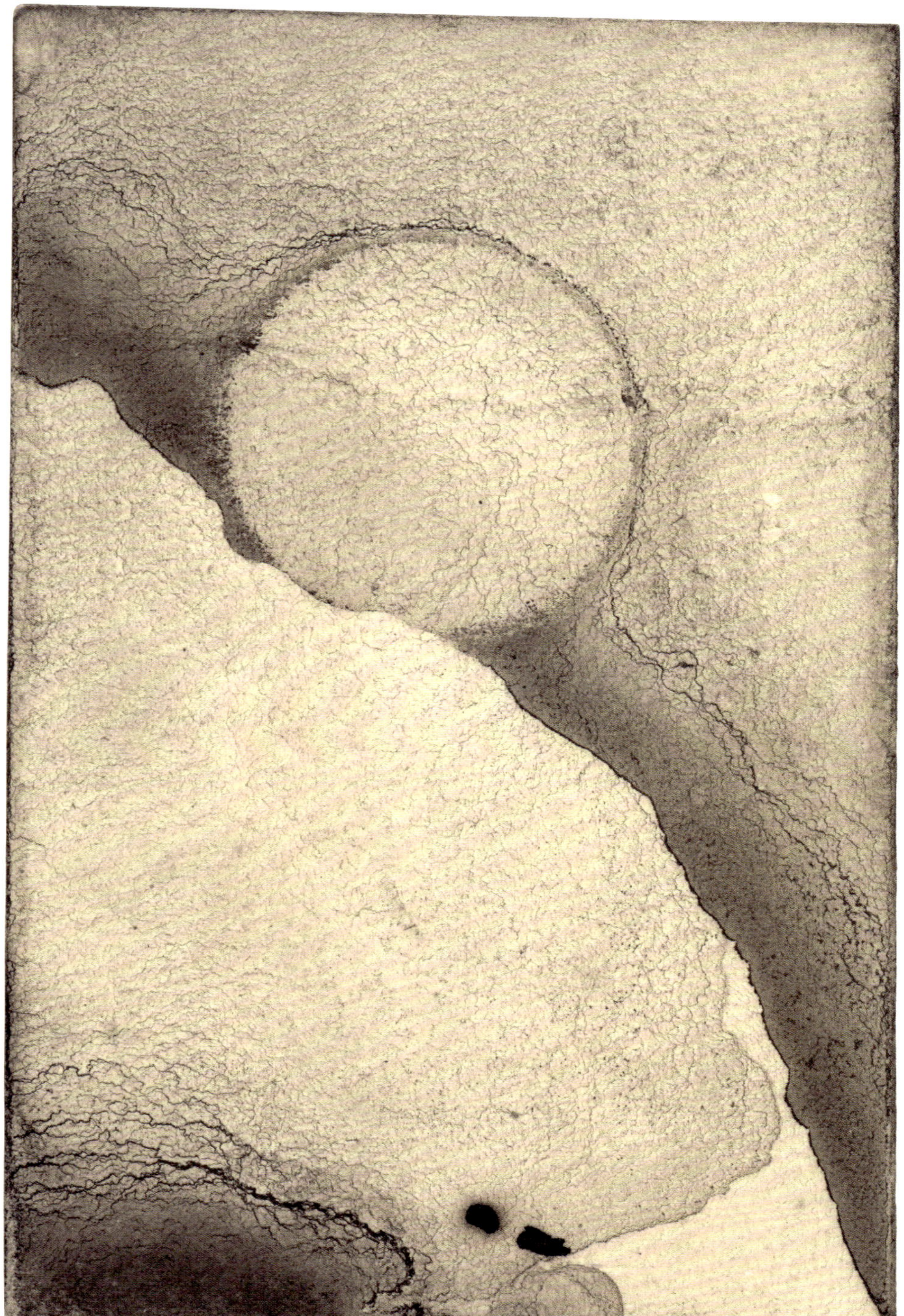

# The Promontory of Dream

## Cosmic Landscapes and Infinite Visions of Night in the Drawings of Victor Hugo

Allegra Pesenti

An unspeakable ceiling of shadows; a depth of obscurity that no diver can fathom; a light mingled with the obscurity, a strange somber vanquished light; brightness reduced to powder: seeds or ashes? millions of torches that give no light; a vast ignition that keeps its secret hidden; a diffusion of light into dust, like a shower of sparks halted in midflight; the turbulence of the whirlpool and the immobility of the tomb; the problem that opens up a precipitous gulf; an enigma that both shows and conceals its face; the infinite masked in blackness: such is the night. All this weighs heavily on man.

*Un indicible plafond de ténèbres; une haute obscurité sans plongeur possible; de la lumière mêlée à cette obscurité, on ne sait quelle lumière vaincue et sombre; de la clarté mise en poudre; est-ce une semence? Est-ce une cendre? Des millions de flambeaux, nul éclairage; une vaste ignition qui ne dit pas son secret, une diffusion de feu en poussière qui semble une volée d'étincelles arrêtée, le désordre du tourbillon et l'immobilité du sépulcre, le problème offrant une ouverture de précipice, l'énigme montrant et cachant sa face, l'infini masqué de noirceur, voilà la nuit. Cette superposition pèse à l'homme.*

—Victor Hugo

The bewildering forces of nature and the towering impressions of man-made monuments form the defining features of Victor Hugo's visual oeuvre. The notion of monumentality is evoked in Hugo's drawings through the primary and material elements of water and stone. In his most descriptive sheets a medieval fort may withstand the tremors of a storm, and a soaring cliff can stand firm against the charge of the sea. The versatility and metamorphosis of water characterize Hugo's more abstract creations, in which pure pools of wash, or "stains," turn into illusory shapes as they touch the paper surface (pp. 142–51). The forms deliquesce and subside into an atmospheric and indefinable sense of mystery that places them closer to ether than to earth. Hugo's interest in the intangible was in fact as profound as his acknowledgment of the physical foundations of terrestrial life. The complexity of humankind and its immediate sphere pervades all his creative endeavors, but so do the limitless expanses of the skies and the cosmic spaces beyond human reach. The free play of his imagination within this realm of infinity is reflected in his celestial landscapes.

Opposite: Victor Hugo, *Tache* (Stain), ca. 1850. Brown ink and wash on paper. 3⅝ × 2⅜ in. (9.2 × 6 cm). Nationalmuseum, Stockholm, NMH 28/1981.

## “Fleeing Spheres” and Hugo’s Consideration of the Skies

There are vast movements of heavenly bodies, the family of the stars, the family of the planets; the pollen of the zodiac; . . . there is sap in the globes, light outside the globes, there are wandering atoms, scattered seeds . . . distances that are like dreams, dizzying movements, worlds plunging into the incalculable, prodigies pursuing one another in the shadows, a mechanism in permanent operation, the breathing of fleeing spheres, wheels that can be felt turning; . . . things are there, and then withdraw; they are unassailable, they are out of reach, they cannot be approached.

*Il y a de vastes évolutions d’astres, la famille stellaire, la famille planétaire, le pollen zodiacal . . . il y a la sève dans les globes, la lumière hors des globes, l’atome errant, le germe épars . . . des distances qui ressemblent à des rêves, des circulations vertigineuses, des enfoncements de mondes dans l’incalculable, des prodiges s’entre-poursuivant dans les ténèbres, un mécanisme une fois pour toutes, des souffles de sphères en fuite, des roues qu’on sent tourner . . . cela est et se dérobe; c’est inexpugnable, c’est hors de portée, c’est hors d’approche.*[1]

A solitary man perched on a tall rock leans back to peer at the flock of birds that hover above him in the form of a halo (fig. 19).[2] The standing figure in this rapidly jotted ink sketch by Hugo is a small but cogent allusion to the author’s own observations of what lies above and, more particularly, of his presence on earth vis-à-vis nature itself and the yonder spheres. Hugo had been in exile in the Channel Islands for more than twelve years when he completed the sketchbook that contains this drawing (1864–65): he and his family settled in Jersey in 1852 and subsequently lived in Guernsey from 1855 to 1870. The self-referencing scene depicted here alludes to an isolated existence marked largely by the confluences of the forces of climate and wilderness.

Exile was a status that suited Hugo’s temperament well, even though it separated him from the culturally and socially engaged life he was accustomed to in France. Proud of his political stance, he stood strong against Louis-Napoléon Bonaparte’s dissolution of the French National Assembly in 1851 and vigorously contested the newly imposed antiparliamentarian constitution. A photograph of the author seated atop a Jersey cliff known as the Rocher des Proscrits (exiles’ rock) portrays him gazing up and beyond the horizon (p. 127). Taken around 1853 by his son Charles, it was undoubtedly staged by Hugo himself, as most of their photographs of this period were.[3] Perhaps not incidentally, Hugo’s pose and placement prefigure those of the man in the sketch mentioned above. The portrait encapsulates the image of himself that he sought to project to the world: distant but undefeated and an idealist as steadfast as the stones beneath him and as tumultuous as the skies above. These aspects of the natural world, which include the ground we walk on and the air we breathe, are shared by all human beings regardless of their origins and however distant they may be from their place of birth. The author professed as much in a speech addressed to a crowd of fellow exiles and locals in Jersey on June 18, 1860: “Know that there is no foreign land; the earth in its entirety is the mother of man, severe and profound. In all the places where he has loved, where he has cried, where he has suffered, everywhere, man is at home.”[4]

Hugo emphasized the universal experience of man’s connection to earth in *Ce que c’est que l’exil*, the volume that serves as an introduction to *Pendant l’exil* (1875):

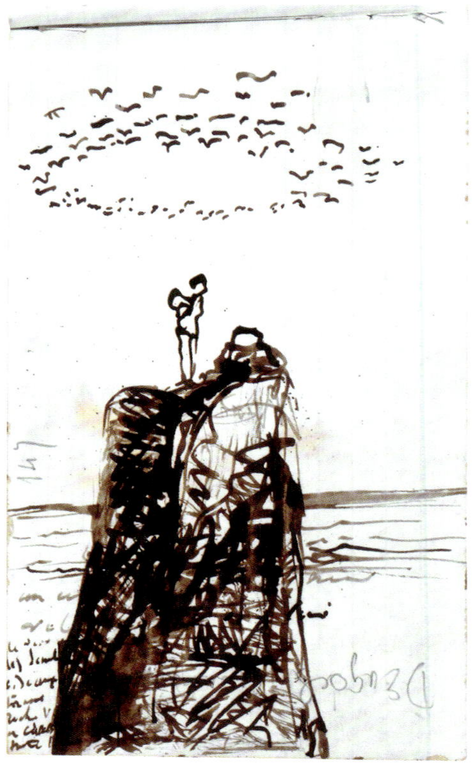

Fig. 19. Victor Hugo, *Gilliatt sur la grande Douvre* (Gilliatt on the Great Douvre), ca. 1864–65. Brown ink on paper. $7\frac{5}{16} \times 4\frac{7}{16}$ in. (18.5 × 11.2 cm). Bibliothèque nationale de France, NAF 13459, f. 73v.

"You can rip a tree from its roots, you will never rip the day from the sky. Tomorrow, dawn."[5] The exile can find truth and confidence in the greater elements above and below since he is, in Hugo's own words, "so deeply entrenched in darkness that he has only the sun to wish for."[6]

The act of looking up and outward was also inherent to the structure of Hauteville House, the Hugo residence on Guernsey, which was carefully arranged and decorated by the author himself. Every object was strategically chosen and displayed within its walls, and each room was filled with symbols and riddles related to Hugo's philosophies of life, with references to God, exile, death, ancient mythologies, and more. A wooden sculpture of Saint John with upturned head and hands personifies the exaltation of heaven (fig. 20). It is placed on a mirrored mantelpiece amid various objets d'art, along with the bold inscription on its plinth, which was likely carved by Hugo himself: "Ad Caelum" (to the sky).

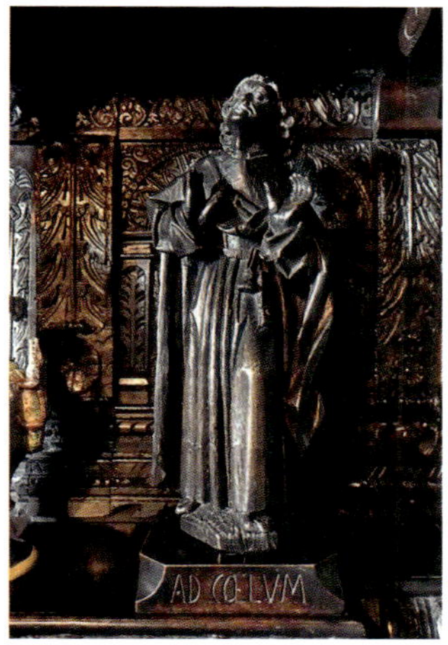


Fig. 20. *Saint John*, n.d. Wood. Hauteville House.

Hugo positioned his own room at the summit of the house. From this intimate and personal den in the terraced niche known as the lookout, he enjoyed sweeping views of the bay below, with a swath of sea in the distance and a wide expanse of sky above. The variegated and often tempestuous climate of the Channel Islands provided an evolving visual drama through the screens of this towered room's bow window (fig. 21). It was presumably in this capsuled space that many of the drawings presented in this exhibition were made and that some of his most renowned books, such as *Les travailleurs de la mer* (*The Toilers of the Sea*) and *Les misérables*, were born. Charles Hugo described it as "a little glass belvedere, open toward all horizons, vast for the soul, narrow for the body, like the cabin of a captain containing everything in an intimate space: the small table, the paper, the ink, the pen, a compact iron bed as rigid as the bed of a soldier."[7] An inscription on the final page of the manuscript of *Les misérables* alludes to the interconnection of Victor Hugo's activities on Guernsey, where writing, drawing, and observation of the skies overlapped. Immediately following "Fin" (indicating the end of the novel), Hugo wrote: "Today June 30, apparition of a comet at 8 o'clock in the evening. It is immense. Its tail is seventeen million leagues long."[8]

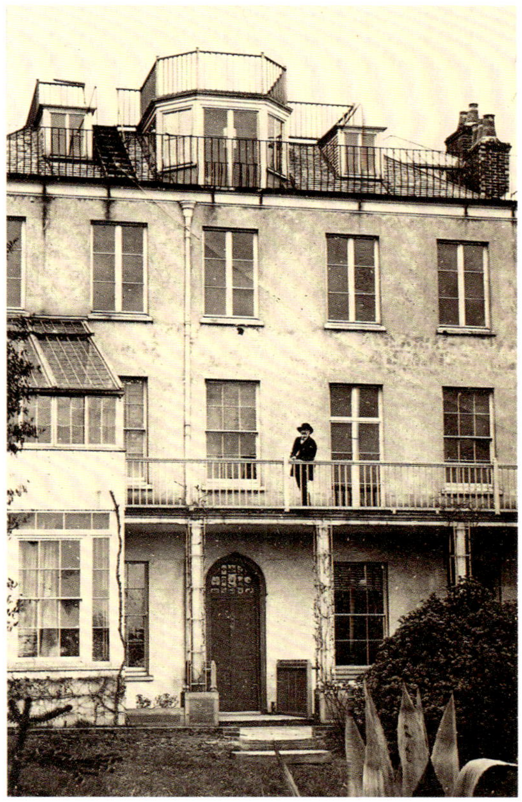

Fig. 21. Arsène Garnier, *Victor Hugo on the Terrace of Hauteville House in Guernsey*, 1868. Salted paper print. 3$\frac{9}{16}$ × 2$\frac{3}{16}$ in. (9 × 5.6 cm). Maisons de Victor Hugo, Paris / Guernesey, MVHP.PH.3334.

We may well imagine him in his lookout conjuring the marbled algae-like sky in a drawing now housed at the Morgan Library, New York, for instance (p. 133). Pasted onto the frontispiece of a copy of *Les travailleurs de la mer* from Pierre-Jules Hetzel's 1880–83 edition of *Œuvres complètes*, the drawing was probably presented as a gift from Hugo to Fortuné-Louis Méaulle in gratitude for his wood-engraved illustrations for the novel.[9] The face of a demon is camouflaged within the simulated storm of this haunting seascape. The reticulated blue ink is a rare occurrence of colored pigment in Hugo's drawn oeuvre, making this one of his most unusual experiments on paper. The effect of the projected vistas from Hauteville House is similarly echoed in *Les misérables*: "He feels buried at once by those two infinites, the ocean and the sky; the one a grave, the other a shroud."[10]

## "Flickering Constellations" and Hugo's Visions of the Night

From fathomless depths weaves Night
a net, with glowing Mars and Venus bright;
and even as the hours tick by,
this net spreads and fills the evening sky.
While in that mesh of darkness, ever thicker,
the constellations flicker.

*La Nuit tire du fond des gouffres inconnus*
*Son filet où luit Mars, où rayonne Vénus,*
*Et, pendant que les heures sonnent,*
*Ce filet grandit, monte, emplit le ciel des soirs,*
*Et dans ses mailles d'ombre et dans ses réseaux noirs*
*Les constellations frissonnent.*[11]

Two large wooden panels carved and painted with scenes from the legend of Saint George flank a window in Hugo's bedroom (fig. 22). At the lower edge of one of them the gilded initials *VH* attribute the conception and execution of these chivalric scenes to the author himself. For the decoration of his most private quarters, Hugo chose a realm of myth interlaced with conquest and courtship, more particularly images that conjure a world of fiction, on the one hand, and of real human instincts, on the other. A prominent star caps the romantic episode in which an elegantly adorned maiden, the princess, holds out a flower to the victorious Saint George, prostrate and adoring below her. The star and the story accompanied Hugo's own visions of the night within the very room in which he wrote, drew, looked out, slept, and dreamed.

For Hugo, night was the time when reality and imagination could conjoin. He sought the night to explore and peruse. When his son Charles derided the island of Jersey, Hugo, disapproving, asked if he had ever walked by its port. "I roam around there every evening as the night falls," the elder Hugo continued. "Yes, every evening at dusk, when the sun has sunken, when the sky is filled with clouds and stars begin to shimmer, I walk alone along the port."[12] His brother-in-law Paul Chenay remembers this habit and the author's love of night excursions through the Guernsey wilderness in a published account of his visits with the family on the island:

> Victor Hugo had long envisaged a nocturnal excursion to that part of the island, so wild and picturesque. . . . The night being clear, the moment seemed right, and he proposed the outing. I accepted enthusiastically, and we immediately set out on foot, sticks in hand. It was nearly midnight . . . in the midst of that vast, lonely plain, drenched in the white moonlight that cast a sinister glow, like a huge shroud, on the buildings from which we were still quite distant, and on the stones lying on the ground. The effect was grandiose and mysterious. It almost seemed as though the famous author of *The Hunchback of Notre Dame* had ordered an ordinary painter to execute this stage set, based on his own imagination.[13]

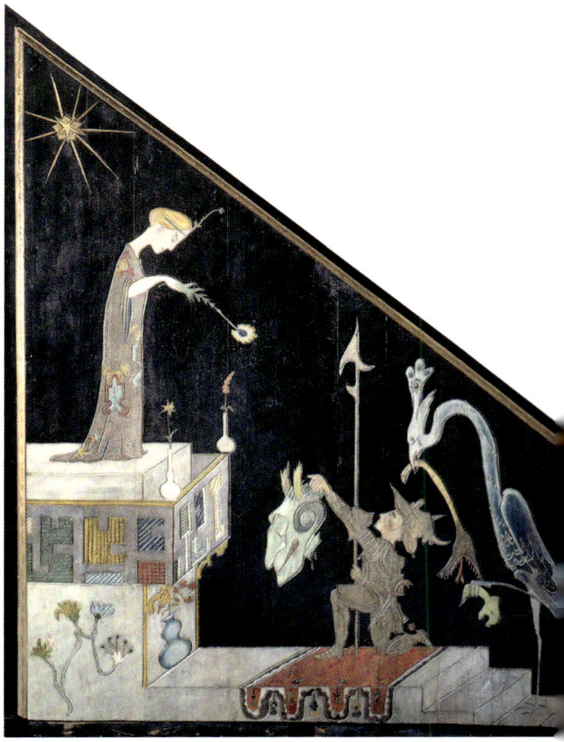

Fig. 22. *Saint George and the Princess*, painted panel in Victor Hugo's bedroom at Hauteville House, Guernsey. Maisons de Victor Hugo, Paris / Guernesey.

The time of day is often indistinguishable in Hugo's drawings, most of which were rendered in a range of brown inks and washes. Far from simple monochromatic works, however, they feature variegated tones and chiaroscuro effects that suggest different atmospheres, from a misty morning to the more somber shadows of crepuscule. One

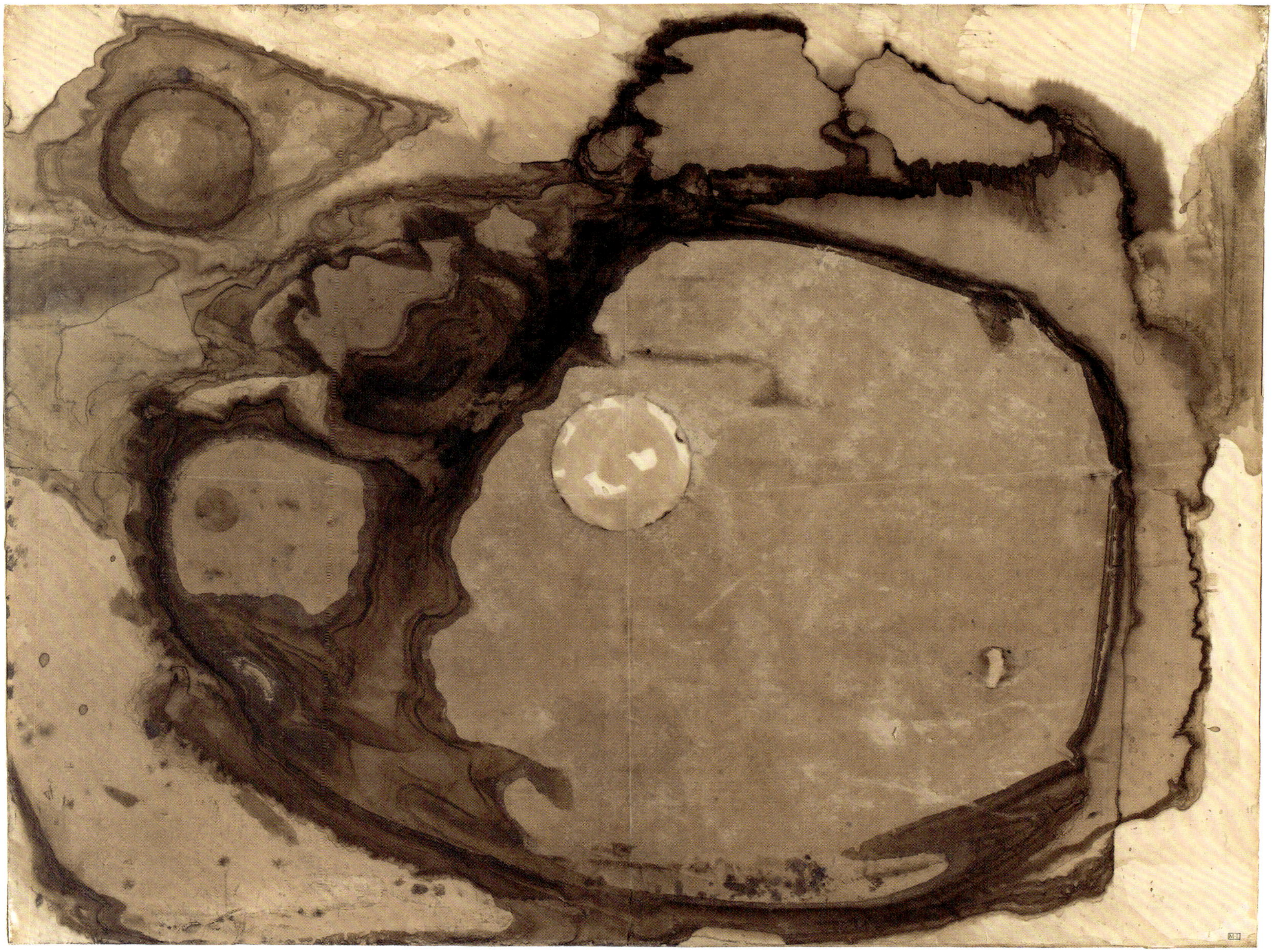

singular series of drawings relates specifically to the skies after nightfall. An intricate technique of ink dilution, the use of both sides of the quill pen (the feathered plume and the nib), and the application of paper or card stencils to create silhouettes of the moon, the sun, or planets distinguish this group within Hugo's drawn oeuvre. The cosmos and its stellar constellations inform a series of semiabstract planetary compositions that are indeed unique to Hugo's experimental and idiosyncratic drawing practice. They are his stones and stains of the night.

*Taches-planètes* (Stains-planets, ca. 1850; fig. 23), now in the collection of the Musée du Louvre in Paris, is among the largest and most striking of a dozen related sheets that survive today.[14] Three disks of different dimensions, one central and two

Fig. 23. Victor Hugo, *Taches-planètes* (Stains-planets), ca. 1850. Brown ink and wash on paper. 17¹¹⁄₁₆ × 23¹⁄₁₆ in. (45 × 58.5 cm). Musée du Louvre, RF 54787-recto.

others to its left, are crowned by alternately shivering and undulating contours. Although the original title is unknown, the hazy aureoles and their luminous matter are reminiscent of nebulae, the clouds of gas and dust in interstellar space.[15] Hugo's attempt to enclose such immensity of form on paper is echoed in his own statement that "beauty is no other than infinity contained within a contour."[16] The clean outline of the central disk, or planet, was likely achieved with the use of a 2½-inch-diameter paper stencil. Spots of unstained paper that had been masked by the stencil introduce light to the composition, while layers of wash and graded intensities of brown ink emanate throughout the sheet. The marbling effect in the contours recalls the Japanese *suminagashi*, or "floating ink," technique, which is achieved by placing a sheet of paper over a shallow container of ink-stained water before gently retrieving the impressed sheet.

The process Hugo used in *Taches-planètes* is difficult to determine, but it likely involved soaking, folding, tilting, blotting, and manipulating the paper to allow the inks to flow freely over the surface of the sheet.[17] He may also have used solvents or gum arabic to create blank reserves within the composition. He adeptly applied a combination of chance and controlled effects in draftsmanship—not unlike the surrealist formulas for automatic drawing processes, such as Max Ernst's adoption of frottage or Oscar Dominguez's use of decalcomania, which postdate Hugo by almost seventy years.

The Louvre drawing is on the same type of paper as works by Hugo that are dated to 1850, and it too has been ascribed to that period, when he was still living in Paris and had set up a studio in his lover Juliette Drouet's apartment. Nonetheless, the dating is hard to ascertain since paper was easily stored and transported and could be used years after it was acquired. The Louvre sheet is in fact very similar in style and subject to a drawing in the Musée des Beaux-Arts in Dijon that is dated between 1853 and 1855.[18] A bolder and more abstract version of *Taches-planètes* at the Musée Victor Hugo in Paris has been assigned to the period between 1864 and 1869, but it seems more in character with works made on the Channel Islands in the mid-1850s (fig. 24).[19] It shares the twirls and drips of another equally whimsical sheet that dates to Hugo's time in Jersey, with the exception of that work's pungent tinge of blue wash on one of its three lunar imprints (p. 149).

Hugo developed the series of cosmic drawings during the period of his exile, particularly from around 1854. In his newly adopted environment, far from the familiar architecture of Paris and the medieval castles along the Rhine, he loosened his compositions and played with a free flow of forms. He became evermore dexterous and resourceful in his use of paper cutouts and stencils, especially in relation to the circular motif and its allusion to the moon and other planetary constellations. A scissored hole in one sheet is echoed by the inky imprints above it (p. 147). Moreover Hugo embraced the magic of form even in works that were used as stencils and that he preserved as objects in and of themselves rather than purely as practical tools of production.

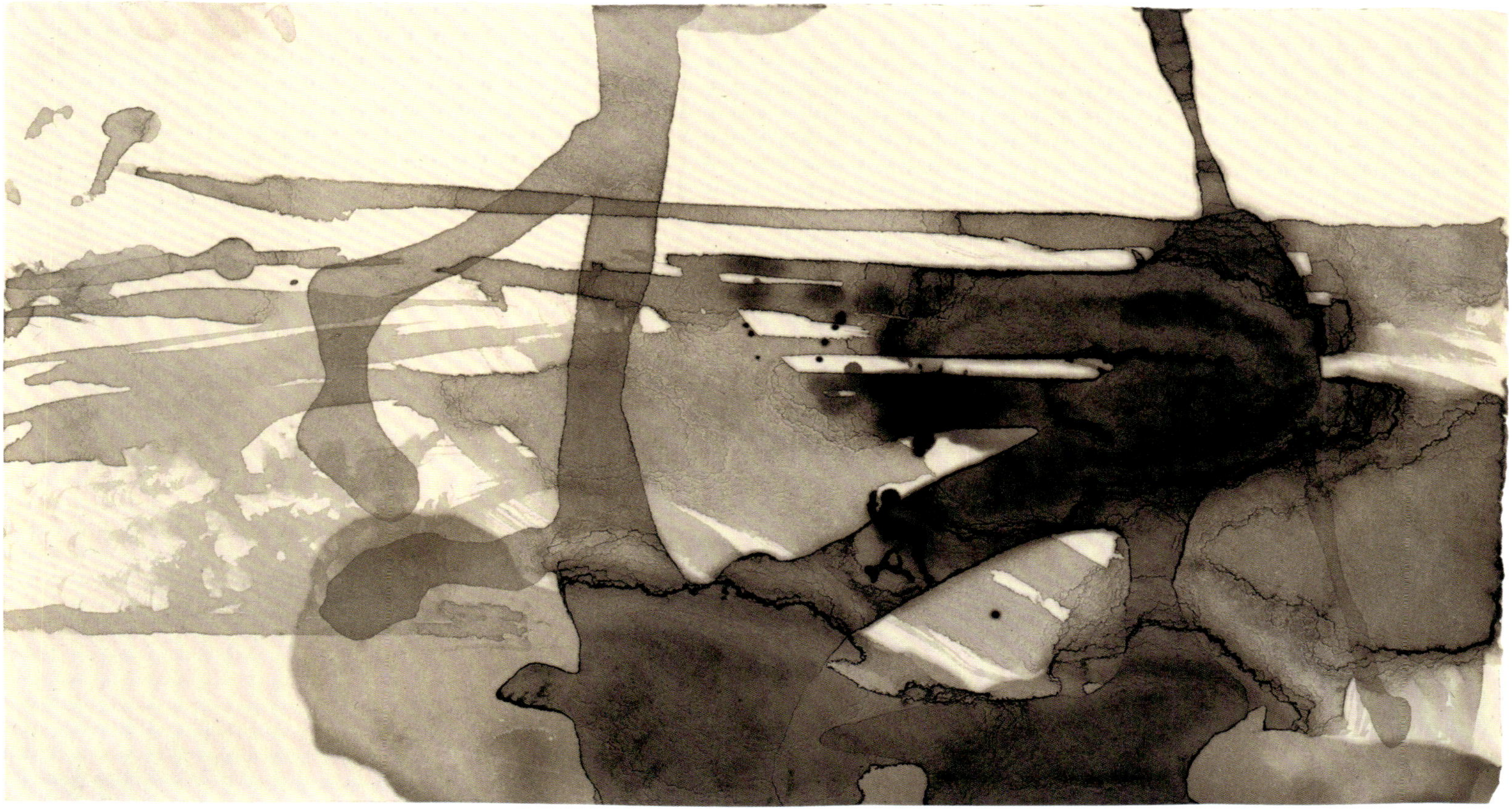

Fig. 24. Victor Hugo, *Composition abstraite* (Abstract composition), ca. 1864–69(?). Brown ink and wash on paper. 5¼ × 9⅝ in. (13.3 × 24.3 cm). Maisons de Victor Hugo, Paris / Guernesey, MVHP.D.2428.

The establishment of a photography studio at Marine Terrace, the family home on Jersey, in 1854 may well have contributed to Hugo's flair for technical experimentation and his curiosity regarding alchemical processes. The other pastime in the Hugo household that undoubtedly fired the writer's inspiration and connection to spirits and worlds beyond was his initiation to table-turning séances in 1853.[20] These activities, combined with his starlit excursions, contributed to the conception of these supranatural compositions. Hugo expresses one interpretation of the wondrous theater of the night in *Post-scriptum de ma vie*, composed of philosophical texts written in 1860 but published posthumously in 1901: "In the midst of this darkness there are lights; what is the purpose of these lights? They utter the unspeakable. They illumine the invisible. They enlighten, for they resemble torches; they gaze on something, for they resemble the eye of man."[21]

Perhaps not incidentally, the mysterious drawing known as *Planète-œil* (Planet-eye, ca. 1854–55; p. 143) was once part of a sketchbook devoted to "spiritualist" images made during séances in 1854 (their papers bear the same watermark, and they were both part of Hugo's gift to the state now housed at the Bibliothèque nationale de France).[22] Here a smoky haze of gray particles is simulated with graphite, stumped and brushed with the plumes of the quill, and a stencil was used to isolate the single planet (or perhaps the moon?) that drifts within it. Although the current title was assigned to this work after Hugo's time, the anthropomorphic association of globes and eyes does appear in his writings,[23] notably in the poems gathered in *Les contemplations*, which he was working on contemporaneously and published in 1856:

Night falls; the globe itself turns dazzlingly bright
Becomes a giant eye, and looks out at the night;

*Le soir vient; et le globe à son tour s'éblouit,*
*Devient un œil énorme et regarde la nuit;*[24]

The séances held in the Hugo home on Jersey were a channel to connect with a full spectrum of individuals, some known and some fictional, and with the planetary world that so fascinated Hugo. On July 26, 1854, Hugo and his fellow participants called on the inhabitants of the planet Mercury, for instance.[25] The Italian astronomer Galileo Galilei was summoned at another sitting. On November 10, 1854, a spirit called Death appeared and communicated: "Study human astronomy in depth. It is filled with germs of truth from which you will be able to extrapolate greater truths. For example, you will find it possible to establish the exact nomenclature of your planetary systems of worlds of reward and punitary worlds, all in function of their distance from the sun."[26]

Little is known about the circulation of Hugo's planetary drawings among his contemporaries beyond his close collaborators and family.[27] He sent a drawing of the Big Dipper to his daughter Léopoldine in 1837, while he was sojourning in Belgium, along with a letter that mentions the celestial constellations he had taught her to identify:[28]

I looked at churches and paintings every day, then in the evening I watched the sky and dreamt of you, my Didine, in seeing this beautiful constellation, this handsome chariot of God which I taught you to distinguish amidst the stars. See, my child, how God is great and how small we are: we place ink stains on paper like God places suns in the skies. It is with these letters that he writes. The sky is his book. . . . Meanwhile here is an image of [the landscape] while the other drawing simulates the Big Dipper. Imagine that my drawing sparkles, and you will believe what I saw.

*Tout le jour je regardais les églises et les peintures, et puis, le soir, je regardais le ciel, et je songeais encore à toi, ma Didine, en voyant cette belle constellation, ce beau chariot de Dieu, que je t'ai appris à distinguer parmi les étoiles. Vois, mon enfant, comme Dieu est grand, et comme nous sommes petits: où nous mettons des taches d'encre, il pose des soleils. C'est avec ces lettres-là qu'il écrit. Le ciel est son livre. . . . En attendant voici qui t'en donnera l'idée à peu près comme l'autre dessin donne l'idée de la Grande-Ourse. Suppose que mon dessin brille, et tu croiras voir ce que j'ai vu.*[29]

It is perhaps the very intimate context of Hugo's draftsmanship that released it from convention and allowed it to diverge from the ordinary. His originality was not lost on the printmaker François Chifflart, who was the favored illustrator of Hugo's writings. The large eye that regards the biblical figure of Cain from a tenebrous background in Chifflart's black chalk drawing *La conscience* (ca. 1860–68; fig. 25) simulates the glaring apparition in the related poem by Hugo ("The Eye was in the tomb and fixed on Cain").[30] Other artists, like the young Odilon Redon, were certainly inspired by Hugo's texts and may also have seen his drawings. The huge head and globular pupil in Redon's *Guardian Spirit of the Waters* (fig. 26), a compelling charcoal drawing from 1878, are particularly reminiscent of Hugo's metaphors, both in writing and on paper.

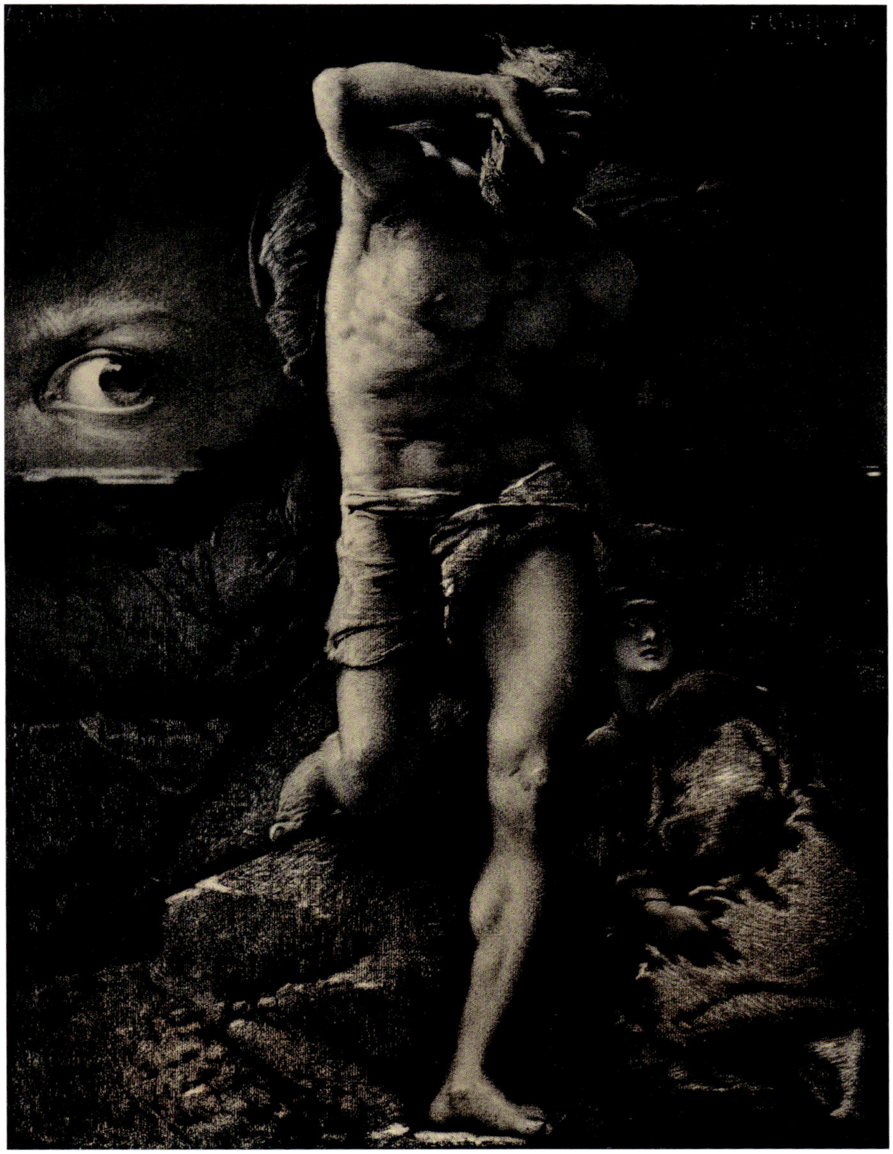

Fig. 25. François Chifflart, *La conscience*, ca. 1860–68. Black chalk on paper. $24\frac{1}{4}$ × $18\frac{1}{2}$ in. (61.6 × 47 cm). Maisons de Victor Hugo, Paris / Guernesey, MVHP.D.447.

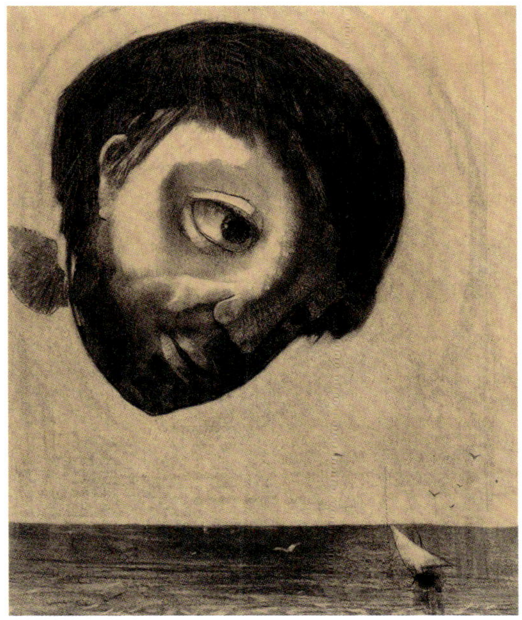

Fig. 26. Odilon Redon, *Guardian Spirit of the Waters*, 1878. Charcoal with touches of white chalk on paper. $18\frac{3}{8}$ × $14\frac{13}{16}$ in. (46.6 × 37.6 cm). The Art Institute of Chicago, David Adler Collection, 1950.1428.

Artists became more aware of Hugo's graphic oeuvre from the 1920s, when Jean Hugo, the author's great-grandson, and his wife, Valentine, introduced the work to their circle of friends, which included the poet Paul Éluard and other members of the surrealist group. Jean was at one time in possession of an enigmatic drawing of a single globe, veiled with somber washes, which Éluard had seen and supposedly titled *Planète* (ca. 1854; p. 151).[31] Valentine gifted two particularly subliminal compositions to André Breton. One is a conceptual interpretation of dawn rendered on a sheet that is minimal in size but infinite in scope, with just a hazy horizon line at its center and the word *AUBE* (dawn) inscribed beneath (fig. 27).[32] The other drawing is more cataclysmic in character, with its amalgamation of ink stains and particles of graphite powder scattered over the paper surface and a lunar disk, likely stenciled from a coin and set apart by its unruptured outline (fig. 28).[33] Breton was certainly attuned to Hugo's spontaneous techniques and to his ability to tap into the unconscious realm.[34] In a letter written to Charles Baudelaire in 1860, Hugo himself referred to his drawing practice as one that "renders more or less what I perceive in my eyes and above all in my mind."[35]

## The Moon between Fact and Fiction

It is the very error of the moon,
She comes more nearer earth than she was wont,
And makes men mad.

—William Shakespeare[36]

The Moon, as Othello recounts, has just passed too close to earth.

*La lune, comme dit Othello, vient de passer trop près de la terre.*

—Victor Hugo[37]

The moon is a poignant and recurring presence in the drawings of Victor Hugo. It often looms above his castles or lingers amid stains. It is also the subject of one of his most transporting yet lesser-known texts in prose. *Promontorium Somnii*, or *Le promontoire du songe* (The promontory of dream), is a personal, scientific, poetic, and historicized treatise on the moon that he wrote in 1863, although the first complete version wasn't published until the following century, in 1937.[38] It was inspired by a visit with the astronomer François Arago at the Observatoire de Paris that had taken place in 1834, about thirty years before Hugo wrote the text. Arago had recently been promoted to director of observations, and knowing of Hugo's interest, he invited him to view the moon with a telescope from one of the domes on the observatory's terrace. At the outset of the evening, Hugo recalled, "The night was clear, the air pure, the sky calm, the moon a crescent; with the naked eye you could make out the dark, mottled curve with

Fig. 27. Victor Hugo, *Aube* (Dawn), n.d. Brown ink and wash on paper. 2⁹⁄₁₆ × 2⁹⁄₁₆ in. (6.5 × 6.5 cm). Centre Pompidou, MNAM-CCI, AM 2003-3 (23).

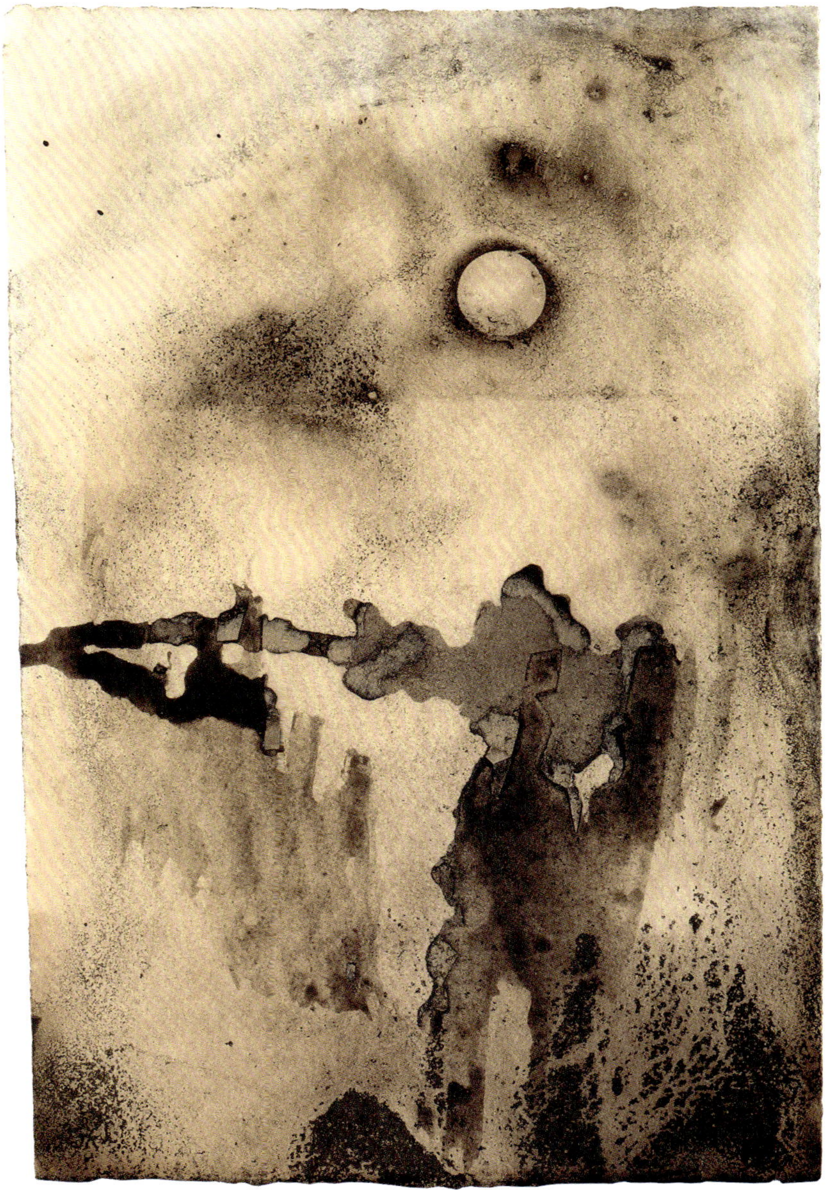

Fig. 28. Victor Hugo, Untitled, n.d. Brown ink and wash on paper. 10¹⁄₁₆ × 6½ in. (25.5 × 16.5 cm). Centre Pompidou, MNAM-CCI, AM 2003-3 (22).

its ashen glow."[39] His account of the turn of events that unfolded is vividly telling of his vision of the outer worlds and provides a parallel context for the drawings.

At first the view through the telescope bewildered Hugo, as all he perceived was darkness and a sense of profound emptiness.[40] Disappointment arose as the pristine form he was accustomed to seeing with the naked eye had all but vanished: "A kind of hole in the darkness is what I beheld; I was like a man who was told, 'Look,' and who saw the inside of a bottle of ink."[41] Moments later a dramatic reversal of perception occurred. The reflections on the moon shifted, and Hugo's eyes adapted to the

7.] MAGASIN PITTORESQUE. 49

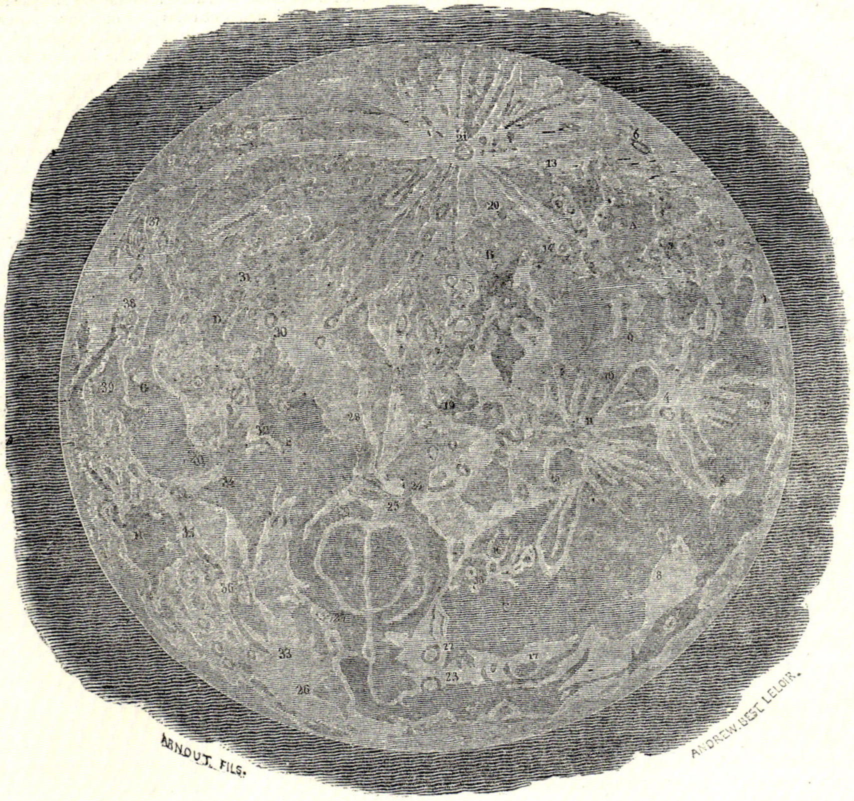


(La Lune.)

NOMS DONNES PAR LES ASTRONOMES AUX TACHES DE LA LUNE.

| | | | |
|---|---|---|---|
| 1 Grimaldus. | 13 Capuanus. | 25 Menelaüs. | 37 Snellius, Turnerius. |
| 2 Galileus. | 14 Bullialdus. | 26 Hermes. | 38 Petavius. |
| 3 Aristarchus. | 15 Erastosthenes. | 27 Possidonius. | 39 Langrenus. |
| 4 Keplerus. | 16 Timocharis. | 28 Dionysius. | 40 Taruntius. |
| 5 Gassendus. | 17 Plato. | 29 Plinius. | *A* Mare Humorum. |
| 6 Shikardus. | 18 Archimedes. | 30 Theophilus. | *B* Mare Nubium. |
| 7 Harpalus. | 19 Insulasinus medii. | 31 Frascatorius. | *C* Mare Imbrium. |
| 8 Heraclides. | 20 Pilatus. | 32 Censorinus. | *D* Mare Nectaris. |
| 9 Lansbergius. | 21 Tycho. | 33 Messala. | *E* Mare Tranquillitatis. |
| 10 Reinoldus. | 22 Eudoxus. | 34 Promontorium somnii. | *F* Mare Serenitatis. |
| 11 Copernicus. | 23 Aristoteles. | 35 Proclus. | *G* Mare Fœcunditatis. |
| 12 Helicon. | 24 Manilius. | 36 Cleomedes. | *H* Mare Critium. |

## DE LA LUNE.

SA FIGURE. — SA ROTATION SUR ELLE-MÊME. — EXPÉRIENCE. — HABITANS DE LA LUNE. — GALILÉE. — LIBRATION.

La lune étant l'astre le plus voisin de notre globe, dont elle se trouve, en quelque sorte, la vassale, puisqu'elle tourne autour de lui et lui sert de lampe pendant l'obscurité des nuits, c'est par elle que nous commencerons à donner des détails sur l'histoire du ciel.

Aujourd'hui nous offrons sa figure, telle qu'elle se présente dans une lunette astronomique qui renverse les objets. C'est le bord supérieur de la gravure qui, dans le ciel, est tourné vers le midi, le bord inférieur vers le nord, celui de droite vers l'orient, celui de gauche vers l'occident. On croit souvent apercevoir dans la lune une espèce de figure humaine; mais en l'examinant avec attention, on n'y voit aucune forme déc idée; aussi, anciennement, a-t-on beaucoup varié dans les opinions à ce sujet, et plusieurs anciens ont-ils pensé que l'aspect de la terre se reproduisait dans cet astre comme dans un miroir.

La figure de la lune demeurant toujours la même à nos yeux, comme chacun peut s'en convaincre, il en résulte que cet astre nous montre toujours la même face; ainsi, s'il pouvait y exister des habitans, la moitié n'aurait jamais vu la terre. A moins d'avoir fait son tour de lune, comme on fait chez nous le tour du monde, le Lunarien de l'hémisphère opposé serait, pour toute sa

TOME I. 7

De l'Imprimerie de LACHEVARDIERE, rue du Colombier, nº 30.
LES BUREAUX SONT RUE DU COLOMBIER, Nº 28, PRÈS LA RUE DES PETITS-AUGUSTINS.
UN DÉPOT EST ÉTABLI RUE DU COQ-SAINT-HONORÉ, Nº 4.

Fig. 29. Giovanni Domenico Cassini, map of the moon, *Magasin Pittoresque*, March 23, 1833, 49.

magnification of the lens. The sudden effect of seeing the surface of the moon as if it were at the tip of his nose was simultaneously terrific and petrifying. Was this unfamiliar vision of the real moon actually an illusion? Or had his own idea of the moon been a delusion all along? The memory of that lightning moment when the boundary between fact and fiction collapsed was so tangible that it stayed with Hugo for decades to come: "The impression of profundity and loss of reality was terrific. And yet that was reality. I touched the crease of my coat—I existed, me. Well, it existed, too. That reverie was a world. . . . That sight was a place where *we* were the dream."[42]

Beyond his poetic and spiritual odes to the moon, Hugo was entrenched in the field of astronomy and the scientific discoveries of some of the great minds of the past, such as Isaac Newton and Robert Hooke, both referred to in *Promontorium Somnii*.[43] Other sources document his interaction with researchers of his own time. Apart from Arago, Hugo corresponded with the French astronomer Camille Flammarion, for instance, to whom he expressed his passion for the field in a letter from Guernsey on December 17, 1862: "The subjects you address . . . are the constant obsession of my thoughts, and exile has merely increased these meditations by placing me between two infinities—ocean and sky. I feel a close affinity to minds like yours. Your studies are my studies. Let us pursue the infinite, yes—that is making true use of the mind's wings."[44]

Perhaps the most revealing document related to Hugo's ongoing investigations of the moon is a page from the French journal *Magasin Pittoresque* that the author preserved for decades after its publication on March 23, 1833, and subsequently attached to the final folio of the *Promontorium Somnii* manuscript, where it remains today (fig. 29).[45] It features a reproduction of a famous map of the surface of the moon based on the findings of the seventeenth-century astronomer Giovanni Domenico Cassini. The drawing for this first scientific map of the moon was executed using a telescope in Paris in the 1670s, while Cassini was director of the Observatoire de Paris.[46] Therein lies the inspiration for Hugo's text and a tie to his verbal and visual depictions of the cosmos.

Among the list of lunar features, numbered on the map and identified in a key below the image, number 34, *Promontorium Somnii*, struck a chord in Hugo's psyche.[47] A year after the publication of the map, he saw the mountainous surface with his own eyes through the telescope and could no longer consider it a figment of his imagination. In his own words, "The light transformed this suddenly lifelike shadow into something like a mask that becomes a face."[48] Yet the moon and its mysterious anthropomorphic features also touched his soul and fed his fantasies. (Cassini himself reproduced the face of a "moon maiden" he had perceived in the crater known as Promontorium Heraclides.) Hugo's drawings of planets and constellations are derived from the same sense of magic and bewilderment: "In the mysterious realm of art—as in that moon our eye accosted just now—lies the pinnacle of dream."[49]

A moon that Hugo knew well was the moon of myths. His extensive references include the ancient Greek poet Pindar, the Roman lyric poet Horace, the prophet

Zoroaster, the witches of Thessaly, and more.[50] He mentions the associations of the moon in all countries, beliefs, and cultures, like the symbolic crescent that appears on the head of the goddess Diana or beneath the feet of the Madonna.[51] Moreover the author partook of two opposing realms—the real, on the one hand, and the surreal, on the other—and with his own revelatory vision through the telescope, an instrument of truth, came the realization that "his" moon encapsulated both.

Poets have invented a metaphorical moon, scientists an
algebraic moon. The real moon is halfway between the two.
That is the moon my eyes beheld.

*Les poètes ont créé une lune métaphorique et les savants une*
*lune algébrique. La lune réelle est entre les deux.*
*C'est cette lune là que j'avais sous les yeux.*[52]

It was with these notions in mind that Hugo drew the expansive and illusory pools of wash in the Louvre *Taches-planètes*, for instance, and the mottled, biomorphic forms in the lunar landscape that later belonged to Breton. In an interesting twist, the French word *tache* translates as "stain" but is also used to describe lunar features such as craters. The list of named features in the *Magasin Pittoresque* version of Cassini's map is headed: "Noms donnés par les astronomes aux taches de la lune" (Names given by astronomers to lunar features). Hugo relates the moon's *taches* to empires in *Promontorium Somnii*, but he also used the term loosely in relation to drawings.[53] "We place ink stains (*taches*) on paper," he states in the letter to Léopoldine cited above, "like God places suns in the skies."[54] In a letter to his friend and executor Paul Meurice, dated December 21, 1858, he refers to "quatre taches d'encre sur du papier" (four ink stains on paper). "Let me know if in their quality as ink stains," he continues, "they appear too black (due to the paper that imbibes a lot), and I shall replace them."[55] Hugo mentions these sheets in relation to his collection of poems *Les contemplations*, but he gives no further clues as to what they represented. Was he referring to the more stain-like, abstract type of composition, or was he using the term *tache* more generally to include all drawings? Since many of his "astral" compositions are echoed in writing in *Les contemplations*, it seems probable that the term *tache* relates to these works in particular, as well as to his more indefinite compositions of pure wash and stains.

Saturn! Heaven's vast sphere, so grim of sight!
Sky's fierce prison, whose barred windows gleam!
World beset by mists, by blasts, by gloom!
A hell composed of winter and of night!

*Saturne ! sphère énorme ! astre aux aspects funèbres !*
*Bagne du ciel ! prison dont le soupirail luit !*
*Monde en proie à la brume, aux souffles, aux ténèbres !*
*Enfer fait d'hiver et de nuit !*[56]

While Hugo's visual renditions of the moon and the cosmos were idiosyncratic and uncommon for their time, they can be considered within the wider realm of the artistic trends and developments of the nineteenth century. A fascination with the moon—accompanied by pious contemplation, melancholy, atmospheric drama, and a leaning toward the sublime—was a signature trait of artists associated with European romanticism. Among the best-known examples are Caspar David Friedrich's famous painting *Two Men Contemplating the Moon* (ca. 1825–30) and Francisco de Goya's

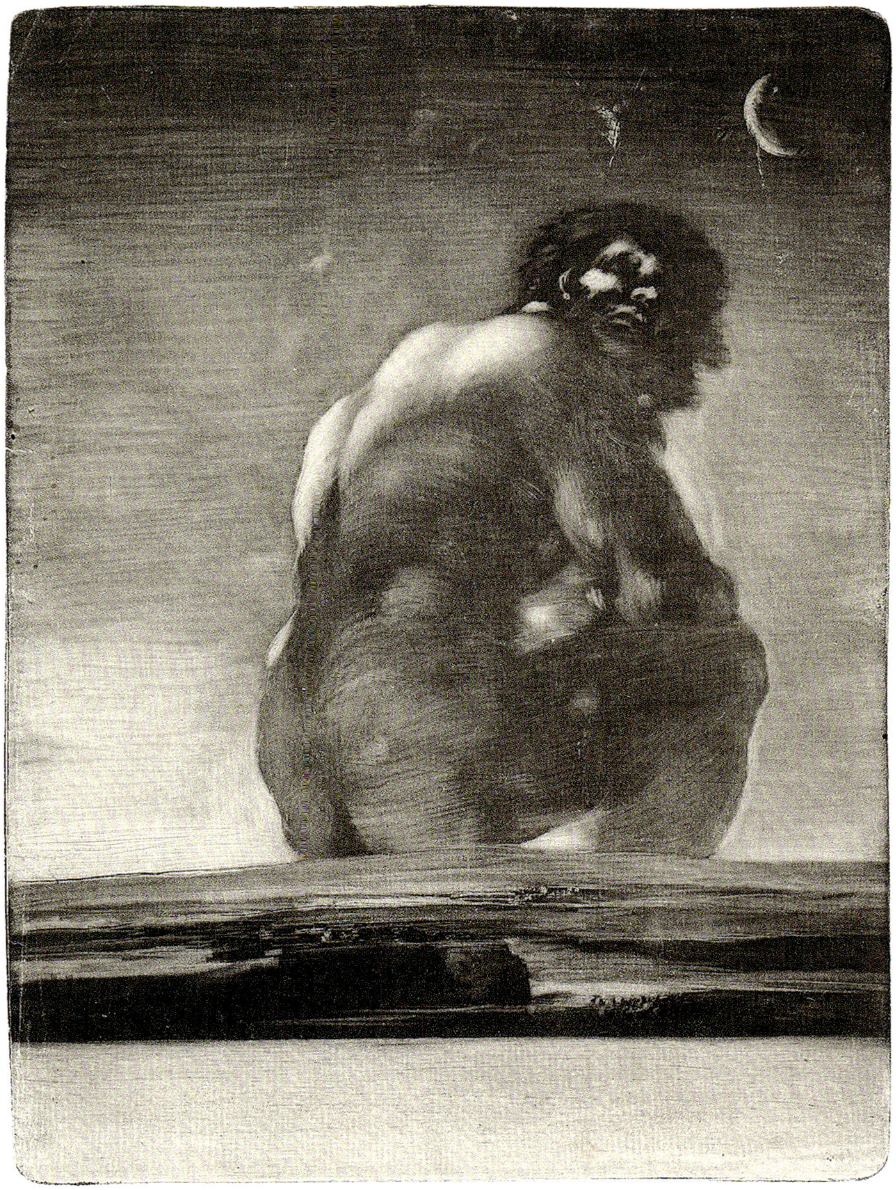

Fig. 30. Francisco de Goya, *A Giant Seated in a Landscape*, sometimes called *The Colossus*, by 1818. Aquatint. Plate: 11³⁄₁₆ × 8³⁄₁₆ in. (28.4 × 20.8 cm). The Metropolitan Museum of Art, New York, Purchase, Harris Brisbane Dick Fund, 1935, 35.42.

tender portrayal of a colossal male figure, pensive and powerless beneath the crescent moon, in his print *A Giant Seated in a Landscape* (by 1818; fig. 30). It is highly likely that Hugo encountered the works of British artists with similar inclinations during his travels to mainland England. John Martin, William Blake, and J. M. W. Turner are but a few of the painters who rendered crepuscular scenes and the mystical forces of the atmosphere between the late 1700s and the first half of the 1800s.

The mid-nineteenth century was also a fundamental time of discovery in the field of photography, and the technological developments in the art of capturing an image

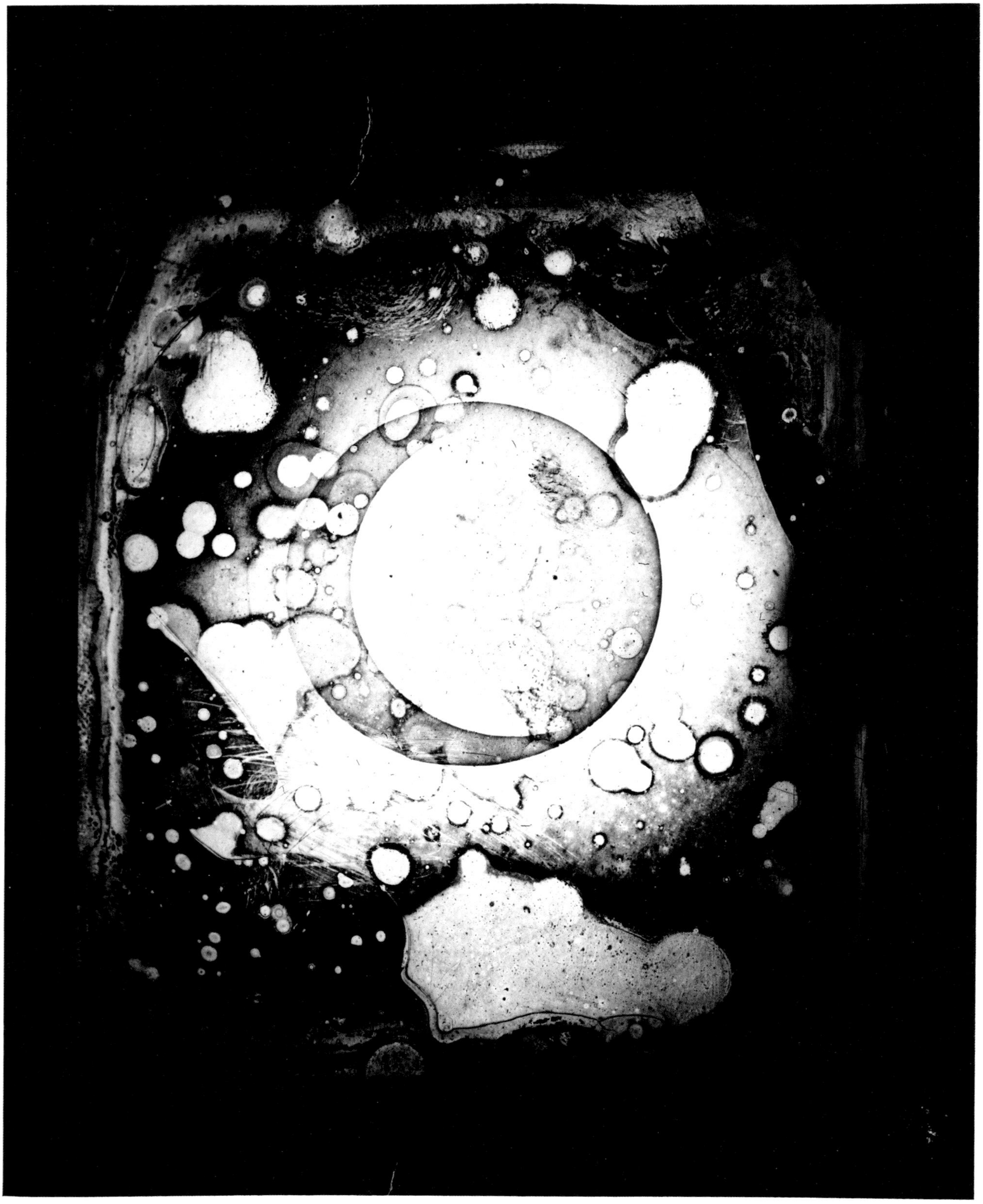

were due mostly to the experiments and curiosity of scientists. In 1839 Arago announced the invention of the daguerreotype and its patenting by the French government to the members of Paris's Académie des sciences. Some of the earliest daguerreotypes of the moon were made around this time in the United States by the British-born New York University professor John William Draper. One example attributed to him, dated March 1840, is tentative and blurred, with the same alluring mystique as Hugo's *taches* (fig. 31).[57] Surely aware of the radical effect these new technologies would have on the course of history, Hugo kept himself keenly informed through journals such as *La Lumière*, the first publication devoted to photography, which began in 1851.[58] He was fascinated by the endeavors of Nadar, and in a letter to the French photographer and adventurer, he praises him for his journal *L'Aéronaute* and for his mission to launch a hot-air balloon.[59] The new findings in the field of astronomy and the desire among specialists to "conquer" the cosmos filtered through to the general public, engendering a popular fascination with the moon. Jules Verne's notable novel *De la terre à la lune* (*From the Earth to the Moon*, 1865) was inspired by contemporaneous discoveries, in particular by Nadar's aerial ventures. Honoré Daumier, a friend of Hugo's, characterized the vogue for moon gazing in illustrations such as *Effet de lunes* (Moonstruck), published in *Le Charivari* on May 10, 1840 (fig. 32). Moreover, even satirical journals with a political slant were named after heavenly bodies and their phenomena, such as *Le Soleil*, *L'Éclipse*, and *La Lune*, which featured Hugo on its cover on May 19, 1867 (fig. 33).

In England too, researchers were making great strides in the combined subjects of science and photography. We may wonder if Hugo had seen the evocative

Fig. 31 (opposite). Attributed to Dr. John William Draper, *Surface of the Moon*, March 1840. Photographic copy of a lost daguerreotype. New York University Archives, New York.

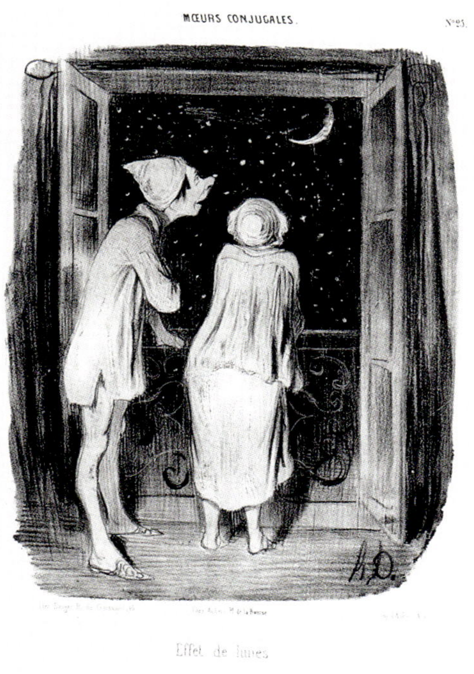


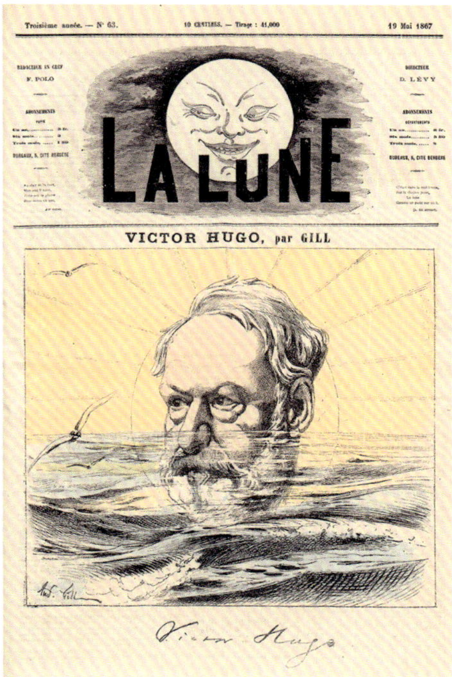


Fig. 32. Honoré Daumier, *Effet de lunes* (Moonstruck), May 10, 1840. Lithograph. $13\frac{7}{16} \times 10\frac{1}{4}$ in. (34.1 × 26 cm). Hammer Museum, Los Angeles, The Armand Hammer Daumier and Contemporaries Collection, Gift of Dr. Armand Hammer, AH.1991.1.747.

Fig. 33. Cover of *La Lune*, May 19, 1867.

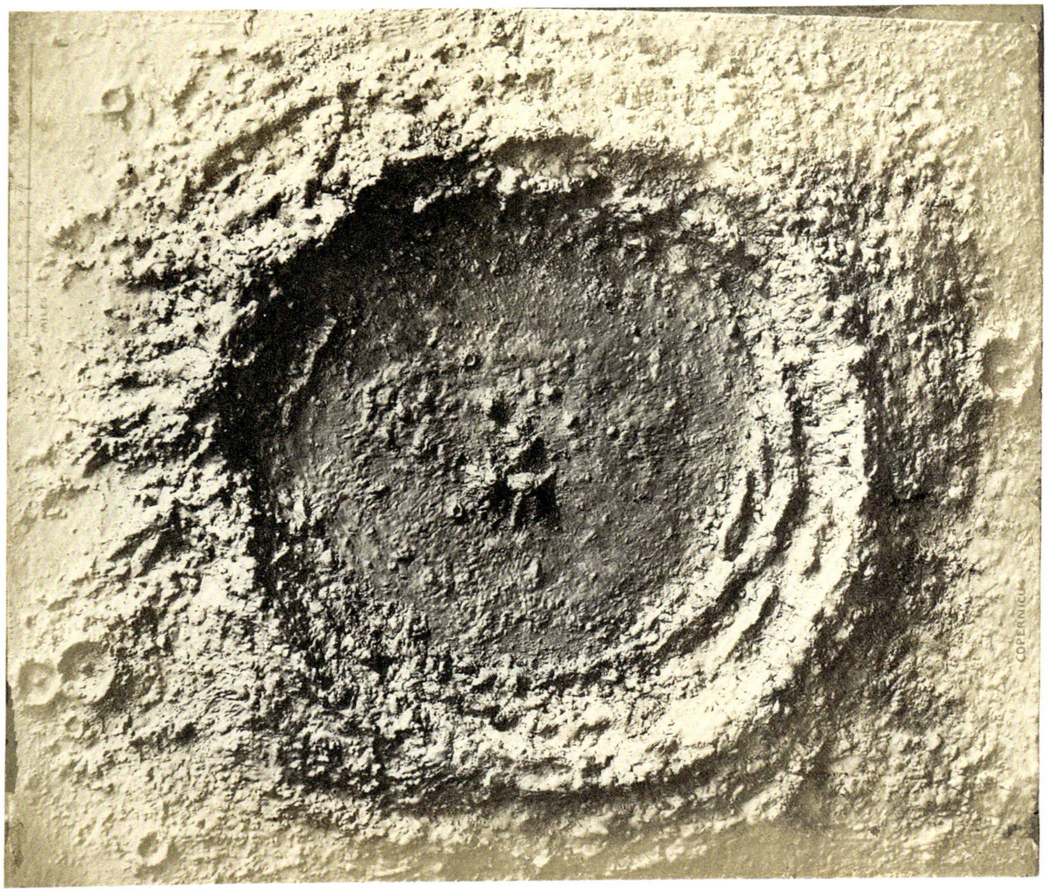

Fig. 34. Unknown photographer, Untitled (papier-mâché or clay model of a moon crater), late 1850s. Salted paper print from a collodion negative. 5⅛ × 6½ in. (13 × 16.5 cm). The J. Paul Getty Museum, 84.XP.259.16.

photographs of models of the moon's surface that belonged to the British astronomer and inventor of the cyanotype Sir John Herschel (fig. 34). He could certainly have known about the pioneering work of the Guernsey-born astronomical photographer Warren De la Rue, who took some of the first photographic prints of the moon in the 1850s (fig. 35). Thus Hugo witnessed dramatic evolutions on two fronts from his homes in the Channel Islands: the rapprochement of the cosmic sphere and the dramatic shift in the visual arts triggered by the invention of photography, from its use as a scientific tool to its development as an artistic medium. As he announced to his sons in Jersey, their time would not be wasted in exile: "So we want to carry out the photographic revolution [in the meantime]."[60]

The real and the surreal conjoin in Victor Hugo's visions of the night. He was patently aware of the reality of what he saw in the skies, whether from the window of his attic at

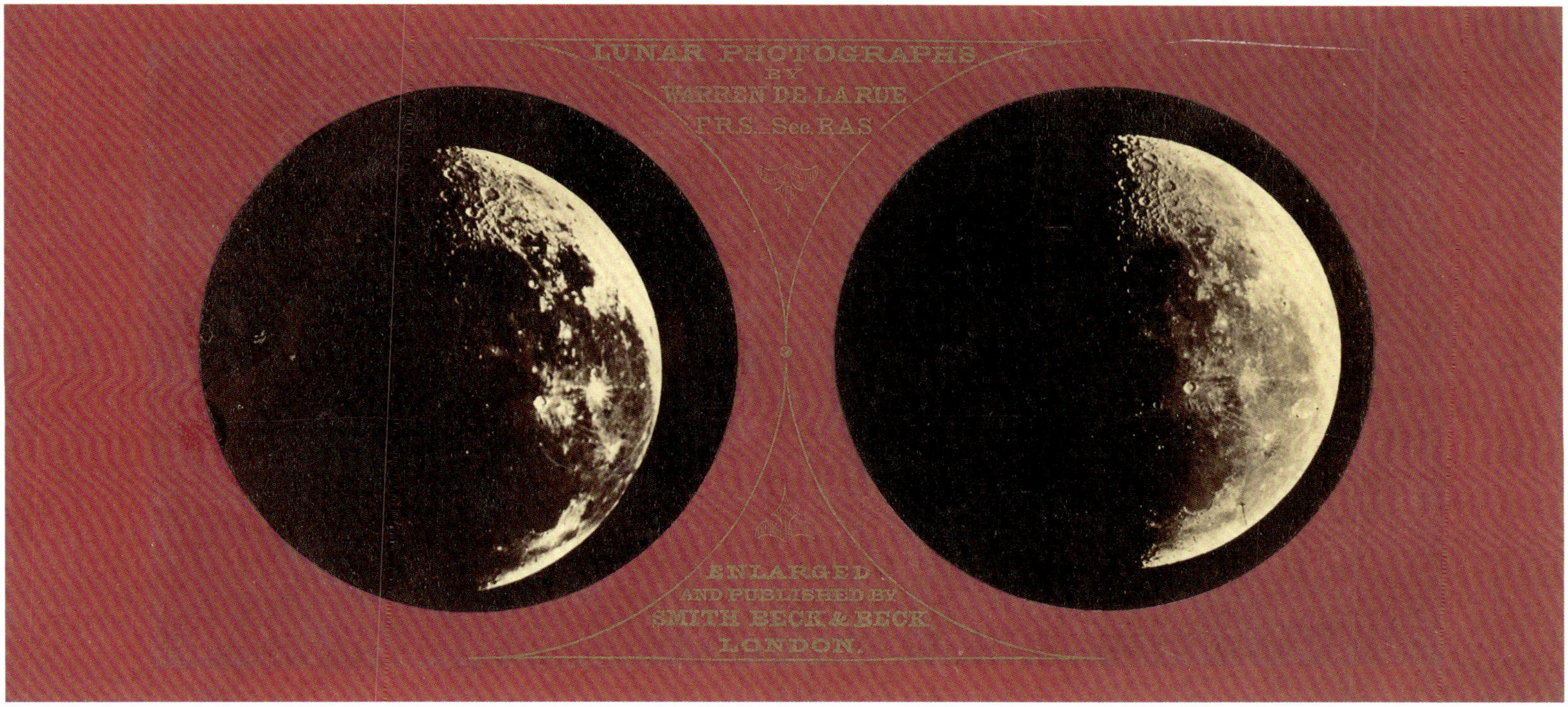


Fig. 35. Warren De la Rue, Untitled (the moon, [left] December 7, 1857, [right] September 15, 1862), negatives 1857 and 1862, print ca. 1862. Albumen silver print. 3⅜ × 6⅞ in. (8.6 × 17.5 cm). The J. Paul Getty Museum, 84.XC.729.484.

Hauteville House, during his twilight walks, or through a telescope. He could not, however, let go of the magic tied to these scintillating sights that are the realm of dreams and the source of ever-inspiring myths. The breadth of knowledge that backs Hugo's drawings of the moon and other celestial spheres is paired with introspection and a deeply personal aesthetic. The subjects of his ink-and-wash renderings range from recognizable objects to less definable forms, but they all jostle the components of stone and stain, light and shadow, ethereality and tactility. None can be defined as abstract in the modern sense of the term, but his freedom of expression and flair for experimentation leave them open to interpretation. They are effectively works that stand outside their time, and thus it seems fitting that the innovative Swiss curator Harald Szeemann, known for his progressive exhibitions of avant-garde art, presented a selection of Hugo's drawings in 1987.[61] Just as Hugo created drawings based at the crux between mystery and materiality, he placed his own persona between heaven and earth as he prepared for the afterlife: "I will close the terrestrial eye, but the spiritual eye will remain open, more than ever."[62]

## Notes

This essay is dedicated to Luna Maya Widmaier Picasso. A special thank-you to Evgenia Citkowitz for her insightful comments on my text and to Natalya Sands for her time researching the moon in my company. Unless otherwise noted, translations are by the author.

Epigraph: Victor Hugo, *The Toilers of the Sea*, trans. James Hogarth (New York: Modern Library, 2002), 294–95; Hugo, *Les travailleurs de la mer*, in *Œuvres complètes* (Paris: Club Français du Livre, 1967), 12:704–5.

1. Hugo, *Toilers of the Sea*, 297–98; Hugo, *Travailleurs de la mer*, 12:706.

2. See Roger Pierrot, Judith Petit, and Marie-Laure Prévost, *Soleil d'encre: Manuscrits et dessins de Victor Hugo* (Paris: Musée du Petit Palais and Bibliothèque nationale de France, 1985), 184, no. 252, and Marie-Laure Prévost, *Victor Hugo: L'homme océan* (Paris: Bibliothèque nationale de France and Seuil, 2002), 275, no. 246. This drawing is related to a printed illustration by François Chifflart in the 1869 illustrated edition of *Les travailleurs de la mer* (Paris: Hetzel).

3. For a survey of the photographs taken in Jersey, see Françoise Heilbrun and Danielle Molinari, *En collaboration avec le soleil: Victor Hugo; Photographies de l'exil* (Paris: Réunion des musées nationaux, Musée d'Orsay, and Maisons de Victor Hugo, 1998).

4. "Sachez-le, il n'y a pas de terre étrangère; partout la terre est la mère de l'homme, sévère et profonde. Dans tous les lieux où il a aimé, où il a pleuré, où il a souffert, c'est à dire partout, l'homme est chez lui." Victor Hugo, *Actes et paroles*, pt. 2, *Pendant l'exil*, in *Œuvres complètes*, 12:846.

5. "Vous pouvez arracher un arbre de ses racines, vous n'arracherez pas le jour du ciel. Demain, l'aurore." Victor Hugo, *Ce que c'est que l'exil*, in *Œuvres complètes*, 15:602.

6. "Tellement jeté aux ténèbres qu'il ne lui reste plus que le soleil." Ibid.

7. Charles Hugo, *Chez Victor Hugo par un passant* (Paris: Cadart & Luquet, 1864), 64.

8. "Aujourd'hui 30 juin, apparition à 8 h. du soir d'une comète. Elle est immense. Sa queue a dix-sept millions de lieues." René Journet and Guy Robert, *Le manuscrit des Misérables* (Paris: Les Belles Lettres, 1963), 260.

9. See Gordon Norton Ray, *The Art of the French Illustrated Book, 1700 to 1914* (New York: Pierpont Morgan Library, 1982), 324, ill. 355.

10. "Il se sent enseveli à la fois par ces deux infinis, l'océan et le ciel; l'un est une tombe, l'autre est un linceul." Victor Hugo, *Les Misérables*, trans. Julie Rose (New York: Modern Library, 2008), 81; Hugo, *Les misérables*, in *Œuvres complètes*, 11:116.

11. Victor Hugo, *La légende des siècles*, in *Œuvres complètes*, 10:649; translated by Deke Dusinberre.

12. "Moi, je m'y promène chaque soir à la nuit tombante. Oui, tous les soirs au crépuscule, quand le soleil est couché, quand le ciel est chargé de nuages et que les étoiles commencent à s'allumer, je me promène tout seul devant le port." Heilbrun and Molinari, *En collaboration*, 41; Adèle Hugo, *Le journal d'Adèle Hugo* (Paris: Minard, 1968–84), 2:347–48.

13. Paul Chenay, *Victor Hugo à Guernesey: Souvenirs inédits de son beau-frère Paul Chenay* (Paris: Félix Juven, 1902), 59; translated by Deke Dusinberre.

14. See Prévost, *Victor Hugo*, 130, no. 106.

15. Since Hugo didn't categorically title his drawings, it is unclear when the term *tache* was first associated with "stained" sheets such as this one. An inscription on the verso of the Louvre sheet suggests the term *tache* was assigned to it in the 1960s: "Cette tache / de Victor Hugo / provient de la collection / Georges Victor Hugo" and "pour Janine et Georges Herscher / en souvenir du / merveilleux livre / sur les dessins de Victor Hugo / avec l'affection / de Valentine Hugo / 19 mars 1964."

16. "La beauté n'est pas autre chose que l'infini contenu dans un contour." Victor Hugo, *Post-scriptum de ma vie* (Paris: Calman Lévy, 1901), 170.

17. The creases on *Taches-planètes* indicate that the sheet was once folded into four.

18. Victor Hugo, *La planète* (Planet), ca. 1853–55; ink wash on paper; 11¼ × 17½ in. (28.5 × 44.5 cm); Dijon, Musée des Beaux-Arts, Donation Granville, inv. DG 624. See Florian Rodari et al., *Shadows of a Hand: The Drawings of Victor Hugo* (New York: Drawing Center; London: Merrell Holberton, 1998), 147, no. 96.

19. See ibid., 49, no. 16; Marie-Laure Prévost and Jean-Jacques Lebel, *Du chaos dans le pinceau: Victor Hugo; Dessins* (Paris: Éditions des Musées de la Ville de Paris, 2000), 291, no. 245. Danielle Molinari dates this drawing to 1864–69 in *Victor Hugo: Visions graphiques* (Paris: Éditions des Musées de la Ville de Paris, 2010), 66, ill. 39.

20. See Pierrot, Petit, and Prévost, *Soleil d'encre*, 132–34.

21. "Il y a des lumières dans la nuit, qu'est-ce que ces lumières font là? Elles disent l'indicible: Elles illuminent l'invisible, elles éclairent, car elles ressemblent à des flambeaux; Elles regardent, car elles ressemblent à des prunelles." Victor Hugo, "Things of the Infinite," in *Victor Hugo's Intellectual Autobiography (Postscriptum de Ma Vie)*, trans. Lorenzo O'Rourke (New York: Funk & Wagnalls, 1907), 253; Hugo, "Choses de l'infini," in *Post-scriptum de ma vie* (Paris: Calman Lévy, 1901), 231.

22. Pierrot, Petit, and Prévost, *Soleil d'encre*, 41, no. 5, and 134, no. 162. More recently Marie-Laure Prévost dated these works to 1857 (Prévost, *Victor Hugo*, 199, no. 155).

23. On Hugo and anthropomorphic associations, see Georges Didi-Huberman, *Ninfa profunda: Essai sur le drapé-tourmente* (Paris: Gallimard, 2017), 67–76.

24. Victor Hugo, "The Clarity That Fills . . . ," in *Selected Poetry*, trans. Steven Monte (New York: Routledge, 2002), 97; Hugo, in *Les contemplations*, in *Œuvres complètes*, 9:69.

25. John Chambers, *Victor Hugo's Conversations with the Spirit World: A Literary Genius's Hidden Life*, 2nd ed. (Rochester, VT: Destiny, 2008), 209.

26. Ibid., 222.

27. More than 150 drawings were exhibited at the Galerie Georges Petit shortly after Hugo's death (*Exposition des dessins et manuscrits de Victor Hugo, au benefice de la souscription pour sa Statue*, Galerie Particulière Georges Petit, Paris, May 1888).

28. "Sur les lettres de voyage de Victor Hugo," *L'Artiste*, February 18, 1844, 104–5. I thank Matthieu Vahanian for this reference.

29. Victor Hugo to Léopoldine Hugo, September 3, 1837, in Hugo, *Œuvres complètes*, 5:1125–26.

30. "L'œil était dans la tombe et regardait Caïn." Victor Hugo, *La légende des siècles*, in *Œuvres complètes*, 10:442. Translation by various authors in *Works of Victor Hugo* (London: Chesterfield Society, n.d.), 9:181.
31. Gaétan Picon et al., *Victor Hugo: Dessins* (Paris: Gallimard, 1985), 268, no. 265.
32. Gérard Audinet et al., *La cime du rêve: Les surréalistes et Victor Hugo* (Paris: Paris-Musées, 2013), 21.
33. See Jean-Jacques Lebel, "Le rhizome Hugo," in Prévost and Lebel, *Du chaos dans le pinceau*, 35–36.
34. See Luc Sante, "The Octopus Bearing the Initials VH," in Rodari et al., *Shadows of a Hand*, 12.
35. "Qui arrivent à rendre à peu près ce que j'ai dans l'œil et surtout dans l'esprit." Victor Hugo to Charles Baudelaire, April 29, 1860, in Hugo, *Œuvres complètes*, 12:1098.
36. William Shakespeare, *Othello* (5.2), in *The Complete Works* (Oxford: Clarendon, 1986), 960.
37. Victor Hugo, *Promontorium Somnii*, in *Œuvres complètes*, 12:463.
38. See Victor Hugo, *Promontorium Somnii*, ed. René Journet and Guy Robert (Paris: Belles Lettres, 1961), and Hugo, *Le promontoire du songe*, ed. Annie Le Brun (Paris: Gallimard, 2012).
39. "La nuit était claire, l'air pur, le ciel serein, la lune à son croissant; on distinguait à l'œil nu la rondeur obscure modelée, la lueur cendrée." Hugo, *Promontorium Somnii*, in *Œuvres complètes*, 12:451; translated by Deke Dusinberre.
40. According to Laurence Bobis, curator and director of the library at the Observatoire de Paris, the instrument that Arago had introduced Hugo to "was not a telescope in the strict sense of the word, but an astronomical refractor: in effect, a refractor has an objective lens, while a telescope has a mirror to concentrate the light." https://www.obspm.fr/victor-hugo-et-le-promontoire-des-songes.html?lang=en.
41. "Une espèce de trou dans l'obscur, voilà ce que j'avais devant les yeux; j'étais comme un homme à qui l'on dirait: regardez, et qui verrait l'intérieur d'une bouteille à l'encre." Hugo, *Promontorium Somnii*, in *Œuvres complètes*, 12:452; translated by Deke Dusinberre.
42. "L'effet de profondeur et de perte du réel était terrible. Et cependant le réel était là. Je touchais les plis de mon vêtement, j'étais, moi. Eh bien, cela aussi était. Ce songe était une terre. . . . cette vision était un lieu pour lequel nous étions le rêve." Ibid.; translated by Deke Dusinberre.
43. Ibid., 12:454.
44. "Les matières que vous traitez, . . . sont la perpétuelle obsession de ma pensée, et l'exil n'a fait qu'augmenter en moi cette méditation, en me plaçant entre deux infinis, l'océan et le ciel. Je me sens en étroite affinité avec des esprits comme le vôtre. Vos études sont mes études. Oui, creusons l'infini. C'est là le véritable emploi des ailes de l'âme." As quoted in René Journet and Guy Robert's annotated edition of *Promontorium Somnii*, 74; translated by Deke Dusinberre. See also http://gallica.bnf.fr/ark:/12148/bpt6k80614z/texteBrut.
45. The manuscript is conserved at the Bibliothèque nationale de France (NAF 24776, f. 89-142). See Hugo, *Promontoire du songe*, 27–28. According to the inscriptions below the illustration, this version of Cassini's map was drawn by Jean-Baptiste Arnout or his son Jules Arnout and printed by the wood engravers John Andrew, Jean Best, and Isidore Leloir.
46. See Zdeněk Kopal and Robert W. Carder, *Mapping of the Moon: Past and Present* (Dordrecht: Reidel, 1974), 21. The map was supplemented with drawings by Sébastien Leclerc and Jean Patigny.
47. The seventeenth-century astronomer Giovanni Battista Riccioli first identified and named the form Palus Somni (Marsh of Sleep), situated near the Lacus Somiorum (Lake of Dreams). Thus the title *Promontorium Somnii* might be an error on Cassini's part. See Ewen A. Whitaker, *Mapping and Naming the Moon: A History of Lunar Cartography and Nomenclature* (Cambridge: Cambridge University Press, 2003), 87.
48. "La lumière avait fait de toute cette ombre soudain vivante quelque chose comme un masque qui devient visage." Hugo, *Promontorium Somnii*, 12:455; translated by Deke Dusinberre.
49. "Dans le monde mystérieux de l'art, comme dans cette lune ou notre regard abordait tout à l'heure, il y a la cime du rêve." Ibid., 12:456; translated by Deke Dusinberre.
50. Ibid., 12:453.
51. Ibid., 12:453–54. As mentioned by René Journet and Guy Robert in their annotated edition of the text, many references cited by Hugo were sourced from Diderot and d'Alembert's *Encyclopédie* (1751–72). Journet and Robert, *Promontorium Somnii*, 74–75.
52. Hugo, *Promontorium Somnii*, 12:454; translated by Deke Dusinberre.
53. Ibid., 12:455.
54. "Où nous mettons des taches d'encre, il pose des soleils." See note 29 above.
55. "Si, en leur qualité de taches d'encre, elles poussaient trop au noir (par la faute du papier qui boit beaucoup) vous me le diriez et je vous les remplacerais." Victor Hugo to Paul Meurice, December 21, 1858, in Hugo, *Œuvres complètes*, 10:1294. For another example of Hugo's use of the term *tache*, see http://expositions.bnf.fr/hugo/arret/taches.htm.
56. Hugo, *Les contemplations*, in *Œuvres complètes*, 9:158; translated by Deke Dusinberre.
57. The spots in this photograph are caused by mold and water damage on the original daguerreotype.
58. Jean-Marc Hovasse, *Victor Hugo*, vol. 2, *Pendant l'exil I (1851–1864)* (Paris: Fayard, 2008), 159.
59. Ibid., 852. Victor Hugo to Nadar, February 20, 1864, in Hugo, *Œuvres complètes*, 12:1250.
60. "C'est donc la révolution photographique que nous voulons faire [en attendant]." Victor Hugo to Pierre-Jules Hetzel, June 2, 1853, in Sheila Gaudon, ed., *Correspondance entre Victor Hugo et Pierre-Jules Hetzel* (Paris: Klincksieck, 1979), 1:311; translated by Deke Dusinberre.
61. *Victor Hugo (1802–1885): Phantasien in Tusche*, Kunsthaus Zürich, 1987.
62. "Je vais fermer l'œil terrestre, mais l'œil spirituel restera ouvert, plus que jamais." Victor Hugo, Testament olographe: Codicille du 31 août 1881, Archives nationales, minutier central des notaires, étude XCXI.

# PLATES

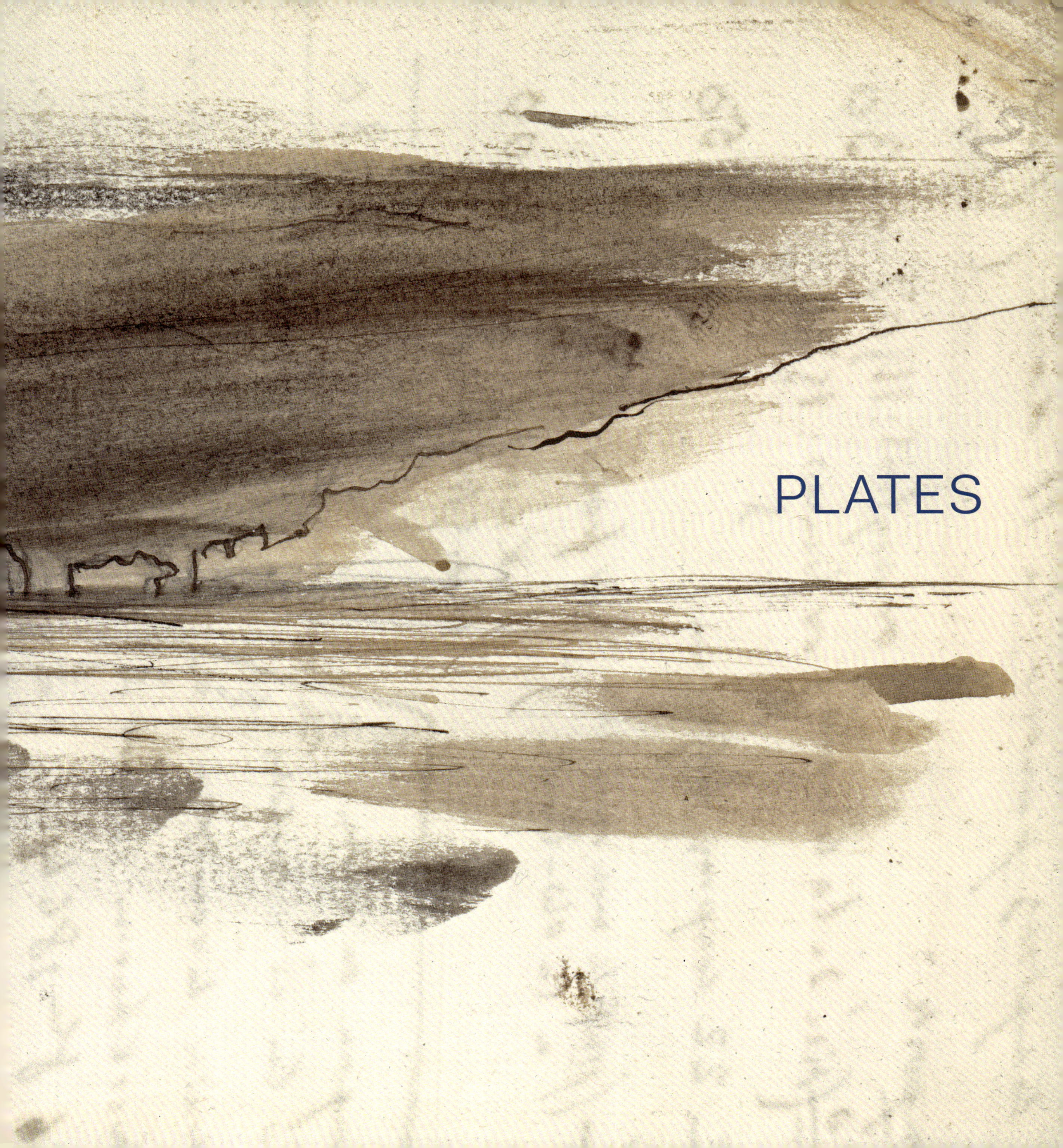

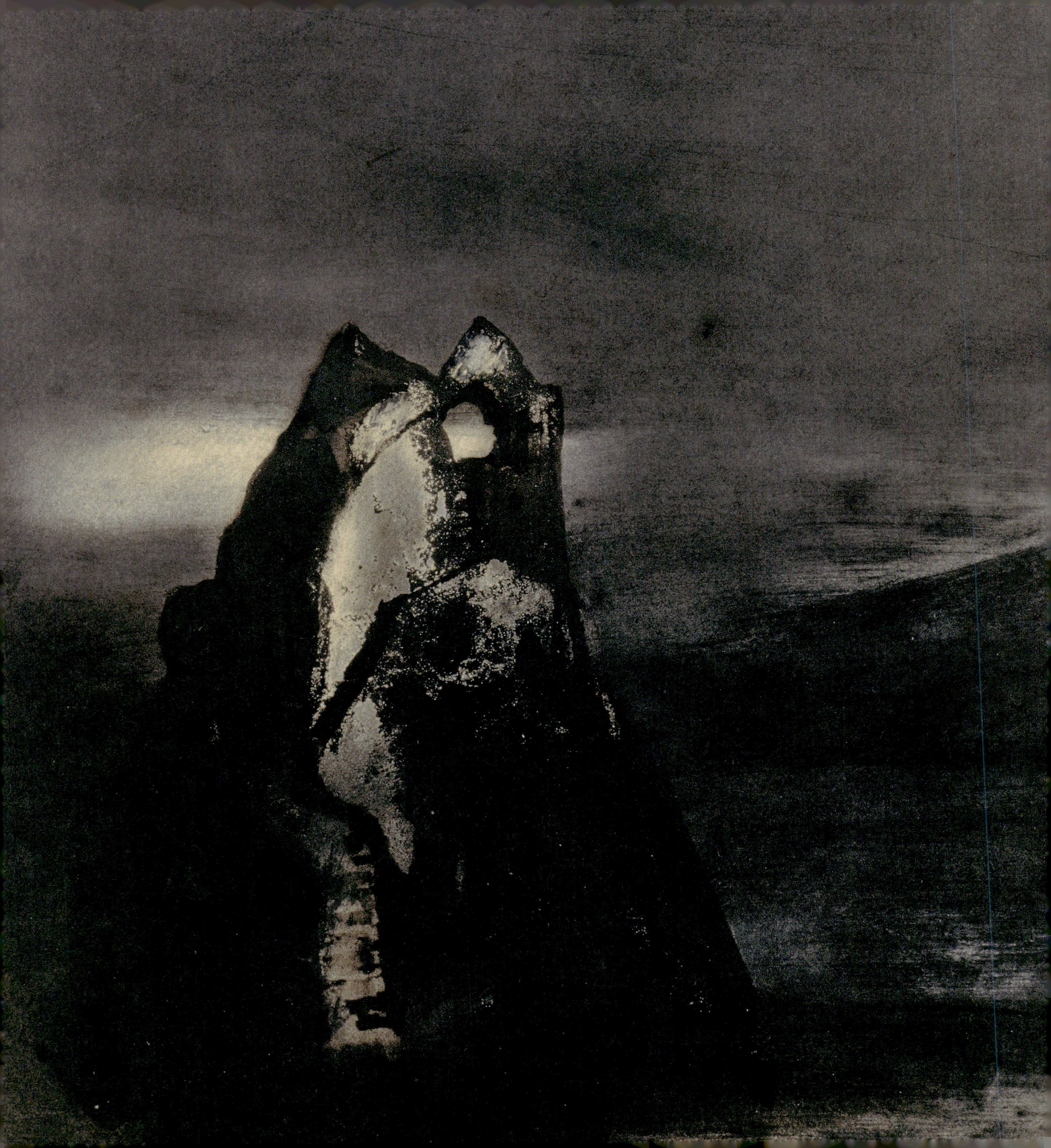

# STONES

*Le beffroi de Lierre* (The belfry of Lier), August 1837. Brown ink and wash on paper. $9\frac{7}{16} \times 6\frac{15}{16}$ in. (24 × 17.7 cm). Yale University Art Gallery, Gift of Mr. and Mrs. Douglas Williams, B.A. 1940.

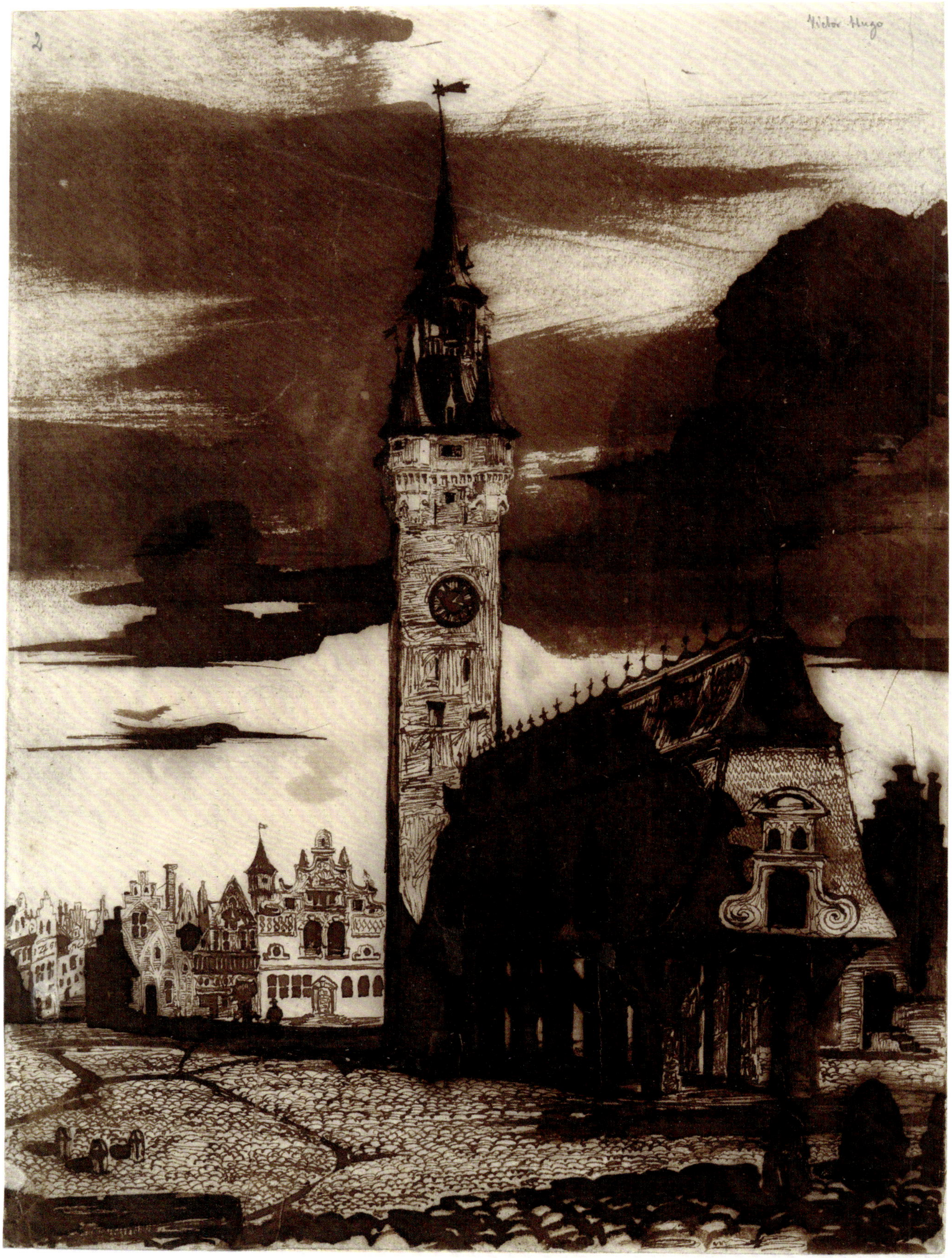
Victor Hugo

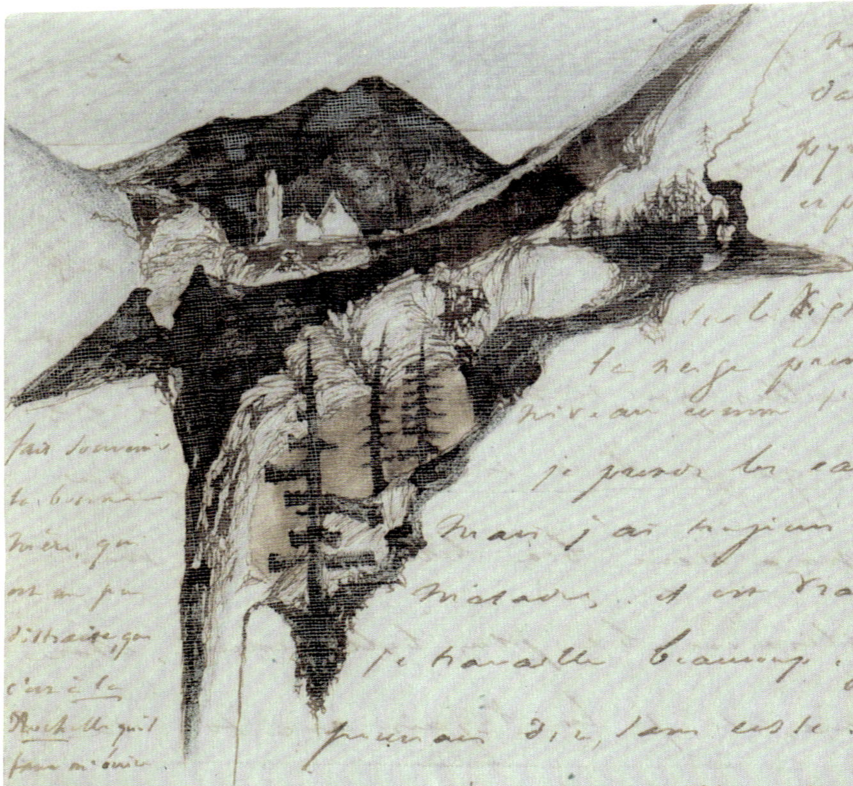

neige dans certaines Pyrénées, et particulièrement sur le Vignemale la neige paraît de niveau comme l'océan.

je prends les eaux. Mais j'ai toujours les yeux malades. il est vrai que je travaille beaucoup. je pourrais dire, sans cesse. Mais c'est ma vie. travailler, et aussi m'occuper de vous tous.

fais souvenir ta bonne mère, qui est un peu distraite, que c'est à la Rochelle qu'il faut m'écrire désormais.

Tu as maintenant deux Charles pour te rendre heureuse. avant peu, tu auras aussi ton père. donc, certaine d'ensoleiller de rire, tu te porteras toujours, mon enfant. tu es dans l'âge.

je charge ta mère de mes souvenirs pour madame Lefèvre et Mme Reynaud. et puis je t'embrasse, ton Charles et toi du fond du cœur.

N° 180 d^tt 160

écris-moi maintenant, à la Rochelle, poste restante.

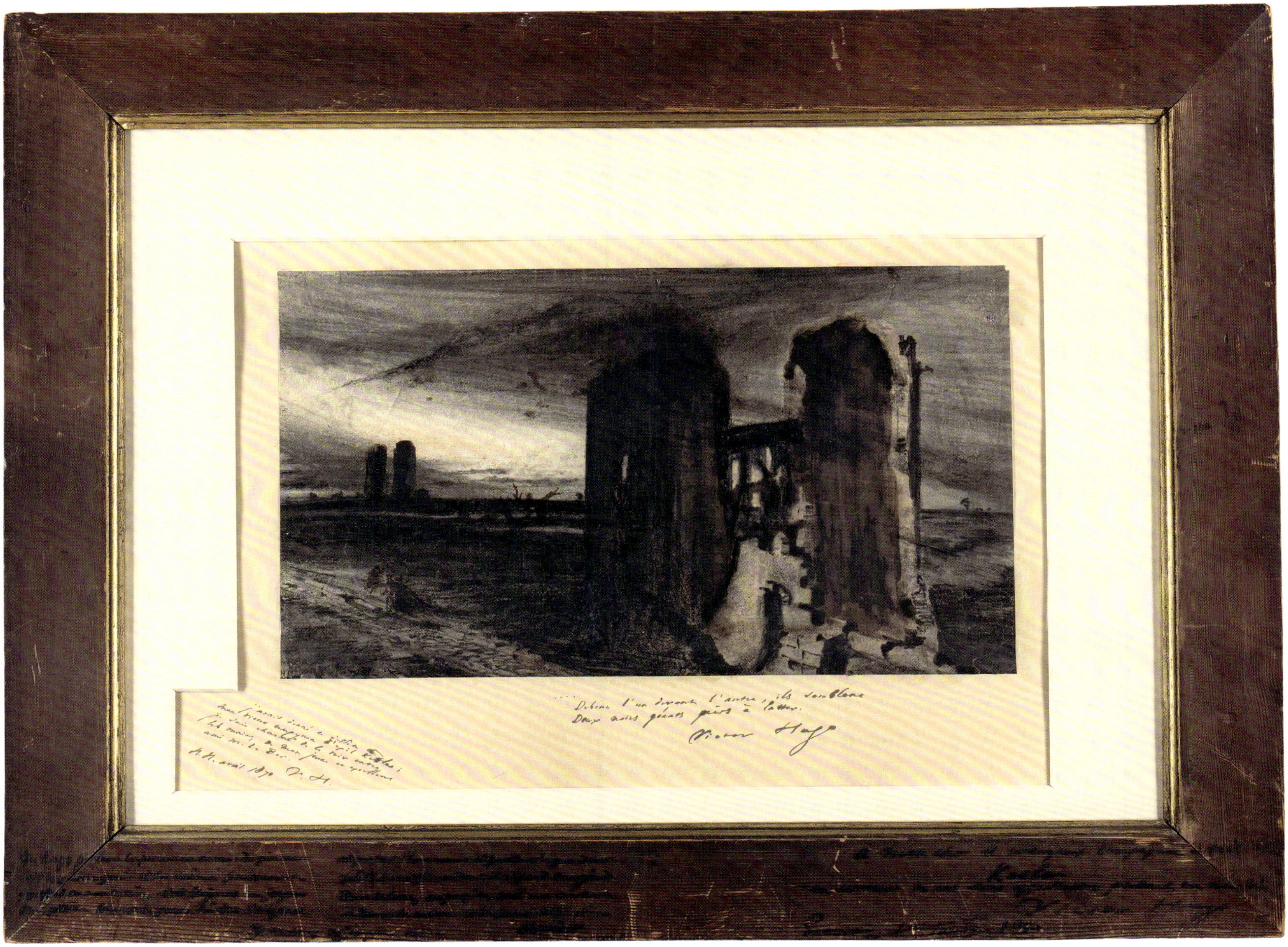

OPPOSITE *Lettre avec vue de Luz* (Letter with view of Luz), August 25, 1843. Brown ink and wash and graphite on paper. 8⅛ × 5⁵⁄₁₆ in. (20.7 × 13.5 cm). Maisons de Victor Hugo, Paris / Guernesey.

ABOVE *Paysage avec deux châteaux en ruine* (Landscape with two derelict castles), 1847. Brown ink and wash over black crayon and graphite, with shellac, on paper, laid down. 10⁹⁄₁₆ × 18⁵⁄₁₆ in. (26.8 × 46.5 cm). The Art Institute of Chicago, Marjorie Blum-Kovler Collection and the Harry and Maribel G. Blum Foundation.

*Château surplombant une rivière* (Castle overlooking a river), 1847. Brown ink and wash and black crayon on paper. 11 × 13 3/16 in. (27.9 × 33.5 cm). Private collection, New York.

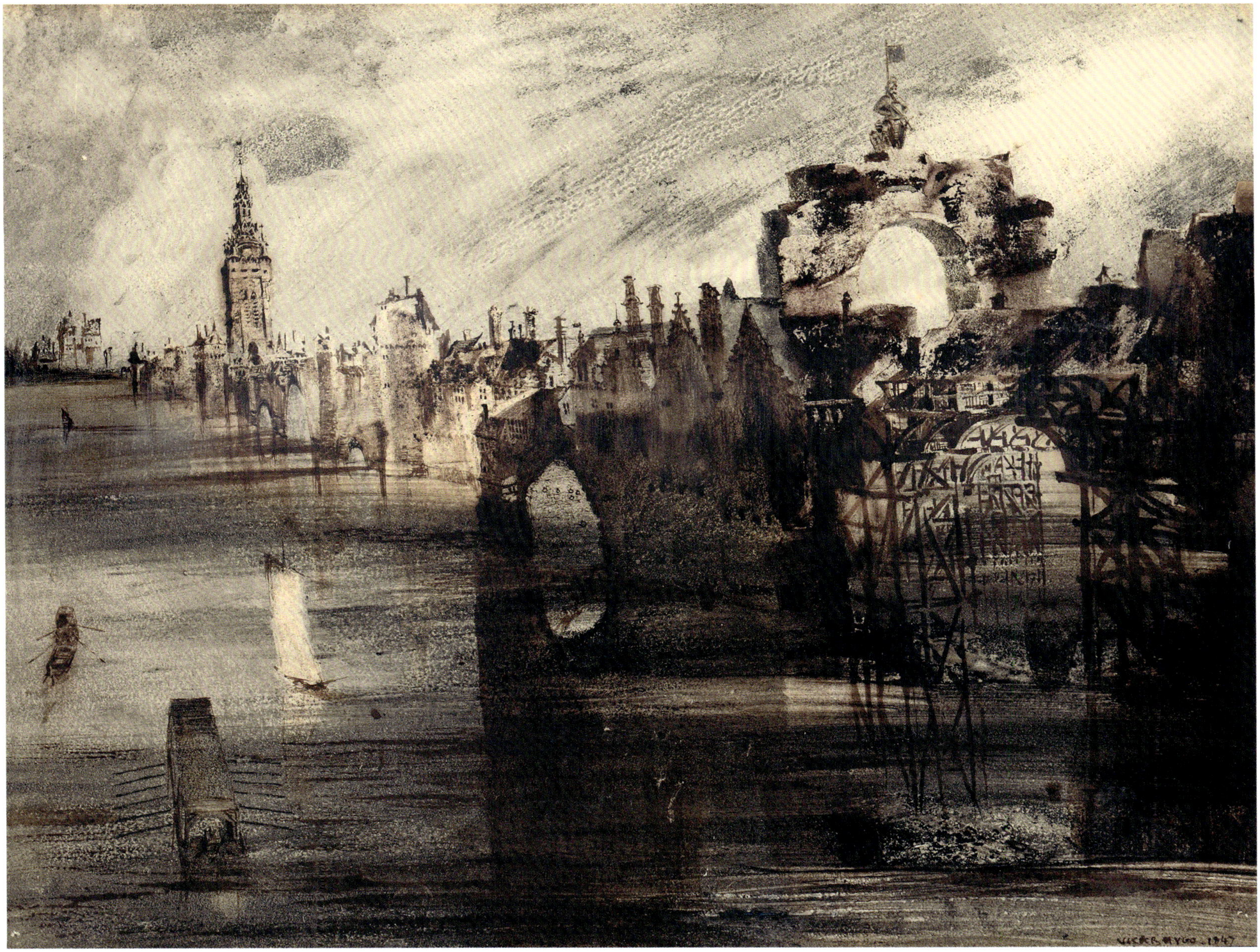

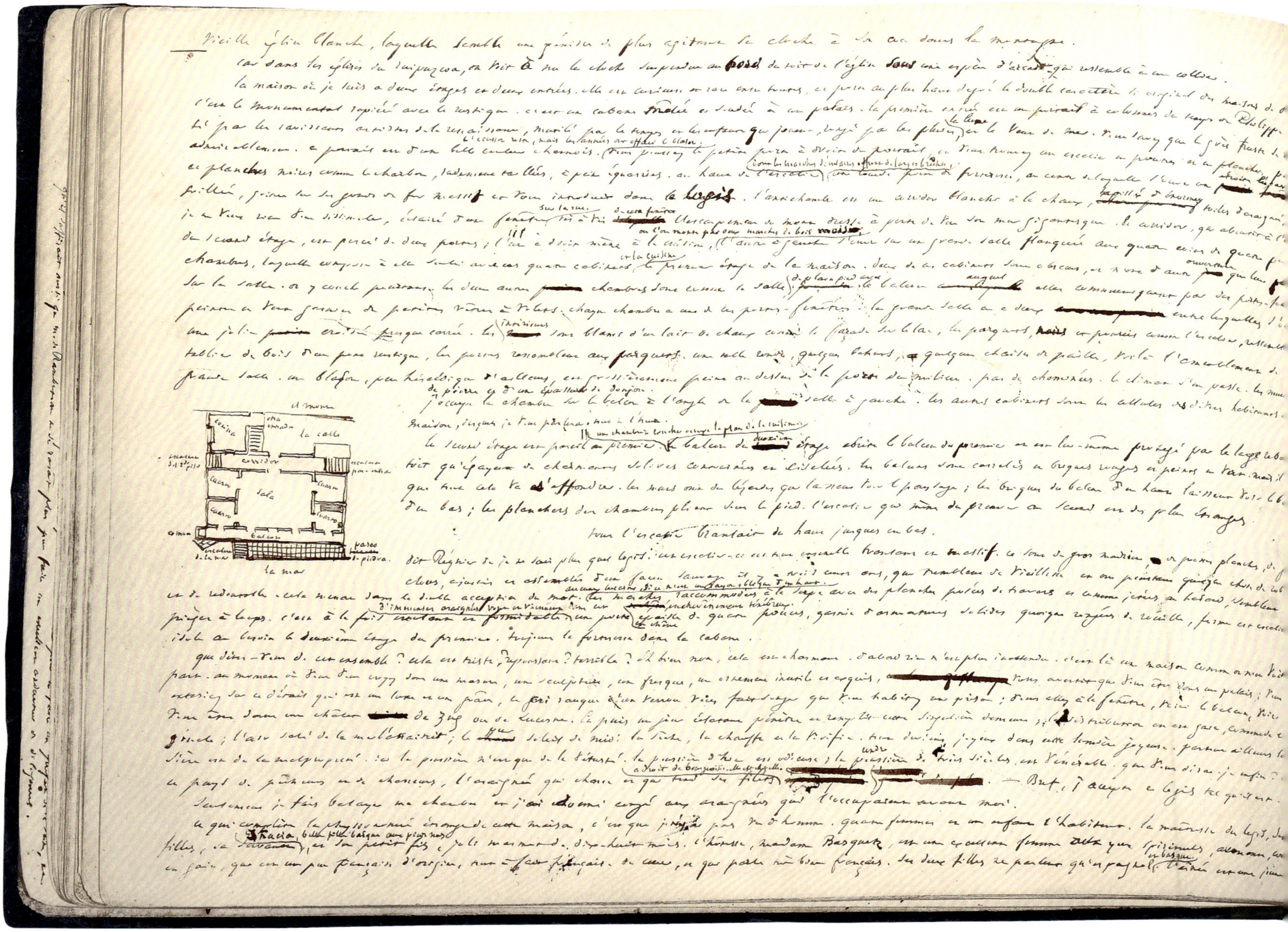

*Voyage de 1843 aux Pyrénées* (1843 voyage to the Pyrenees), 1843. Bound sketchbook with drawings in brown ink and wash and graphite on paper. 9⁷⁄₁₆ × 25⁹⁄₁₆ in. (24 × 65 cm) open. Bibliothèque nationale de France.

malade, douce et pensive. La cadette s'appelle Pepa comme toutes les espagnoles. Elle a vingt ans, la taille svelte, le corsage souple, la main bien faite, le pied petit, chaussé à la Guipuzcoa, les yeux noirs et grands, les cheveux séparés, et elle s'assied le soir sur le balcon dans une attitude triste, et elle se retourne, si sa mère l'appelle, avec une vivacité joyeuse. Elle est à cet âge où l'ingénuité de la jeune fille commence à disparaître, incessamment voilée par la mélancolie de la femme. L'enfant qui rampe dans l'escalier d'un étage à l'autre, va et vient sous le feu, rit, remplit la maison, et la réchauffe avec son innocence, sa grâce et sa naïveté. Un enfant dans une maison, c'est un poêle de gaîté.

Comme il avoisine près de ma chambre, le soir, je l'entends qui murmure doucement pendant que les quatre femmes l'endorment avec une chanson.

Je vous ai dit que la maison avait une autre entrée. C'est un escalier sans rampe, formé de grosses pierres de taille, qui mène de la rue à la cuisine, et va de là rejoindre d'autres escaliers de pierre qui s'en vont dans la montagne à travers les feuillages.

La maison est posée en travers sur la rue comme le château de Chenonceaux sur le Cher, et la rue passe dessous au moyen d'une espèce d'arche de pont longue, étroite, voûtée et obscure qu'une lanterne éclaire la nuit, et où brûle, dans une niche, à côté d'un soupirail fermé d'une grille du quinzième siècle, une cire bénie recommandée aux passants mortels qui passent par l'inscription que voici :

VNA LIMOSNA PARA
ALVMBRAR AL S.^TO C.^TO
D. BVEN BIAJE.
AÑO 1756

(une aumône pour éclairer le saint-christ du bon voyage an 1756)

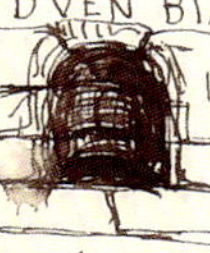

Maintenant vous connaissez la maison ; vous connaissez les habitants. Je vous ai dit où est ma chambre ; mais je ne vous ai pas dit ce qu'elle est. Figurez-vous quatre murs blancs, deux chaises de paille, une console sur trépied, [illegible], un chapeau d'enfant orné de plumes et de verroteries suspendu à un clou, une tablette portant quelques pots de pommade et trois volumes dépareillés de Jean-Jacques Rousseau, un lit à baldaquin antique de fort belle forme, avec deux matelas durs comme marbre, et un chef de bois peint le plus joli du monde, un miroir penché à encadrement exquis accroché au mur, et une porte de cave qui ne ferme pas. Voilà ma chambre. Ajoutez-y la porte-fenêtre dont je vous ai déjà parlé et ma table qui est sur le balcon. De mon lit je vois la mer et la montagne.

Vous voyez que, malgré les prédictions sinistres des gens civilisés de St Sébastien, j'ai réussi à me loger chez les hurons de Pasages. Maintenant ai-je réussi à y vivre ? Jugez-en. Sur ma table à tapis vert qui ne quitte pas le balcon, la gracieuse Pepa qui jase avec l'aube riante vers dix heures pose une serviette blanche, puis elle m'apporte des huîtres détachées le matin même des roches de la baie, deux côtelettes d'agneau, une ouïe plus fraîche que ne l'est un délicieux poisson, des œufs sur le plat sucrés ;

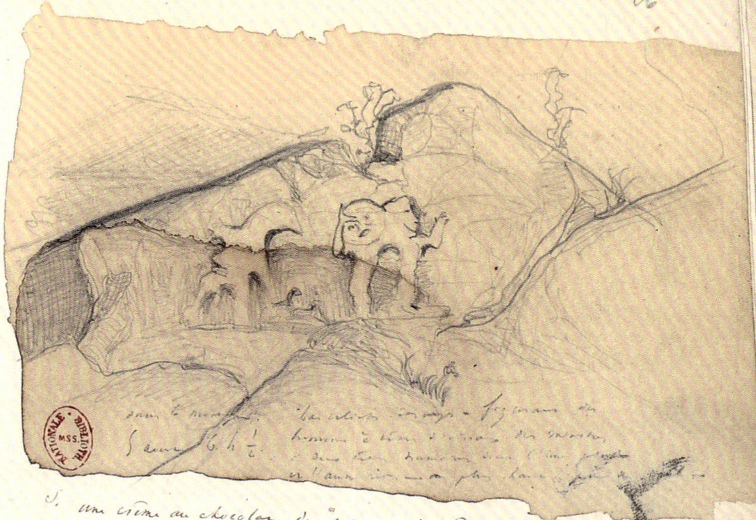







une crème au chocolat, des poires et des pêches, une tasse de fort bon café, et un verre de vin de Malaga. Je bois d'ailleurs du cidre, ne pouvant me faire au vin de peau de bouc. Cela est mon déjeuner ; voici mon dîner, que à lieu le soir vers sept heures, quand je suis revenu de mes courses dans la baie ou sur la côte. Une excellente soupe, le puchero avec le lard et les pois-chiches sans le safran et les piments, des tranches de merluche frites dans l'huile, un poulet rôti, une salade de cresson cueilli dans le ruisseau du lavoir, des petits pois aux œufs durs, un gâteau de maïs au lait et à la fleur d'orange, des brugnons, des fraises et un verre de vin de Malaga. Pendant que Pepita qui sert, allant et venant autour de moi, toutes ces choses qui sollicitent mon appétit de montagnard, le soleil se couche, et la lune se lève, un bateau-pêcheur sort de la baie, tous les spectacles de l'océan et des montagnes se déploient devant moi mêlés à tous les spectacles du ciel. (je parle basque et espagnol à Pepita.) Je lui conte des histoires de sorciers que j'invente incroyables et auxquelles j'ai l'air de croire, elle rit et tâche de me dissuader, j'entends chanter au loin les batelières, et je ne m'aperçois pas que la porcelaine est en faïence et l'argenterie en étain.

Tout cela me coûte cinq francs par jour.

À St Sébastien, on me croit probablement mort de faim et dévoré par les sauvages.

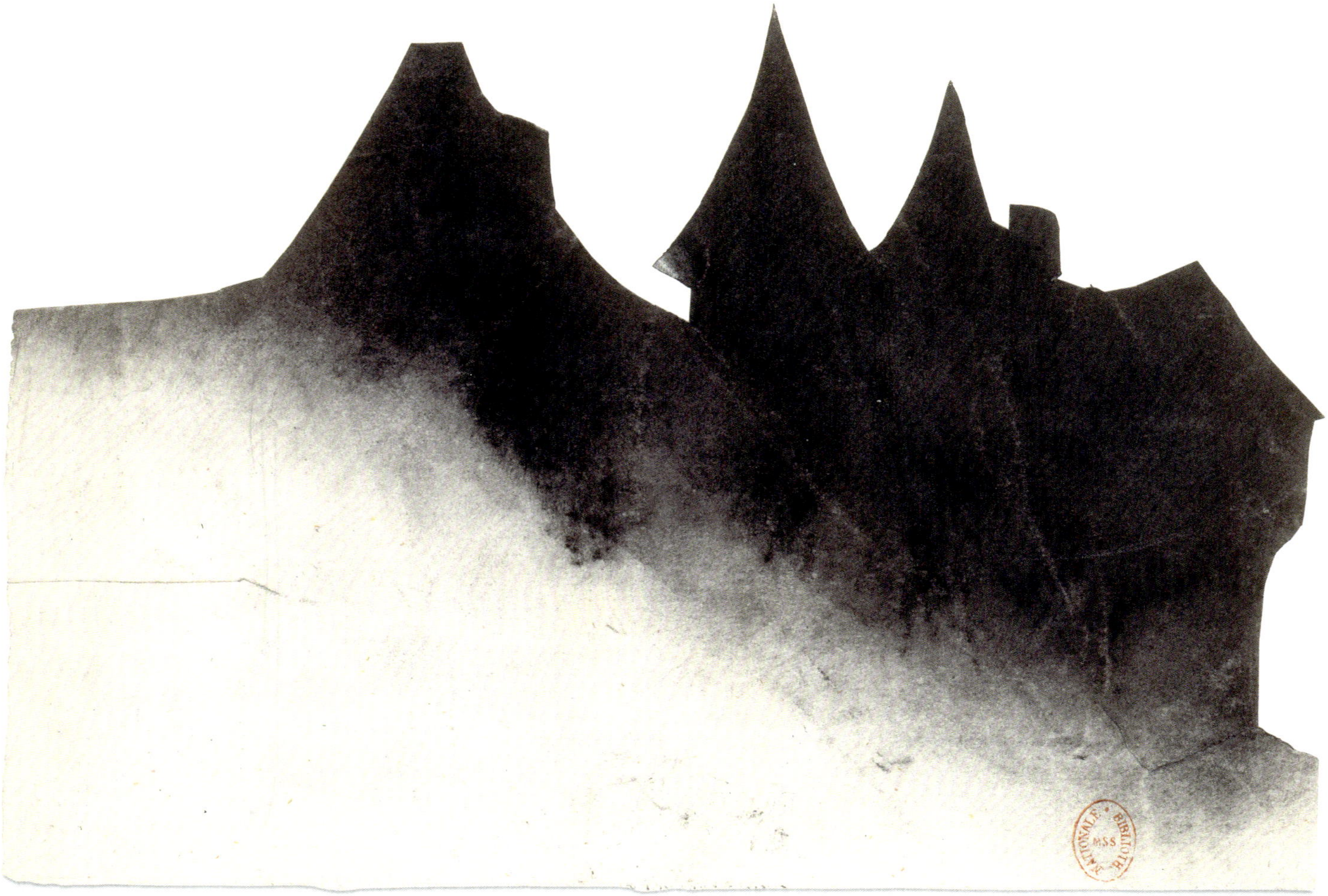

*Silhouette de toits et tourelles* (Silhouette of roofs and turrets), ca. 1855–56. Stencil cut from paper with charcoal. 5½ × 7⅞ in. (13.9 × 20 cm). Bibliothèque nationale de France.

*Silhouette de toits et tourelles* (Silhouette of roofs and turrets), ca. 1855–56. Stencil cut from paper with graphite. 6 × 8 11/16 in. (15.3 × 22 cm). Bibliothèque nationale de France.

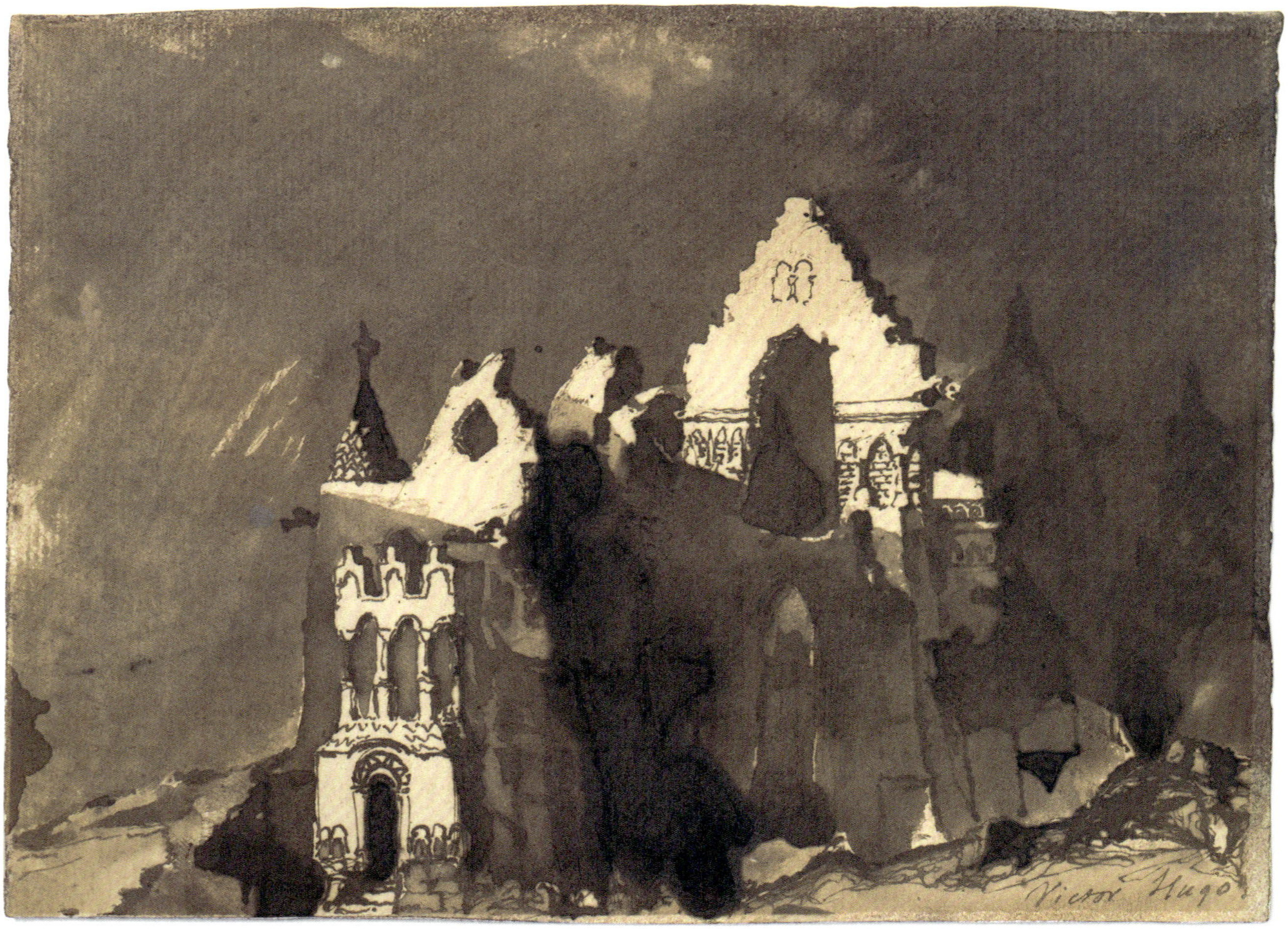


*L'abbaye* (The abbey), ca. 1860. Brown ink and wash on paper.
$5\frac{3}{16} \times 6\frac{7}{8}$ in. (13.2 × 17.5 cm). Private collection, New York.

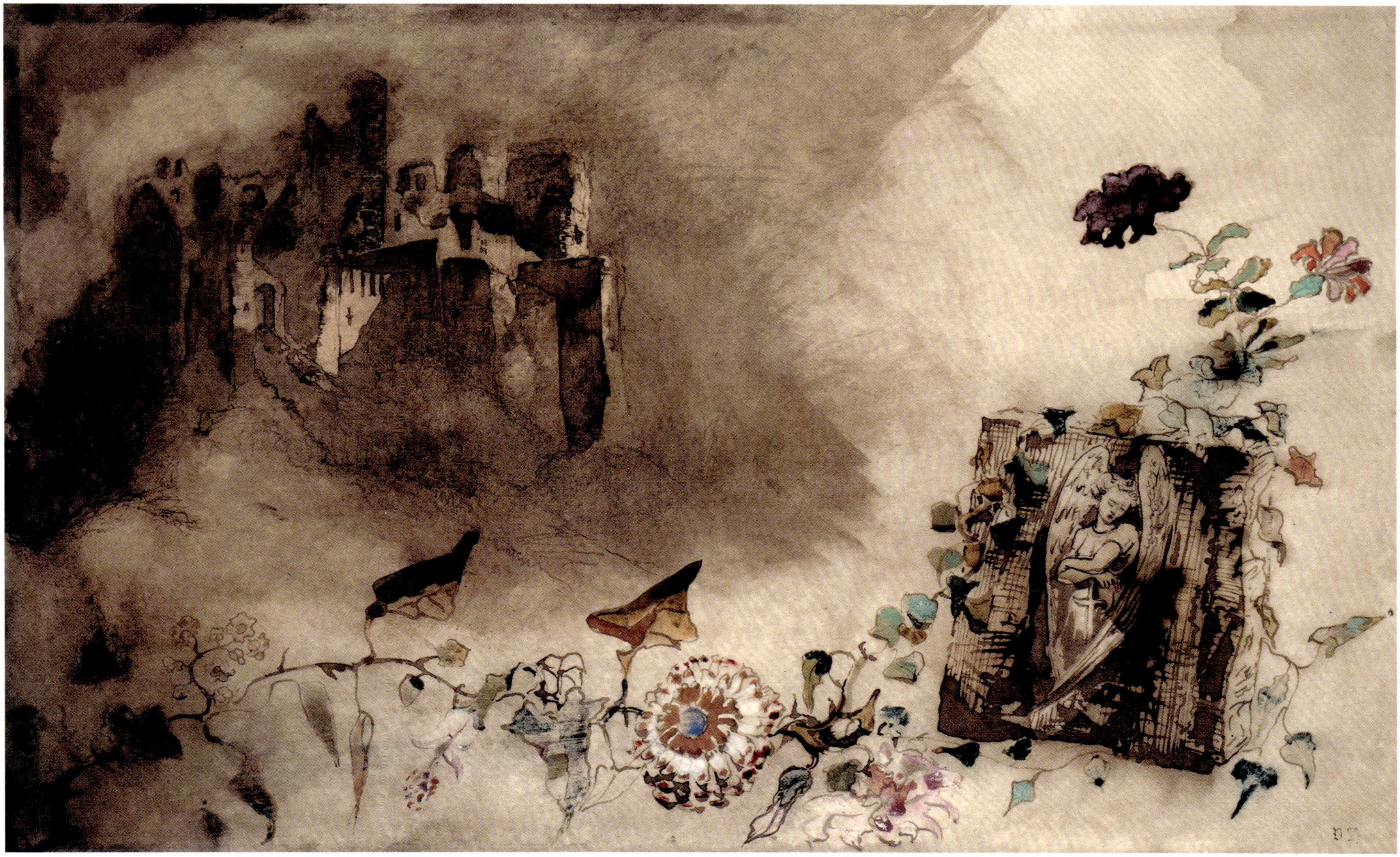

*Le burg à l'ange* (The castle with the angel), ca. 1871. Brown ink and wash, graphite, watercolor, and white gouache on paper. 8⅜ × 13$\frac{7}{16}$ in. (21.2 × 34.2 cm). Maisons de Victor Hugo, Paris / Guernesey.

OPPOSITE *Silhouette de château illuminé par un orage* (Silhouette of a castle illuminated by lightning), ca. 1854–57(?). Stencil cut from card with charcoal and brown ink and wash. 7 5/16 × 6 1/4 in. (18.5 × 15.8 cm). Bibliothèque nationale de France.

FOLLOWING PAGES
*Souvenir d'un burg des Vosges* (Souvenir of a castle in the Vosges), 1857. Brown ink and wash, white gouache, and blue wash on paper. 18 1/2 × 12 3/16 in. (47 × 31 cm). The Metropolitan Museum of Art, New York, Purchase, Harris Brisbane Dick Fund, Donald Young Foundation Gift, Harry G. Sperling Fund, and David M. Tobey Gift, 2012.

*Le burg* (The castle), ca. 1854–57(?). Brown ink and wash and charcoal on paper. 13 3/16 × 10 5/16 in. (33.5 × 26.2 cm). Collection of Véronique and Louis-Antoine Prat, Paris.

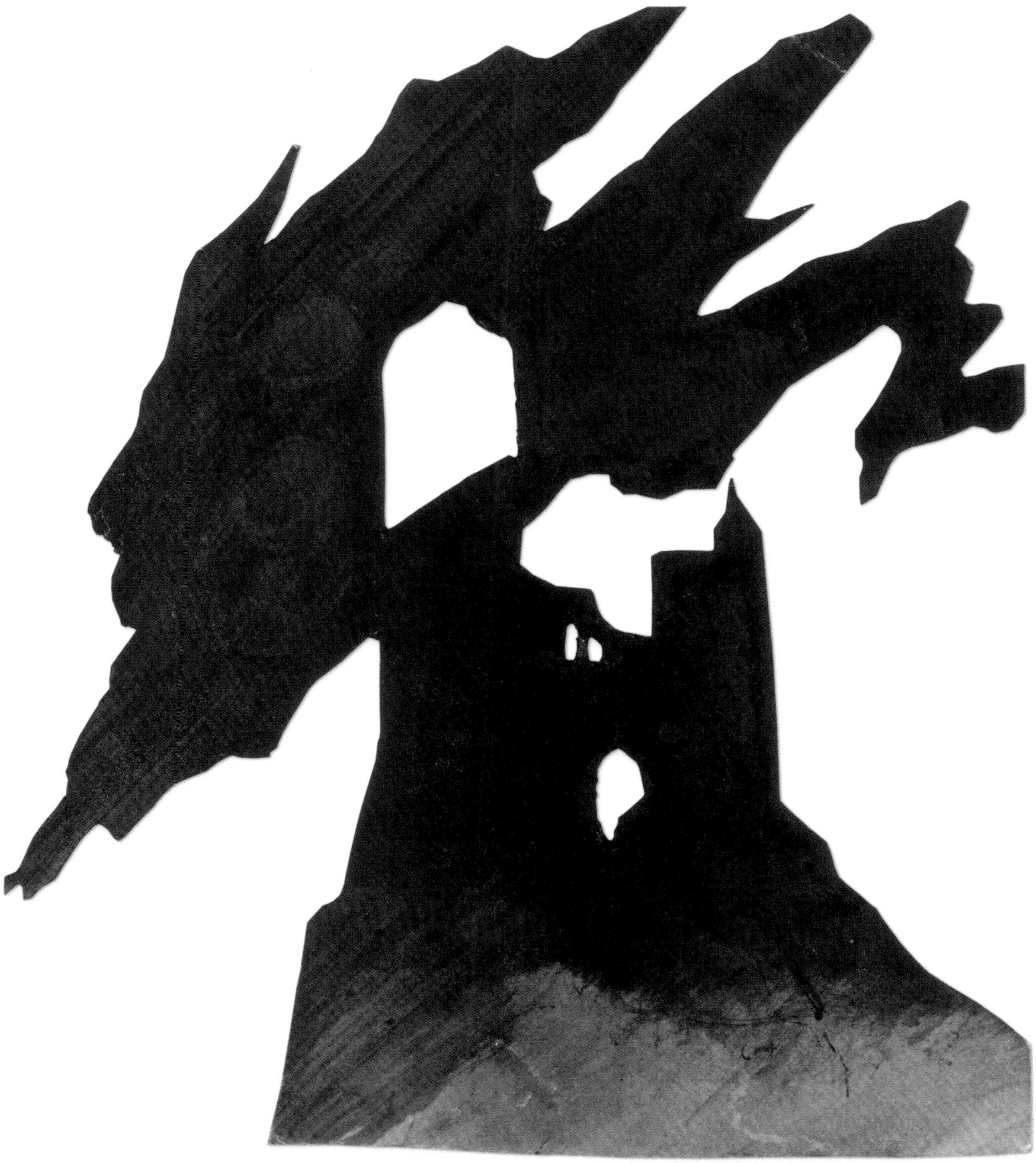

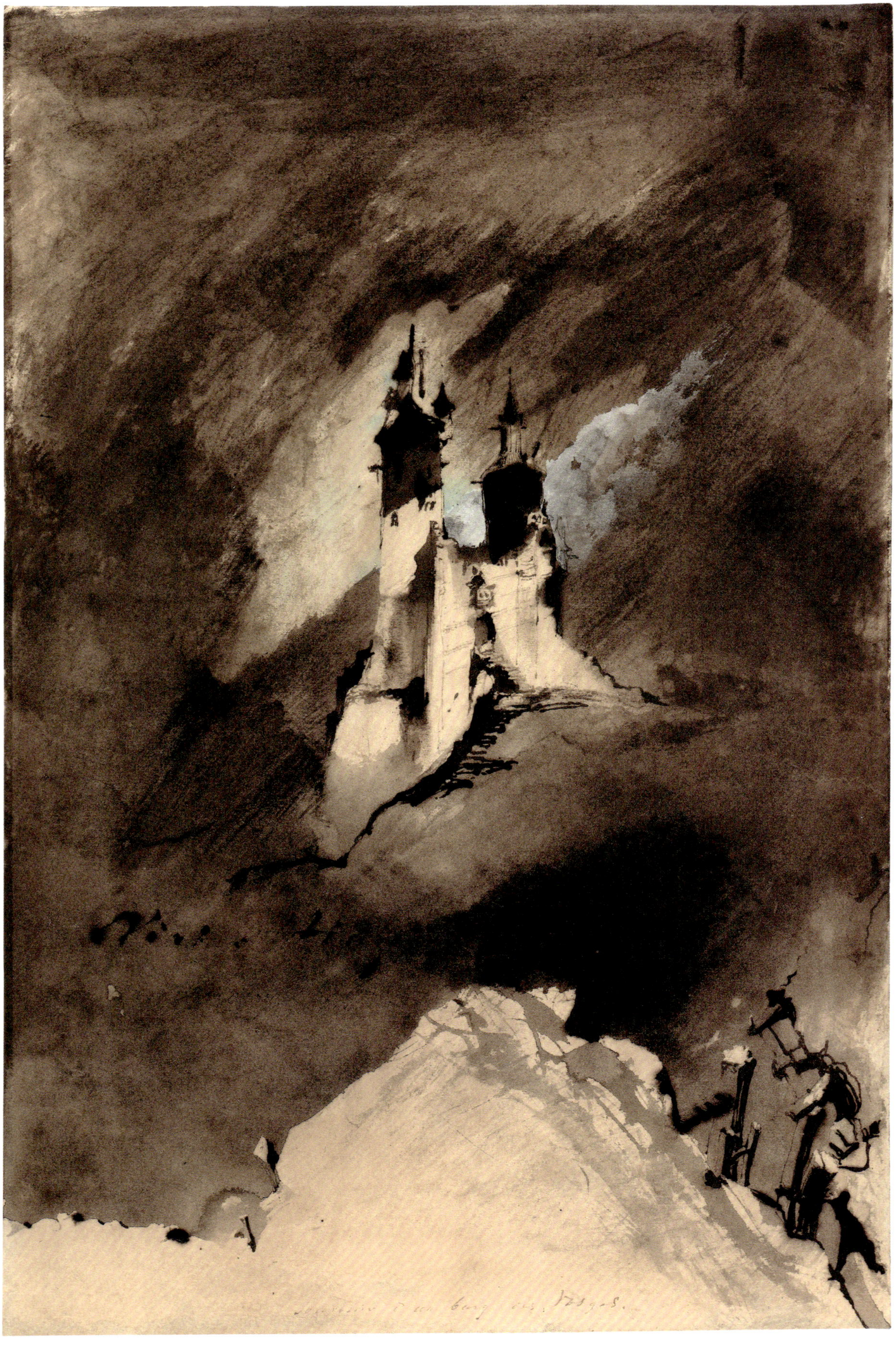

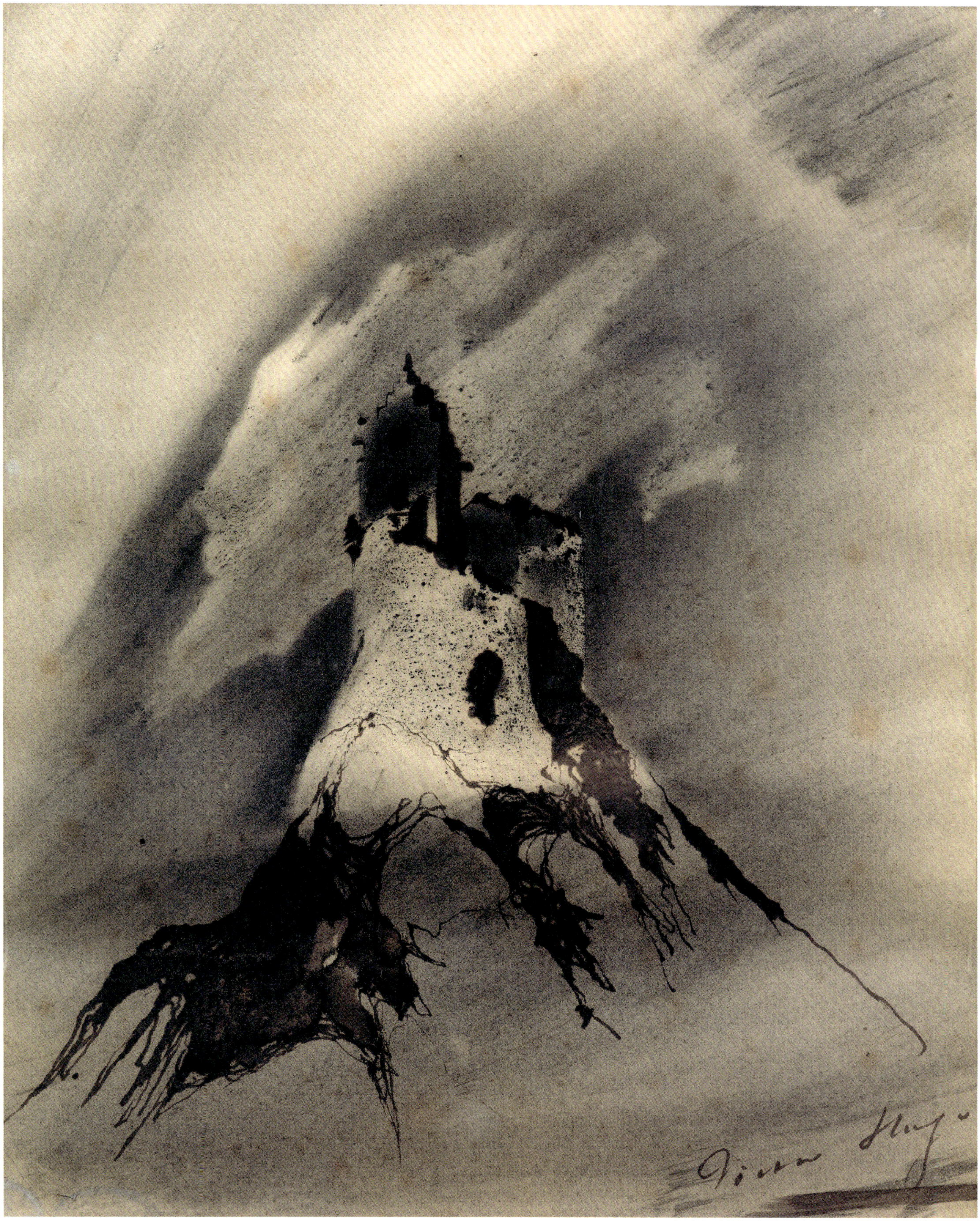

*Forteresse médiévale* (Medieval fortress), ca. 1863. Brown ink and wash on paper. 5⅝ × 8¾ in. (14.3 × 22.3 cm). Bibliothèque nationale de France.

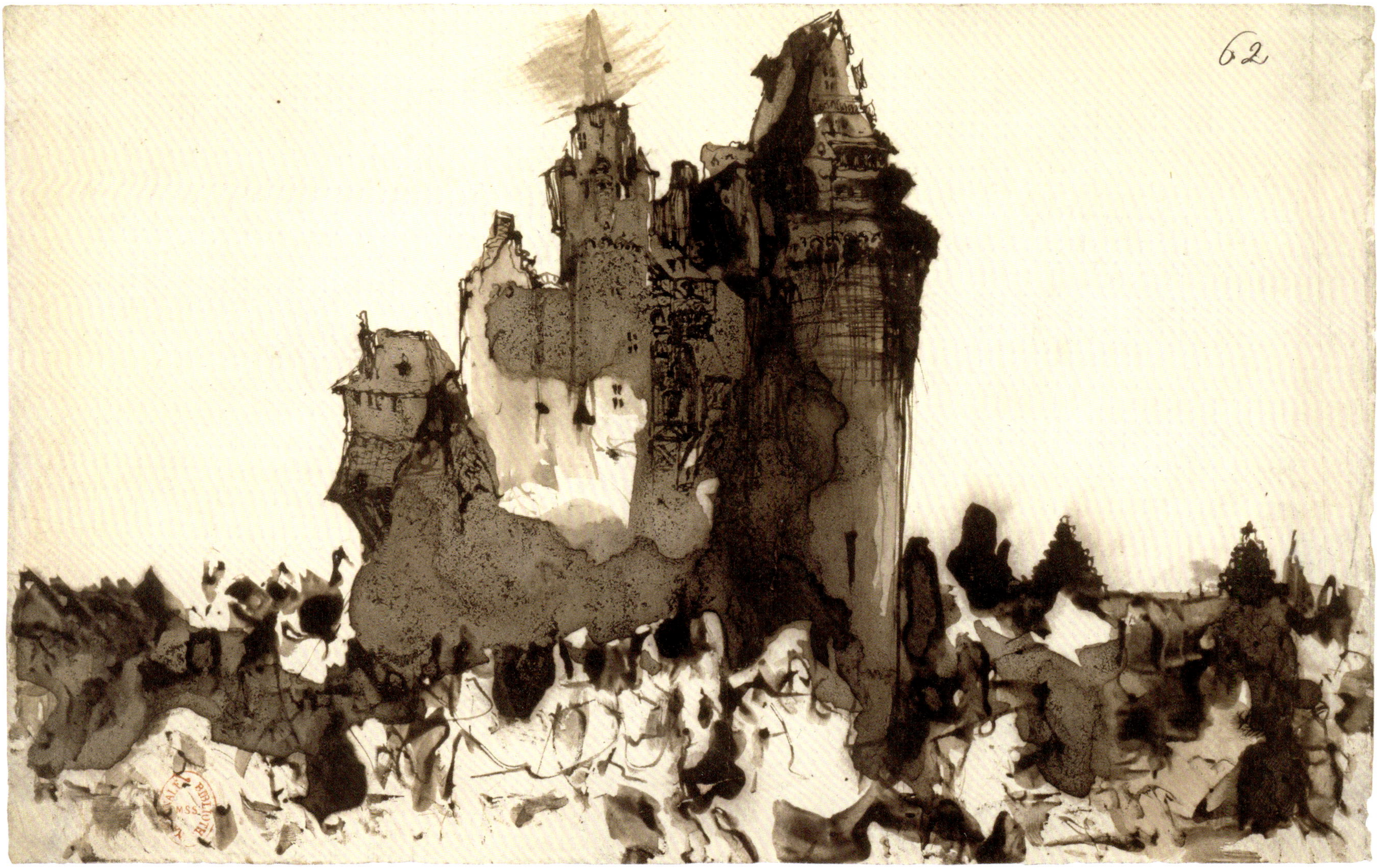
62

Charles Hugo (French, 1826–1871) and/or Auguste Vacquerie (French, 1819–1895). *Le château Mont Orgueil* (The castle of Mont Orgueil), ca. 1853. Salted paper print. 7⅜ × 6½ in. (18.8 × 16.5 cm). Musée d'Orsay, Paris.

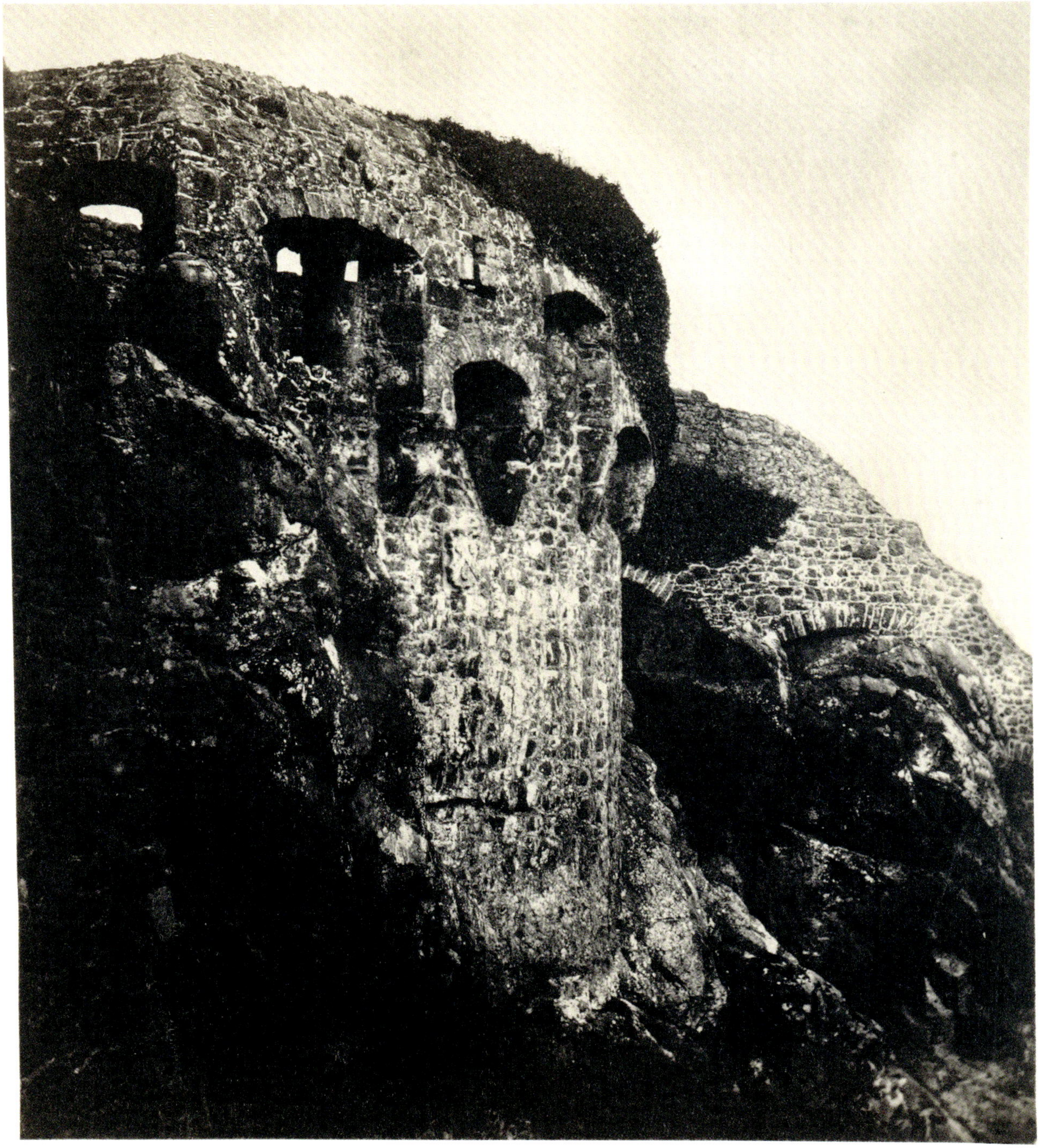

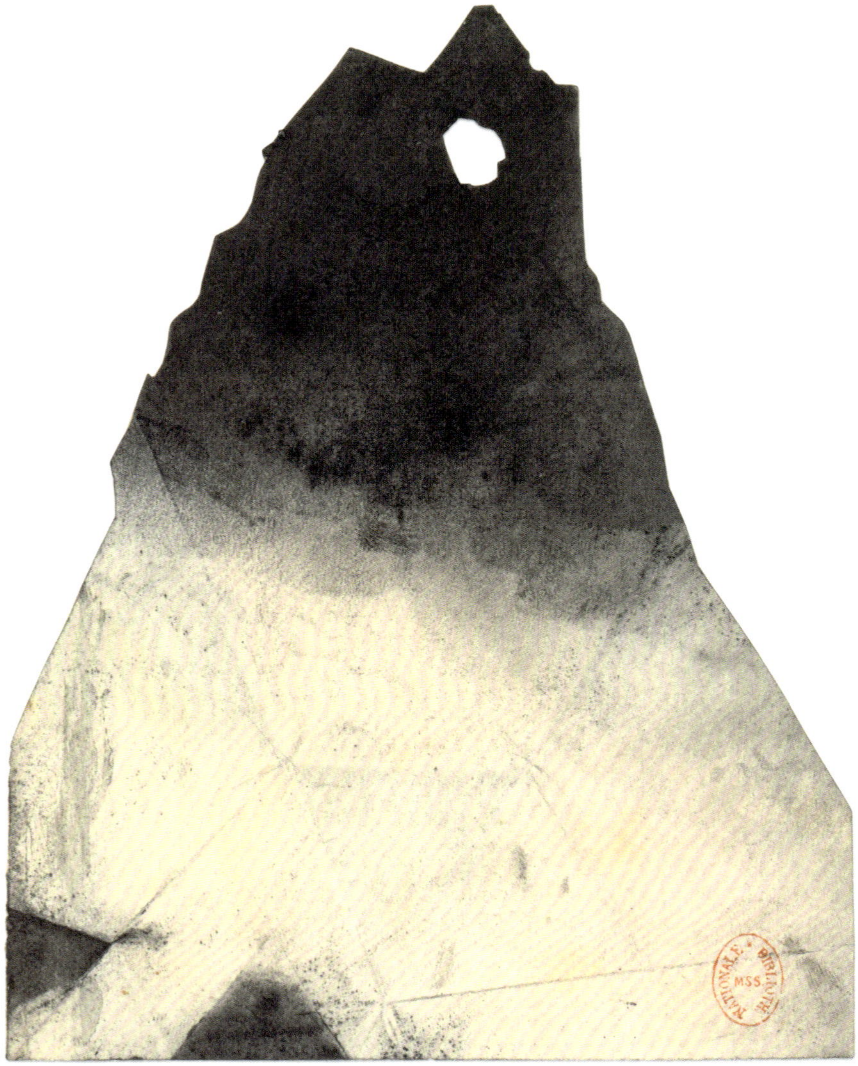

*Silhouette de l'Ermitage* (Silhouette of l'Ermitage), ca. 1855 (recto and verso). Stencil cut from paper with charcoal. $5\frac{13}{16} \times 4\frac{1}{2}$ in. (14.7 × 11.5 cm). Bibliothèque nationale de France.

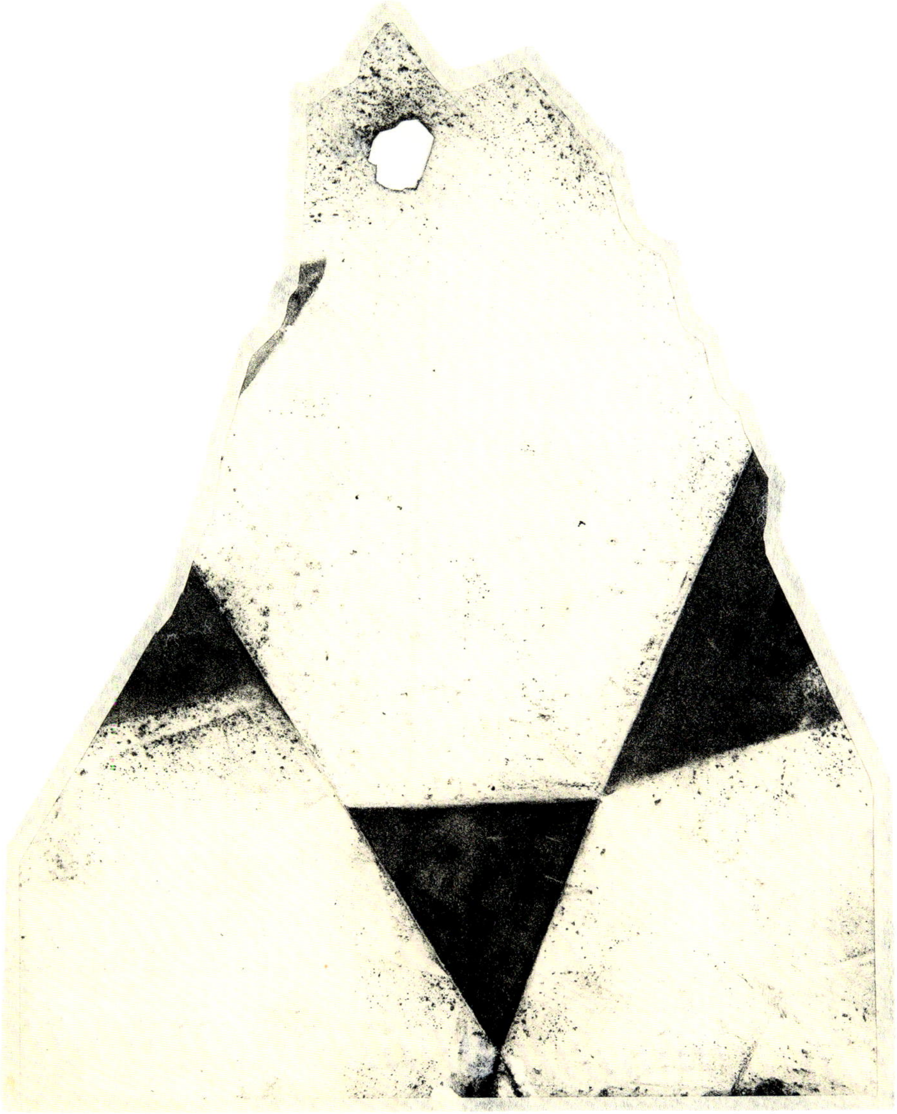

Charles Hugo (French, 1826–1871). *Le Rocher de l'Ermitage* (The Rocher de l'Ermitage), ca. 1853. Salted paper print. 8 1/16 × 6 1/2 in. (20.5 × 16.5 cm). Musée d'Orsay, Paris.

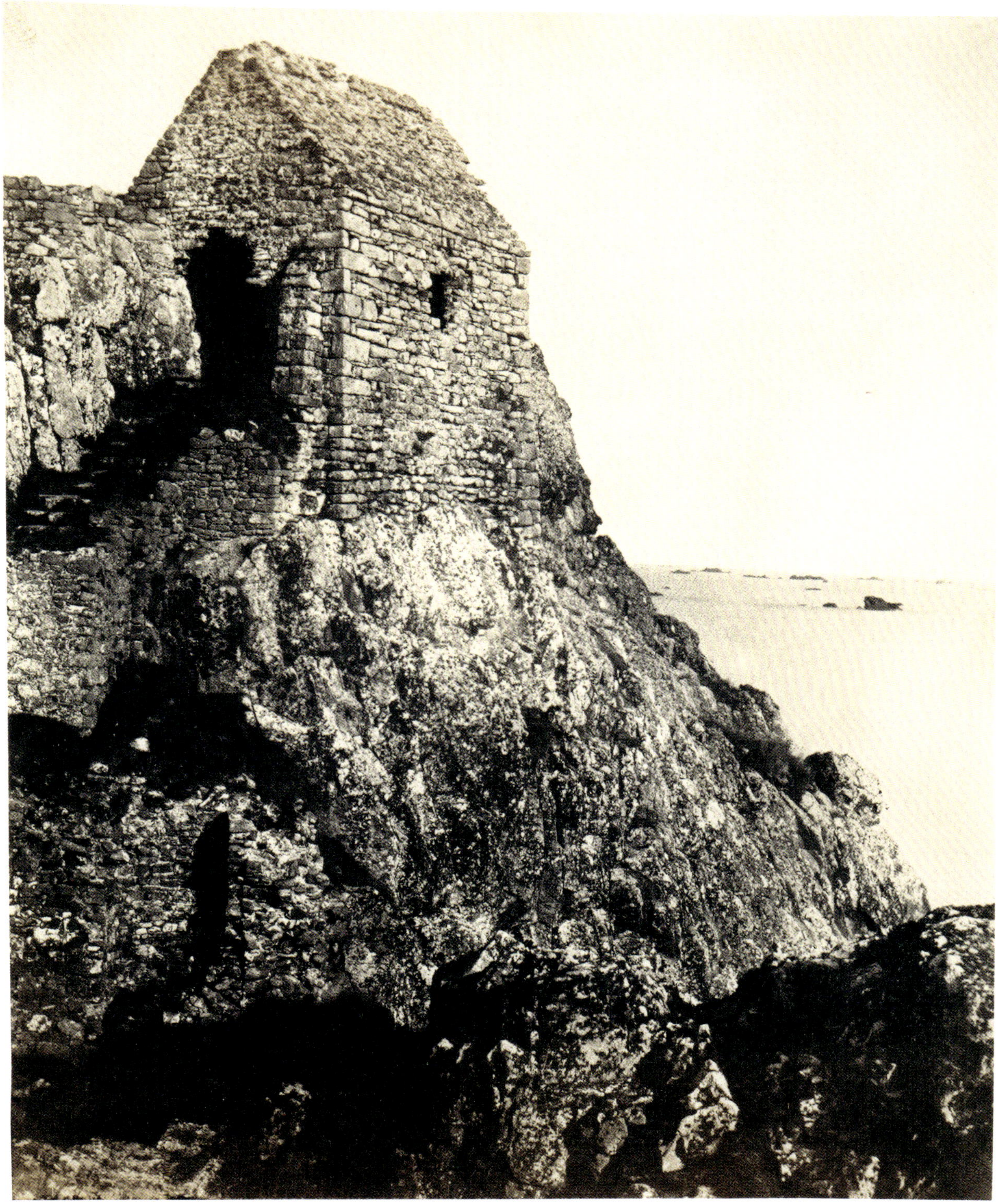

*Souvenir de Suisse* (Souvenir of Switzerland), ca. 1854–55. Brown and black ink, brown and gray wash, black powdered pigment, and unidentified black medium with white gouache on paper in pyrographed and painted frame. 9¼ × 8⁹⁄₁₆ in. (23.5 × 21.7 cm). Maisons de Victor Hugo, Paris / Guernesey.

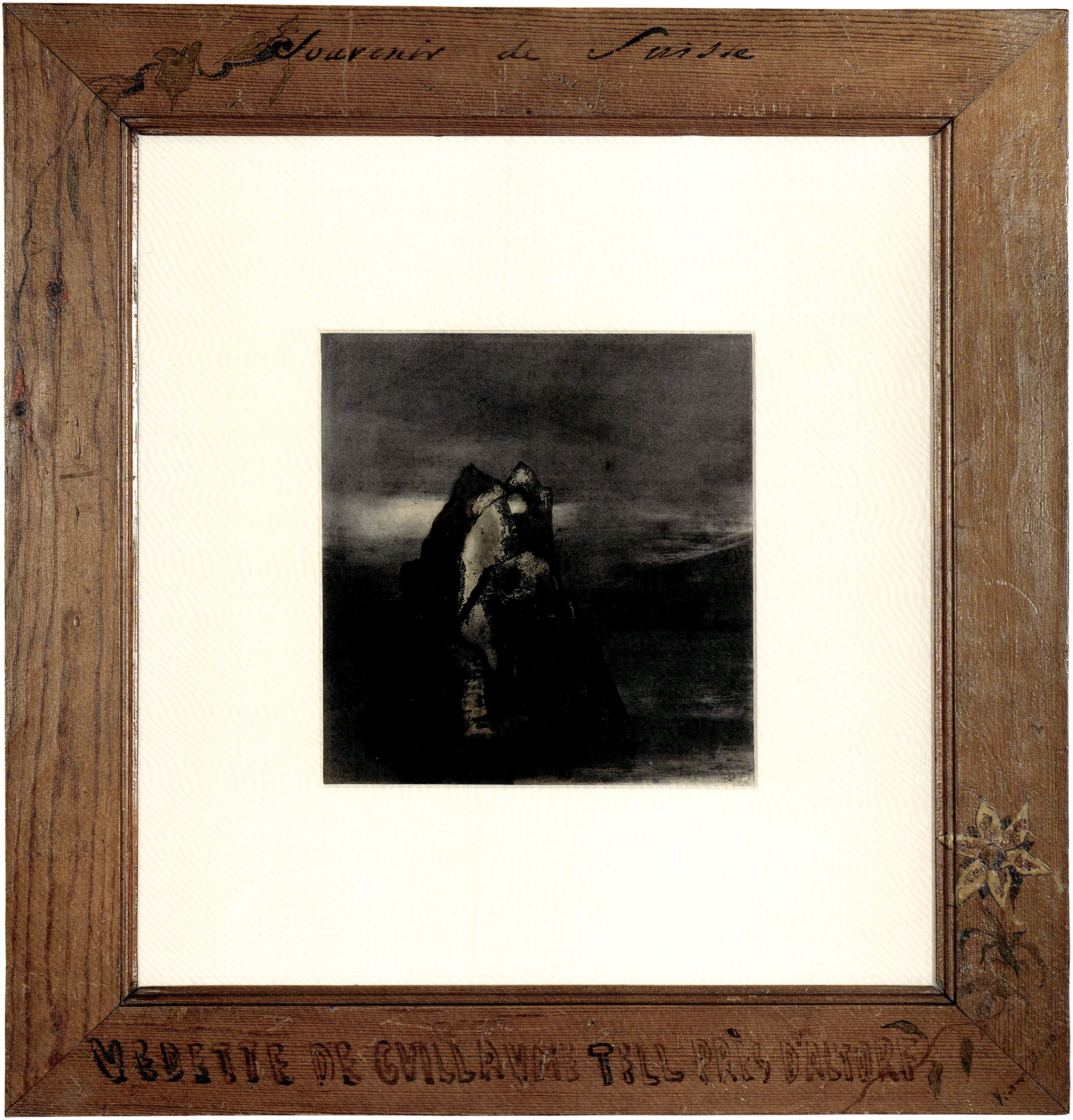
Souvenir de Suisse

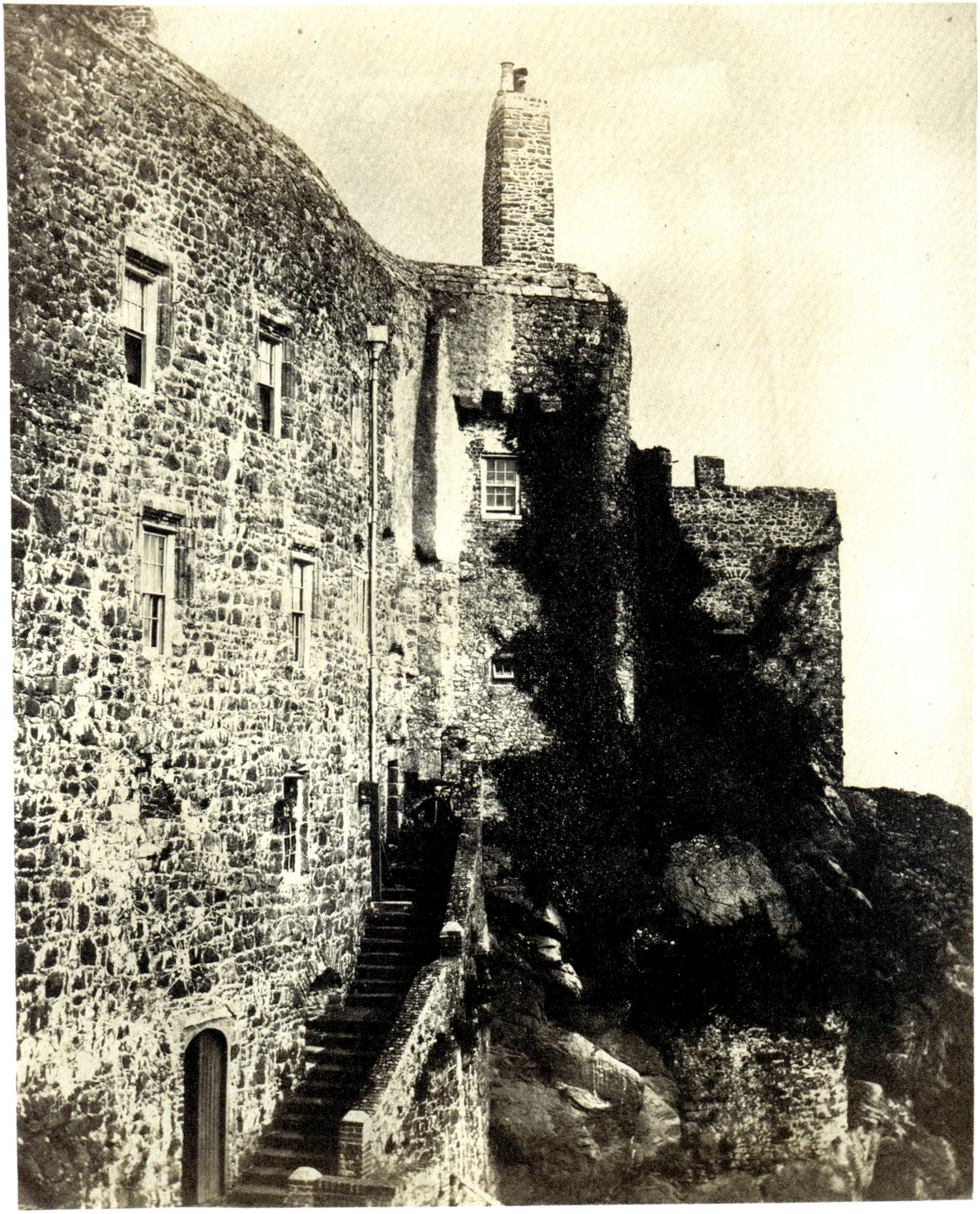

Charles Hugo (French, 1826–1871) and/or Auguste Vacquerie (French, 1819–1895). *Le château Mont Orgueil* (The castle of Mont Orgueil), ca. 1853. Salted paper print. 8⅜ × 6½ in. (21.2 × 16.5 cm). Musée d'Orsay, Paris.

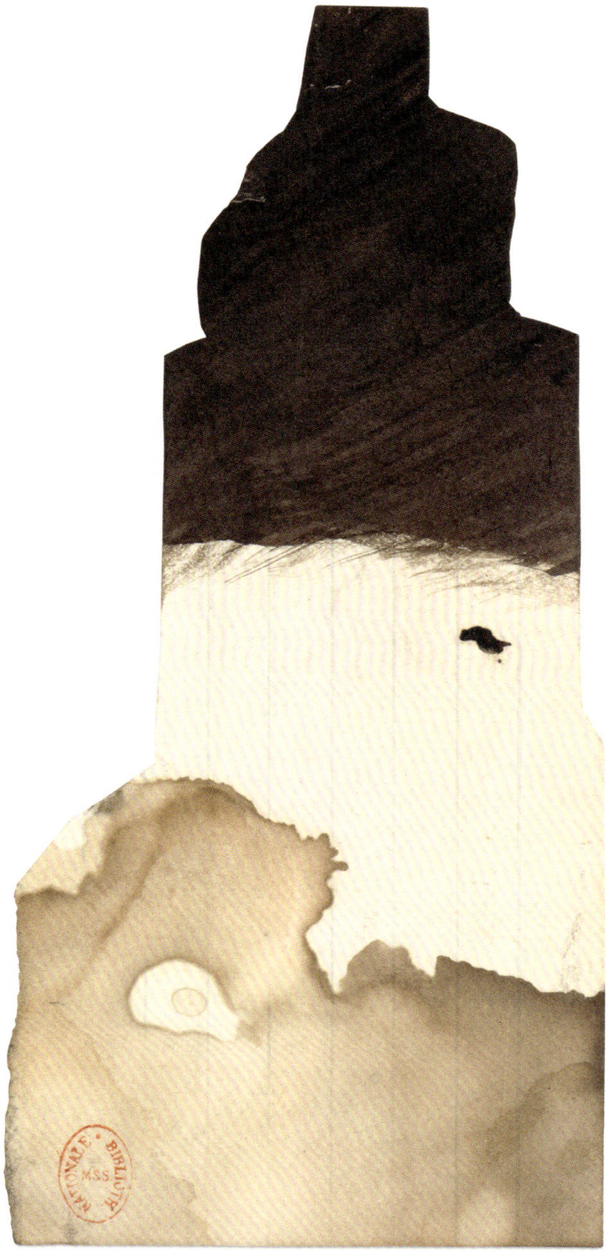

*Silhouette d'une tour* (Silhouette of a tower), ca. 1855. Stencil cut from ruled notepaper with brown ink and wash. $6\frac{1}{2} \times 3\frac{1}{16}$ in. (16.5 × 7.8 cm). Bibliothèque nationale de France.

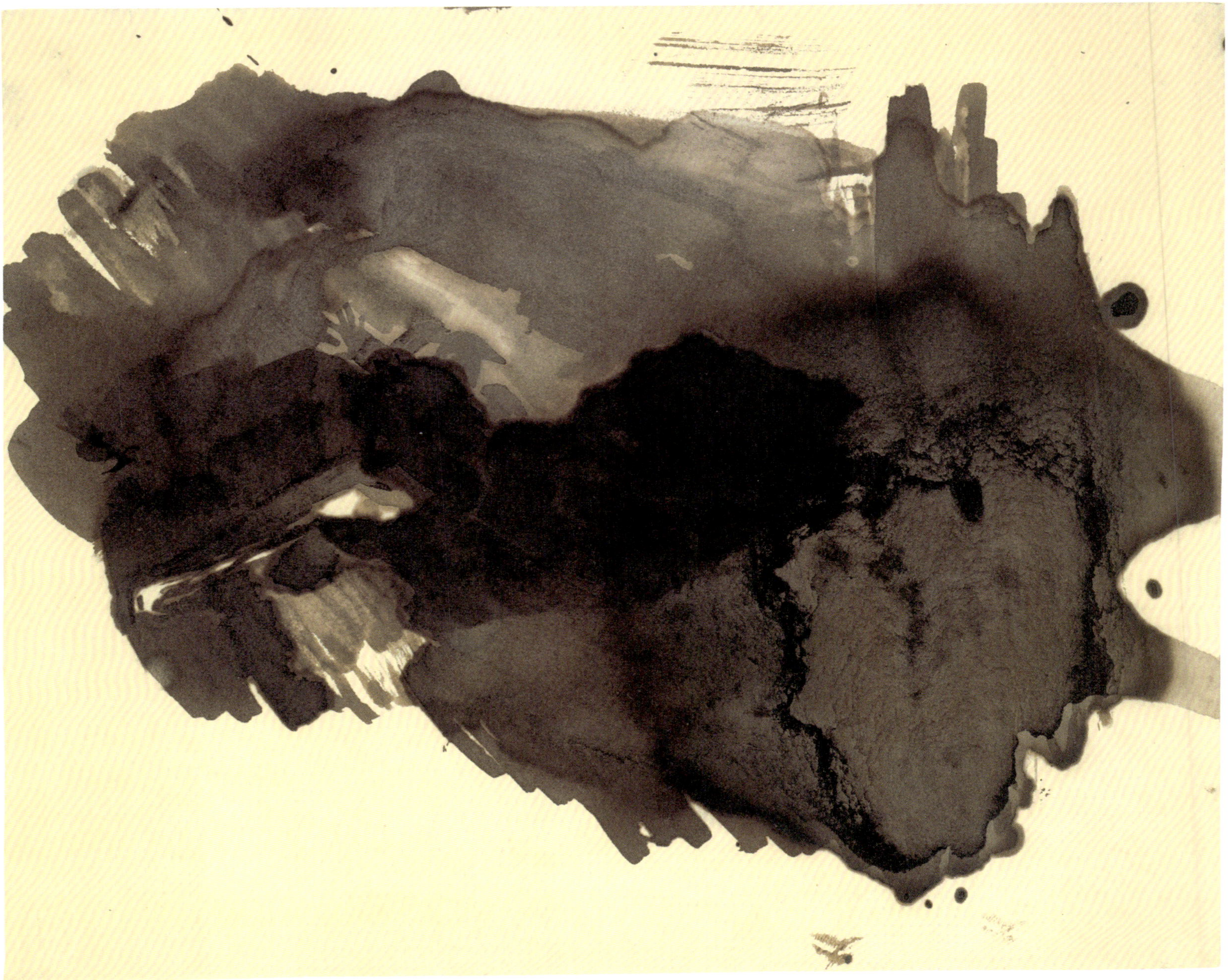

ABOVE *Château sur une colline* (Castle on a hill), ca. 1860–70(?). Brown ink and wash on paper. 7⁵⁄₁₆ × 8⁷⁄₈ in. (18.5× 22.5 cm). Maisons de Victor Hugo, Paris / Guernesey.

OPPOSITE Charles Hugo (French, 1826–1871). *Auguste Vacquerie au pied d'un rocher (La Collette)* (Auguste Vacquerie at the foot of a rock [La Collette]), ca. 1853. Salted paper print. 8¹³⁄₁₆ × 7³⁄₁₆ in. (22.4 × 18.2 cm). Musée d'Orsay, Paris, Don de Mme Marie-Thérèse et M. André Jammes, 1984.

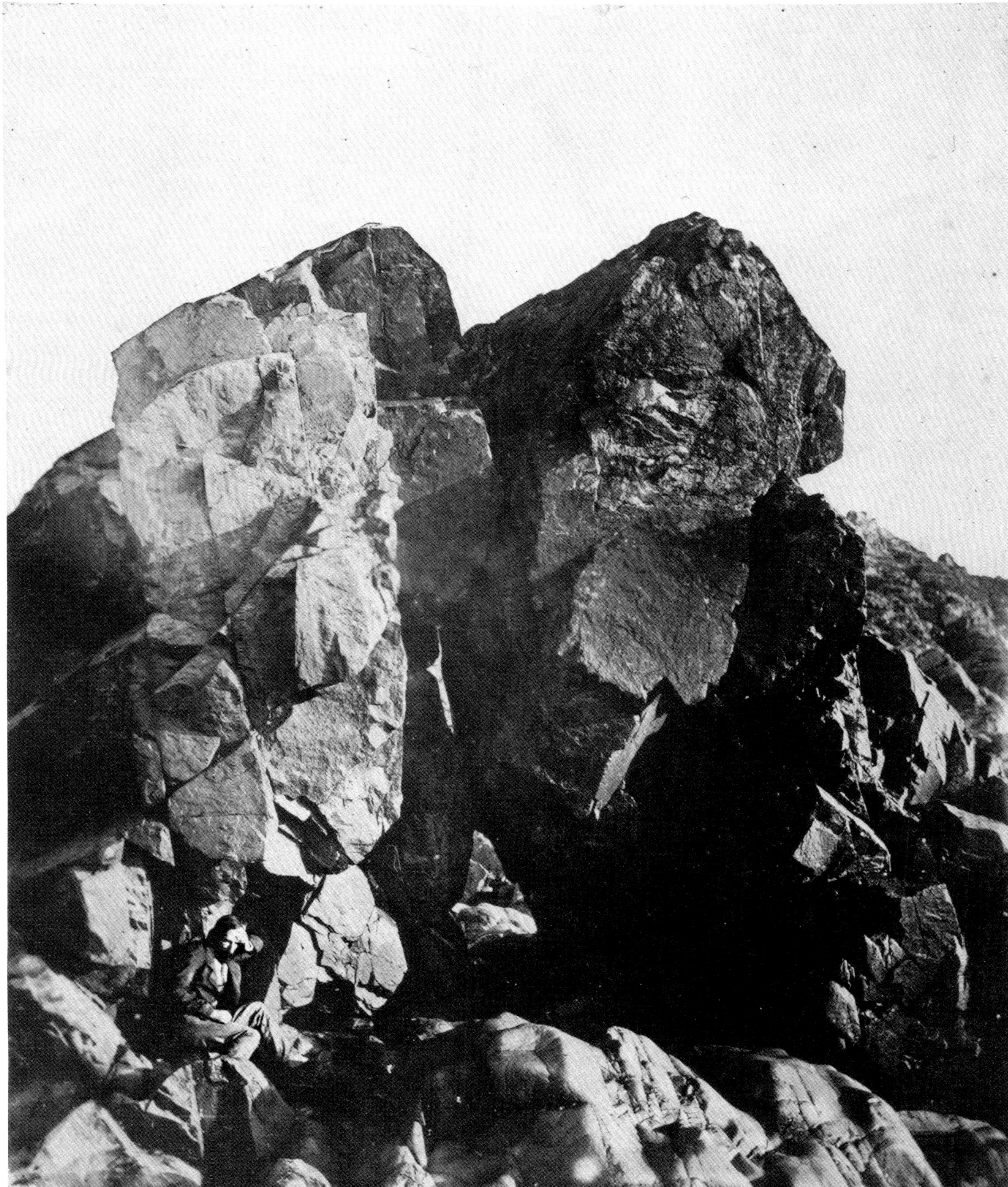

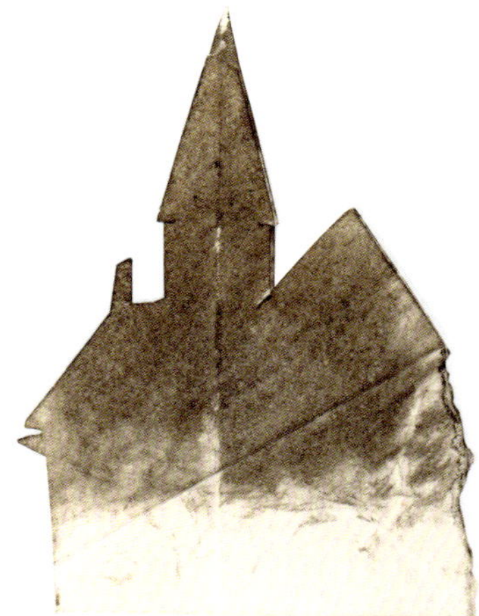

LEFT *Silhouette d'un burg* (Silhouette of a castle), ca. 1854. Stencil cut from paper from a printed concert program dated October 20, 1854. 4 13/16 × 4 11/16 in. (12.3 × 11.9 cm). Bibliothèque nationale de France.

RIGHT *Silhouette de clocher* (Silhouette of a bell tower), ca. 1855. Stencil cut from a paper envelope with brown ink and wash. 4 15/16 × 1 3/4 in. (12.5 × 4.5 cm) unfolded. Maisons de Victor Hugo, Paris / Guernesey.

*Silhouette du château de Vianden* (Silhouette of the castle of Vianden), 1871. Stencil cut from paper with brown and purple ink. 2¾ × 4¾ in. (7 × 12 cm). Private collection.

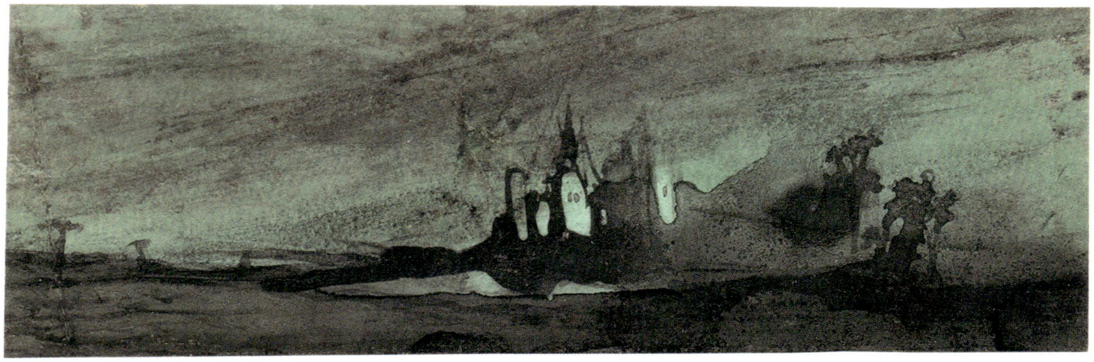

ABOVE *Paysage avec château* (Landscape with castle), ca. 1855–57. Brown ink and green-blue wash on paper. 1¾ × 4½ in. (4.4 × 11.4 cm). Collection of Gordon VeneKlasen.

OPPOSITE *Château au bord d'un lac* (Castle by a lake), 1858. Black and brown ink and wash with white chalk and black Conté crayon, heightened with white gouache. 9⅝ × 9¾ in. (24.5 × 24.8 cm). Collection of Frances Beatty and Allen Adler.

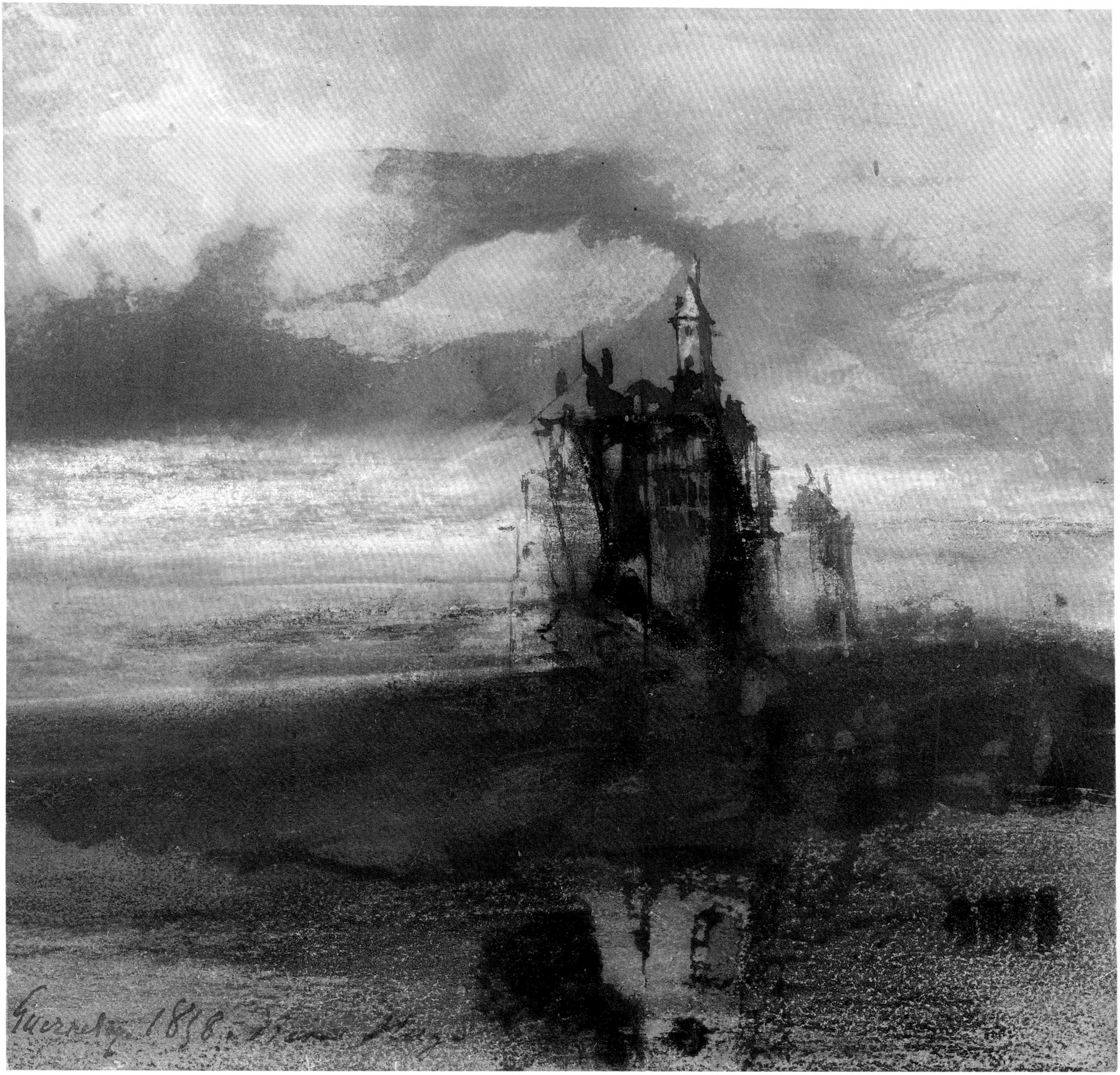
Guernesey 1858.

*La Tourgue en 1835* (La Tourgue in 1835), May 30, 1876. Brown ink and wash on paper. $11\frac{15}{16} \times 7\frac{13}{16}$ in. (30.3 × 19.8 cm). Maisons de Victor Hugo, Paris / Guernesey.

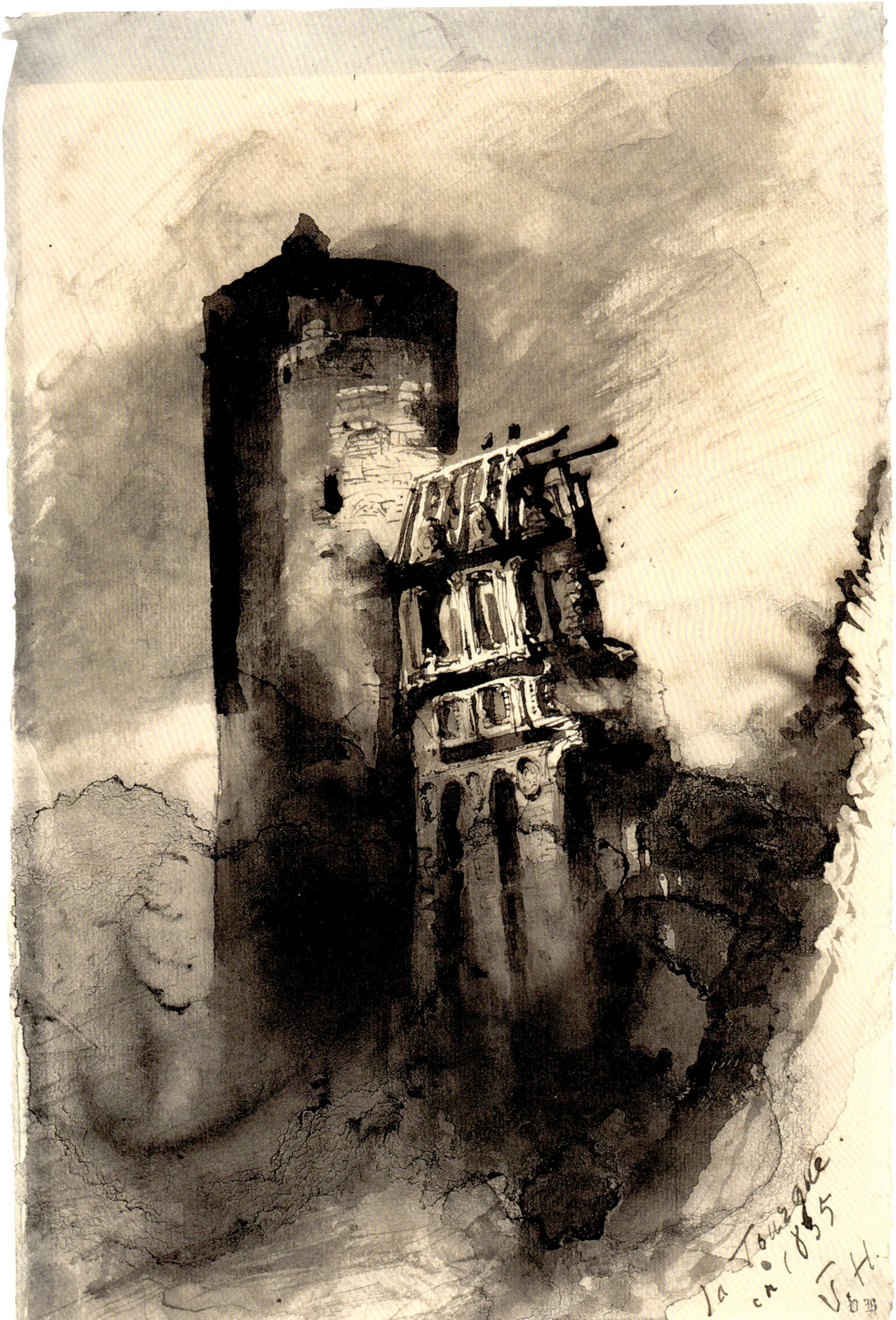
la Tourgue
en 1835
V.H.

*Le phare des Casquets* (The Casquets lighthouse), 1866. Brown ink and wash, black crayon, black chalk, and white gouache on paper. 35⅜ × 18⅞ in. (89.8 × 48 cm). Maisons de Victor Hugo, Paris / Guernesey.

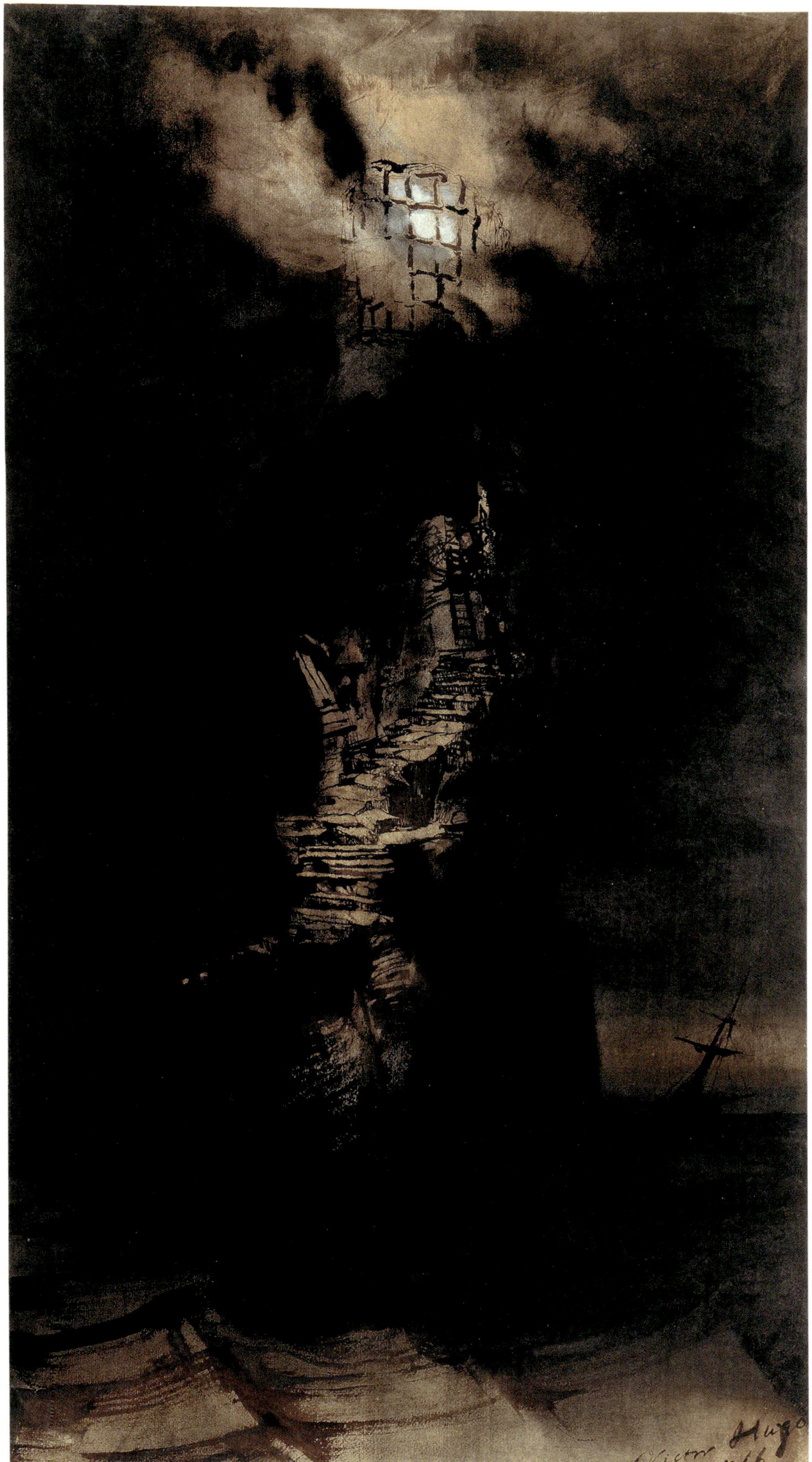
Victor Hugo
1866

OPPOSITE *Silhouette d'un château* (Silhouette of a castle), 1856. Stencil cut from ruled notepaper with charcoal and traces of white gouache. 9 9⁄13 × 6 15⁄16 in. (24.3 × 17.6 cm). Maisons de Victor Hugo, Paris / Guernesey.

ABOVE *Silhouette d'église* (Silhouette of a church), 1855. Stencil cut from paper with charcoal and traces of brown ink. 3 7⁄8 × 2 15⁄16 in. (9.8 × 7.5 cm). Bibliothèque nationale de France.

*Vianden 1871*, 1871. Brown and black ink, brown and purple wash, graphite, and varnish on sketchbook paper. 9⅞ × 13¹¹⁄₁₆ in. (25.1 × 34.7 cm). Bibliothèque nationale de France.

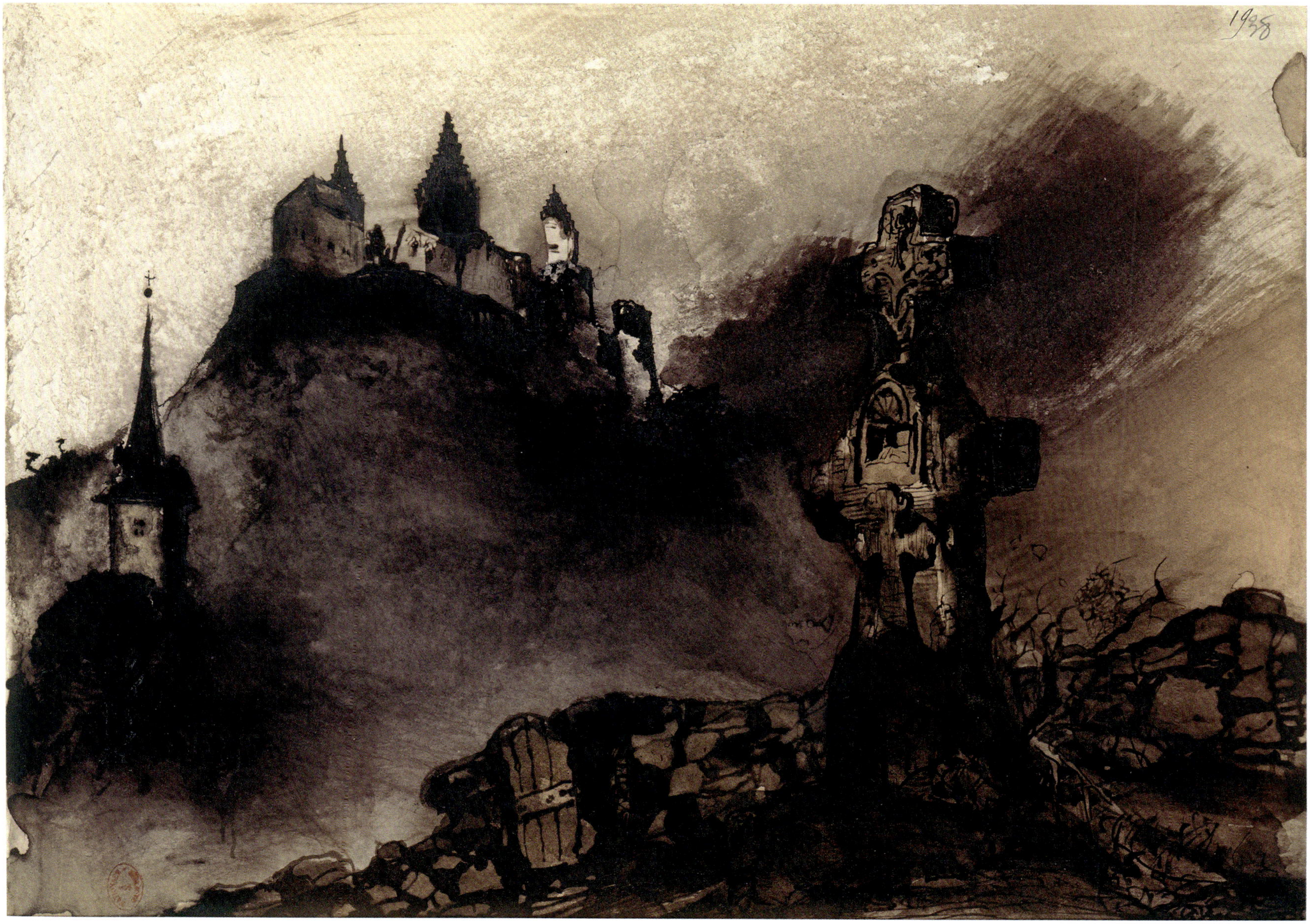

*Vianden à travers une toile d'araignée* (The town of Vianden seen through a spiderweb), August 13, 1871. Brown ink and wash and blue watercolor over graphite on paper. 10 1/16 × 11 15/16 in. (25.5 × 30.3 cm). Maisons de Victor Hugo, Paris / Guernesey.

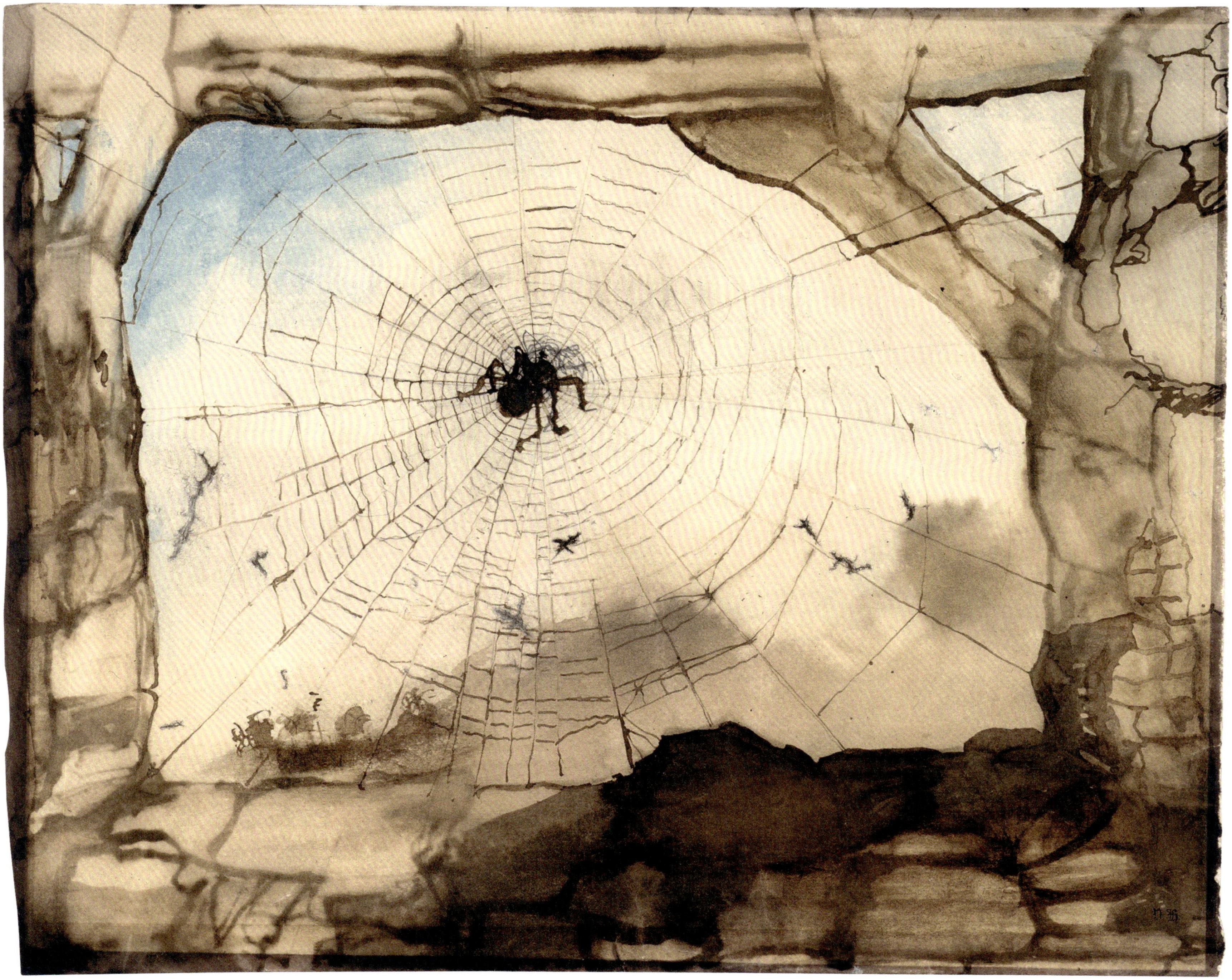

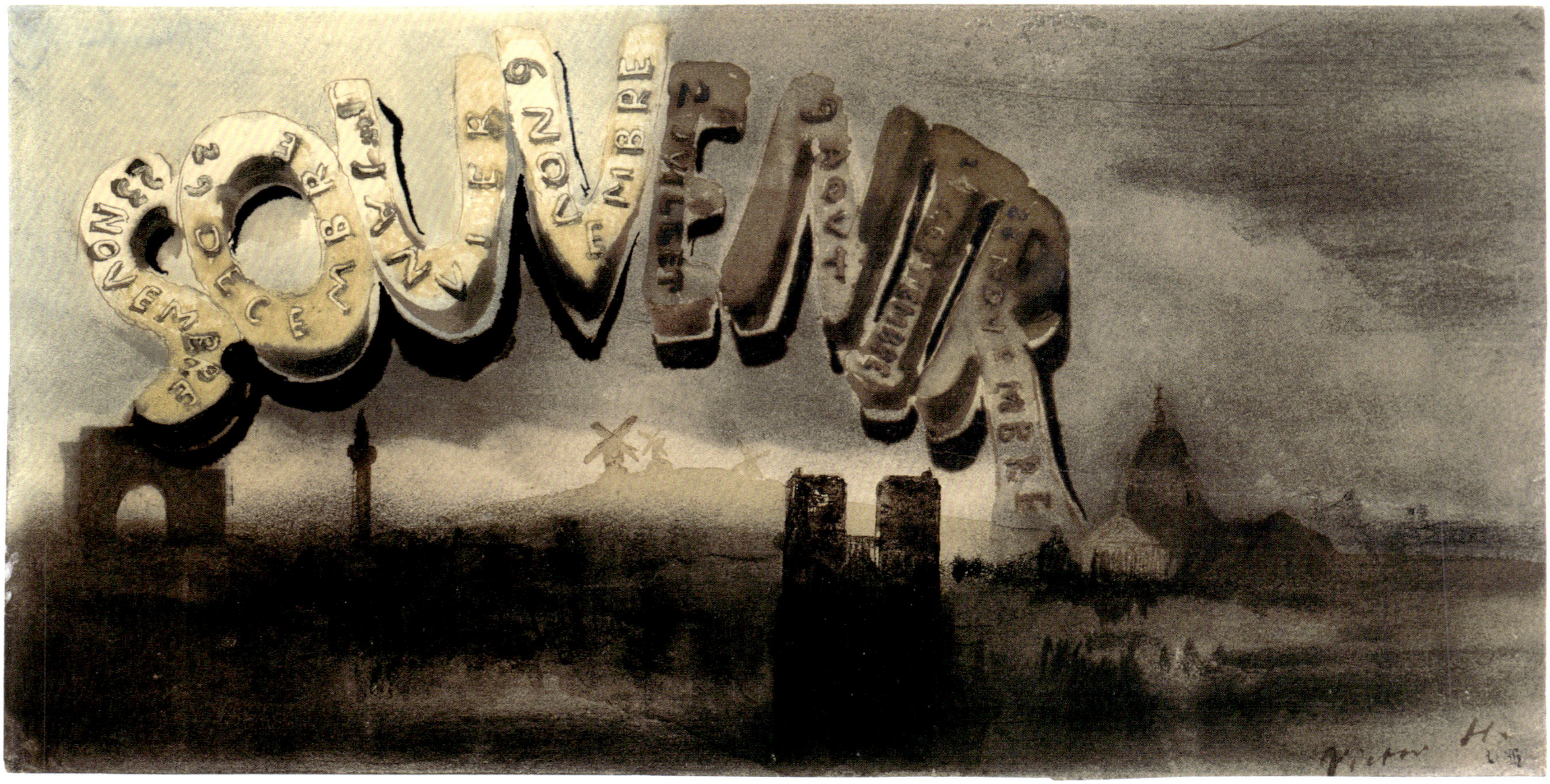

*Souvenir*, ca. 1855(?). Brown ink; brown, black, and blue wash; charcoal; graphite; and black crayon with traces of gold medium on paper. 6 × 11⅝ in. (15.3 × 29.6 cm). Maisons de Victor Hugo, Paris / Guernesey.

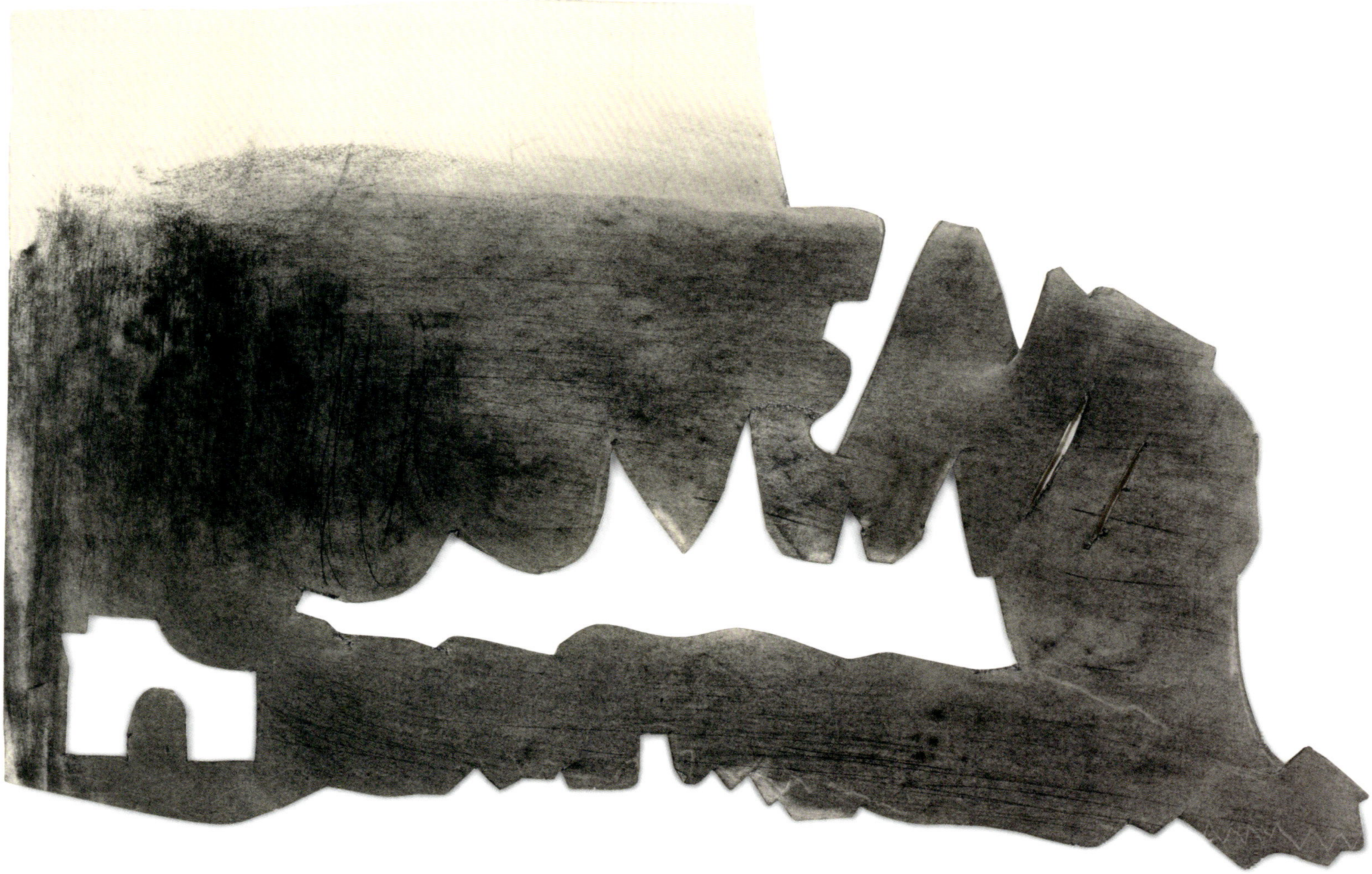

Pochoir pour *Souvenir* (Stencil for Souvenir), ca. 1855(?). Stencil cut from paper with charcoal and brown and black ink. 5⅜ × 8¾ in. (13.7 × 22.3 cm). Maisons de Victor Hugo, Paris / Guernesey.

FROM TOP

Signed pebble, 1856. Ink on pebble. 2¾ × 4⁷⁄₁₆ × 1¹⁵⁄₁₆ in. (7 × 11.3 × 5 cm). Maisons de Victor Hugo, Paris / Guernesey.

Signed pebble, September 1856. Ink on pebble. 4¹⁵⁄₁₆ × 4⁵⁄₁₆ × 1⅞ in. (12.5 × 11 × 4.7 cm). Maisons de Victor Hugo, Paris / Guernesey.

Signed pebble, 1856. Ink on pebble. 3¹⁵⁄₁₆ × 4⁵⁄₁₆ × 2¹⁄₁₆ in. (10 × 11 × 5.3 cm). Maisons de Victor Hugo, Paris / Guernesey.

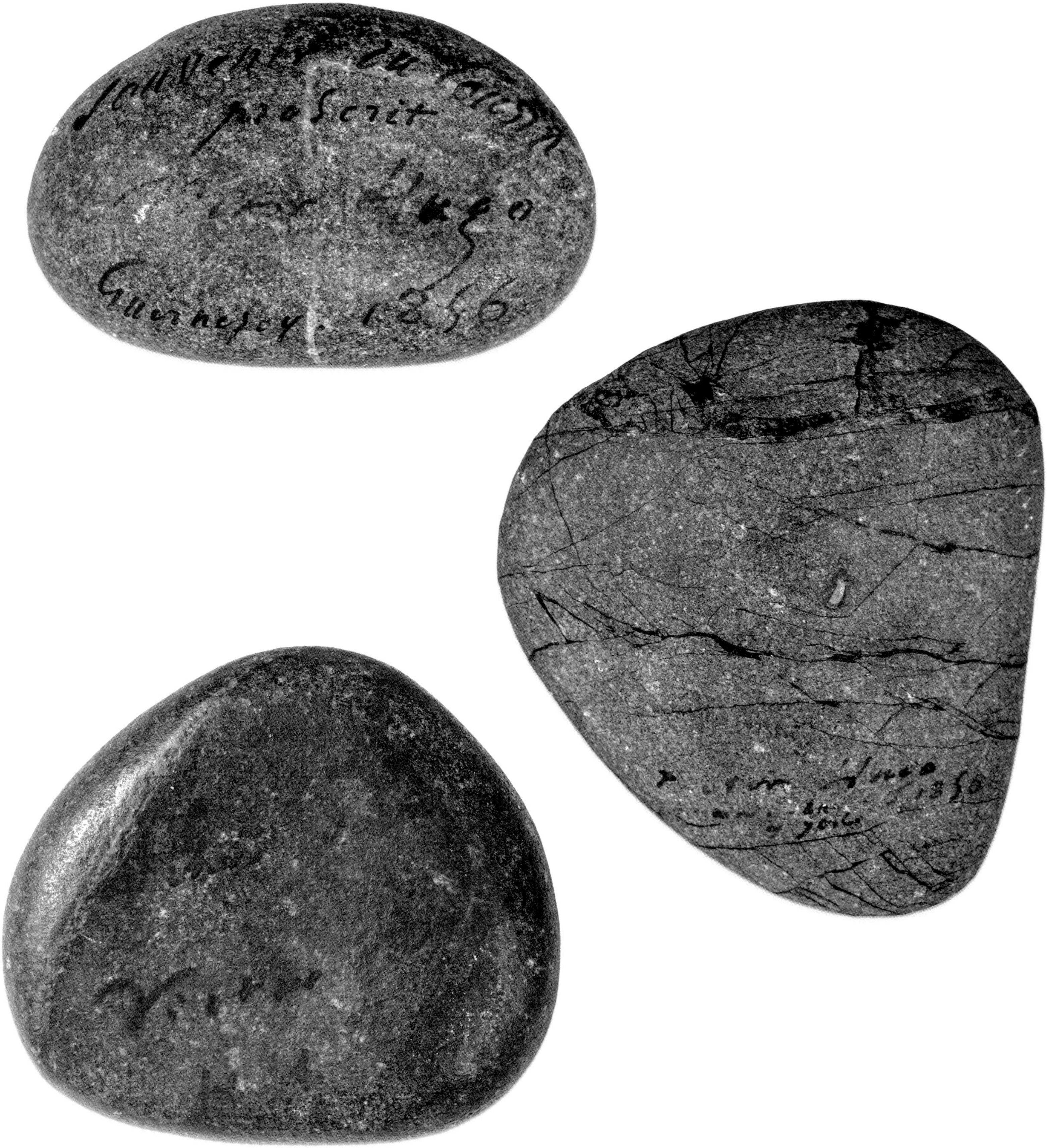
proscrit
Hugo
Guernesey 1856

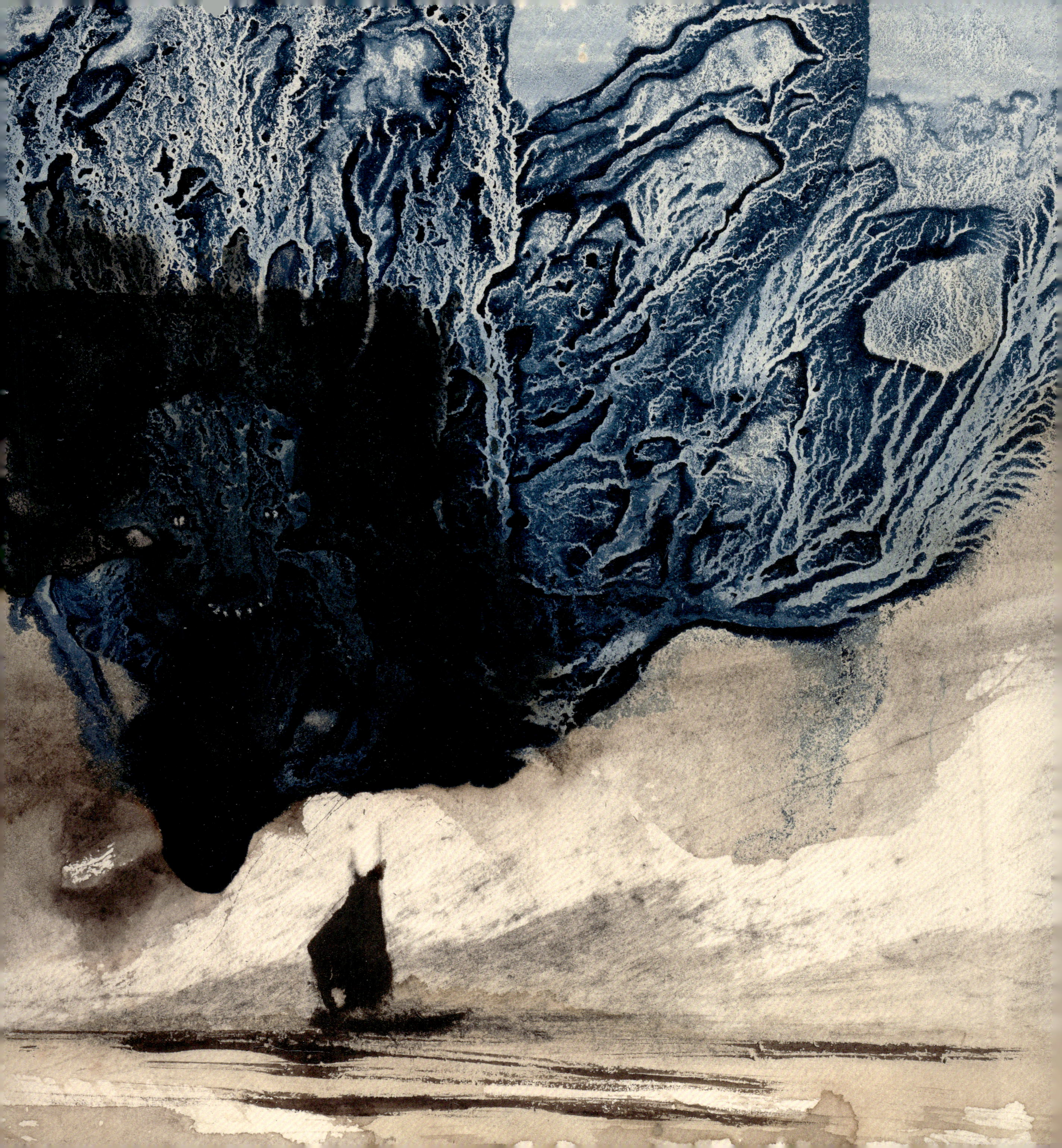

# WATER

Charles Hugo (French, 1826–1871). *Marine Terrace*, ca. 1852–53. Salted paper print. $2\frac{13}{16} \times 4\frac{1}{16}$ in. (7.1 × 10.3 cm). Grunwald Center for the Graphic Arts, Hammer Museum, Purchased with funds provided by the Lloyd E. Rigler–Lawrence E. Deutsch Acquisition Endowment Fund.

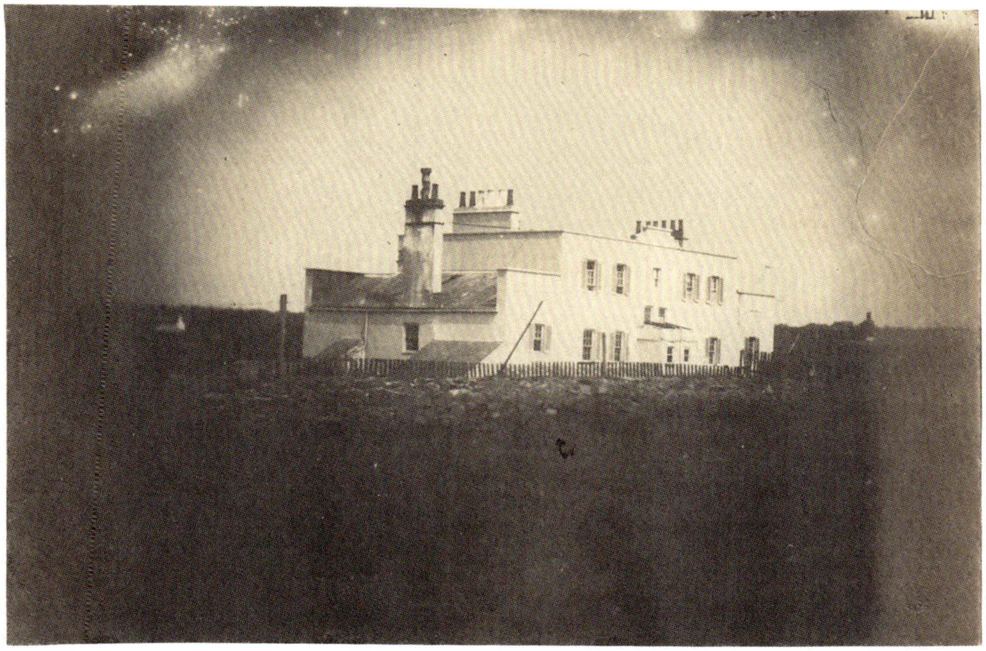

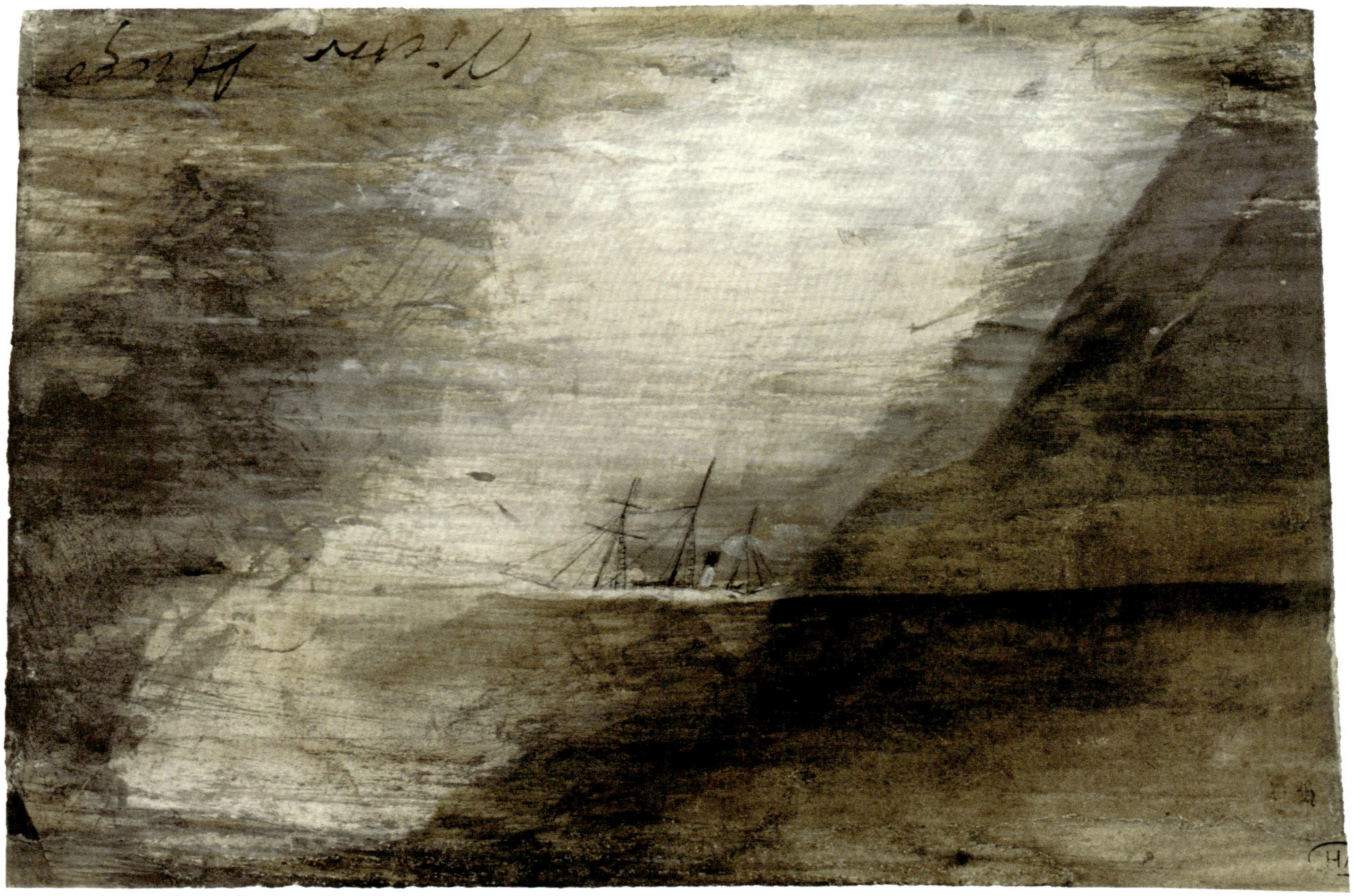

*Un trois-mâts à vapeur* (A three-masted steamboat), ca. 1856. Brown and black ink, brown and gray wash, graphite, watercolor, and white gouache on paper. 5⅛ × 7½ in. (13 × 19 cm). Maisons de Victor Hugo, Paris / Guernesey.

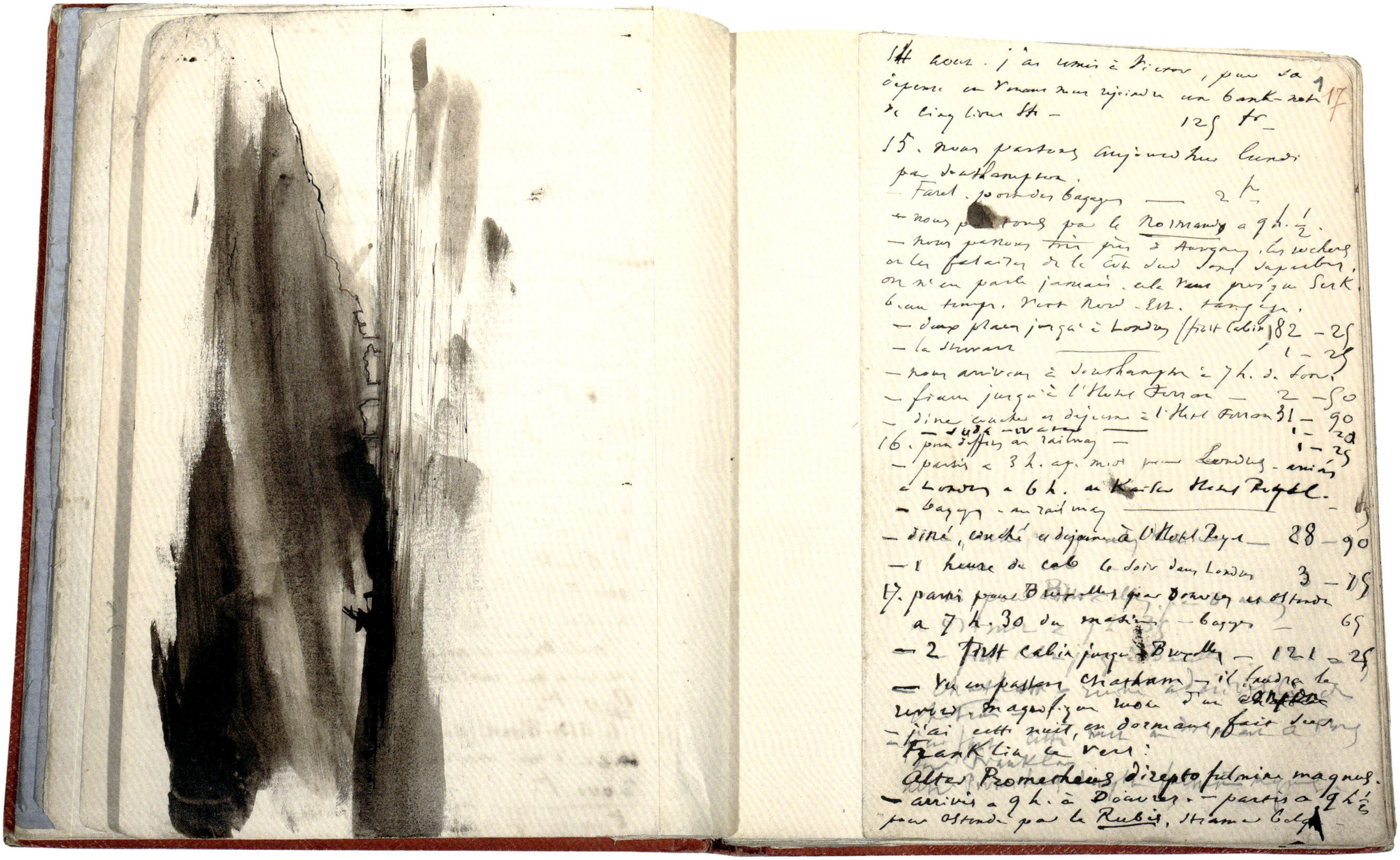

*Les Needles, île de Wight* (The Needles, Isle of Wight), 1865. Bound sketchbook with drawings in brown ink and wash on paper. 7³⁄₁₆ × 11¹⁵⁄₁₆ in. (18.3 × 30.3 cm) open. Bibliothèque nationale de France.

Charles Hugo (French, 1826–1871). *Victor Hugo sur le Rocher des Proscrits* (Victor Hugo seated on the Rocher des Proscrits [exiles' rock]), ca. 1853. Salted paper print. $8\frac{3}{8} \times 7\frac{1}{16}$ in. (21.2 × 18 cm). Maisons de Victor Hugo, Paris / Guernesey.

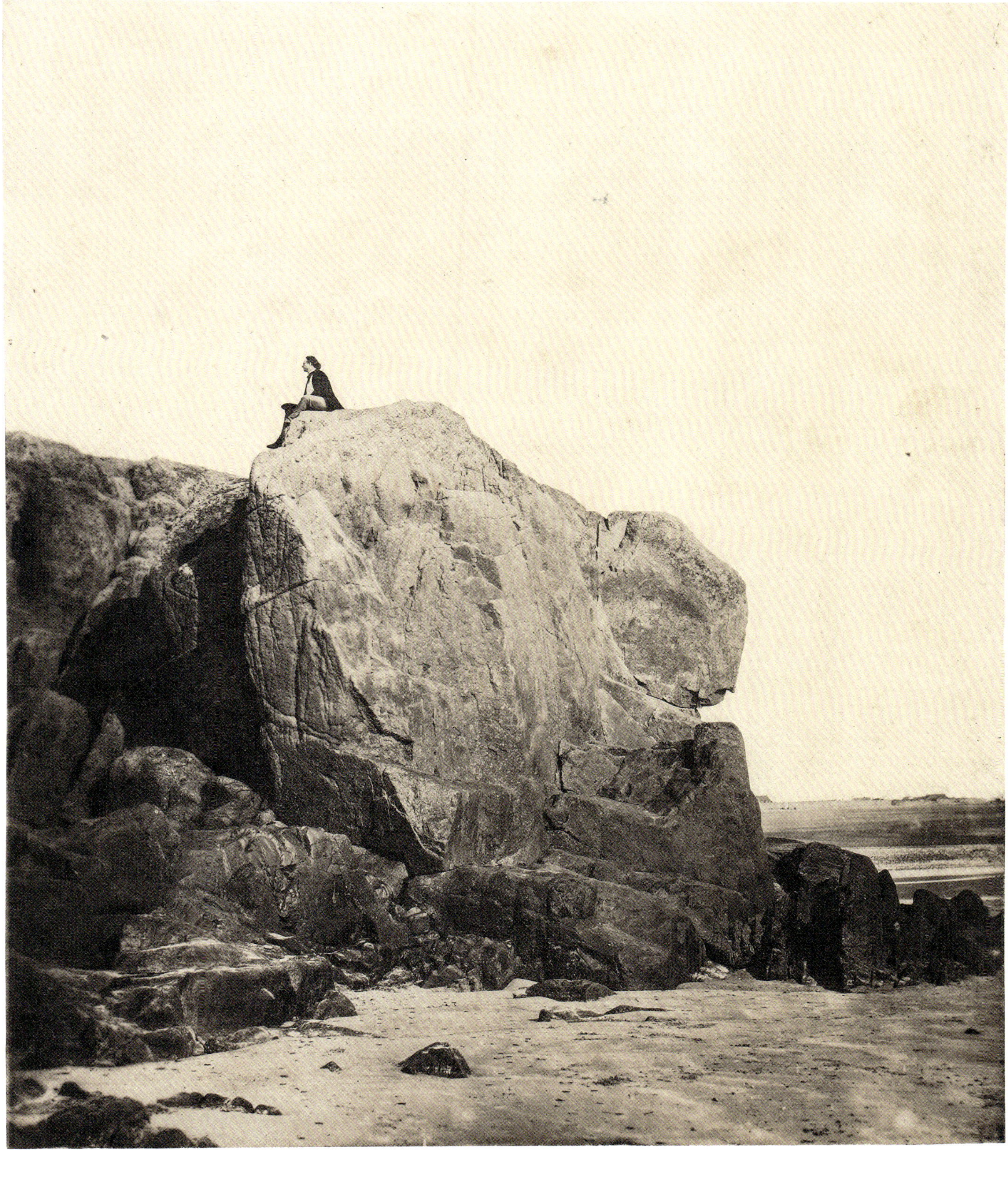

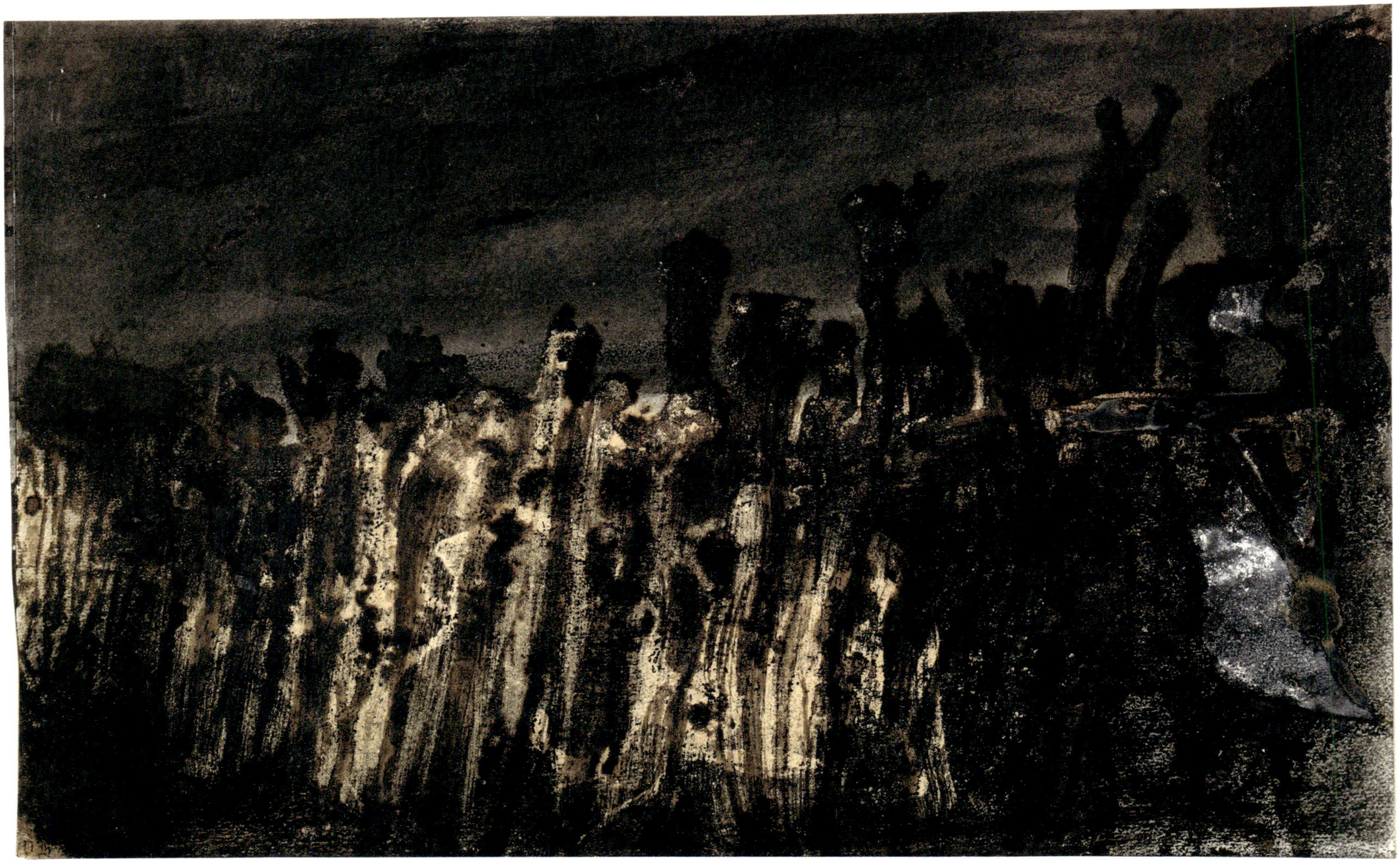

*Brise-lames à Jersey* (A breakwater in Jersey), ca. 1854–55. Brown and black ink, charcoal with white gouache, and traces of varnish on paper. 11⅜ × 18 in. (28.9 × 45.7 cm). Maisons de Victor Hugo, Paris / Guernesey.

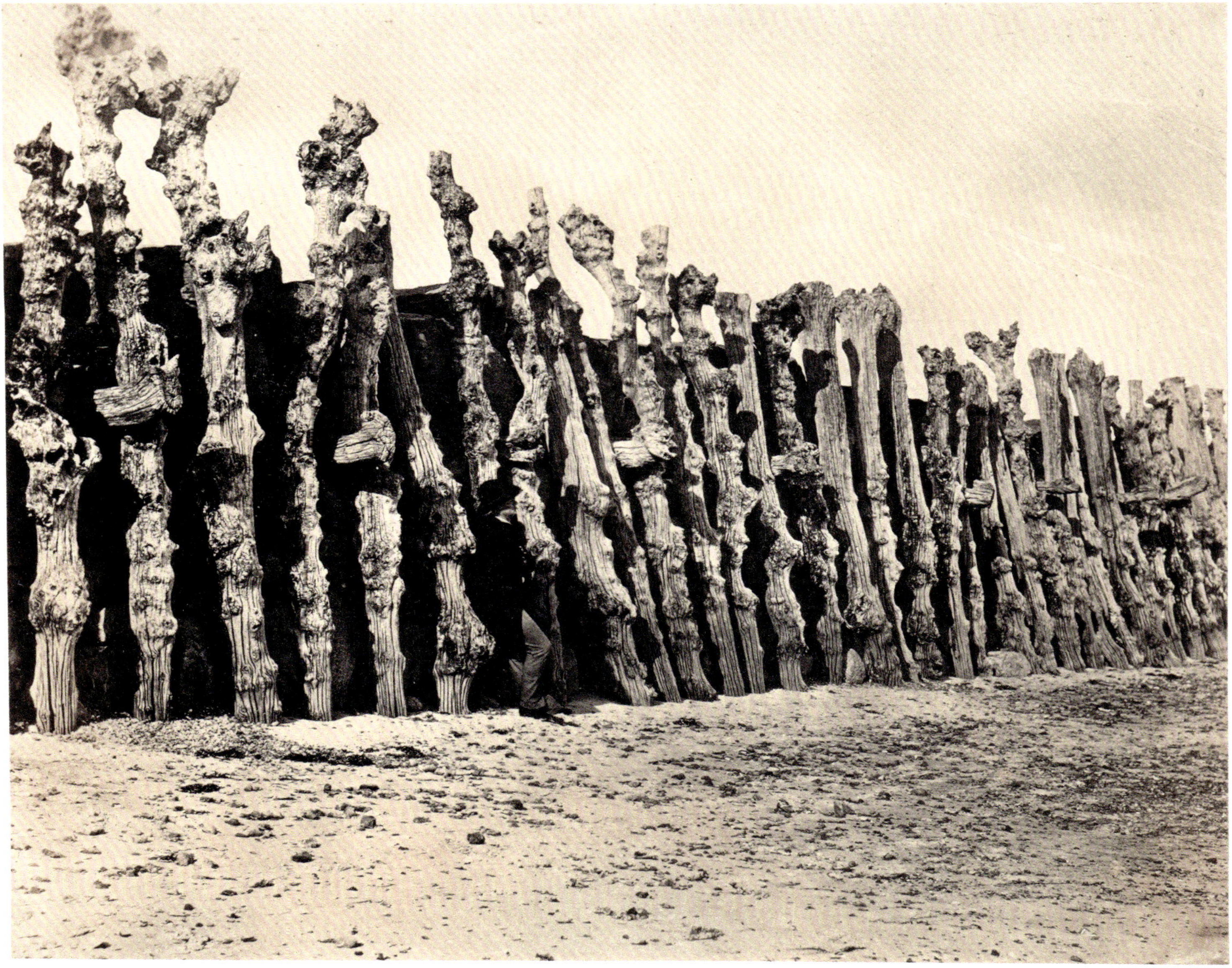

Charles Hugo (French, 1826–1871). *Victor Hugo au Dicq, Jersey* (Victor Hugo at the Dicq, Jersey), ca. 1853. Salted paper print. 6¼ × 7⅝ in. (15.8 × 19.3 cm). Musée d'Orsay, Paris.

*Le serpent* (The snake), ca. 1856. Brown ink, brown and black wash, charcoal, white and red gouache, and traces of varnish and glue on paper. 12⅜ × 19$\frac{5}{16}$ in. (31.5 × 49.1 cm). Maisons de Victor Hugo, Paris / Guernesey.

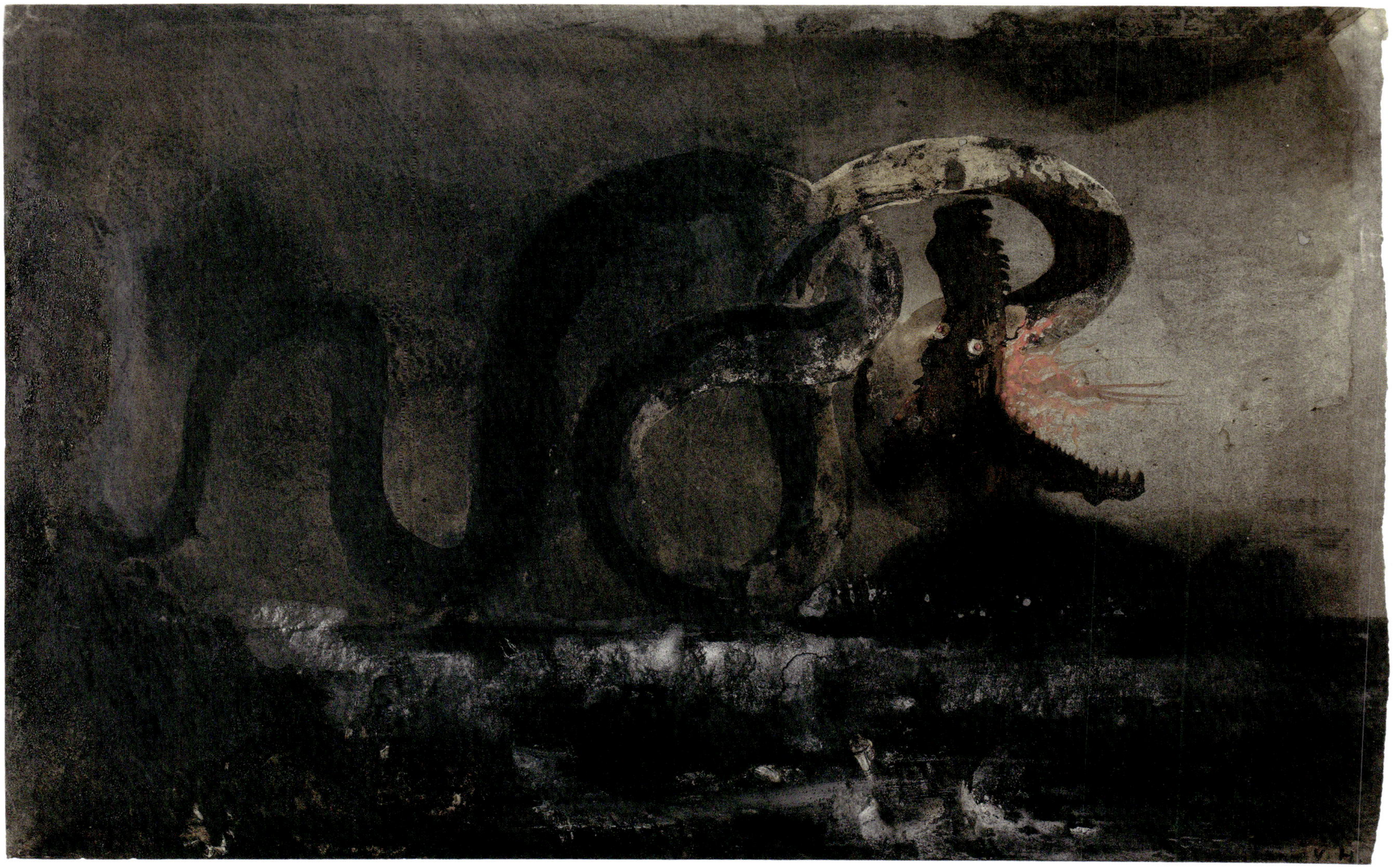

*Marine avec bateau à voile et figure monstrueuse dans le ciel* (Seascape with sailboat and a monstrous figure in the sky), pasted in *Les travailleurs de la mer*, vol. 2 of *Œuvres complètes* (Paris: Hetzel, 1880–83), ca. 1874–78. Brown ink and wash, blue ink and wash, and gouache(?) on paper, laid down. $8\frac{11}{16} \times 5\frac{7}{16}$ in. (22 × 13.8 cm). The Morgan Library and Museum, Bequest of Gordon N. Ray, 1987.

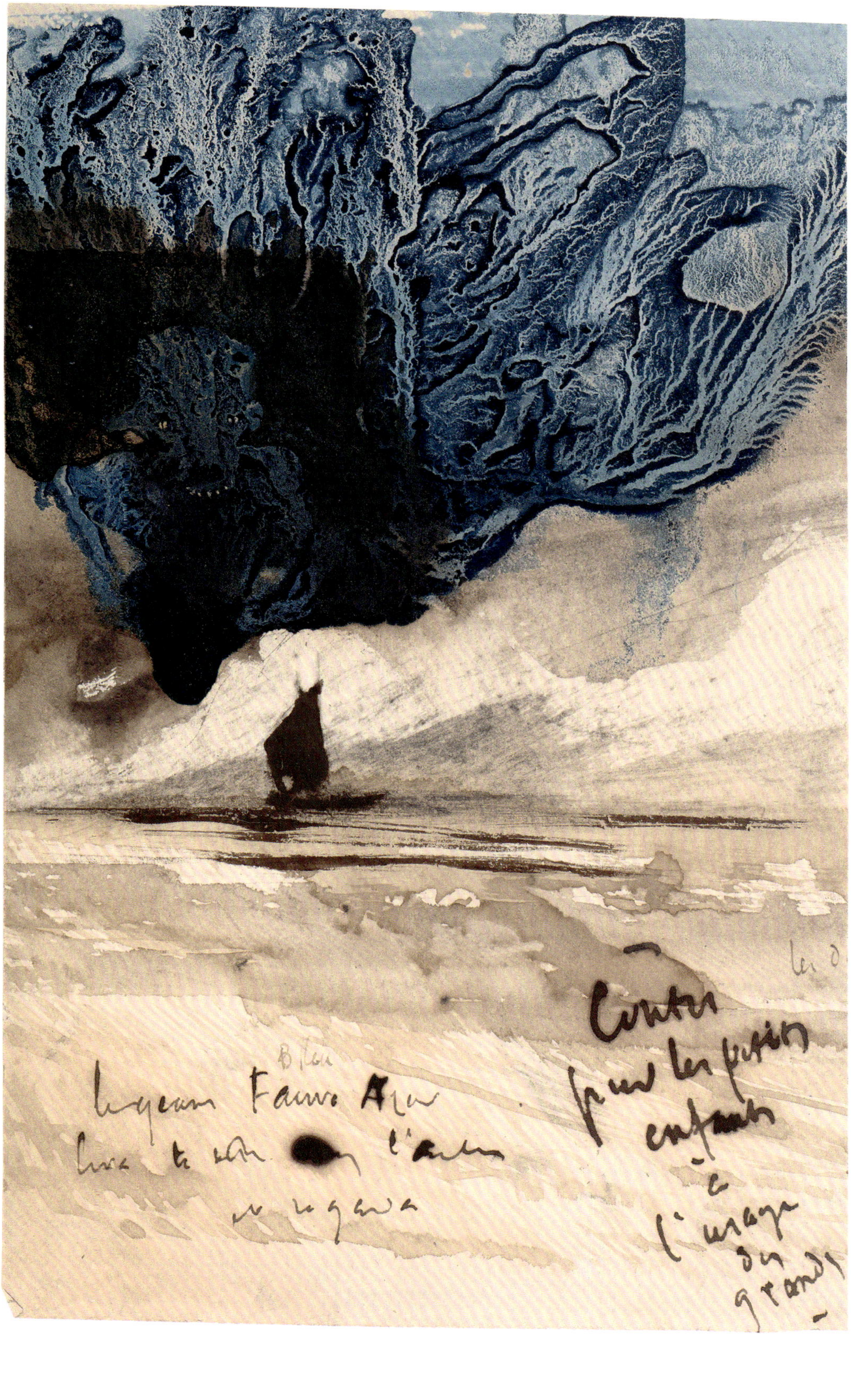
Contes
pour les petits
enfants
à
l'usage
des
grands

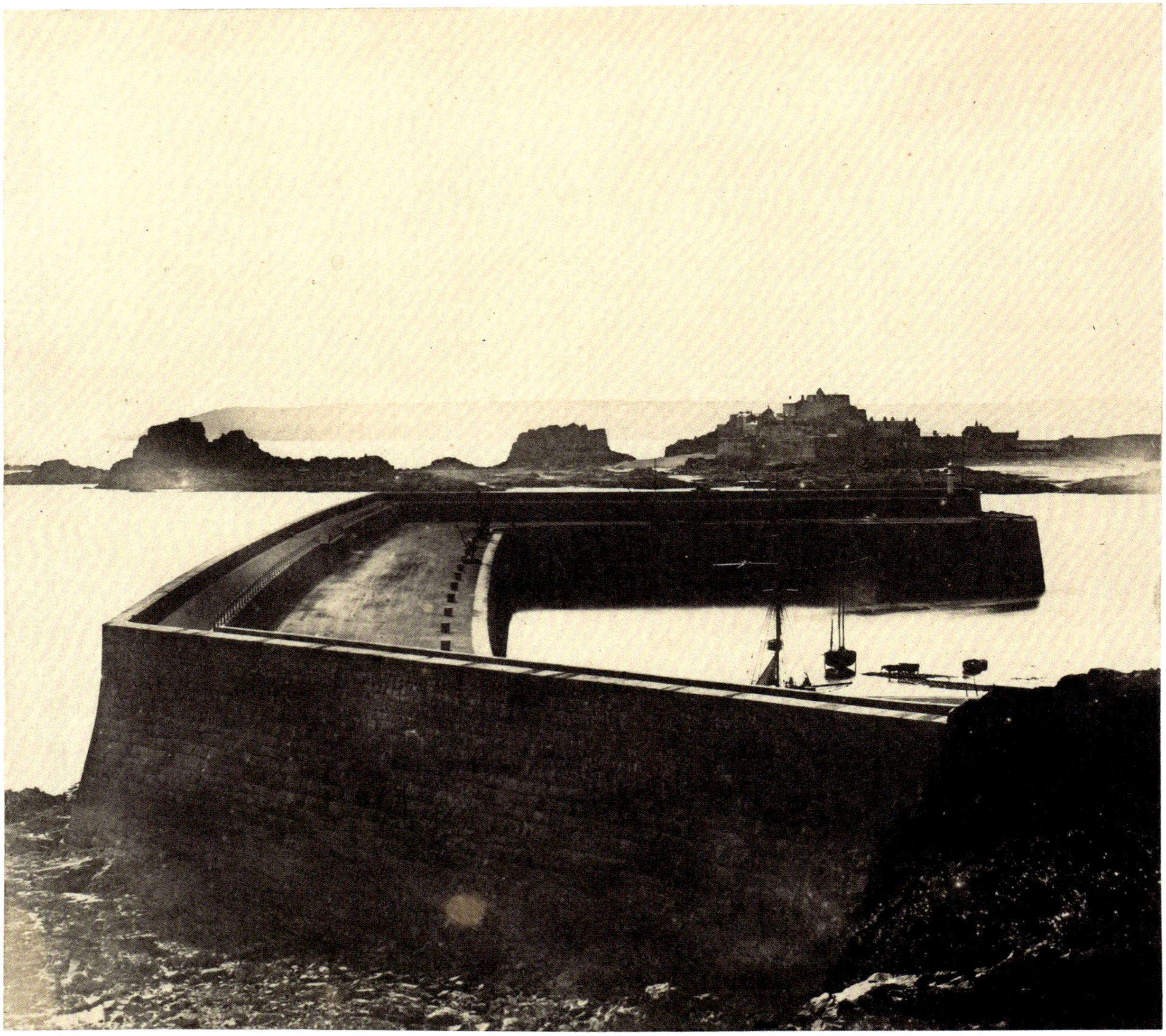

Charles Hugo (French, 1826–1971) and/or Auguste Vacquerie (French, 1819–1895). *"Jersey – la jetée 1853"* (Jersey—the jetty 1853), 1853. Salted paper print. 5 13⁄16 × 6 5⁄16 in. (14.7 × 16.1 cm). Maisons de Victor Hugo, Paris / Guernesey.

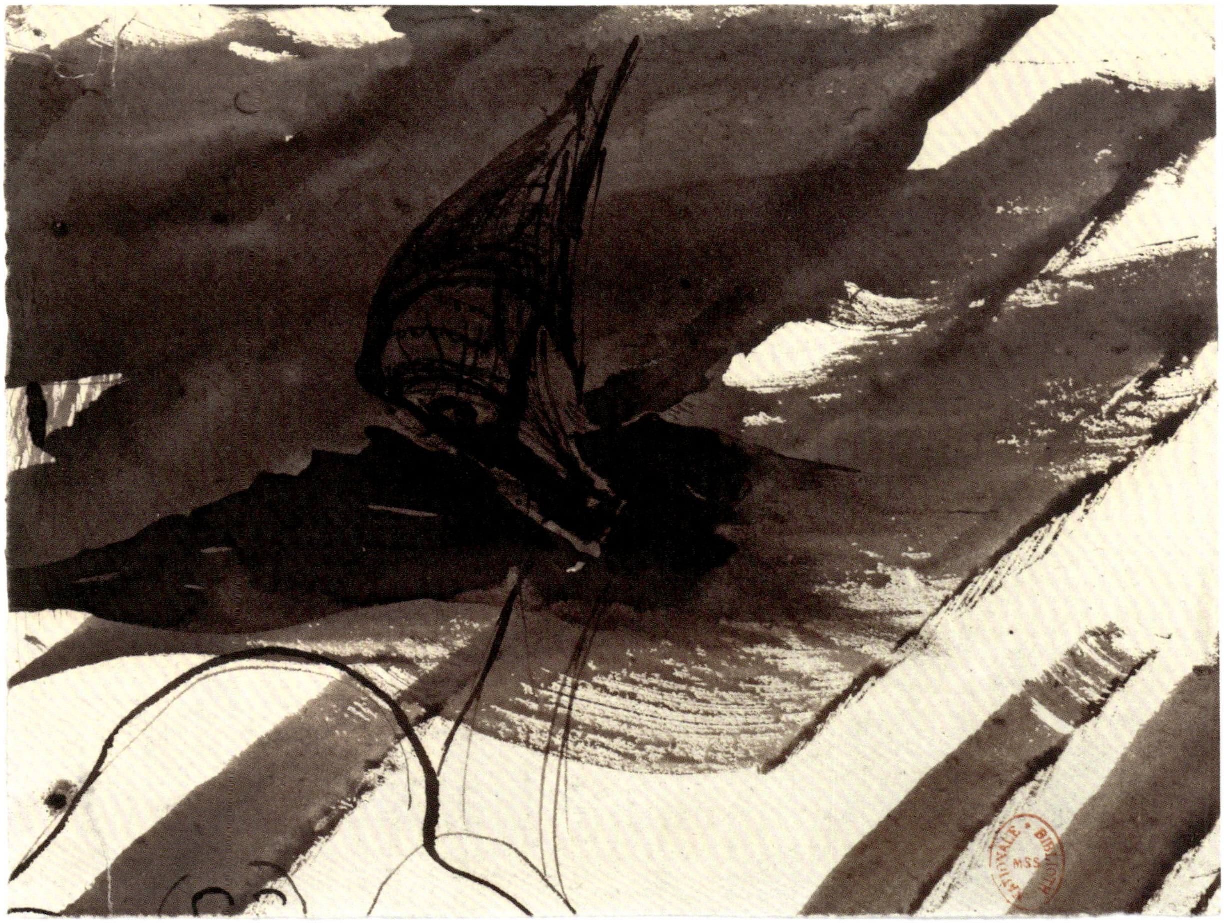

*Barque à la voile gonflée* (Boat in full sail), ca. 1866–69. Brown ink and wash on paper. 4⅞ × 6¼ in. (12.4 × 15.8 cm). Bibliothèque nationale de France.

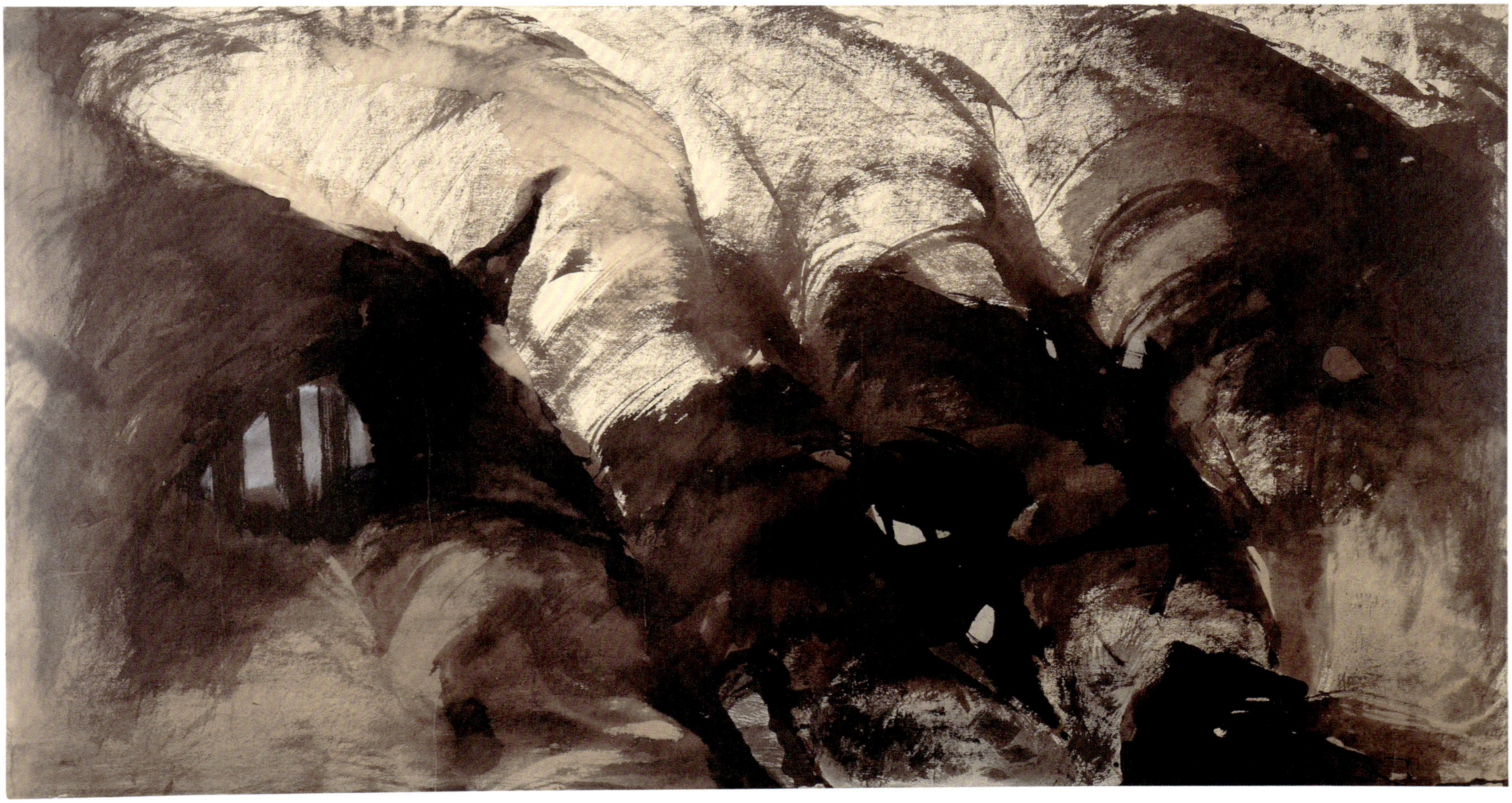

*L'intestin de Léviathan* (The bowels of Leviathan), 1866. Brown and black ink and wash and white gouache on paper. 19¼ × 35⁹⁄₁₆ in. (48.9 × 90.4 cm). Maisons de Victor Hugo, Paris / Guernesey.

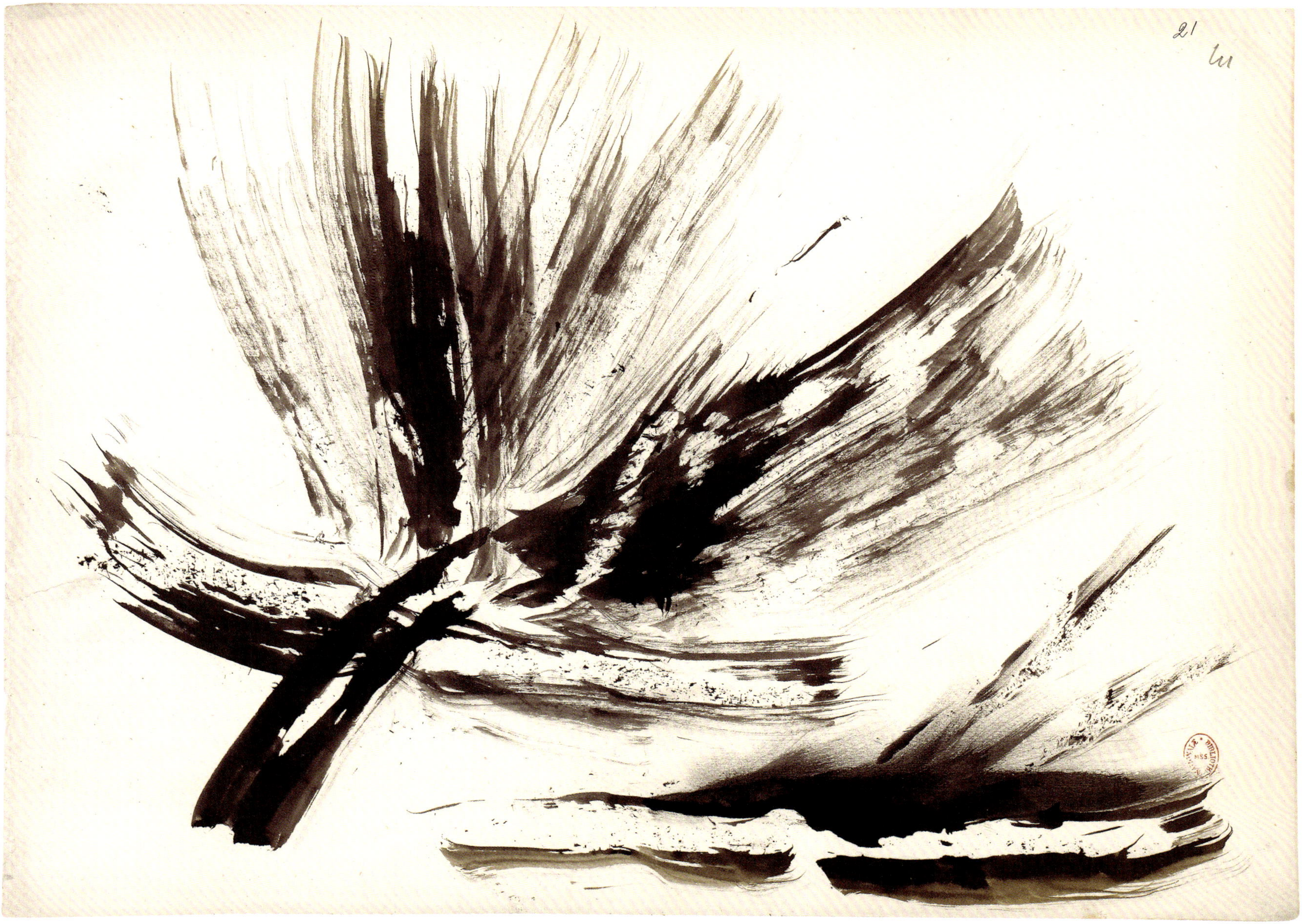

*Taches* (Stains), ca. 1870–71. Brown ink and wash and graphite on paper.
$10\frac{1}{16} \times 13\frac{7}{8}$ in. (25.5 × 35.3 cm). Bibliothèque nationale de France.

*Ma destinée* (My destiny), 1867. Brown ink and wash and white gouache on paper. 6¾ × 10⅜ in. (17.2 × 26.4 cm). Maisons de Victor Hugo, Paris / Guernesey.

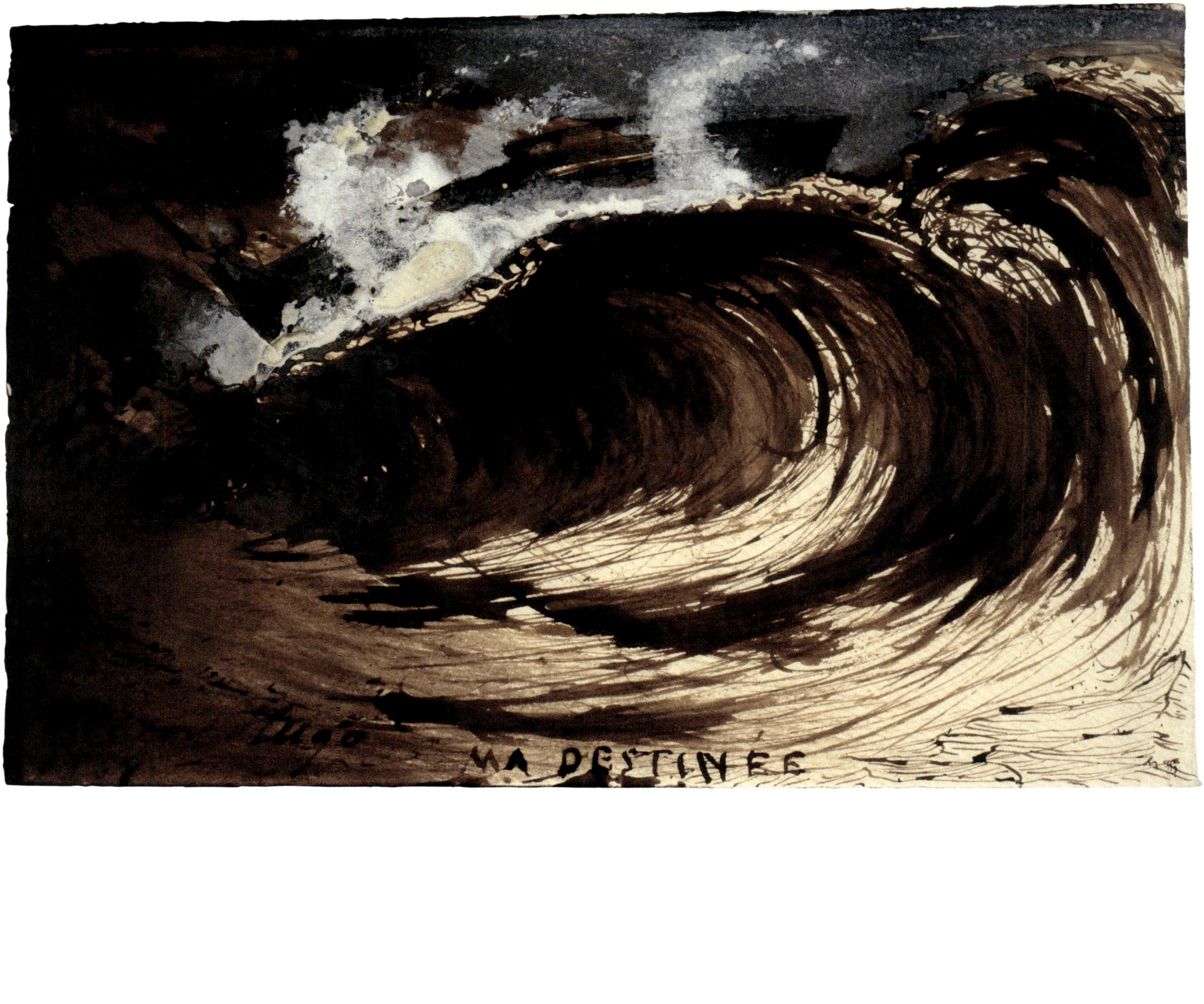
Hugo
MA DESTINEE

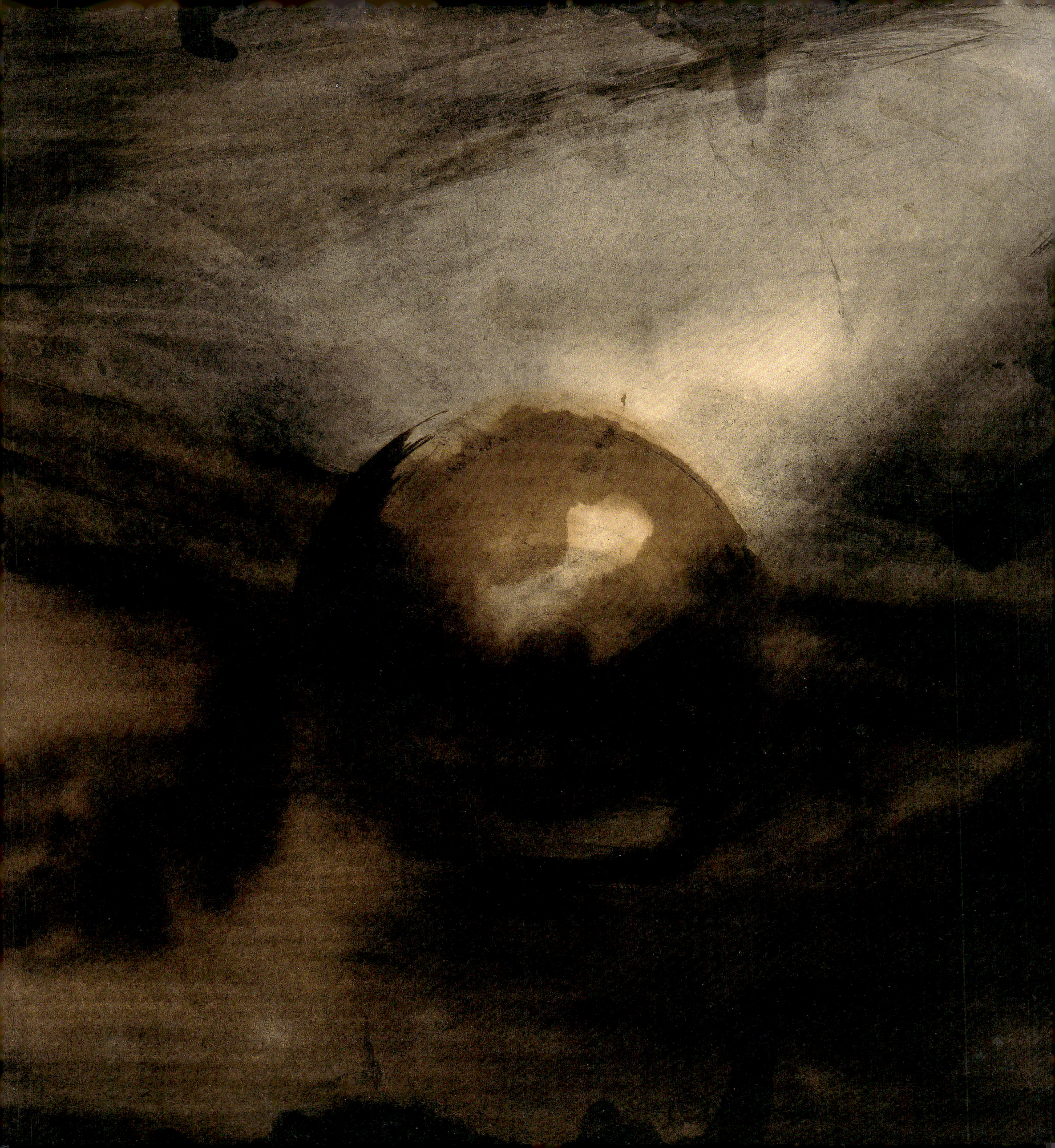

# SPHERES

*Planète-œil* (Planet-eye), ca. 1854–55. Graphite and black ink and wash on paper. 11⁹⁄₁₆ × 8⁷⁄₁₆ in. (29.3 × 21.4 cm). Bibliothèque nationale de France.

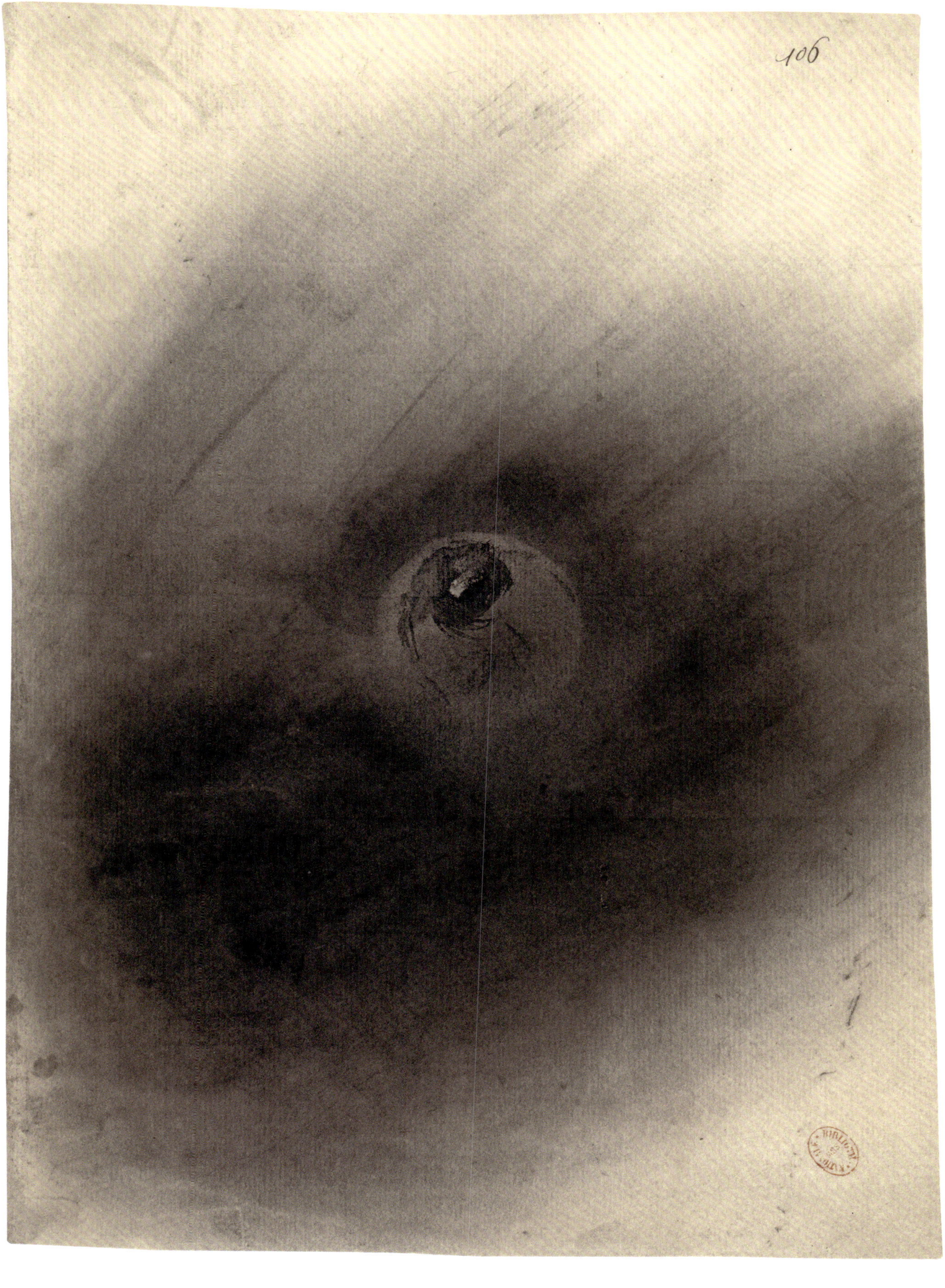

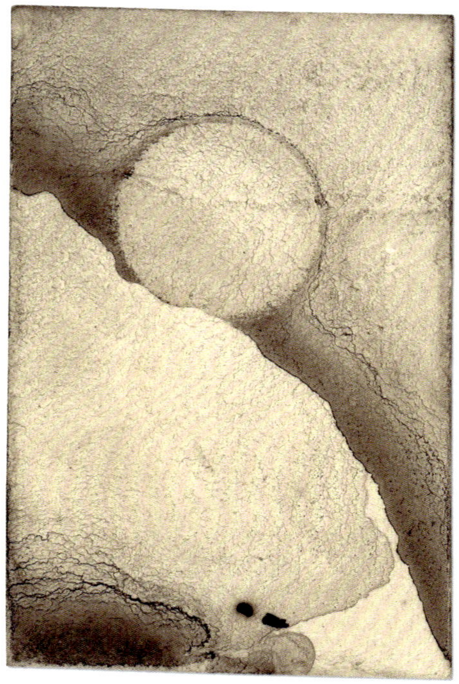

*Tache* (Stain), ca. 1850. Brown ink and wash on paper.
3⅝ × 2⅜ in. (9.2 × 6 cm). Nationalmuseum, Stockholm.

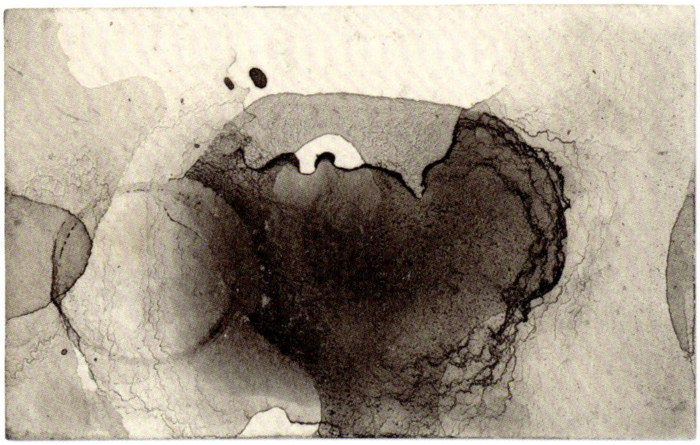

*Taches* (Stains), ca. 1850. Brown ink and wash on paper.
$2\frac{5}{16} \times 3\frac{9}{16}$ in. (5.8 × 9 cm). Nationalmuseum, Stockholm.

*Tache* (Stain), ca. 1850–55(?). Cut paper with brown wash and graphite. 9 × 5 9/16 in. (22.9 × 14.1 cm). Private collection.

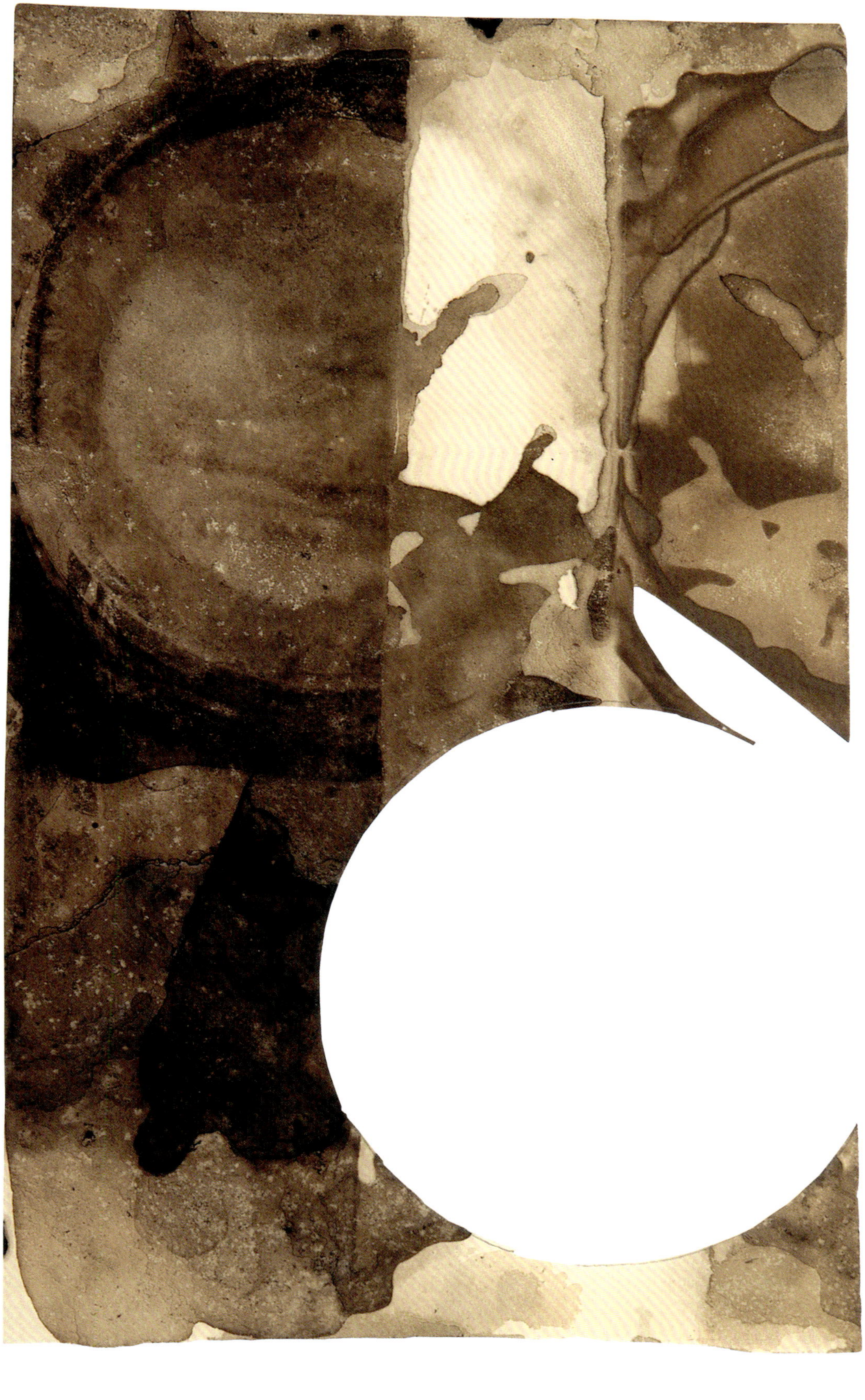

*Taches* (Stains), ca. 1853–55. Brown and blue wash on paper.
$14\frac{15}{16} \times 9\frac{1}{2}$ in. (37.9 × 24.1 cm). Private collection.

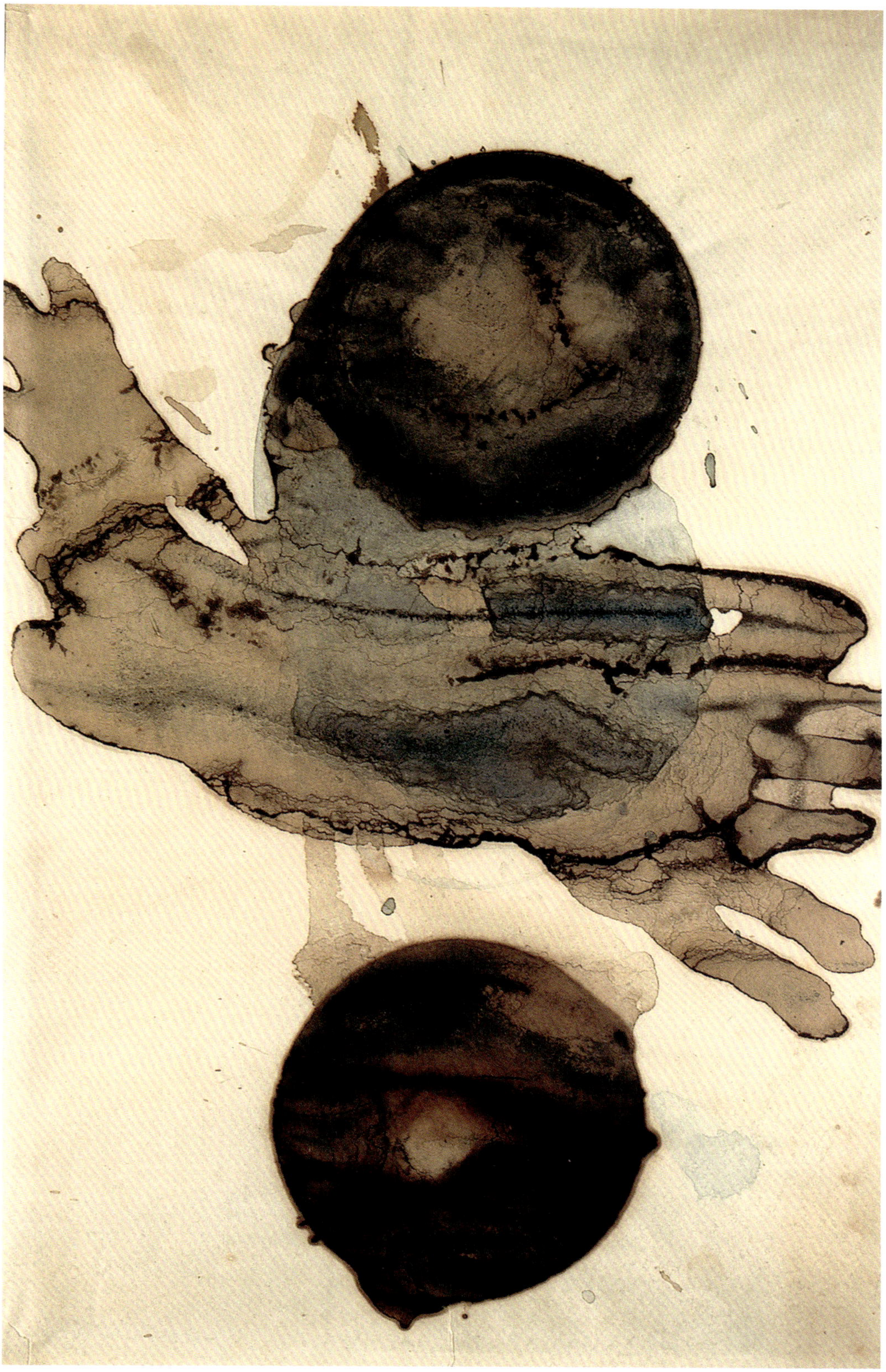

*Planète* (Planet), ca. 1854. Brown ink and wash over charcoal with touches of white gouache on paper. 12⅛ × 14 9/16 in. (30.8 × 37 cm). Collection of David Lachenmann.

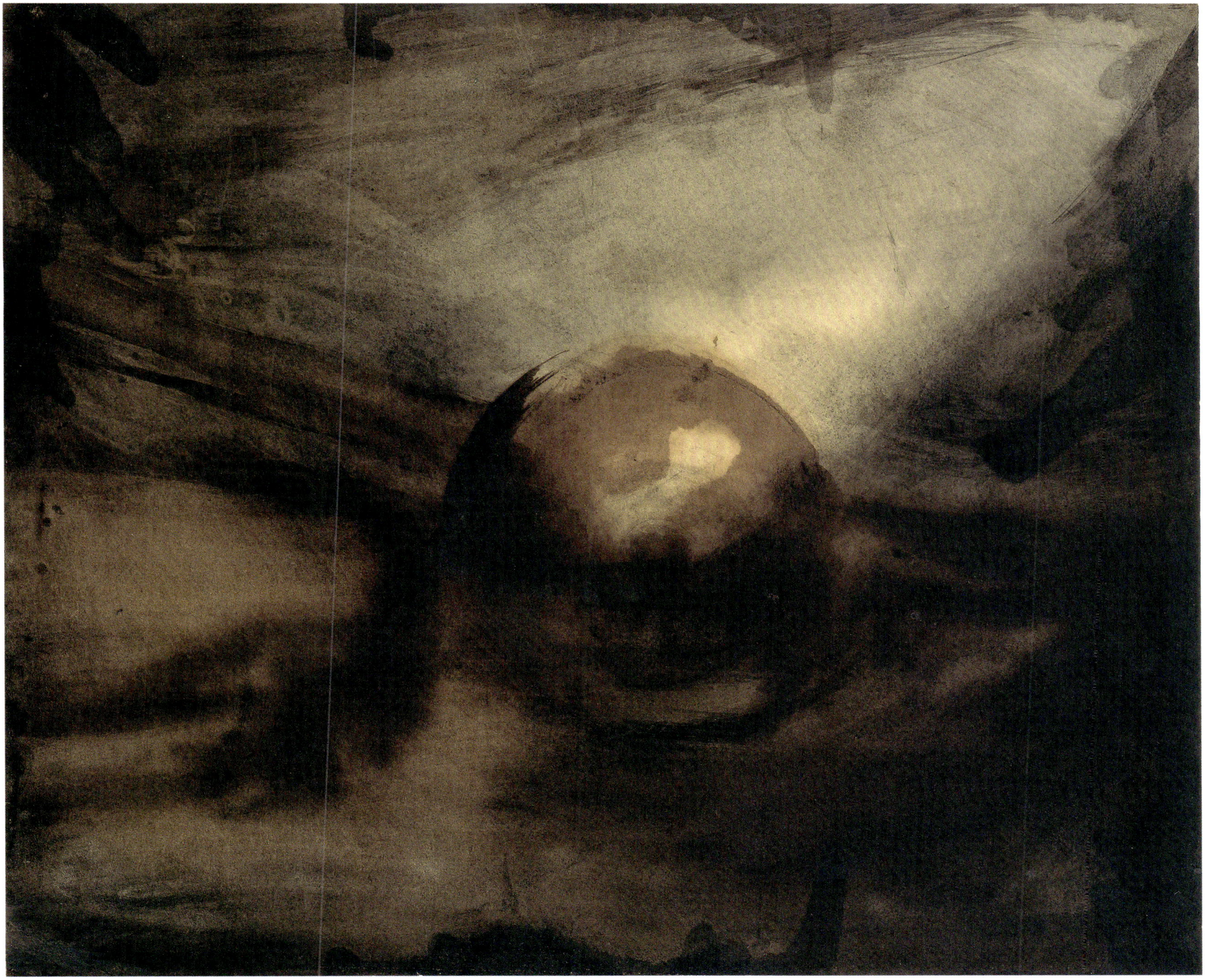

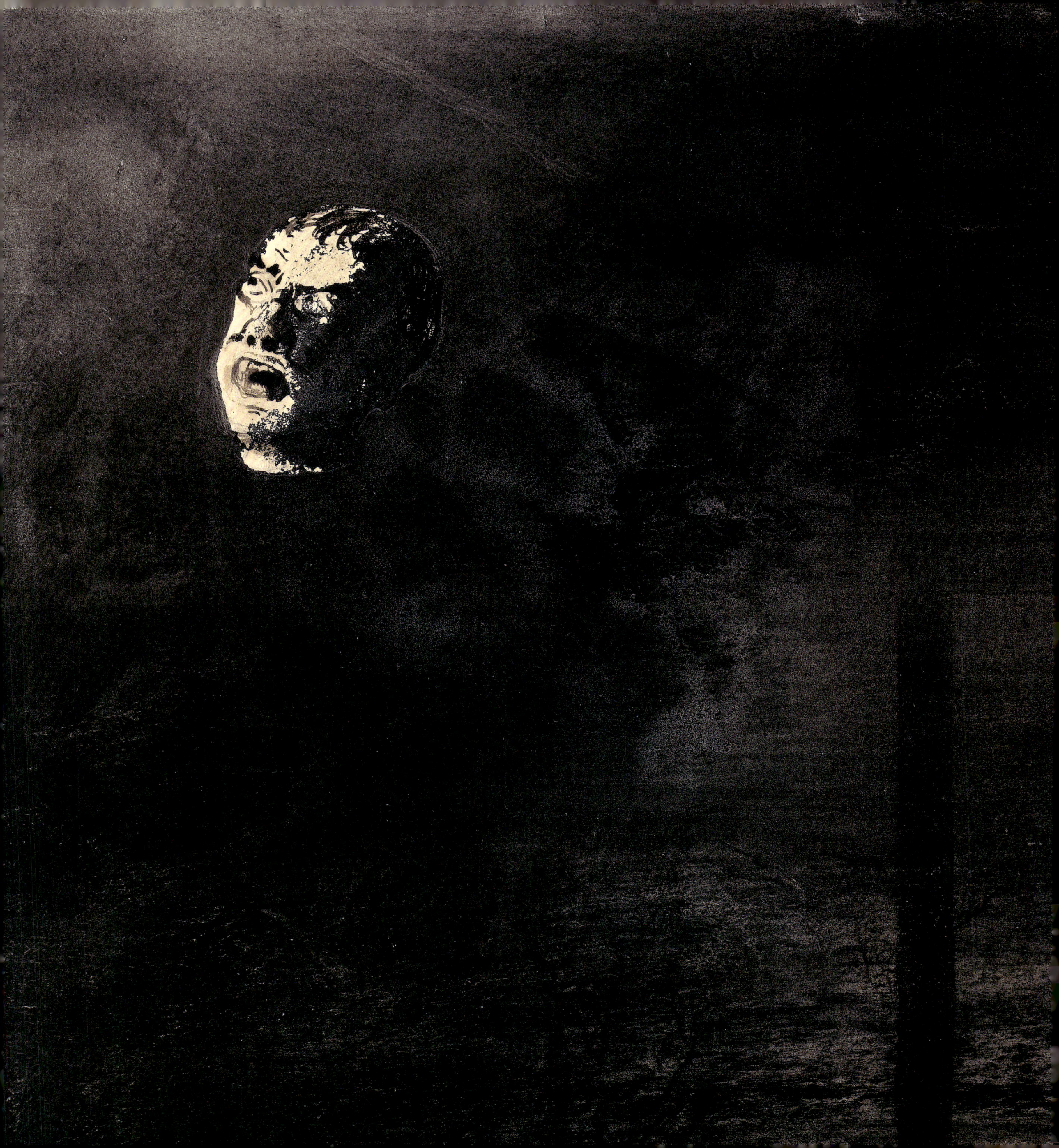

# JUSTICE

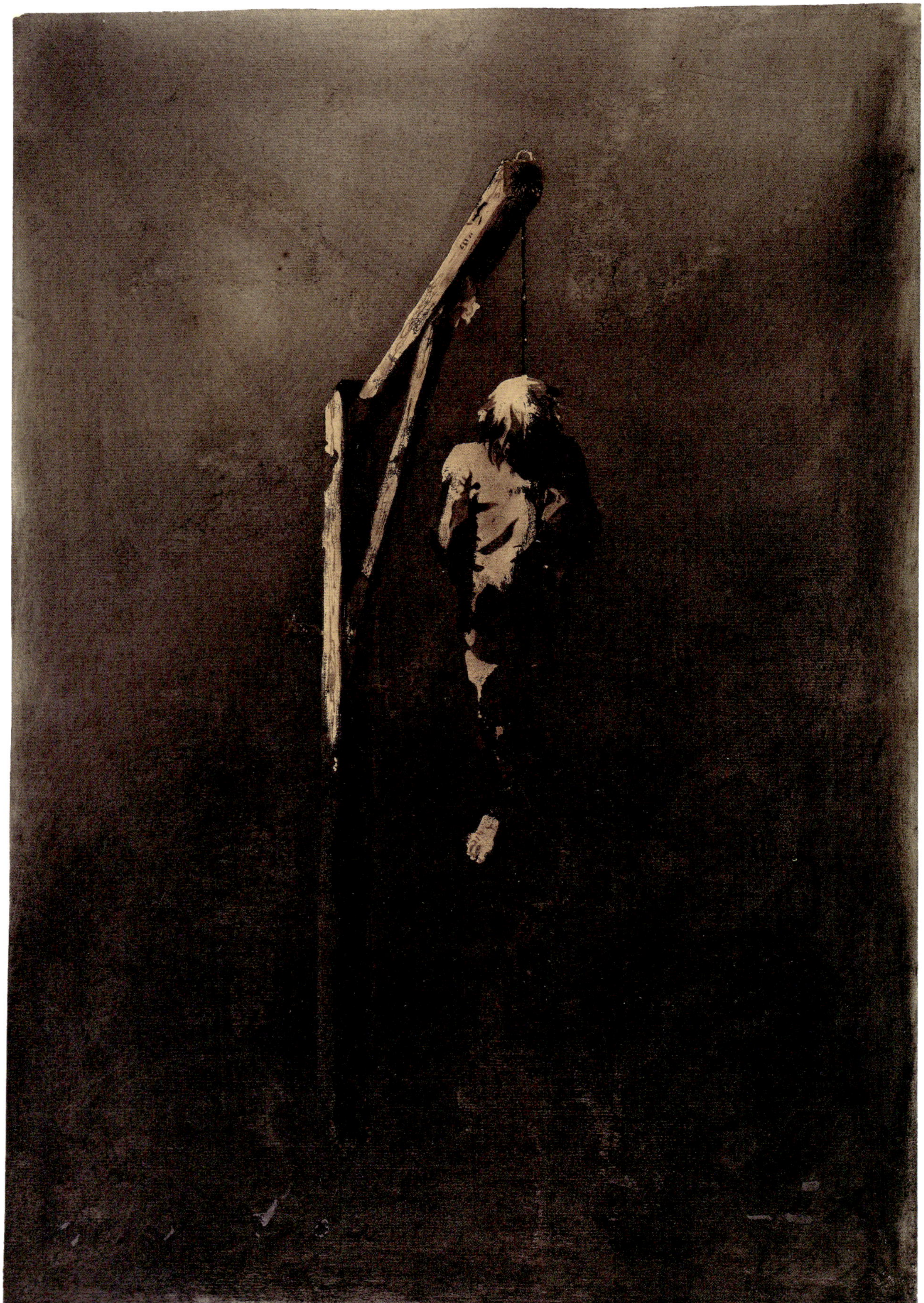

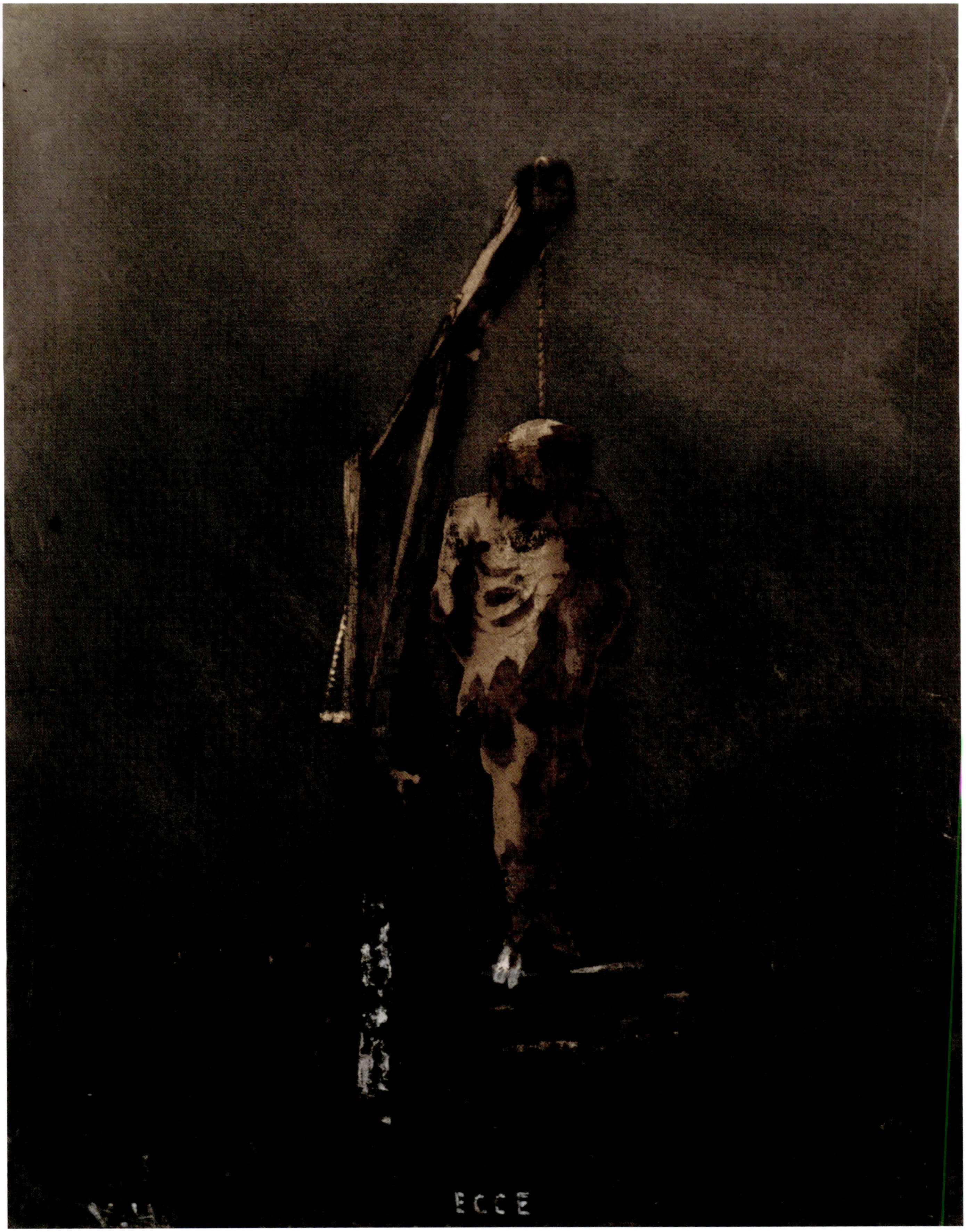
ECCE

PREVIOUS PAGES

*Ecce Lex (Le pendu)* (Ecce Lex [hanged man]), 1854. Brown ink, brown and black wash, graphite, charcoal, and white gouache on paper. 20 × 13¾ in. (50.8 × 34.9 cm). Maisons de Victor Hugo, Paris / Guernesey.

*Ecce (Le pendu)* (Ecce [hanged man]), 1854. Brown ink, brown and black wash, charcoal, and white gouache on paper. 16 7/16 × 12 13/16 in. (41.7 × 32.5 cm). Maisons de Victor Hugo, Paris / Guernesey.

ABOVE AND OPPOSITE *"Prenant le frais avec ses sept frères"* (Taking in the fresh air with his seven brothers), ca. 1854–57. Brown and black ink and wash, graphite, charcoal, black crayon, white gouache, and watercolor on paper. Left: 6¾ × 14⅛ in. (17.2 × 35.8 cm). Right: 11⅜ × 18 in. (28.9 × 45.7 cm). Maisons de Victor Hugo, Paris / Guernesey.

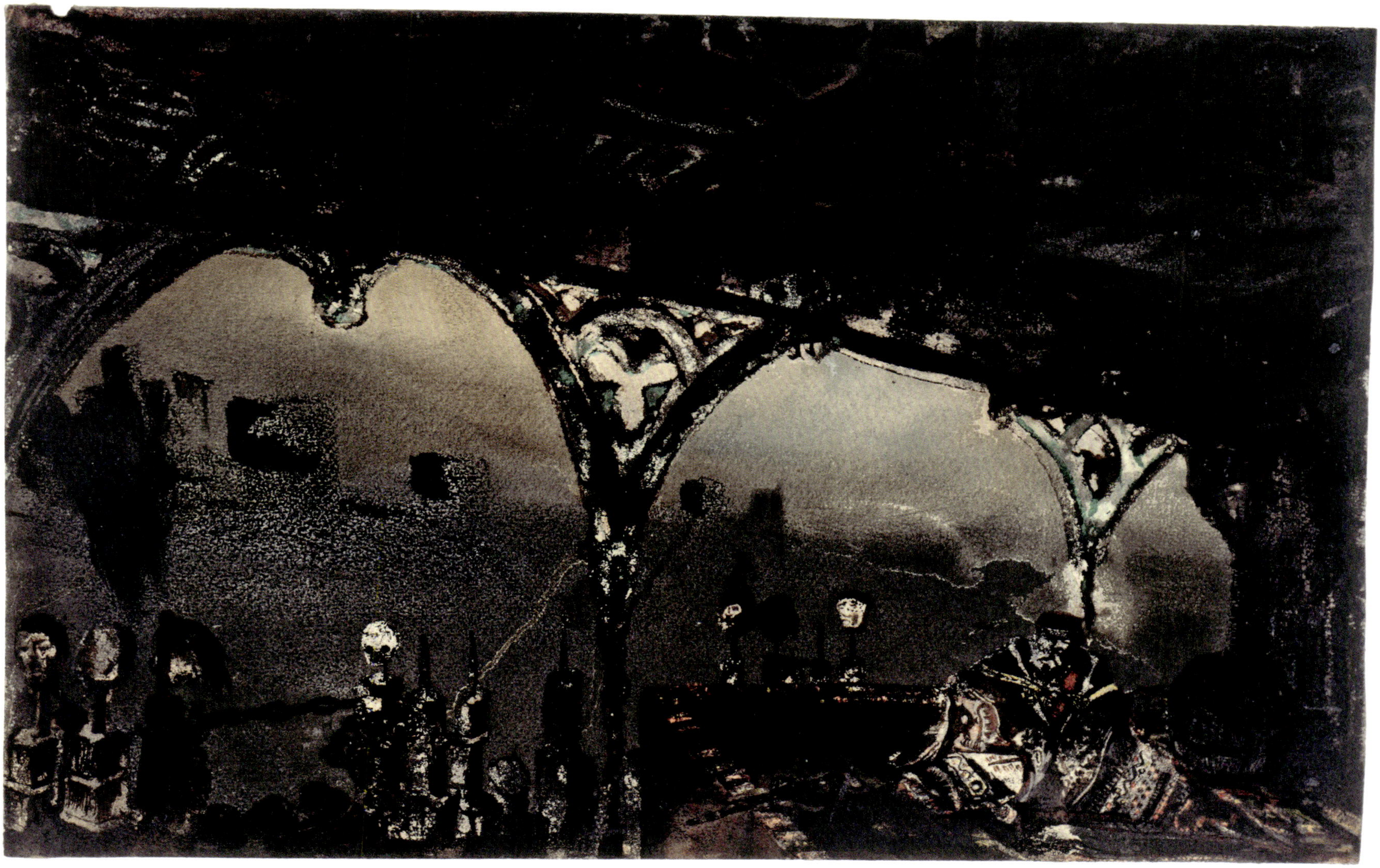

*Justitia* (Justice), 1857. Graphite; brown and black ink; brown, black, and red wash; charcoal; and traces of red gouache on paper. 21 × 13¾ in. (53.4 × 35 cm). Maisons de Victor Hugo, Paris / Guernesey.

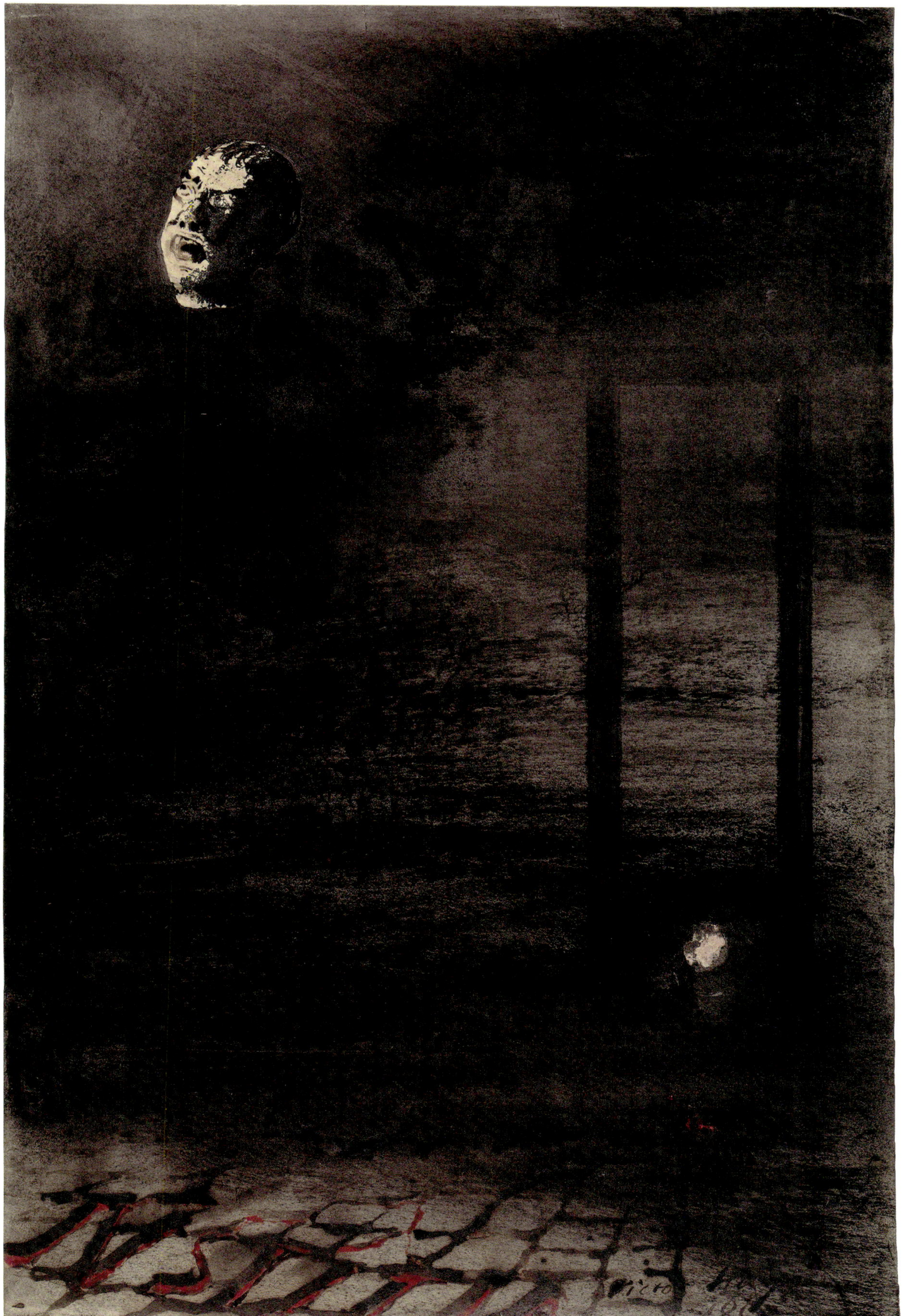

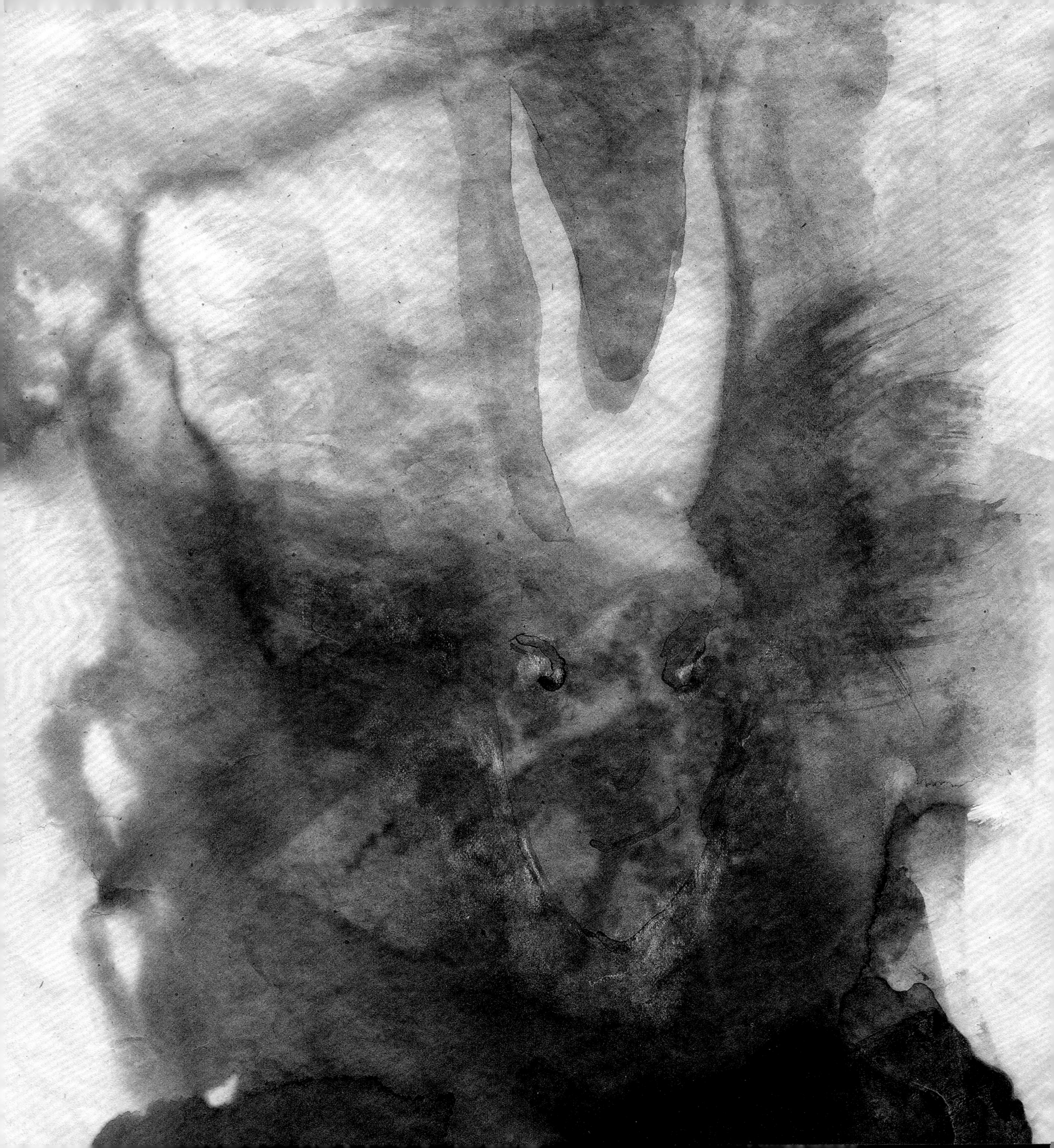

# STAINS

*Taches avec empreintes de doigts* (Abstract composition with fingerprints), ca. 1864–65.
Brown ink and wash on paper. 10⁵⁄₁₆ × 7½ in. (26.2 × 19 cm). Bibliothèque nationale de France.

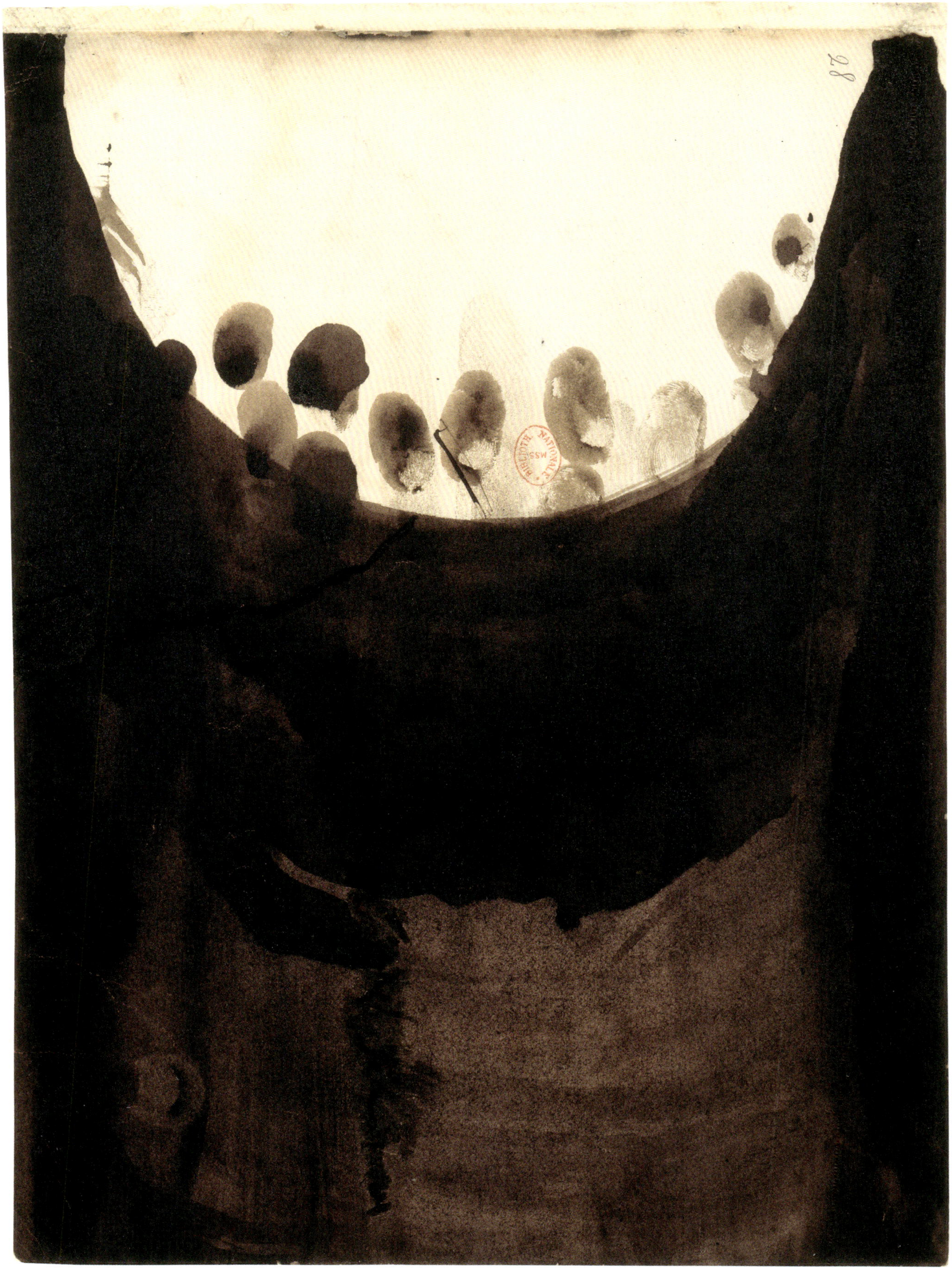

*Étude pour la tombe de Léopoldine* (Study for the tomb of Léopoldine), 1858. Stencil cut from paper with brown ink and wash. 5¼ × 3⅛ in. (13.4 × 8 cm). Maisons de Victor Hugo, Paris / Guernesey.

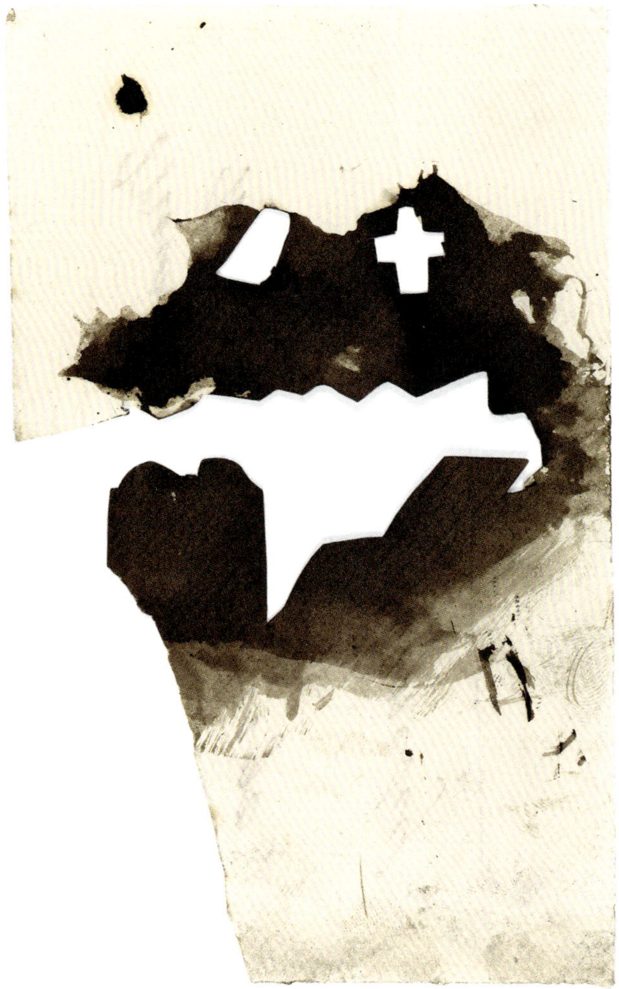

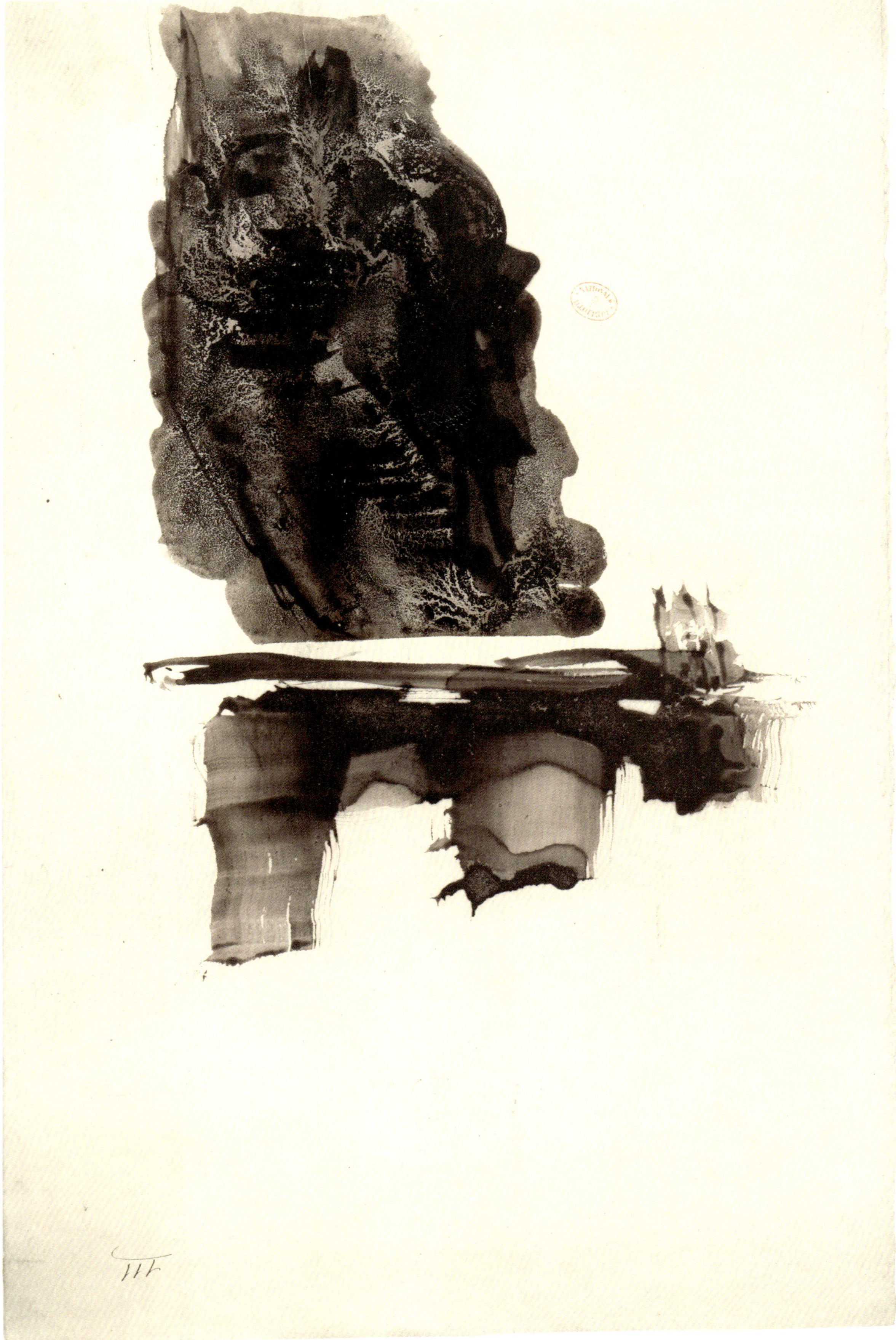

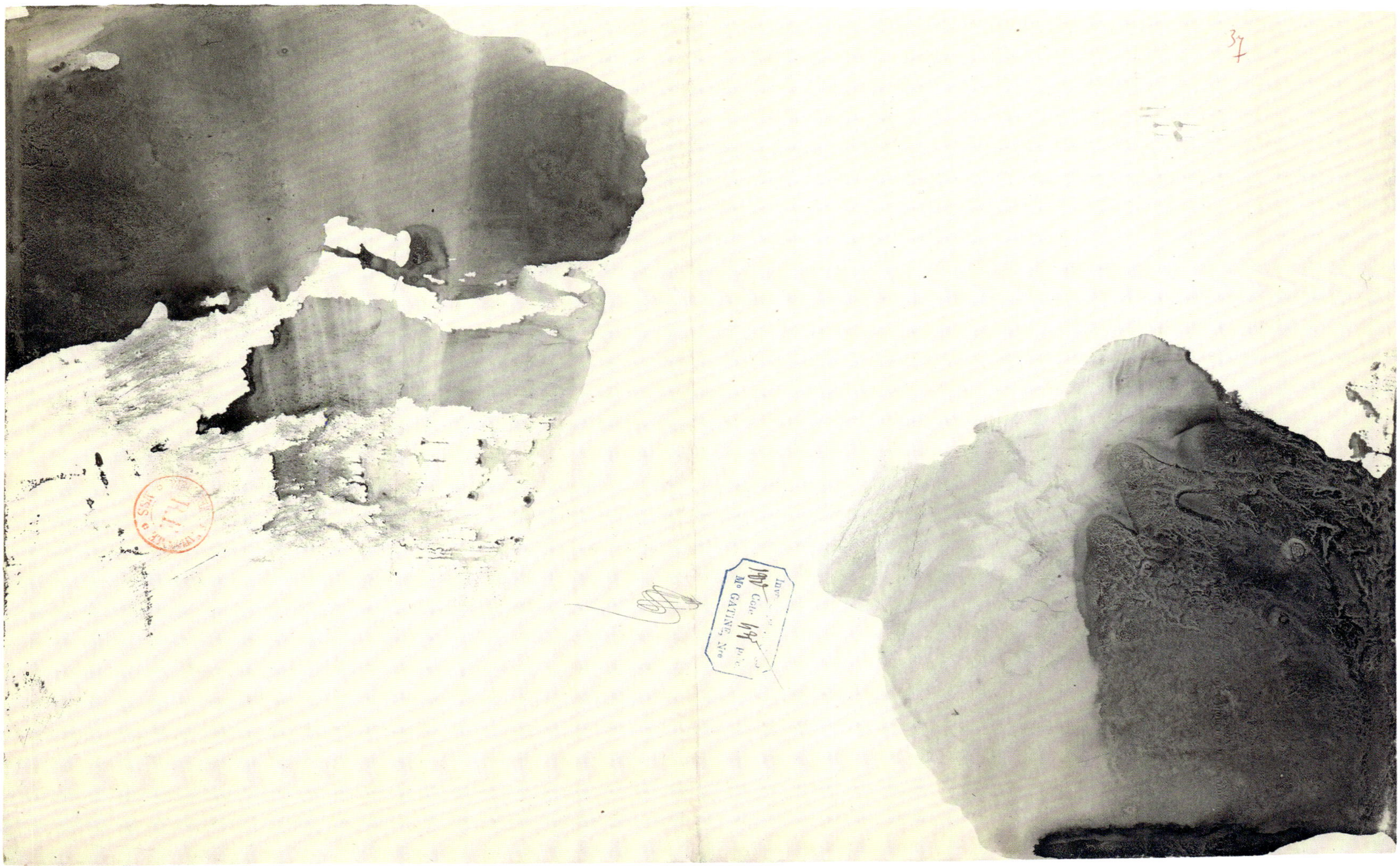

OPPOSITE *Taches* (Stains), ca. 1866–68(?). Graphite powder, graphite wash, and brown ink and wash on paper. $14\frac{1}{16} \times 9\frac{1}{4}$ in. ($35.7 \times 23.5$ cm). Bibliothèque nationale de France.

ABOVE *Taches* (Stains), ca. 1875(?). Brown ink and wash on paper. $9\frac{1}{8} \times 14\frac{1}{4}$ in. ($23.1 \times 36.2$ cm). Bibliothèque nationale de France.

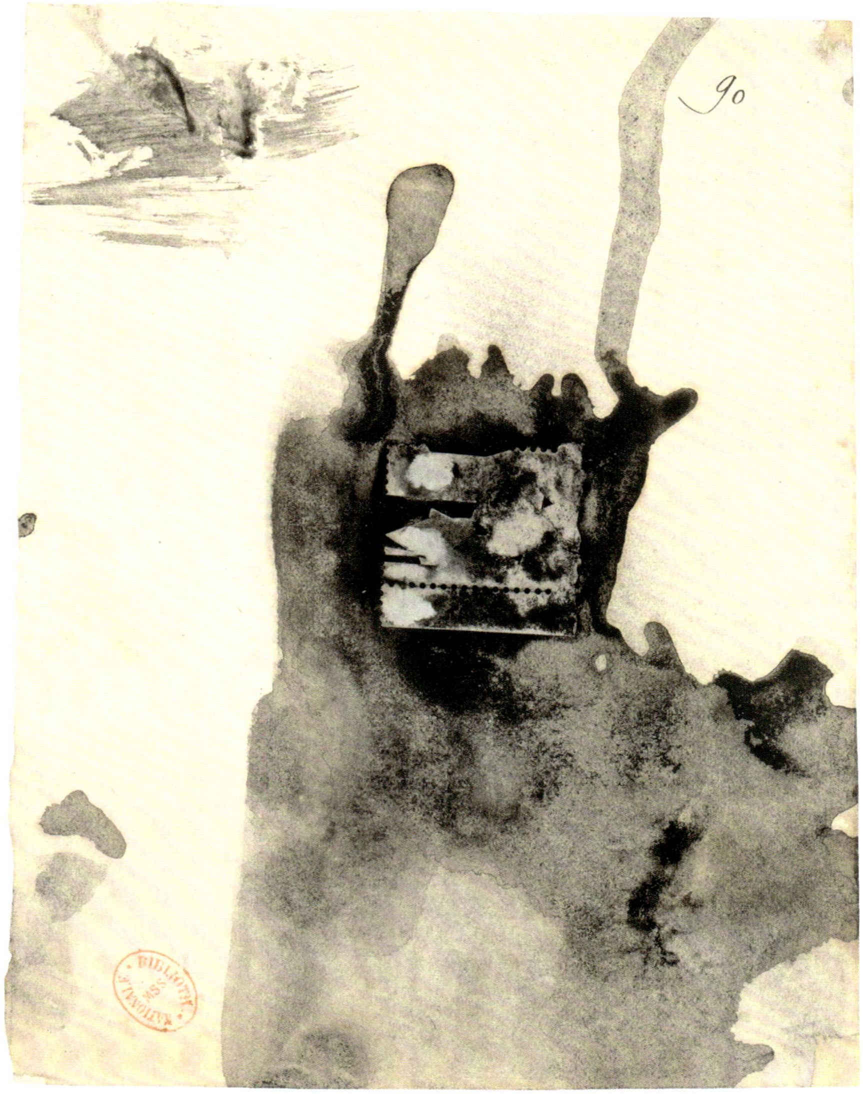

*Taches et collage* (Stains and collage), ca. 1855–56. Graphite powder, graphite wash, and a cut postal stamp pasted onto paper, with traces of white gouache. 6⅛ × 4⅝ in. (15.5 × 11.8 cm). Bibliothèque nationale de France.

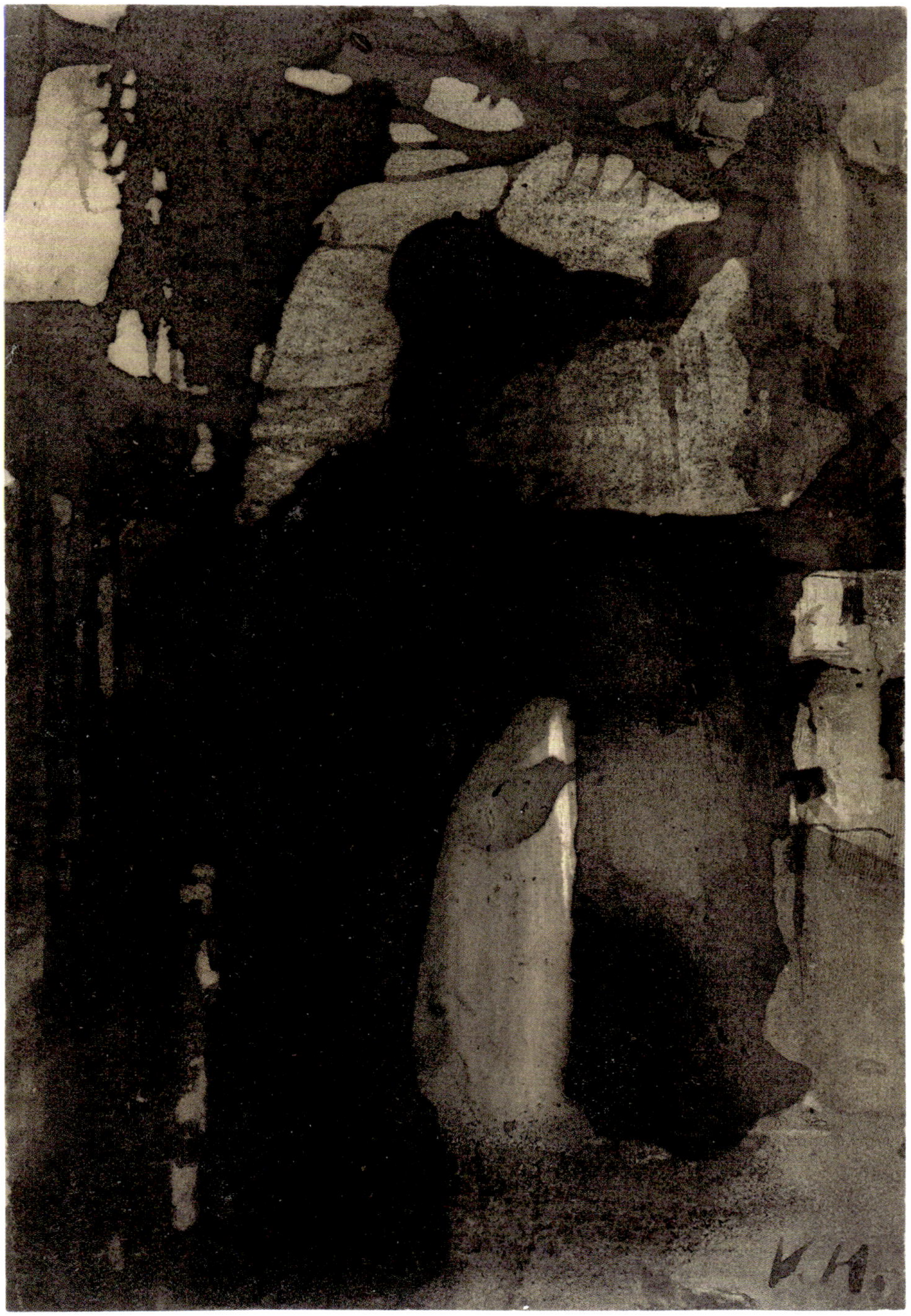

*La bouche d'ombre* (The mouth of darkness), ca. 1855–57(?). Brown ink and wash on paper. 7 5/16 × 4 13/16 in. (18.5 × 12.3 cm). Maisons de Victor Hugo, Paris / Guernesey.

*Tache* (Stain), ca. 1864–69. Brown ink and wash on paper. 8 13/16 × 5 9/16 in. (22.4 × 14.2 cm). Maisons de Victor Hugo, Paris / Guernesey.

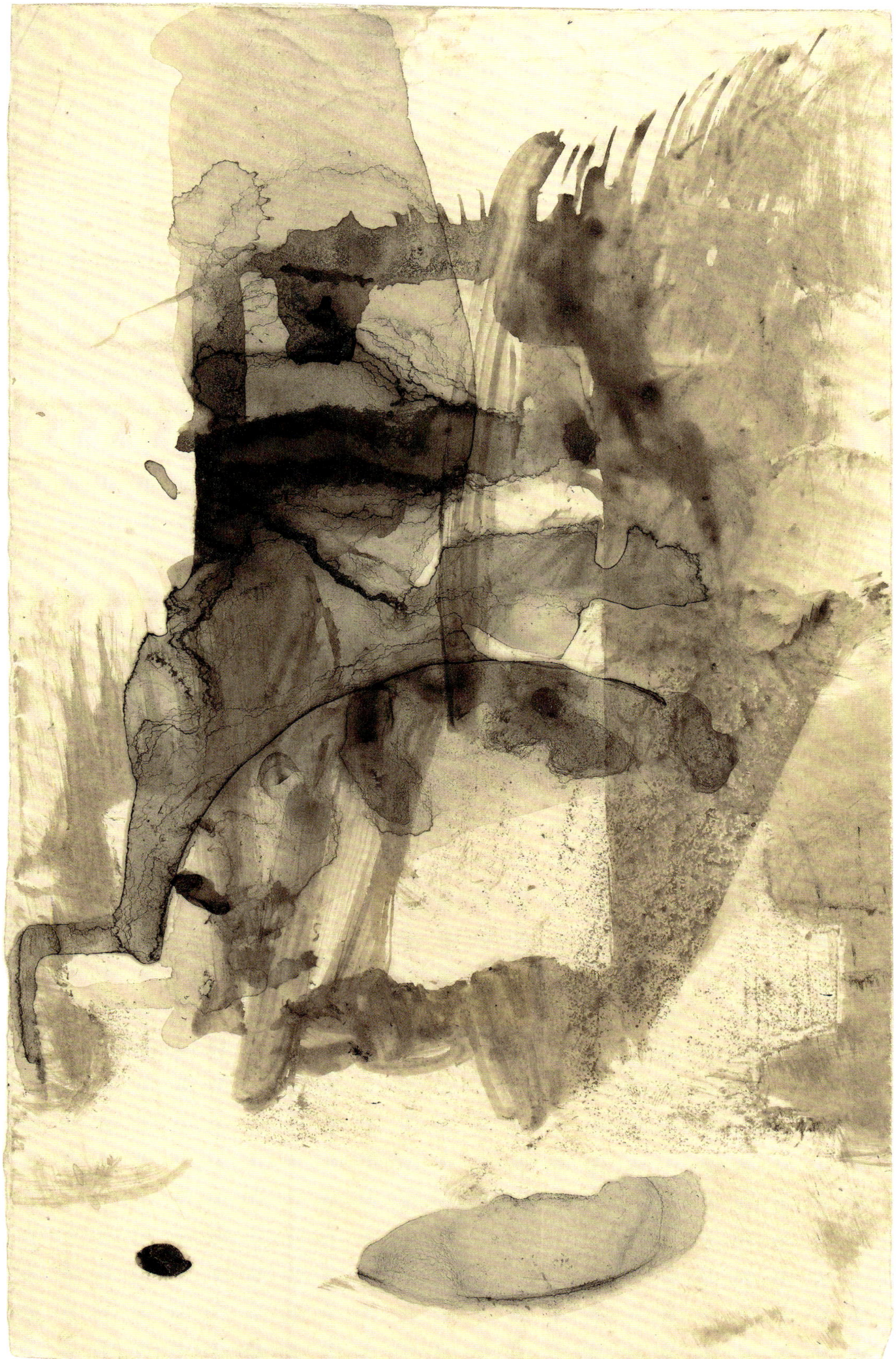

*Tache* (Stain). Brown ink and wash on paper. $4\frac{5}{16} \times 3\frac{15}{16}$ in. (11 × 10 cm). Private collection.

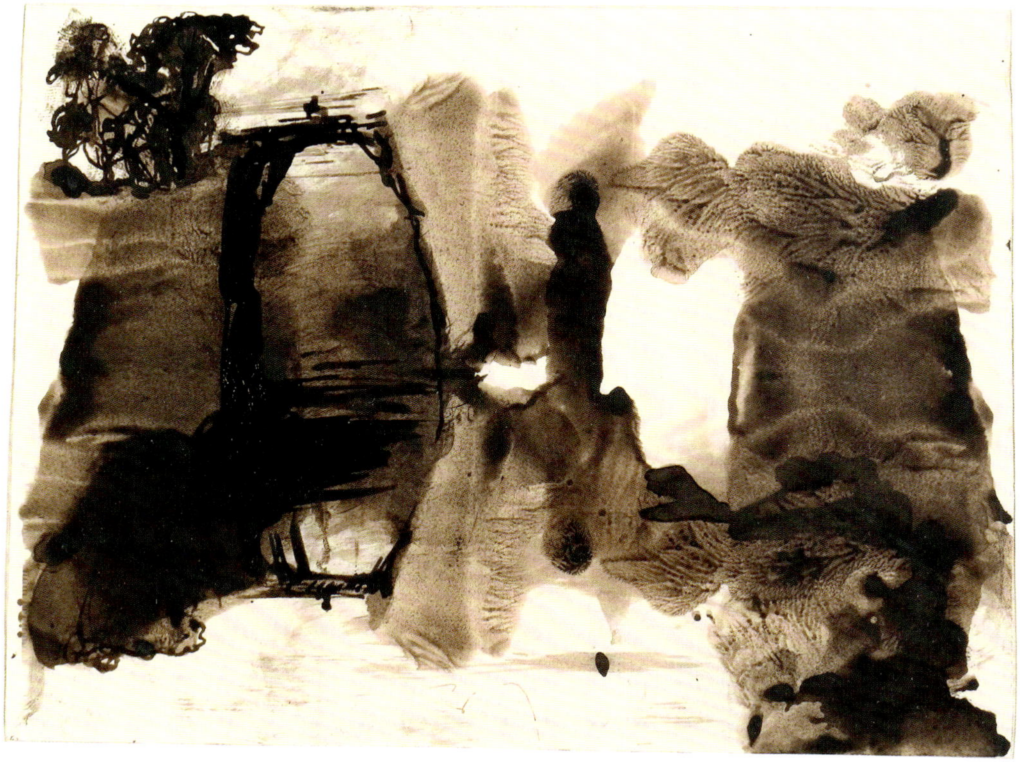

*Paysage au pont* (Landscape with bridge), ca. 1855–56. Brown ink and wash on paper. 4 × 5¼ in. (10.1 × 13.3 cm). Ville de Dijon—Direction des Musées et du Patrimoine—Musée des Beaux-Arts, Donation Pierre et Kathleen Granville, 1999.

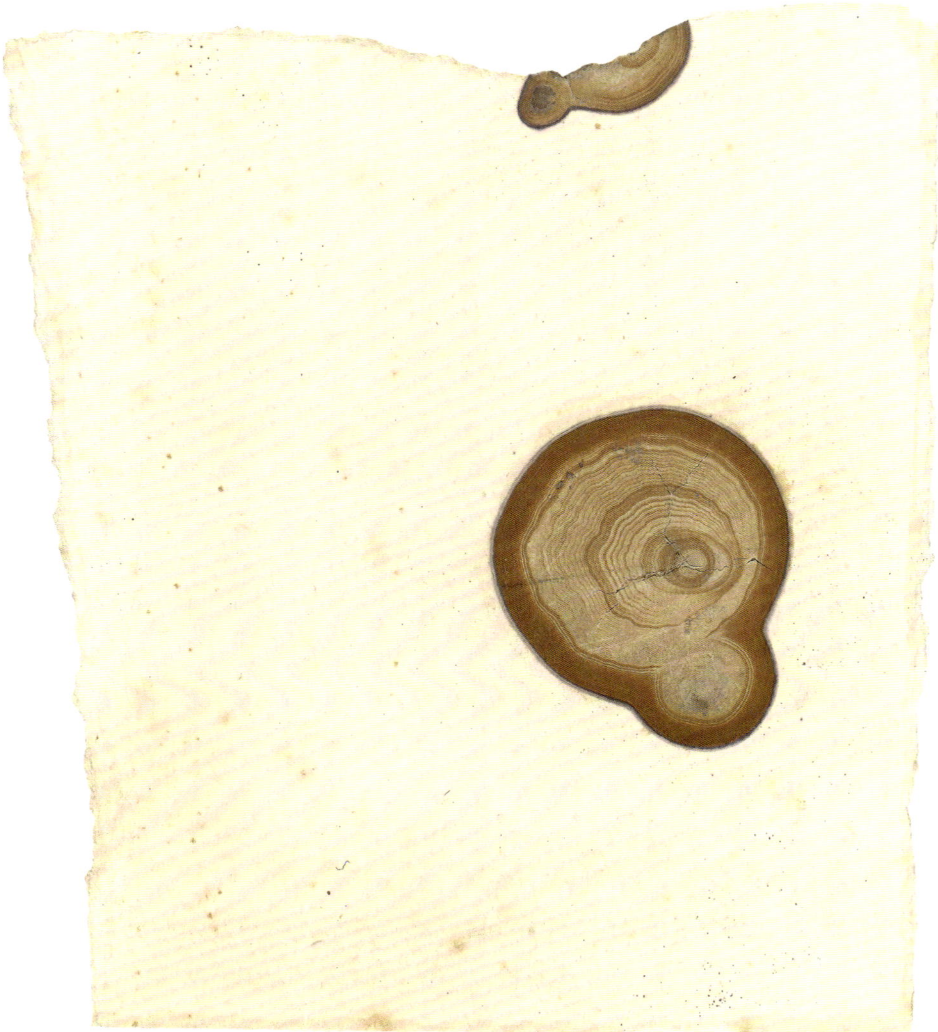

ABOVE *Tache* (Stain). Brown ink and wash on paper. 5 9/16 × 4 15/16 in. (14.2 × 12.5 cm). Maisons de Victor Hugo, Paris / Guernesey.

OPPOSITE *Rosace* (Rosette), ca. 1859. Brown ink and wash on paper. 8 7/8 × 7 1/16 in. (22.6 × 18 cm). Maison Vacquerie–Musée Victor Hugo, Villequier–Dept. 76.

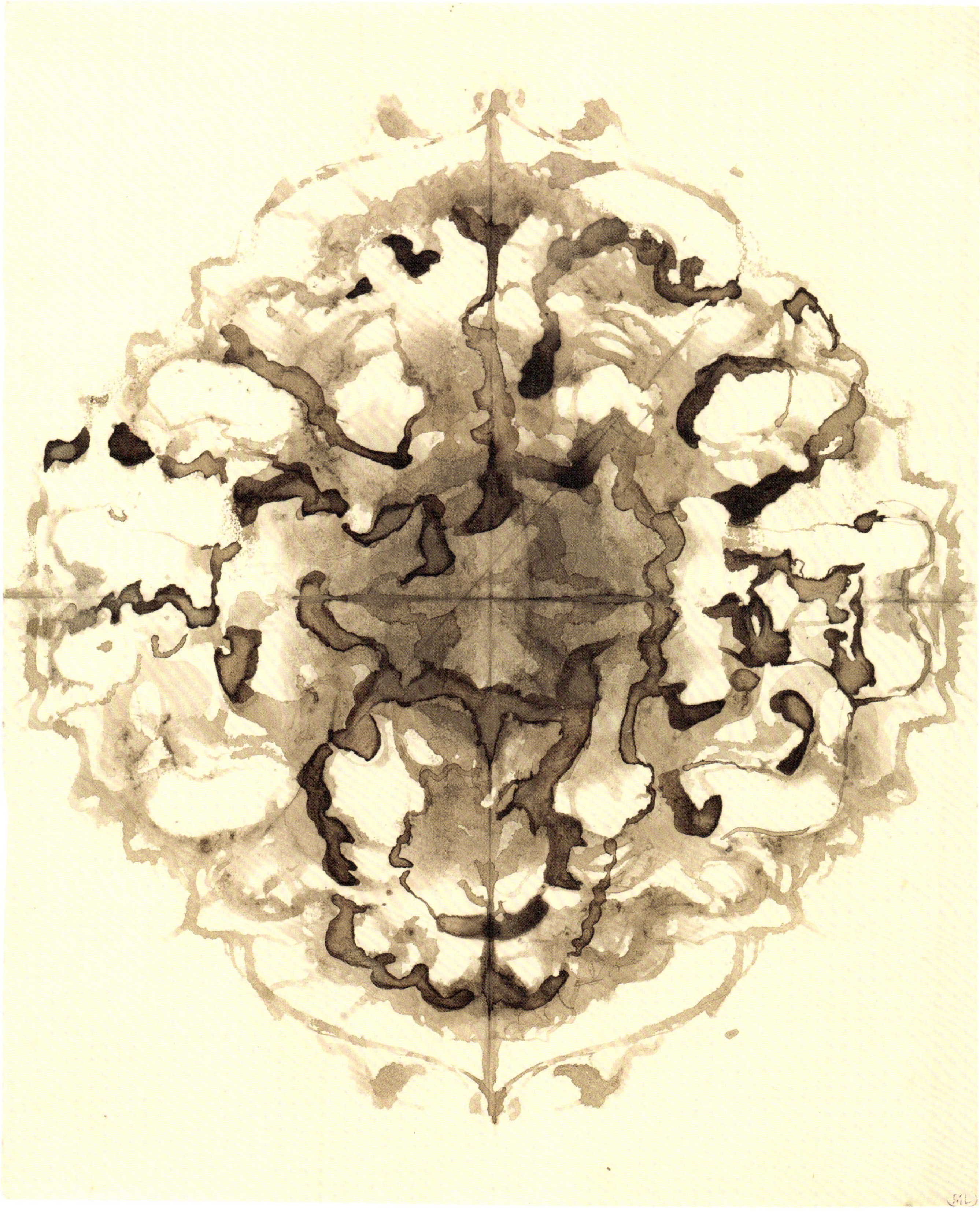

*Tache* (Stain), ca. 1850–70(?). Brown ink on paper.
3$\frac{1}{8}$ × 6$\frac{11}{16}$ in. (8 × 17 cm). Private collection.

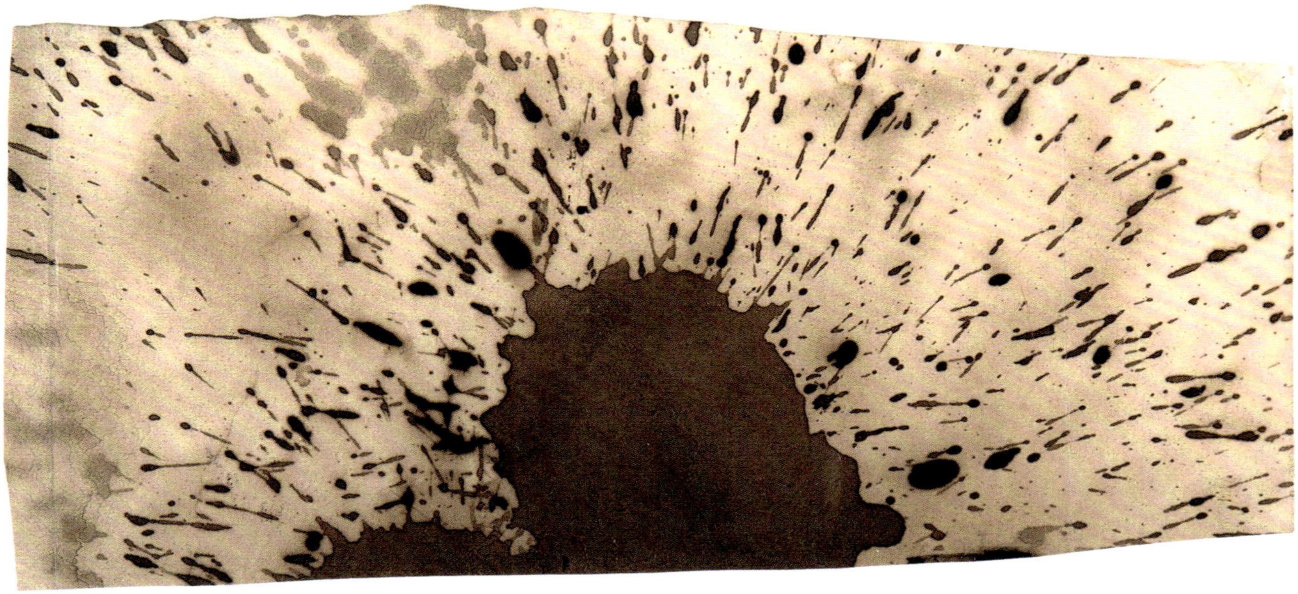

ABOVE *Taches* (Stains), ca. 1852–59(?). Brown ink and wash on paper. 14⁹⁄₁₆ × 17¹⁵⁄₁₆ in. (37 × 45.5 cm). Nationalmuseum, Stockholm.

OPPOSITE *Tache (avec tête de caractère)* (Stain with head), ca. 1869. Brown ink and wash on paper. 8¾ × 5¹¹⁄₁₆ in. (22.3 × 14.4 cm). Maisons de Victor Hugo, Paris / Guernesey.

*Tête de diable* (Head of a devil), ca. 1864–69. Brown ink and wash with white gouache on paper. 15 3/16 × 9 3/8 in. (38.5 × 23.8 cm). Fundación Almine y Bernard Ruiz-Picasso para el Arte.

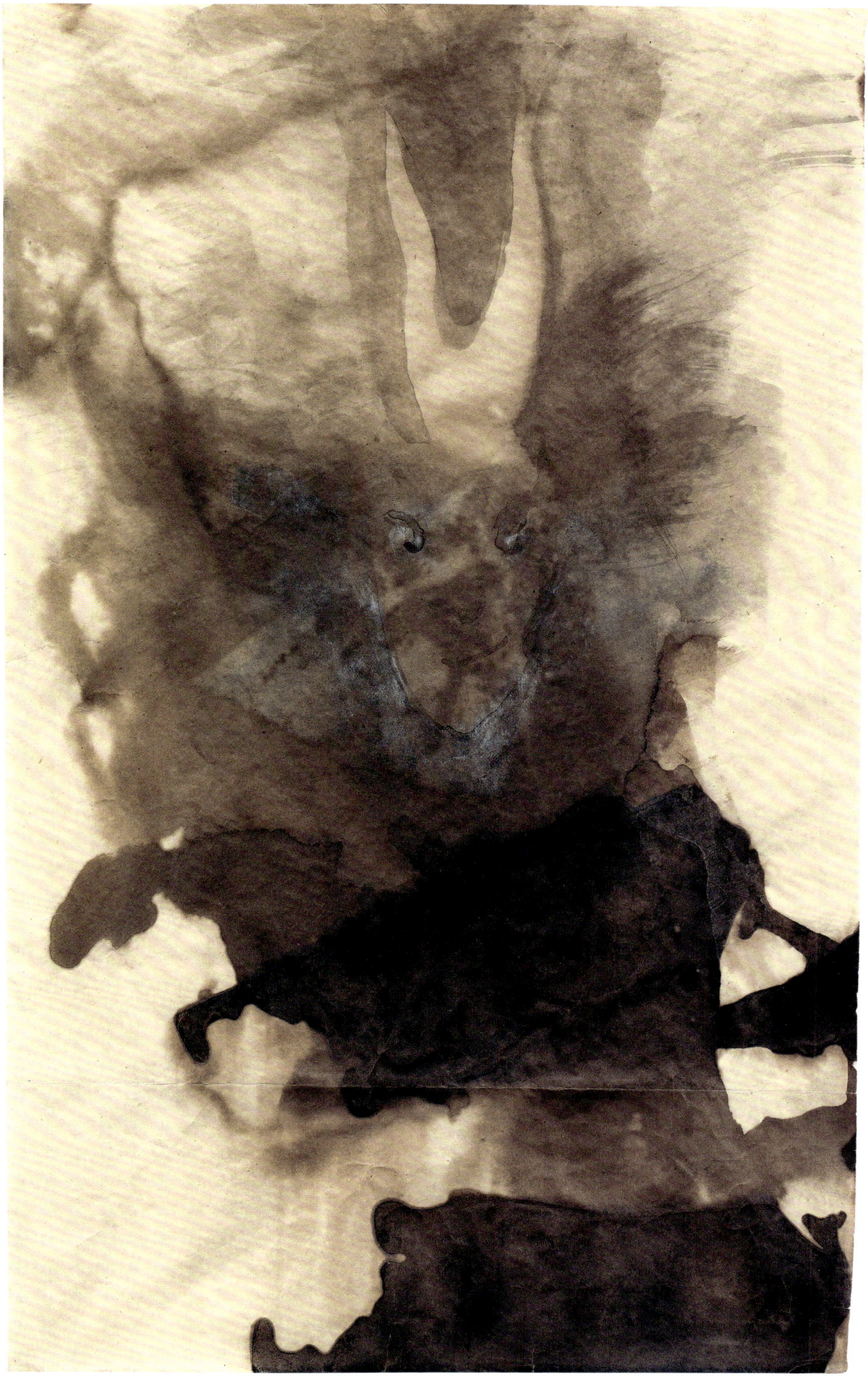

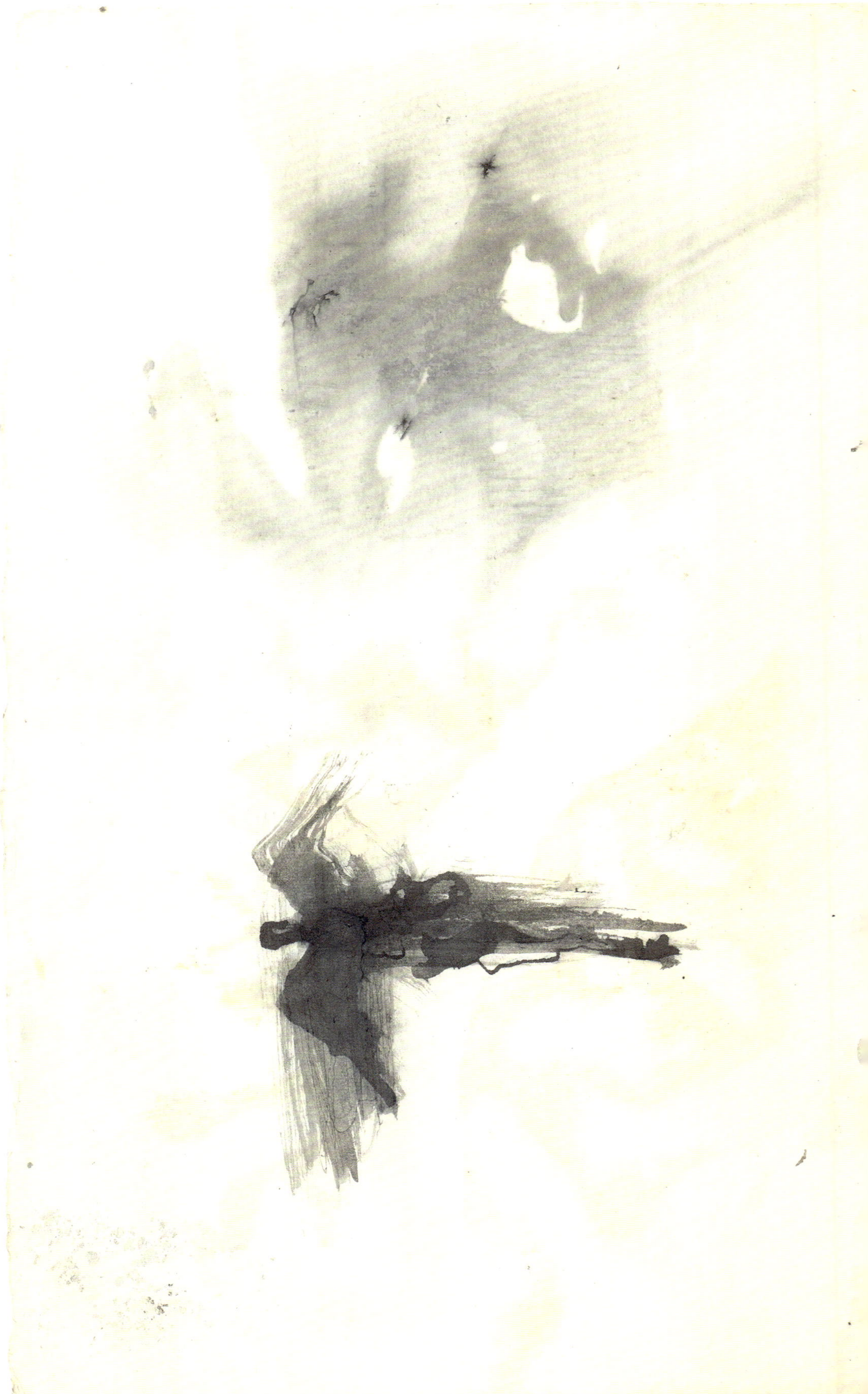

*Taches* (Stains), ca. 1875(?). Black and gray-blue ink and wash on paper. 17 7/16 × 21 5/8 in. (44.3 × 55 cm). Bibliothèque nationale de France.

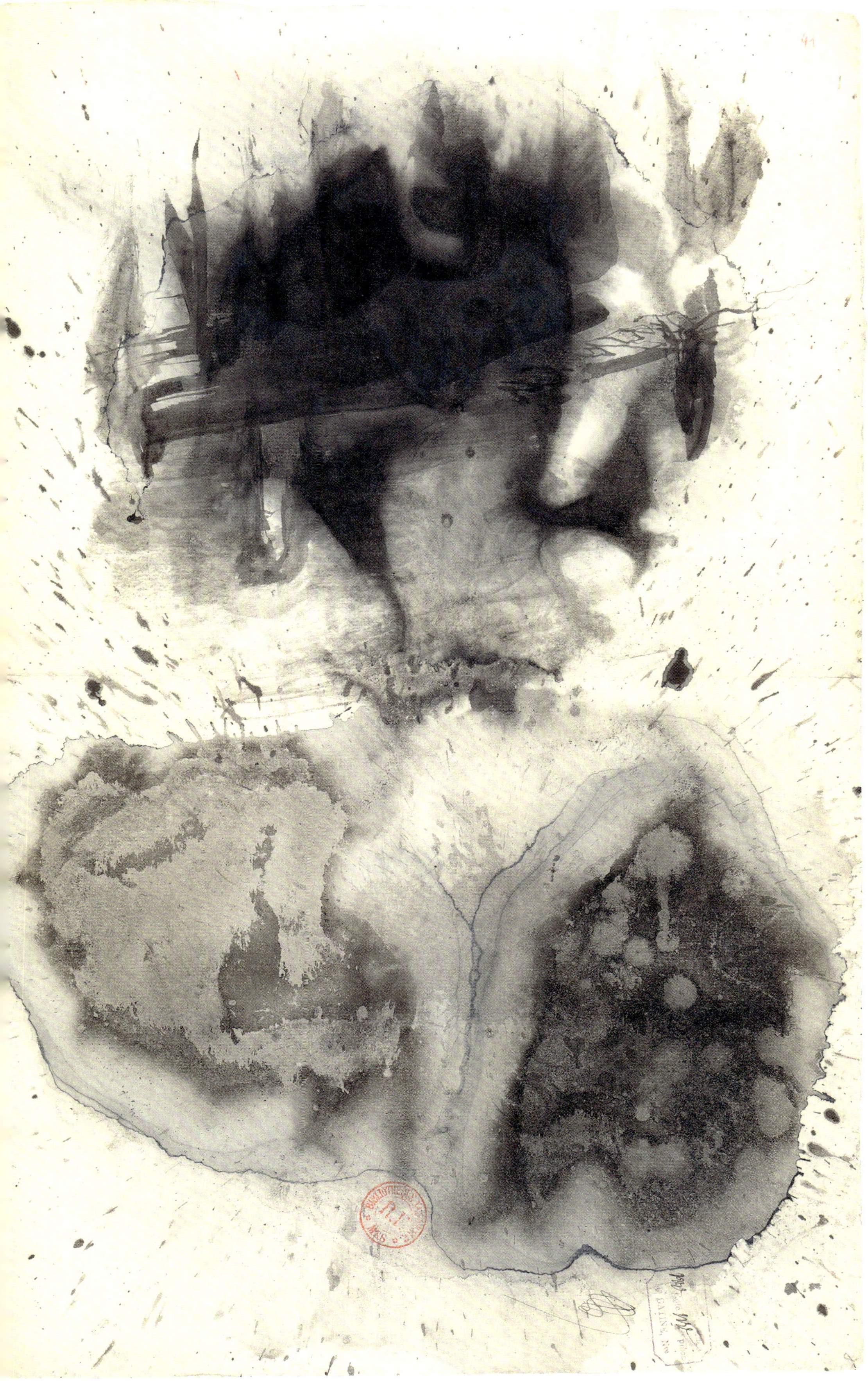

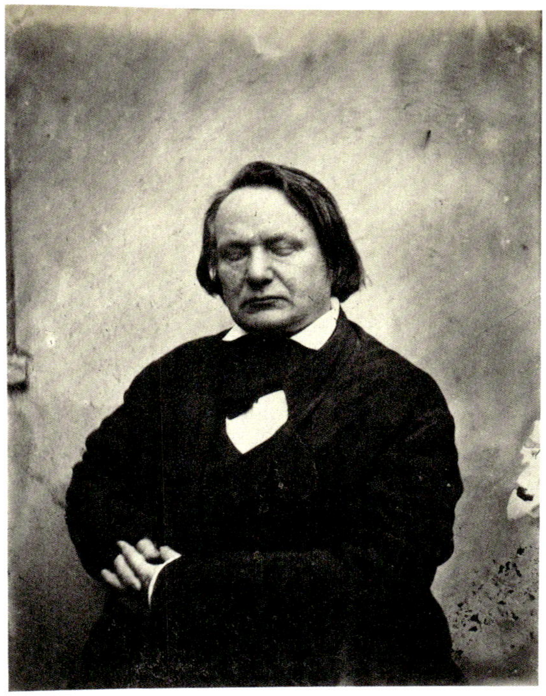

Auguste Vacquerie (French, 1819–1895). *Victor Hugo écoutant Dieu* (Victor Hugo listening to God), ca. 1853. Salted paper print. 3¾ × 2¹³⁄₁₆ in. (9.5 × 7.2 cm). Musée d'Orsay, Paris.

# CHRONOLOGY

Matthieu Vahanian

Victor Hugo's publications (blue)
Historical context (brown)
Victor Hugo's life (black)

**1802**
August 2: Napoléon Bonaparte is proclaimed consul for life.
February 26: Victor-Marie Hugo is born in Besançon (Doubs) to Léopold Hugo, an army officer, and Sophie Trébuchet. He has two older brothers, Abel and Eugène.

**1804**
December 2: Napoléon I is crowned emperor of the French. Beginning of the First Empire.

**1805**
Napoléon I defeats the Austro-Russian armies at Austerlitz, which leads to the dissolution of the Holy Roman Empire in 1806.

**1807–8**
Sophie Hugo and her sons join Léopold Hugo in Naples.

**1809**
Sophie Hugo and her sons move back to Paris.

**1811–12**
Léopold Hugo is an aide-de-camp to Joseph Bonaparte, newly anointed king of Spain. The Hugo family is reunited in Madrid for a year.

**1814**
April 4: Napoléon I abdicates and is exiled to the island of Elba, in Italy.
Louis XVIII establishes a constitutional monarchy in France.

**1815**
Napoléon I escapes Elba and returns to France for a brief period, known as the Hundred Days.
Defeated at Waterloo, Napoléon I abdicates and is banished to Saint Helena, a remote British island in the south Atlantic Ocean. End of the First Empire. Louis XVIII returns to the throne.

**1817**
Victor Hugo, aged fifteen, is honored by the Académie française for a poem he submitted to a competition.

**1818**
Léopold and Sophie Hugo obtain legal separation.

**1819**
Victor Hugo and his brothers launch *Le Conservateur Littéraire*, a royalist literary journal, in which he publishes his poems.

**1820**
*Bug-Jargal* (first version)
Victor Hugo is granted a royal pension for his ode "La mort du duc de Berry."
Secret correspondence with Adèle Foucher, a childhood friend.
Meets his literary idol, the French author François-René de Chateaubriand.

**1821**
*Iñez de Castro*
Death of Napoléon I on Saint Helena.
June 27: Death of Sophie Hugo, mother of Victor Hugo.
Marriage of Léopold Hugo and his longtime mistress, Catherine Thomas.
Engagement of Victor Hugo and Adèle Foucher.

**1822**
*Odes et poésies diverses*
Victor Hugo is granted an annual royal pension by Louis XVIII.
Marriage of Victor Hugo and Adèle Foucher at the church of Saint-Sulpice in Paris.

**1823**
*Han d'Islande* (*Hans of Iceland*)
Death of Léopold Hugo, first child of Victor and Adèle Hugo.

**1824**
*Nouvelles odes*
Death of Louis XVIII.
August 28: Birth of Léopoldine Hugo, daughter of Victor and Adèle Hugo
Victor Hugo participates in artistic and literary salons organized by the French writer and librarian Charles Nodier at Nodier's home in the Bibliothèque de l'Arsenal.
Friendship with the painters Achille Devéria and Louis Boulanger.

**1825**
Coronation of Charles X.
Victor Hugo is made a chevalier of the Légion d'honneur. Invited to Charles X's coronation, for which he writes an ode.
Travels to the Alps with Charles Nodier.

**1826**
*Bug-Jargal*
*Odes et ballades* (*Odes and Ballads*)
Joseph Nicéphore Niépce captures the earliest surviving photographic image.
November 2: Birth of Charles Hugo, son of Victor and Adèle Hugo.

**1827**
*Cromwell*
Victor Hugo's preface to *Cromwell* becomes a foundational text for the new literary movement of romanticism.

**1828**
January 29: Death of Léopold Hugo, father of Victor Hugo.
October 27: Birth of Victor Hugo (who becomes François-Victor Hugo in 1849), son of Victor and Adèle Hugo.

**1829**
*Les orientales* (*Orientalia*)
*Le dernier jour d'un condamné* (*The Last Day of a Condemned Man*)
The play *Marion de Lorme* is censored.

**1830**
February 23: Premiere of *Hernani*, performed amid riots as scuffles break out between Hugo's followers and the defenders of classicism.
July 27–29: July Revolution. Charles X abdicates. Louis-Philippe is crowned king of the French.
July 28: Birth of Adèle Hugo, daughter of Victor and Adèle Hugo.
Victor Hugo's wife, Adèle, becomes romantically involved with his friend the literary critic Charles Augustin Sainte-Beuve. Several years of marital conflict follow.

**1831**
*Notre-Dame de Paris* (*The Hunchback of Notre-Dame*)
*Marion de Lorme*

**1832**
*Les feuilles d'automne* (*Autumn Leaves*)
*Le roi s'amuse*
The Hugo family moves to the Place Royale in Paris (now Place des Vosges, home to the Maison de Victor Hugo).

**1833**
*Lucrèce Borgia* (*Lucrezia Borgia*)
*Marie Tudor*
Slavery is abolished in the British Empire.
Death of Joseph Nicéphore Niépce. His partner Louis Daguerre picks up his research in the nascent field of photography.
Beginning of a long affair between Victor Hugo and the French actress Juliette Drouet.

**1834**
*Claude Gueux*
Victor Hugo begins a series of trips with Juliette Drouet. They travel to Brittany, to Normandy, along the Loire River, and around Paris.
Visits the astronomer François Arago at the Paris observatory, where he sees the surface of the moon for the first time through a refracting telescope.

**1835**
*Angelo, tyran de Padoue* (*Angelo, Tyrant of Padua*)
*Les chants du crépuscule* (*Songs of the Half Light*)
Victor Hugo travels to Normandy and Picardy with Juliette Drouet.

**1836**
Failed coup d'état by Louis-Napoléon Bonaparte (future Napoléon III) in Strasbourg.
Victor Hugo travels to Brittany and Normandy, accompanied by Juliette Drouet and the painter Célestin Nanteuil, who created frontispieces for several of his early publications.
Meets Auguste Vacquerie and Paul Meurice, two young admirers who become lifelong friends and associates of Hugo and his family.

**1837**
*Les voix intérieures*
Death of Eugène Hugo, brother of Victor Hugo.
Victor Hugo is promoted to rank of *officier* of the Légion d'honneur.
Travels to Belgium and Normandy.

**1838**
*Ruy Blas*
Victor Hugo travels to Champagne.
The poet and critic Théophile Gautier praises Hugo's landscape and architecture drawings in *La Presse* (June 27).

**1839**
François Arago presents Louis Daguerre's invention, the daguerreotype, to the French Académie des sciences. A few weeks later, on January 25, William Henry Fox Talbot presents his invention of the calotype to the Royal Society in London.
Victor Hugo travels with Juliette Drouet to Alsace, the Rhine Valley, Switzerland, Provence, and Burgundy.

**1840**
Failed coup d'état by Louis-Napoléon Bonaparte in Boulogne.
New laws limiting child labor.
*Les rayons et les ombres*
Victor Hugo travels with Juliette Drouet to the Rhine Valley.

**1841**
Victor Hugo is elected to the Académie française.

**1842**
*Le Rhin*

**1843**
*Les burgraves*
February 15: Marriage of Léopoldine Hugo and Charles Vacquerie.
Victor Hugo travels with Juliette Drouet to Spain and the Pyrenees.
September 4: Léopoldine Hugo and Charles Vacquerie drown in the Seine. Hugo learns of their deaths five days later, through a newspaper announcement. He stops traveling, and no new works are published until 1852.
Victor Hugo begins an affair with Léonie Biard d'Aunet, wife of the French painter François-Auguste Biard.

**1844**
*Extinction du paupérisme* (*The Extinction of Pauperism*) by Louis-Napoléon Bonaparte is published in London.

**1845**
Begins *Les misères*, later to become *Les misérables*.
Victor Hugo is appointed peer of France.
Léonie Biard d'Aunet is jailed because of her adulterous affair with Hugo.

**1846**

Death of Claire Pradier, the only child of Juliette Drouet.

**1847**

Victor Hugo favors the return of the Bonaparte family to France in a speech before the Chamber of Peers.

Selects four drawings to be etched by Alfred Marvy for a charity organized by his wife, Adèle Hugo.

**1848**

The February Revolution leads to Louis-Philippe's abdication. Proclamation of the Second Republic. Louis-Napoléon Bonaparte elected president. The provisional government abolishes the Chamber of Peers.

April 7: Slavery is abolished in the French colonies.

Work on *Les misères* interrupted.

Victor Hugo is elected Paris deputy to the Constituent Assembly; he supports the Republican left but refuses to be part of the provisional government.

*L'Événement*, a journal supporting Louis-Napoléon Bonaparte's candidacy for presidency, is launched by Hugo's sons together with Auguste Vacquerie and Paul Meurice.

Hugo gives a speech supporting freedom of the press and arguing against the death penalty.

**1849**

Victor Hugo is elected Paris deputy to the Legislative National Assembly.

Calls for the creation of the United States of Europe as president of the Peace Congress.

Gives a speech condemning poverty.

Travels to Normandy.

**1850**

Victor Hugo gives a speech supporting secular education, universal suffrage, and freedom of the press.

Joins the left wing of the Legislative National Assembly in Paris.

Sets up a studio in Juliette Drouet's apartment.

**1851**

December 2: Coup d'état by Louis-Napoléon Bonaparte marks the end of the Second Republic.

Victor Hugo proclaims his deep discontent with the current class divisions in a speech against Louis-Napoléon Bonaparte at the Legislative National Assembly in Paris.

Charles Hugo is sentenced to jail after signing an article against the death penalty in *L'Événement*. François-Victor Hugo, Paul Meurice, and Auguste Vacquerie are also jailed for their involvement with the journal.

In December, Victor Hugo leads the resistance against Louis-Napoléon Bonaparte's coup d'état. Threatened with arrest, he goes into hiding with Juliette Drouet's help before his escape to Brussels. This marks the beginning of a nearly twenty-year exile.

**1852**

The pamphlet *Napoléon le petit* (*Napoleon the Little*) is published in Brussels.

December 2: Proclamation of the Second Empire with Napoléon III as emperor.

Publication of *The Eighteenth Brumaire of Louis Napoléon* by Karl Marx.

Louis-Napoléon Bonaparte signs Hugo's expulsion warrant.

The publication of Victor Hugo's attack against Louis-Napoléon Bonaparte in *Napoléon le petit* forces him to leave Brussels for Jersey, one of the Channel Islands. The Hugo family moves into Marine Terrace, a large house overlooking the sea.

Charles Hugo is introduced to photography and sets up a photographic studio at Marine Terrace.

Writing in *La Presse*, Théophile Gautier praises Hugo's drawings.

A few drawings are sold at auction alongside Victor Hugo's Parisian belongings.

**1853**

*Les châtiments*

Beginning of spiritualist séances and table-turning sessions with Delphine de Girardin in the Hugo household.

Jean-Jacques Sabatier, a fellow exile, teaches Charles Hugo and Auguste Vacquerie the basic process of photography. Charles Hugo trains with the photographer Edmond Bacot in Normandy. Victor Hugo initiates plans to integrate photographs into future publications, including a book on the Channel Islands and a new edition of *Le Rhin*, which are never published.

**1854**

*Lettre à Lord Palmerston*, in which Hugo describes the execution of John Charles Tapner to Lord Palmerston, the home secretary.

February 10: John Charles Tapner, found guilty of murdering his wife, is hanged in Guernsey.

Victor Hugo reacts against Tapner's execution. He makes drawings titled *Le pendu* (The hanged man).

**1855**

Spiritualist séances end due to the illness and dementia of one of the participants, Jules Allix.

Victor Hugo is expelled from Jersey after protests among exiles against the rapprochement between Queen Victoria and Napoléon III. The Hugo family moves to the neighboring island of Guernsey.

**1856**

*Les contemplations*

Victor Hugo acquires Hauteville House, the family home on Guernsey, with the proceeds from *Les contemplations*. He will work on the design and decoration of the house for the following three years.

**1857**

The French author Alexandre Dumas visits Victor Hugo in Guernsey.

Juliette Drouet moves to Guernsey.

**1859**
*La légende des siècles* (*The Legend of the Ages*)
December 2: The American abolitionist John Brown is hanged in Charlestown, Virginia.
The French government of Napoléon III offers a general amnesty to exiles.
Victor Hugo refuses to return to France under the current government.
Takes a public stance in favor of John Brown in a letter addressed to the United States of America.
A photography studio is set up in Hauteville House.
Baudelaire praises Hugo's drawings in his review of the Salon of 1859.

**1860**
Resumes work on *Les misérables*
Brief visit to Jersey. Victor Hugo's brother-in-law, Paul Chenay, etches the drawing *Le pendu* (The hanged man), dated 1854, under the title *John Brown*. The first version, etched with the date December 2, 1859, is censored for its implicit reference to the December 2, 1851, coup d'état. A revised second version of the print is widely distributed.

**1861**
Victor Hugo completes the interior of Hauteville House with the creation of a lookout, a glass room overlooking the ocean.
Resumes travel for the first time since the beginning of exile. He sojourns in Belgium with Charles Hugo and visits Waterloo. Charles Hugo remains on the Continent.

**1862**
*Les misérables*
Victor Hugo travels to Belgium, Luxembourg, and the Rhine Valley.
The Hugo family begins to host weekly meals for the poor and destitute children of Guernsey.
Edmond Bacot spends two weeks in Guernsey to photograph Hauteville House. His photographs will later be engraved by Maxime Lalanne for the book *Chez Victor Hugo par un passant* (1864).
Victor Hugo approves Paul Chenay's project to reproduce a selection of his drawings in a publication highlighting the author's draftsmanship. The album *Dessins de Victor Hugo* is published by Castel in Paris the following year with twelve engravings by Chenay, eleven woodcuts by Alphonse Gérard after Victor Hugo's drawings, and a preface by Théophile Gautier.

**1863**
Adèle Hugo publishes *Victor Hugo raconté par un témoin de sa vie*.
Victor Hugo travels to Luxembourg, the Rhine Valley, and Belgium.

**1864**
Begins *Les travailleurs de la mer* (*The Toilers of the Sea*).
Victor Hugo travels to the Ardennes, the Rhine Valley, and Belgium.
Adèle Hugo returns to Guernsey after an absence of more than sixteen months.
Juliette Drouet moves to a house in Guernsey named Hauteville Fairy, not far from Hauteville House.

**1865**
*Chansons des rues et des bois* (*Songs of Street and Wood*)
The Thirteenth Amendment abolishes slavery in the United States.
Adèle Hugo settles with her two sons in Brussels. Charles Hugo marries Alice Lehaene.
Victor Hugo visits Brussels and travels to Germany and Luxembourg.

**1866**
*Les travailleurs de la mer* (*The Toilers of the Sea*)
Victor Hugo binds thirty-six drawings into his manuscript of *Les travailleurs de la mer*.
Spends the summer in Belgium.

**1868**
Victor Hugo travels again to Belgium. His wife, Adèle Hugo, dies in Brussels on August 27.
Birth of Georges, son of Charles and Alice Hugo.

**1869**
*L'homme qui rit* (*The Man Who Laughs*)
*Torquemada*
First illustrated edition of *Les travailleurs de la mer*. Engravings by François Chifflart, published by Hetzel.
Victor Hugo is appointed president of the Peace Congress in Lausanne, Switzerland.
Birth of Jeanne, daughter of Charles and Alice Hugo.

**1870**
First legal French edition of *Les châtiments*.
July 19: Beginning of the Franco-Prussian War.
September 4: Fall of Napoléon III and proclamation of the Third Republic.
Charles Hugo and his family visit Guernsey.
August 15: Victor Hugo leaves Guernsey when the French imperial army is first defeated.
September 5: Victor Hugo returns triumphantly to France.

**1871**
The Paris Commune is suppressed by the French army.
May 10: End of the Franco-Prussian War.
Victor Hugo is elected deputy for Paris at the National Assembly, then resigns.
Sudden death of Charles Hugo. Victor Hugo is the guardian of Georges and Jeanne Hugo until Alice Hugo's remarriage in 1877.
Leaves for Brussels but is expelled following his offer to shelter communards. He takes up residence in Vianden, Luxembourg.

**1872**
*L'année terrible*
Victor Hugo is defeated in the elections and returns to Guernsey, where he remains for another year.
His daughter Adèle Hugo is committed to a mental health facility in Saint-Mandé, near Paris.

**1873**
Death of François-Victor Hugo, son of Victor and Adèle Hugo.

**1874**
*Quatrevingt-treize* (*Ninety-Three*)
*Mes fils*

**1875**
*Actes et paroles* (*Deeds and Words*)
Philippe Burty publishes a thorough study of Hugo's drawings in the journal *L'Art*.
Victor Hugo drafts his literary testament.

**1876**
First edition of *Victor Hugo illustré* by Eugène Hugues, an affordable and popular publication of his complete works, illustrated with reproductions of some of his drawings and works by other artists.
Victor Hugo is elected senator for the department of the Seine.

**1877**
*L'art d'être grand-père* (*The Art of Being a Grandfather*)
*Histoire d'un crime* (*History of a Crime*)

**1878**
Victor Hugo suffers a stroke and stops writing.

**1881**
French laws grant free primary education, freedom of assembly, and freedom of the press.
*Les quatre vents de l'esprit* (*The Four Winds of the Spirit*)
Victor Hugo draws up his will and chooses to leave his manuscripts and drawings to the Bibliothèque nationale de France.

**1882**
French laws establish free, mandatory secular education.
*Dessins de Victor Hugo: Les travailleurs de la mer* is published with wood engravings by Fortuné-Louis Méaulle after drawings by Hugo.

**1883**
Publication of *L'archipel de la Manche*.
Death of Juliette Drouet.
Victor Hugo meets Auguste Rodin, who sculpts his bust.

**1885**
May 22: Victor Hugo dies in Paris.
June 1: State funeral of Victor Hugo, reportedly attended by two million people.

**1886**
Posthumous publication of *La fin de Satan*.

**1888**
First exhibition of drawings and manuscripts by Victor Hugo in Paris is organized by his lifelong friend Paul Meurice.

**1903**
Inauguration of the Maison de Victor Hugo in Paris at 6, place des Vosges, thanks to the efforts and gifts of Paul Meurice.

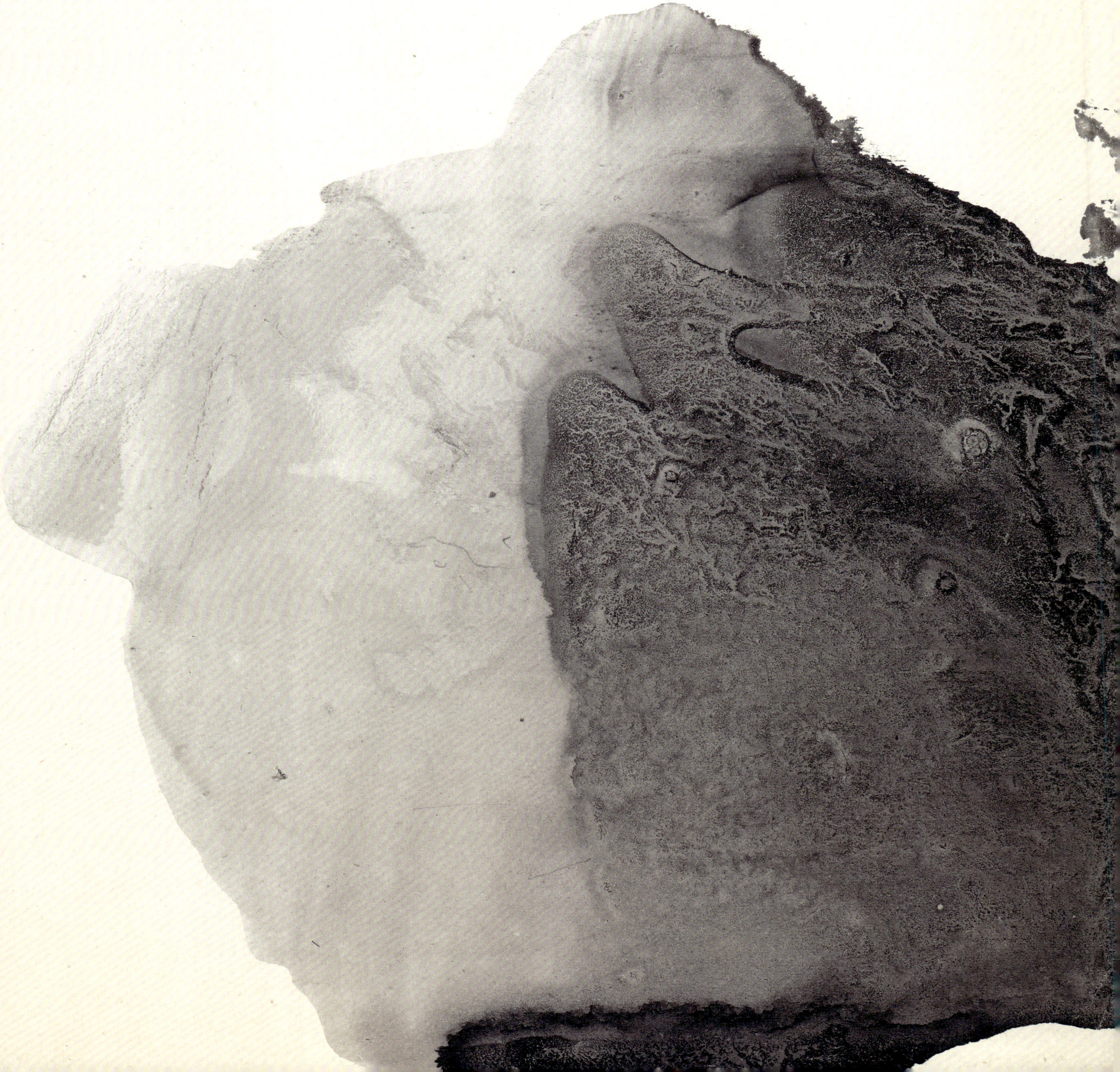

## Drawings

*Le beffroi de Lierre* (The belfry of Lier), August 1837
Brown ink and wash on paper
9 7/16 × 6 15/16 in. (24 × 17.7 cm)
Yale University Art Gallery, Gift of Mr. and Mrs. Douglas Williams, B.A. 1940, 1977.7
Page 73

*Lettre avec vue de Luz* (Letter with view of Luz), August 25, 1843
Brown ink and wash and graphite on paper
8 1/8 × 5 5/16 in. (20.7 × 13.5 cm)
Maisons de Victor Hugo, Paris / Guernesey, MVHP.D.1392
Page 74

*Voyage de 1843 aux Pyrénées* (1843 voyage to the Pyrenees), 1843
Bound sketchbook with drawings in brown ink and wash and graphite on paper
9 7/16 × 25 9/16 in. (24 × 65 cm) open
Bibliothèque nationale de France, NAF 13346, fols. 22–23
Pages 78–79

*Château surplombant une rivière* (Castle overlooking a river), 1847
Brown ink and wash and black crayon on paper
11 × 13 3/16 in. (27.9 × 33.5 cm)
Private collection, New York
Page 77

*Paysage avec deux châteaux en ruine* (Landscape with two derelict castles), 1847
Brown ink and wash over black crayon and graphite, with shellac, on paper, laid down
10 9/16 × 18 5/16 in. (26.8 × 46.5 cm)
Inscribed on mount "Debout l'un devant l'autre, ils semblent / Deux noirs géants prêts à la lutte. / Victor Hugo" [Standing facing one another they resemble / Two dark giants ready for the fight / Victor Hugo] and "J'avais donné ce dessin à / mon vieux compagnon d'exil Kesler ; / je suis charmé de le voir entre / les mains de mon jeune et excellent / ami M. Le Ber / V.H. / H.H. avril 1870" [I had given this drawing to my old companion in exile Kesler. I am charmed to see it in the hands of my excellent young friend M. Le Ber V.H. H.H. April 1870]
Inscribed on frame: "À mon cher et courageux compagnon d'exil / Kesler / en souvenir des soins affectueux pendant ma maladie / Victor Hugo / Guernesey 1 janvier / 1859" [To my dear and courageous companion in exile Kesler for the affection with which he cared for me during illness. Victor Hugo, Guernsey, January 1, 1859], with a largely illegible inscription by Kesler
The Art Institute of Chicago, Marjorie Blum-Kovler Collection and the Harry and Maribel G. Blum Foundation, 1989.168
Page 75

*Tache* (Stain), ca. 1850
Brown ink and wash on paper
3 5/8 × 2 3/8 in. (9.2 × 6 cm)
Nationalmuseum, Stockholm, NMH 28/1981
Page 144

*Taches* (Stains), ca. 1850
Brown ink and wash on paper
2 5/16 × 3 9/16 in. (5.8 × 9 cm)
Nationalmuseum, Stockholm, NMH 34/1981
Page 145

*Tache* (Stain), ca. 1850–55(?)
Cut paper with brown wash and graphite
9 × 5 9/16 in. (22.9 × 14.1 cm)
Private collection
Page 147

*Tache* (Stain), ca. 1850–70(?)
Brown ink on paper
3 1/8 × 6 11/16 in. (8 × 17 cm)
Private collection
Page 177

*Taches* (Stains), ca. 1852–59(?)
Brown ink and wash on paper
14 9/16 × 17 15/16 in. (37 × 45.5 cm)
Nationalmuseum, Stockholm, NMH 27/1981
Page 178

*Taches* (Stains), ca. 1853–55
Brown and blue wash on paper
14 15/16 × 9 1/2 in. (37.9 × 24.1 cm)
Private collection
Page 149

*Ecce (Le pendu)* (Ecce [hanged man]), 1854
Brown ink, brown and black wash, charcoal, and white gouache on paper
16 7/16 × 12 13/16 in. (41.7 × 32.5 cm)
Signed and inscribed "V.H. ECCE"
Maisons de Victor Hugo, Paris / Guernesey, MVHP.D.124
Page 155

*Ecce Lex (Le pendu)* (Ecce Lex [hanged man]), 1854
Brown ink, brown and black wash, graphite, charcoal, and white gouache on paper
20 × 13 3/4 in. (50.8 × 34.9 cm)
Signed "Victor Hugo ECCE LEX"
Maisons de Victor Hugo, Paris / Guernesey, MVHP.D.967
Page 154

*Planète* (Planet), ca. 1854
Brown ink and wash over charcoal with touches of white gouache on paper
12 1/8 × 14 9/16 in. (30.8 × 37 cm)
Collection of David Lachenmann
Page 151

*Silhouette d'un burg* (Silhouette of a castle), ca. 1854
Stencil cut from paper from a printed concert program dated October 20, 1854
4 13/16 × 4 11/16 in. (12.3 × 11.9 cm)
Bibliothèque nationale de France, NAF 13351, fol. 35[3]
Page 102

*Brise-lames à Jersey* (A breakwater in Jersey), ca. 1854–55
Brown and black ink, charcoal with white gouache, and traces of varnish on paper
11 3/8 × 18 in. (28.9 × 45.7 cm)
Maisons de Victor Hugo, Paris / Guernesey, MVHP.D.127
Page 128

*Planète-œil* (Planet-eye), ca. 1854–55
Graphite and black ink and wash on paper
$11\frac{9}{16} \times 8\frac{7}{16}$ in. (29.3 × 21.4 cm)
Bibliothèque nationale de France, NAF 13355,
fol. 106
Page 143

*Souvenir de Suisse* (Souvenir of Switzerland),
ca. 1854–55
Brown and black ink, brown and gray wash,
black powdered pigment, and unidentified black
medium with white gouache on paper in
pyrographed and painted frame
$9\frac{1}{4} \times 8\frac{9}{16}$ in. (23.5 × 21.7 cm)
Signed and inscribed on the frame "Souvenir de
Suisse / VEDETTE DE GUILLAUME TELL PRÈS
D'ALTORF / Victor Hugo" [Souvenir of Switzerland,
Watchtower of William Tell near Altorf, Victor Hugo]
Maisons de Victor Hugo, Paris / Guernesey,
MVHP.D.963
Page 97

*Le burg* (The castle), ca. 1854–57(?)
Brown ink and wash and charcoal on paper
$13\frac{3}{16} \times 10\frac{5}{16}$ in. (33.5 × 26.2 cm)
Signed "Victor Hugo"
Collection of Véronique and Louis-Antoine Prat,
Paris
Page 87

*"Prenant le frais avec ses sept frères"* (Taking in
the fresh air with his seven brothers), ca. 1854–57
Brown and black ink and wash, graphite, charcoal,
black crayon, white gouache, and watercolor
on paper
$11\frac{3}{8} \times 18$ in. (28.9 × 45.7 cm) and $6\frac{3}{4} \times 14\frac{1}{8}$ in.
(17.2 × 35.8 cm)
Inscribed "PRENANT LE FRAIS / AVEC SES
SEPT FRERES" [Taking in the fresh air with his
seven brothers]
Maisons de Victor Hugo, Paris / Guernesey,
MVHP.D.819
Pages 156, 157

*Silhouette de château illuminé par un orage*
(Silhouette of a castle illuminated by lightning),
ca. 1854–57(?)
Stencil cut from card with charcoal and brown
ink and wash
$7\frac{5}{16} \times 6\frac{1}{4}$ in. (18.5 × 15.8 cm)
Bibliothèque nationale de France, NAF 13351,
fol. 34[1]
Page 85

Pochoir pour *Souvenir* (Stencil for Souvenir),
ca. 1855(?)
Stencil cut from paper with charcoal and brown
and black ink
$5\frac{3}{8} \times 8\frac{3}{4}$ in. (13.7 × 22.3 cm)
Maisons de Victor Hugo, Paris / Guernesey,
MVHP.D.2648
Page 117

*Silhouette de clocher* (Silhouette of a bell tower),
ca. 1855
Stencil cut from a paper envelope with brown
ink and wash
$4\frac{15}{16} \times 1\frac{3}{4}$ in. (12.5 × 4.5 cm) unfolded
Maisons de Victor Hugo, Paris / Guernesey,
MVHP.D.2250
Page 102

*Silhouette d'église* (Silhouette of a church), 1855
Stencil cut from paper with charcoal and traces
of brown ink
$3\frac{7}{8} \times 2\frac{15}{16}$ in. (9.8 × 7.5 cm)
Bibliothèque nationale de France, NAF 13351,
fol. 35[2]
Page 111

*Silhouette de l'Ermitage* (Silhouette of l'Ermitage),
ca. 1855
Stencil cut from paper with charcoal
$5\frac{13}{16} \times 4\frac{1}{2}$ in. (14.7 × 11.5 cm)
Bibliothèque nationale de France, NAF 13355,
fol. 107[1]
Pages 92, 93

*Silhouette d'une tour* (Silhouette of a tower),
ca. 1855
Stencil cut from ruled notepaper with brown
ink and wash
$6\frac{1}{2} \times 3\frac{1}{16}$ in. (16.5 × 7.8 cm)
Bibliothèque nationale de France, NAF 13355,
fol. 107[2]
Page 99

*Souvenir*, ca. 1855(?)
Brown ink; brown, black, and blue wash; charcoal;
graphite; and black crayon with traces of gold
medium on paper
$6 \times 11\frac{5}{8}$ in. (15.3 × 29.6 cm)
Signed "Victor H."
Maisons de Victor Hugo, Paris / Guernesey,
MVHP.D.926
Page 116

*Paysage au pont* (Landscape with bridge),
ca. 1855–56
Brown ink and wash on paper
$4 \times 5\frac{1}{4}$ in. (10.1 × 13.3 cm)
Ville de Dijon—Direction des Musées et du
Patrimoine—Musée des Beaux-Arts, Donation
Pierre et Kathleen Granville, 1999-DG623
Page 173

*Silhouette de toits et tourelles* (Silhouette of
roofs and turrets), ca. 1855–56
Stencil cut from paper with charcoal
$5\frac{1}{2} \times 7\frac{7}{8}$ in. (13.9 × 20 cm)
Bibliothèque nationale de France, NAF 13351,
fol. 32
Page 80

*Silhouette de toits et tourelles* (Silhouette of
roofs and turrets), ca. 1855–56
Stencil cut from paper with graphite
$6 \times 8\frac{11}{16}$ in. (15.3 × 22 cm)
Bibliothèque nationale de France, NAF 13351,
fol. 33[1]
Page 81

*Taches et collage* (Stains and collage), ca. 1855–56
Graphite powder, graphite wash, and a cut
postal stamp pasted onto paper, with traces of
white gouache
$6\frac{1}{8} \times 4\frac{5}{8}$ in. (15.5 × 11.8 cm)
Bibliothèque nationale de France, NAF 13355,
fol. 90
Page 168

*La bouche d'ombre* (The mouth of darkness),
ca. 1855–57(?)
Brown ink and wash on paper
$7\frac{5}{16} \times 4\frac{13}{16}$ in. (18.5 × 12.3 cm)
Signed "V.H."
Maisons de Victor Hugo, Paris / Guernesey,
MVHP.D.2010.7.1
Page 169

*Paysage avec château* (Landscape with castle), ca. 1855–57
Brown ink and green-blue wash on paper
1¾ × 4½ in. (4.4 × 11.4 cm)
Collection of Gordon VeneKlasen
Page 104

*Le serpent* (The snake), ca. 1856
Brown ink, brown and black wash, charcoal, white and red gouache, and traces of varnish and glue on paper
12⅜ × 19⁵⁄₁₆ in. (31.5 × 49.1 cm)
Signed "V.H."
Maisons de Victor Hugo, Paris / Guernesey, MVHP.D.818
Page 131

*Silhouette d'un château* (Silhouette of a castle), 1856
Stencil cut from ruled notepaper with charcoal and traces of white gouache
9⁹⁄₁₆ × 6¹⁵⁄₁₆ in. (24.3 × 17.6 cm)
Maisons de Victor Hugo, Paris / Guernesey, MVHP.D.1384
Page 110

*Un trois-mâts à vapeur* (A three-masted steamboat), ca. 1856
Brown and black ink, brown and gray wash, graphite, watercolor, and white gouache on paper
5⅛ × 7½ in. (13 × 19 cm)
Signed "Victor Hugo"
Maisons de Victor Hugo, Paris / Guernesey, MVHP.D.127
Page 124

*Justitia* (Justice), 1857
Graphite; brown and black ink; brown, black, and red wash; charcoal; and traces of red gouache on paper
21 × 13¾ in. (53.4 × 35 cm)
Signed and dated "Victor Hugo / 1857"
Maisons de Victor Hugo, Paris / Guernesey, MVHP.D.966
Page 159

*Souvenir d'un burg des Vosges* (Souvenir of a castle in the Vosges), 1857
Brown ink and wash, white gouache, and blue wash on paper
18½ × 12³⁄₁₆ in. (47 × 31 cm)
Signed, dated, and inscribed "Victor Hugo / Guernesey 1857 / Souvenir d'un burg des Vosges" [Victor Hugo, Guernsey, 1857. Souvenir of a castle in the Vosges]
The Metropolitan Museum of Art, New York, Purchase, Harris Brisbane Dick Fund, Donald Young Foundation Gift, Harry G. Sperling Fund, and David M. Tobey Gift, 2012, 2012.17
Page 86

*Château au bord d'un lac* (Castle by a lake), 1858
Black and brown ink and wash with white chalk and black Conté crayon, heightened with white gouache
9⅝ × 9¾ in. (24.5 × 24.8 cm)
Signed, dated, and inscribed "Guernesey 1858 Victor Hugo"
Collection of Frances Beatty and Allen Adler
Page 105

*Étude pour la tombe de Léopoldine* (Study for the tomb of Léopoldine), 1858
Stencil cut from paper with brown ink and wash
5¼ × 3⅛ in. (13.4 × 8 cm)
Inscribed on the back "Monsieur. M[illegible] onsieur Victor Hugo, Guernesey" [postmarked 08/22/58]
Maisons de Victor Hugo, Paris / Guernesey, MVHP.D.2012.5.1
Page 165

*Rosace* (Rosette), ca. 1859
Brown ink and wash on paper
8⅞ × 7¹⁄₁₆ in. (22.6 × 18 cm)
Maison Vacquerie–Musée Victor Hugo, Villequier–Dept. 76, inv. 1981.1.3
Page 175

*L'abbaye* (The abbey), ca. 1860
Brown ink and wash on paper
5³⁄₁₆ × 6⅞ in. (13.2 × 17.5 cm)
Signed "Victor Hugo"
Private collection, New York
Page 82

*Château sur une colline* (Castle on a hill), ca. 1860–70(?)
Brown ink and wash on paper
7⁵⁄₁₆ × 8⅞ in. (18.5 × 22.5 cm)
Maisons de Victor Hugo, Paris / Guernesey, MVHP.D.2775
Page 100

*Forteresse médiévale* (Medieval fortress), ca. 1863
Brown ink and wash on paper
5⅝ × 8¾ in. (14.3 × 22.3 cm)
Bibliothèque nationale de France, NAF 13355, fol. 62
Page 89

*Taches avec empreintes de doigts* (Abstract composition with fingerprints), ca. 1864–65
Brown ink and wash on paper
10⁵⁄₁₆ × 7½ in. (26.2 × 19 cm)
Bibliothèque nationale de France, NAF 13345, fol. 28
Page 163

*Tache* (Stain), ca. 1864–69
Brown ink and wash on paper
8¹³⁄₁₆ × 5⁹⁄₁₆ in. (22.4 × 14.2 cm)
Maisons de Victor Hugo, Paris / Guernesey, MVHP.D.2012.4.1
Page 171

*Tête de diable* (Head of a devil), ca. 1864–69
Brown ink and wash with white gouache on paper
15³⁄₁₆ × 9⅜ in. (38.5 × 23.8 cm)
Fundación Almine y Bernard Ruiz-Picasso para el Arte
Page 181

*Les Needles, île de Wight* (The Needles, Isle of Wight), 1865
Bound sketchbook with drawings in brown ink and wash on paper
7³⁄₁₆ × 11¹⁵⁄₁₆ in. (18.3 × 30.3 cm) open
Bibliothèque nationale de France, NAF 13462, fols. 16–17
Page 125

*L'intestin de Léviathan* (The bowels of Leviathan), 1866
Brown and black ink and wash and white gouache on paper
$19\frac{1}{4} \times 35\frac{9}{16}$ in. (48.9 × 90.4 cm)
Maisons de Victor Hugo, Paris / Guernesey, MVHP.D.808
Page 136

*Le phare des Casquets* (The Casquets lighthouse), 1866
Brown ink and wash, black crayon, black chalk, and white gouache on paper
$35\frac{3}{8} \times 18\frac{7}{8}$ in. (89.8 × 48 cm)
Signed and dated "Victor Hugo / 1866"
Maisons de Victor Hugo, Paris / Guernesey, MVHP.D.185
Page 109

*Taches* (Stains), ca. 1866–68(?)
Graphite powder, graphite wash, and brown ink and wash on paper
$14\frac{1}{16} \times 9\frac{1}{4}$ in. (35.7 × 23.5 cm)
Bibliothèque nationale de France, NAF 13355, fol. 111
Page 166

*Barque à la voile gonflée* (Boat in full sail), ca. 1866–69
Brown ink and wash on paper
$4\frac{7}{8} \times 6\frac{1}{4}$ in. (12.4 × 15.8 cm)
Bibliothèque nationale de France, NAF 13351, fol. 21
Page 135

*Ma destinée* (My destiny), 1867
Brown ink and wash and white gouache on paper
$6\frac{3}{4} \times 10\frac{3}{8}$ in. (17.2 × 26.4 cm)
Signed, dated, and inscribed "Victor Hugo / 1867 / MA DESTINÉE" [Victor Hugo, 1867. My destiny]
Maisons de Victor Hugo, Paris / Guernesey, MVHP.D.927
Page 139

*Tache (avec tête de caractère)* (Stain with head), ca. 1869
Brown ink and wash on paper
$8\frac{3}{4} \times 5\frac{11}{16}$ in. (22.3 × 14.4 cm)
Maisons de Victor Hugo, Paris / Guernesey, MVHP.D.2384
Page 179

*Taches* (Stains), ca. 1870–71
Brown ink and wash and graphite on paper
$10\frac{1}{16} \times 13\frac{7}{8}$ in. (25.5 × 35.3 cm)
Bibliothèque nationale de France, NAF 13349, fol. 21
Page 137

*Le burg à l'ange* (The castle with the angel), ca. 1871
Brown ink and wash, graphite, watercolor, and white gouache on paper
$8\frac{3}{8} \times 13\frac{7}{16}$ in. (21.2 × 34.2 cm)
Maisons de Victor Hugo, Paris / Guernesey, MVHP.D.36
Page 83

*Silhouette du château de Vianden* (Silhouette of the castle of Vianden), 1871
Stencil cut from paper with brown and purple ink
$2\frac{3}{4} \times 4\frac{3}{4}$ in. (7 × 12 cm)
Private collection
Page 103

*Vianden à travers une toile d'araignée* (The town of Vianden seen through a spiderweb), August 13, 1871
Brown ink and wash and blue watercolor over graphite on paper
$10\frac{1}{16} \times 11\frac{15}{16}$ in. (25.5 × 30.3 cm)
Maisons de Victor Hugo, Paris / Guernesey, MVHP.D.83
Page 115

*Vianden 1871*, 1871
Brown and black ink, brown and purple wash, graphite, and varnish on sketchbook paper
$9\frac{7}{8} \times 13\frac{11}{16}$ in. (25.1 × 34.7 cm)
Bibliothèque nationale de France, NAF 13349, fol. 19
Page 113

*Marine avec bateau à voile et figure monstrueuse dans le ciel* (Seascape with sailboat and a monstrous figure in the sky), pasted in *Les travailleurs de la mer*, vol. 2 of *Œuvres complètes* (Paris: Hetzel, 1880–83), ca. 1874–78
Brown ink and wash, blue ink and wash, and gouache(?) on paper, laid down
$8\frac{11}{16} \times 5\frac{7}{16}$ in. (22 × 13.8 cm)
Inscribed "Contes / pour les petits / enfants / à / l'usage / des / grands" [Stories for little children to be used by grown-ups] with a second illegible inscription
The Morgan Library and Museum, Bequest of Gordon N. Ray, 1987, PML140540
Page 133

*Taches* (Stains), ca. 1875(?)
Brown ink and wash on paper
$9\frac{1}{8} \times 14\frac{1}{4}$ in. (23.1 × 36.2 cm)
Bibliothèque nationale de France, NAF 24807, fols. 37–38
Page 167

*Taches* (Stains), ca. 1875(?)
Black and gray-blue ink and wash on paper
$17\frac{7}{16} \times 21\frac{5}{8}$ in. (44.3 × 55 cm)
Bibliothèque nationale de France, NAF 24807, fols. 41–42
Pages 182–83

*La Tourgue en 1835* (La Tourgue in 1835), May 30, 1876
Brown ink and wash on paper
$11\frac{15}{16} \times 7\frac{13}{16}$ in. (30.3 × 19.8 cm)
Signed and inscribed "La Tourgue / en 1835 / V.H."
Maisons de Victor Hugo, Paris / Guernesey, MVHP.D.96
Page 107

*Tache* (Stain)
Brown ink and wash on paper
$4\frac{5}{16} \times 3\frac{15}{16}$ in. (11 × 10 cm)
Private collection
Page 172

*Tache* (Stain)
Brown ink and wash on paper
$5\frac{9}{16} \times 4\frac{15}{16}$ in. (14.2 × 12.5 cm)
Maisons de Victor Hugo, Paris / Guernesey, MVHP.D.1385
Page 174

## Photographs

Charles Hugo (French, 1826–1871)
*Marine Terrace*, ca. 1852–53
Salted paper print
$2\frac{13}{16} \times 4\frac{1}{16}$ in. (7.1 × 10.3 cm)
Grunwald Center for the Graphic Arts, Hammer Museum, Purchased with funds provided by the Lloyd E. Rigler–Lawrence E. Deutsch Acquisition Endowment Fund, 2016.14.1
Page 123

Charles Hugo (French, 1826–1871)
*Auguste Vacquerie au pied d'un rocher (La Collette)* (Auguste Vacquerie at the foot of a rock [La Collette]), ca. 1853
Salted paper print
$8\frac{13}{16} \times 7\frac{3}{16}$ in. (22.4 × 18.2 cm)
Musée d'Orsay, Paris, Don de Mme Marie-Thérèse et M. André Jammes, 1984, PHC 1984 85 2
Page 101

Charles Hugo (French, 1826–1871)
*Le Rocher de l'Ermitage* (The Rocher de l'Ermitage), ca. 1853
Salted paper print
$8\frac{1}{16} \times 6\frac{1}{2}$ in. (20.5 × 16.5 cm)
Musée d'Orsay, Paris, PHO 1986 123 166
Page 95

Charles Hugo (French, 1826–1871)
*Victor Hugo au Dicq, Jersey* (Victor Hugo at the Dicq, Jersey), ca. 1853
Salted paper print
$6\frac{1}{4} \times 7\frac{5}{8}$ in. (15.8 × 19.3 cm)
Musée d'Orsay, Paris, PHO 1986 123 167
Page 129

Charles Hugo (French, 1826–1871)
*Victor Hugo sur le Rocher des Proscrits* (Victor Hugo seated on the Rocher des Proscrits [exiles' rock]), ca. 1853
Salted paper print
$8\frac{3}{8} \times 7\frac{1}{16}$ in. (21.2 × 18 cm)
Inscribed on mount "Le Rocher des Proscrits / à Paul Meurice / mon ami / Charles Hugo / Jersey 1853" [The Rocher des Proscrits. To Paul Meurice, my friend. Charles Hugo, Jersey 1853]
Maisons de Victor Hugo, Paris / Guernesey, MVHP.PH.2119
Page 127

Charles Hugo (French, 1826–1871) and/or Auguste Vacquerie (French, 1819–1895)
*Le château Mont Orgueil* (The castle of Mont Orgueil), ca. 1853
Salted paper print
$7\frac{3}{8} \times 6\frac{1}{2}$ in. (18.8 × 16.5 cm)
Musée d'Orsay, Paris, PHO 1986 123 165
Page 91

Charles Hugo (French, 1826–1871) and/or Auguste Vacquerie (French, 1819–1895)
*Le château Mont Orgueil* (The castle of Mont Orgueil), ca. 1853
Salted paper print
$8\frac{3}{8} \times 6\frac{1}{2}$ in. (21.2 × 16.5 cm)
Musée d'Orsay, Paris, PHO 1986 123 164
Page 98

Charles Hugo (French, 1826–1871) and/or Auguste Vacquerie (French, 1819–1895)
*"Jersey – la jetée 1853"* (Jersey—the jetty 1853), 1853
Salted paper print
$5\frac{13}{16} \times 6\frac{5}{16}$ in. (14.7 × 16.1 cm)
Inscribed "La Jetée / Jersey 1853"
Maisons de Victor Hugo, Paris / Guernesey, MVHP.PH.2525
Page 134

Auguste Vacquerie (French, 1819–1895)
*Victor Hugo écoutant Dieu* (Victor Hugo listening to God), ca. 1853
Salted paper print
$3\frac{3}{4} \times 2\frac{13}{16}$ in. (9.5 × 7.2 cm)
Musée d'Orsay, Paris, PHO 1986 123 107
Page 184

## Objects

Signed pebble, 1856
Ink on pebble
$2\frac{3}{4} \times 4\frac{7}{16} \times 1\frac{15}{16}$ in. (7 × 11.3 × 5 cm)
Signed, dated, and inscribed "Souvenir du cousin / proscrit / Victor Hugo / Guernesey 1856" [Souvenir of the banished cousin Victor Hugo Guernsey 1856]
Maisons de Victor Hugo, Paris / Guernesey, MVHP.OA.1179
Page 119

Signed pebble, 1856
Ink on pebble
$3\frac{15}{16} \times 4\frac{5}{16} \times 2\frac{1}{16}$ in. (10 × 11 × 5.3 cm)
Signed "Victor"
Maisons de Victor Hugo, Paris / Guernesey, MVHP.OA.2721
Page 119

Signed pebble, September 1856
Ink on pebble
$4\frac{15}{16} \times 4\frac{5}{16} \times 1\frac{7}{8}$ in. (12.5 × 11 × 4.7 cm)
Signed and dated "Victor Hugo / [illegible] 1856 / 7bre"
Maisons de Victor Hugo, Paris / Guernesey, MVHP.OA.2720
Page 119

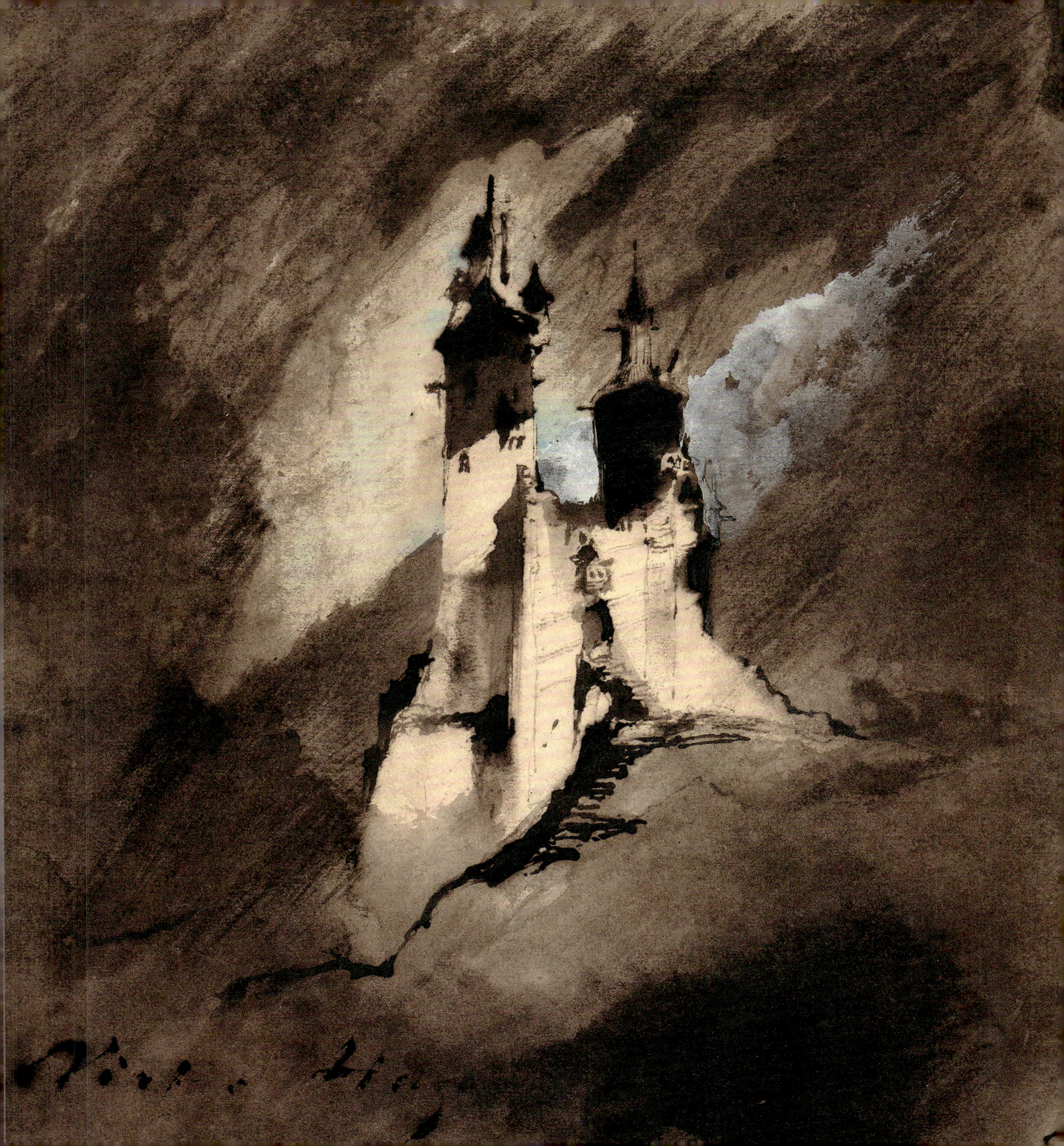

## SELECTED BIBLIOGRAPHY


Alexandre, Arsène, and Victor Hugo. *La maison de Victor Hugo*. Paris: Hachette, 1903.

Audinet, Gérard, and Julie Borgeaud. *Louis Soutter, Victor Hugo: Dessins parallèles*. Exh. cat. Paris: Paris musées, 2015.

Audinet, Gérard, and Jérôme Godeau. *Entrée des médiums: Spiritisme et art de Hugo à Breton*. Exh. cat. Paris: Paris musées, 2012.

Barbou, Alfred. *Victor Hugo et son temps*. Paris: G. Charpentier, 1881.

Bertaux, Émile. "Victor Hugo artiste." Pt. 1, "Le dessinateur," and pt. 2, "Le décorateur." *Gazette des Beaux-Arts* 29 (1903): 465–89; 30 (1903): 146–72.

Bibliothèque nationale de France. *Victor Hugo: Exposition organisée pour commémorer le cent cinquantième anniversaire de sa naissance*. Exh. cat. Paris: Bibliothèque nationale, 1952.

Blanchard, Gérard. "Victor Hugo et les graveurs de son temps." *Communication et langages*, no. 62 (1984): 62–85.

Blondel, Madeleine, and Pierre Georgel. *Victor Hugo et les images: Colloque de Dijon*. Dijon: Aux amateurs de livres, 1989.

Bory, Jean-François. *Victor Hugo: Dessins*. Paris: H. Veyrier, 1980.

Burty, Philippe. "Les dessins de Victor Hugo." *L'Art*, no. 37 (1875): 32–38.

Cardinal, Roger. "Victor Hugo, Somnambulist of the Sea." In *Artistic Relations: Literature and the Visual Arts in Nineteenth-Century France*, ed. Peter Collier and Robert Lethbridge, 209–21. New Haven, CT: Yale University Press, 1994.

Cazaumayou, Henri. *Maison de Victor Hugo, dessins de Victor Hugo*. Paris: Paris musées, 1985.

Charles, Corinne. *Victor Hugo: Visions d'intérieurs; Du meuble au décor / Victor Hugo: Interior Visions; From Furniture to Decoration.* Paris: Paris musées, 2003.

Chenay, Paul. *Victor Hugo à Guernesey: Souvenirs inédits de son beau-frère Paul Chenay*. Paris: Félix Juven, 1902.

*Cinquante dessins de Victor Hugo provenant de la collection de Monsieur Jean Hugo*. Sale cat. Sotheby Parke Bernet Monaco S.A., Sporting d'Hiver, Monte Carlo, June 15, 1981.

Clouard, Maurice. "Notes sur les dessins de Victor Hugo accompagnées de lettres inédites." *Revue d'histoire littéraire de la France*, no. 3 (1898): 341–64.

*Collection Hugo, Victor, Georges, Jean et les autres*. Sale cat. Christie's, Paris, April 4, 2012.

Cornaille, Roger, Gaëton Picon, and Georges Herscher. *Victor Hugo dessinateur*. Paris: Éditions du Minotaure, 1963.

Coural, Natalie, Dominique Cordellier, and Hélène Grollemund. *Le papier à l'œuvre*. Paris: Musée du Louvre; Vanves: Hazan, 2011.

Daubray, Cécile. *Victor Hugo et ses correspondants*. Paris: Albin Michel, 1947.

Delalande, Jean. *Dessins de Victor Hugo*. Paris: Maison de Victor Hugo, 1985.

———. *Victor Hugo à Hauteville House*. Paris: Albin Michel, 1947.

———. *Victor Hugo dessinateur génial et halluciné*. Paris: Nouvelles Éditions Latines, 1964.

Dubois, Madeleine. *Victor Hugo et les artistes romantiques*. Exh. cat. Paris: Maison de Victor Hugo, 1951.

Escholier, Raymond. *Victor Hugo artiste.* Paris: Georges Crès, 1926.

———. *Victor Hugo raconté par l'image*. Exh. cat. Paris: Maison de Victor Hugo, 1930.

Femmel, Gerhard, Pierre Georgel, Göran Söderström, and Börje Magnusson. *Diktaren som bildkonstnär: Goethe, Hugo, Strindberg*. Exh. cat. Stockholm: Rabén & Sjögren, 1974.

Focillon, Henri. "Les dessins de Victor Hugo." *Bulletin des Amis de l'Université de Lyon* 27 (March–April 1914): 72–86. Reprinted in Henri Focillon, *Technique et sentiment: Études sur l'art moderne* (Paris: Laurens, 1919), 46–63.

Focillon, Henri, Sandra Costa, and Victor Hugo. *I disegni di Victor Hugo*. Exh. cat. Bologna: Alfa, 1983.

Galerie Aittouarès. *Victor Hugo: Dessins*. Exh. cat. Paris: Galerie Aittouarès, 1993.

Galerie Georges Petit. *Exposition de dessins et manuscrits de Victor Hugo: Au bénéfice de la souscription pour sa statue, mai 1888*. Exh. cat. Paris: Galerie Georges Petit, 1888.

Gaudon, Jean. *Ce que disent les tables parlantes*. Paris: J. J. Pauvert, 1964.

Gautier, Théophile. "M. Victor Hugo dessinateur." *La Presse*, June 27, 1838.

———. "Vente du mobilier de M. Victor Hugo." *La Presse*, June 7, 1852.

Georgel, Pierre. *L'album de Léopoldine Hugo*. Villequier: Musée Victor Hugo, 1967.

———. "'Le bonhomme est charmant . . .': Victor Hugo et les dessins de ses enfants." *Gazette des Beaux-Arts* 111 (January–June 1988): 55–62.

———. *"Cet immense rêve de l'océan": Paysages de mer et autres sujets marins par Victor Hugo*. Exh. cat. Paris: Paris musées, 2005.

———. *Dessins de Victor Hugo*. Exh. cat. Paris: Maison de Victor Hugo, 1971.

———. "Dessins de Victor Hugo dans les collections publiques françaises." *La Revue du Louvre et des Musées de France*, no. 4–5 (1971): 251–68.

———. *Les dessins de Victor Hugo pour les "Travailleurs de la mer" de la Bibliothèque nationale*. Paris: Herscher, 1985.

———. "De Thomas Couture à Jean Valjean: Une lettre de Charles Hugo à son père, Victor Hugo (1843)." In *The Artist and the Writer in France*, ed. Francis Haskell, Anthony Levi, and Robert Shackleton, 100–110. Oxford: Clarendon, 1974.

——. *Drawings by Victor Hugo*. Exh. cat. London: Victoria and Albert Museum, 1974.
——. *1850, Le burg à la croix, Victor Hugo*. Paris: Paris musées and Maison de Victor Hugo, 2007.
——. "Pour l'intimité." In *Usages de l'image au XIXe siècle*, ed. Stéphane Michaud, Jean-Yves Mollier, and Nicole Savy, 184–203. Paris: Créaphis, 1992.
——. "Le romantisme des années 1860: Correspondance Victor Hugo–Philippe Burty." *Revue de l'Art*, no. 20 (1973): 8–64.
——. "Les 'sources' de quelques dessins de Victor Hugo." *Bulletin de la Société de l'Histoire de l'Art Français*, 1971, 281–95.
——. "Victor Hugo: Dessin dit *La bouche d'ombre*." In *Album amicorum: Œuvres choisies pour Arnauld Brejon de Lavergnée*, ed. Valérie Lavergne-Durey. Trouville-sur-Mer: Librairie des Musées, 2012.
——. *Victor Hugo: Dessins*. Paris: Gallimard, 2002.
——. "La vision en silhouette." *L'Arc*, no. 57 (1974): 24–32.
Georgel, Pierre, Jean-Paul Boulanger, and Geneviève Renisio. *La gloire de Victor Hugo*. Exh. cat. Paris: Réunion des musées nationaux, 1985.
Georgel, Pierre, Delphine Gleizes, and Stéphane Guégan, eds. *L'œil de Victor Hugo: Actes du colloque, 19–21 Septembre 2002*. Paris: Éditions des Cendres and Musée d'Orsay, 2004.
Georgel, Pierre, and Sylvia Lorant-Colle. *Victor Hugo et les siens: Deux siècles d'art et d'artistes*. Exh. cat. Arles: Actes sud, 2001.
Grossiord, Sophie. *Victor Hugo: «Et s'il n'en reste qu'un.»* Paris: Gallimard, 1997.
Heilbrun, Françoise, and Danielle Molinari. *En collaboration avec le soleil: Victor Hugo; Photographies de l'exil*. Exh. cat. Paris: Réunion des musées nationaux, Musée d'Orsay, and Maison de Victor Hugo, 1998.
Herscher, Georges. "Papiers découpés de Victor Hugo." *L'Œil*, no. 107 (November 1963): 34–39.
Hoffmann, Léon-François, and Suzanne Nash. *Hugo et l'histoire*. Fasano, Italy: Schena; Paris: Presses de l'Université de Paris-Sorbonne, 2005.
Hovasse, Jean-Marc. *Victor Hugo*. Vol. 1, *Avant l'exil, 1802–1851*, and vol. 2, *Pendant l'exil, 1851–1864*. Paris: Fayard, 2001–8.
Hugo, Adèle, and Victor Hugo. *Victor Hugo raconté par un témoin de sa vie*. Paris: Librairie internationale, 1863.
Hugo, Marie, Laura Hugo, and Jean-Baptiste Hugo. *Hauteville House: Victor Hugo décorateur*. Paris: Paris musées, 2016.
Hugo, Victor. *Récits et dessins de voyage*. Tournai: Renaissance du livre, 2001.
Journet, René, and Guy Robert. *Le manuscrit des Misérables*. Paris: Les Belles Lettres, 1963.
Lafargue, Jacqueline. *Victor Hugo: Dessins et lavis*. Paris: Hervas, 1983.
Lalanne, Maxime. *Chez Victor Hugo par un passant*. Paris: Cadart & Luquet, 1864.
Lautreppe, Le Cocq de. "Victor Hugo, Draftsman and Decorator." *Century Magazine* 58 (July 1899): 428–34.
Lebel, Jean-Jacques, and Marie-Laure Prévost. *«Du chaos dans le pinceau»: Victor Hugo, dessins*. Exh. cat. Paris: Paris musées, 2000.
——. *Victor Hugo: "Caos en el pincel—"; Dibujos*. Exh. cat. Madrid: Museo Thyssen-Bornemisza, 2000.
Lebel, Jean-Jacques, Marie-Laure Prévost, and Laure-Charlotte Feffer Périn. *Victor Hugo, pittore*. Exh. cat. Venice: Mazzotta, 1993.
Le Brun, Annie. *Les arcs-en-ciel du noir: Victor Hugo*. Exh. cat. Paris: Gallimard, 2012.
Lethève, Jacques. "Dessins de Victor Hugo." Special issue, *Textes et Documents*, no. 11 (September 1962).
Leymarie, Jean. *Victor Hugo and the Romantic Vision: Drawings and Watercolors*. Exh. cat. New York: Jan Krugier Gallery, 1990.
Maison de Victor Hugo (Paris). *La cime du rêve: Les surréalistes et Victor Hugo*. Exh. cat. Paris: Paris musées, 2013.
——. *Enfance et jeunesse de Victor Hugo*. Exh. cat. Paris: Maison de Victor Hugo, 1952.
——. *L'esprit de la lettre*. Exh. cat. Paris: Paris musées, 2007.
——. *Exposition du Rhin: Dessins de Victor Hugo*. Exh. cat. Paris, 1919.
——. *Les misérables, 1862–1962*. Exh. cat. Paris: Maison de Victor Hugo, 1962.
——. *Le Rhin: Le voyage de Victor Hugo en 1840*. Exh. cat. Paris: Maison de Victor Hugo, 1985.
——. *Les séjours de Victor Hugo*. Exh. cat. Paris: Maison de Victor Hugo, 1935.
*Maison de Victor Hugo: Catalogue*. Paris: Ville de Paris, 1934.
*Maison de Victor Hugo: Catalogue*. 2nd ed. Paris: Ville de Paris, 1957.
Menard, Marie-Anne. *Hugo, la main du rêve: Dessins du Musée Victor Hugo de Villequier*. Mont-Saint-Aignan: Centre régional de documentation pédagogique de Haute-Normandie, 2001.
Mercié, Jean-Louis. *Victor Hugo et Julie Chenay*. Paris: Lettres modernes, 1967.
Meurice, Paul. "Victor Hugo, Artist." Pt. 2. *Harper's Monthly,* February 1901, 444–52.
Molinari, Danielle. *Maison de Victor Hugo: Museum Guide*. Paris: Paris musées, 2009.
——. *Les Orientales*. Exh. cat. Paris: Paris musées, 2010.
——. *Victor Hugo: Visions graphiques*. Paris: Paris musées, 2010.
Musée Charlier. *Victor Hugo et la Belgique*. Exh. cat. Brussels: Edimco, 1951.
Musée des beaux-arts et d'archéologie (Besançon). *Victor Hugo au musée: Dessins et souvenirs*. Exh. cat. Besançon: Musée des beaux-arts, 1985.
——. *Victor Hugo: Cent cinquantième anniversaire de sa naissance*. Exh. cat. Besançon: Musée des beaux-arts, 1952.
Picon, Gaëtan. *Dessins et ébauches de Victor Hugo: Provenant de la succession Hugo*. Exh. cat. Paris: Galerie Lucie Weill, 1972.
Picon, Gaëtan, Henri Focillon, Geneviève Picon, and Réjane Bargiel. *Victor Hugo: Dessins*. Paris: Gallimard, 1985.
Pierrot, Roger, Judith Petit, and Marie-Laure Prévost. *Soleil d'encre: Manuscrits et dessins de Victor Hugo*. Exh. cat. Paris: Musée du Petit Palais and Bibliothèque nationale de France, 1985.
Planès, Eugène. *Catalogue de la Maison de Victor Hugo*. Paris: Librairies-Imprimeries Réunies, 1907.
Pouchain, Gérard, and Victor Hugo. *Promenades en Normandie: Avec un guide nommé Victor Hugo*. Condé-sur-Noireau: C. Corlet, 1983.
Prat, Louis-Antoine. "L'autre génie de Victor Hugo (1802–1885)." In *Le dessin français au XIXe siècle*, 392–403. Paris: Louvres éditions, Musée d'Orsay, and Somogy, 2011.
Prévost, Marie-Laure. *Victor Hugo: L'homme océan*. Exh. cat. Paris: Bibliothèque nationale de France and Seuil, 2002.
Recht, Roland, Gennaro Toscano, and Fabien Jamois, eds. *Victor Hugo et le débat patrimonial: Actes du colloque*. Paris: Maison de l'UNESCO, 2003.

Rodari, Florian. *Victor Hugo: Dessins visionnaires*. Exh. cat. Lausanne: Fondation de l'Hermitage; Milan: 5 Continents, 2008.

———. *Victor Hugo, précurseur a posteriori: Encres de Victor Hugo*. Villeurbanne: URDLA, 2007.

Rodari, Florian, Pierre Georgel, Luc Sante, and Marie-Laure Prévost. *Shadows of a Hand: The Drawings of Victor Hugo*. Exh. cat. New York: Drawing Center; London: Merrell Holberton, 1998.

Rosenberg, Raphael. "Was There a First Abstract Painter? Af Klint's Amimetic Images and Kandinsky's Abstract Art." In *Hilma af Klint: The Art of Seeing the Invisible,* ed. Kurt Almqvist and Louise Belfrage, 87–100, 322–23. Stockholm: Axel and Margaret Ax:son Johnson Foundation, 2015.

Rosenberg, Raphael, and Max Hollein. *Turner, Hugo, Moreau: Entdeckung der Abstraktion*. Exh. cat. Frankfurt: Schirn Kunsthalle; Munich: Hirmer, 2007.

Rosi, Arlette, and Marie-Laure Prévost. *Victor Hugo, dessinateur (1802–1885)*. Exh. cat. Brussels: Musée d'Ixelles, 1999.

Seghers, Pierre. *Victor Hugo visionnaire*. Paris: Robert Laffont, 1983.

Sergent, Jean. *Dessins de Victor Hugo*. Paris: Palatine, 1955.

———. *Notice sur trois dessins de Victor Hugo: Le pendu ou John Brown*. Paris: Hemmerlé, 1952.

Sergent, Jean, and Madeleine Dubois. *Maturité de Victor Hugo, 1828–1848*. Exh. cat. Paris: Maison de Victor Hugo, 1953.

Simon, Gustav. *Visite à la Maison de Victor Hugo*. Paris: Ollendorf, 1904.

Solente, Suzanne. *Bibliothèque nationale, nouvelles acquisitions latines et françaises du Département des Manuscrits (1951–57)*. Exh. cat. Paris: Bibliothèque nationale, 1960.

Stahl, Marguerite, and Alexandre Péraud. *Victor Hugo (1802–1885): Photographies et dessins gravés*. Exh. cat. Bordeaux: Conseil général de la Gironde, 2002.

Sueur-Hermel, Valérie. "Fortuné Méaulle, interprète de Victor Hugo, ou la gravure sur bois au service du 'choc des rayons et des ombres.'" *Nouvelles de l'estampe*, no. 185–86 (December 2002–February 2003): 32–45.

Szeemann, Harald. *Aubes: Rêveries au bord de Victor Hugo*. Exh. cat. Paris: Paris musées, 2002.

———. *Victor Hugo (1802–1885): Phantasien in Tusche*. Exh. cat. Zurich: Kunsthaus Zürich, 1987.

Tébar Avila, Victoria. "Concepción técnica en los dibujos de paisaje de Victor Hugo." PhD diss., Universitat de Barcelona, Facultat de Belles Arts, 2001.

Thompson, C. W. *Victor Hugo and the Graphic Arts, 1820–1833*. Geneva: Librairie Droz, 1970.

Université Rennes 2. *Toujours en ramenant la plume: Les travailleurs de la mer; L'œuvre graphique de Victor Hugo*. http://www.ressources.univ-rennes2.fr/toujours-en-ramenant-la-plume/.

Vacquerie, Auguste. *Profils et grimaces*. Paris: Michel Lévy frères, 1856.

*Victor Hugo raconté par l'image*. Exh. cat. Paris: Maison de Victor Hugo, 1930.

Ville de Paris. *Victor Hugo en exil*. Exh. cat. Paris, 1955.

Vouga, Daniel. *Victor Hugo: Dessins et ébauches*. Exh. cat. Neuchâtel: Attinger, 1972.

Weiss, René. *La Maison de Victor Hugo à Guernesey (Hauteville-House)*. Paris: Imprimerie nationale, 1928.

Wild, Adolf. *Victor Hugo und Deutschland: Zeichnungen—Bücher—Dokumente*. Exh. cat. Mainz: Schmidt, 1990.

Wipplinger, Hans-Peter, and Ivan Ristić. *Victor Hugo: Der schwarze Romantiker / The Dark Romanticist.* Exh. cat. Cologne: Walther König, 2017.

# SELECTED EXHIBITION HISTORY

**1888**
*Exposition des dessins et manuscrits de Victor Hugo: Au bénéfice de la souscription pour sa statue*, Galerie Georges Petit, Paris, May 1888

**1919**
*Exposition du Rhin*, Maison de Victor Hugo, Paris, 1919–20

**1930**
*Victor Hugo raconté par l'image*, Maison de Victor Hugo, Paris, June–August 1930

**1935**
*Les séjours de Victor Hugo*, Maison de Victor Hugo, Paris, May 17–July 14, 1935

**1951**
*Dessins de Victor Hugo des collections de la Maison de Victor Hugo*, Musée Rath, Geneva, May 15–June 17, 1951
*Victor Hugo et les artistes romantiques*, Maison de Victor Hugo, Paris, June 23–September 2, 1951
*Victor Hugo et la Belgique*, Musée Charlier, Saint-Josse-ten-Noode, Belgium, December 15, 1951–January 14, 1952

**1952**
*Enfance et jeunesse de Victor Hugo*, Maison de Victor Hugo, Paris, May 1952
*Victor Hugo: Exposition organisée pour commémorer le cent cinquantième anniversaire de sa naissance*, Bibliothèque nationale de France, Paris, June 20–October 20, 1952
*Victor Hugo: Cent cinquantième anniversaire de sa naissance*, Musée des Beaux-Arts, Besançon, September–October 1952

**1953**
*Maturité de Victor Hugo, 1828–1848*, Maison de Victor Hugo, Paris, May–July 1953

**1955**
*Victor Hugo en exil*, Hauteville House, Guernsey, June–October 1955

**1962**
*Les misérables, 1862–1962*, Maison de Victor Hugo, Paris, November 1962–February 1963

**1971**
*Dessins de Victor Hugo,* Musée Victor Hugo, Villequier, June–October 1971; Maison de Victor Hugo, Paris, November 1971–January 1972

**1972**
*Dessins et ébauches de Victor Hugo provenant de la succession Hugo*, Galerie Lucie Weill, Paris, February 16–March 21, 1972
*Victor Hugo: Dessins et ébauches*, Musée d'Art et d'Histoire, Neuchâtel, June 30–September 17, 1972

**1974**
*Drawings by Victor Hugo*, Victoria and Albert Museum, London, February 28–April 14, 1974
*Diktare, bildkonstnärer: Goethe, Hugo, Strindberg,* Nationalmuseum, Stockholm, October–December 1974

**1983**
*I disegni di Victor Hugo*, Palazzo Pepoli Campogrande, Bologna, September 10–October 15, 1983

**1985**
*Le Rhin: Le voyage de Victor Hugo en 1840*, Maison de Victor Hugo, Paris, March 25–June 29, 1985
*Victor Hugo au musée: Dessins et souvenirs*, Musée des Beaux-Arts, Besançon, April 28–June 13, 1985
*Victor Hugo et la Normandie*, Musée Victor Hugo, Villequier, June–October 1985
*La gloire de Victor Hugo*, Galeries nationales du Grand Palais, Paris, October 1, 1985–January 6, 1986
*Soleil d'encre: Manuscrits et dessins de Victor Hugo*, Musée du Petit Palais, Paris, October 3, 1985–January 5, 1986

**1987**
*Victor Hugo (1802–1885): Phantasien in Tusche*, Kunsthaus Zürich, June 5–August 23, 1987

**1990**
*Victor Hugo und Deutschland: Zeichnungen, Bücher, Dokumente*, Gutenberg-Museum, Mainz, February 6–March 31, 1990
*Victor Hugo and the Romantic Vision*, Jan Krugier Gallery, New York, May 4–July 27, 1990; Galerie Jan Krugier, Geneva, January–February 1991

**1993**
*Victor Hugo pittore*, Galleria d'Arte Moderna, Ca' Pesaro, Venice, March 13–May 23, 1993
*Victor Hugo: Dessins*, Galerie Aittouarès, Paris, October 30–November 30, 1993

**1996**
*Le siècle de Victor Hugo*, Odakyu Museum, Tokyo, July 24–August 11, 1996; Kintetsu Art Museum, Osaka, August 23–September 4, 1996; Koriyama Art Museum, October 5–November 10, 1996; Hiroshima Art Museum, November 16–December 23, 1996

**1998**

*Shadows of a Hand: The Drawings of Victor Hugo,* Drawing Center, New York, April 16–June 13, 1998

*"En collaboration avec le soleil": Victor Hugo; Photographies de l'exil*, Musée d'Orsay and Maison de Victor Hugo, Paris, October 27, 1998–January 24, 1999

**1999**

*Victor Hugo dessinateur*, Musée d'Ixelles, Brussels, February 5–April 25, 1999

**2000**

*Caos en el pincel . . . : Victor Hugo, dibujos / Du chaos dans le pinceau . . . : Victor Hugo, dessins*, Museo Thyssen-Bornemisza, Madrid, June 2–September 10, 2000; Maison de Victor Hugo, Paris, October 12, 2000–January 7, 2001

**2002**

*Victor Hugo et les siens: Deux siècles d'art et d'artistes*, Galerie d'art du Conseil Général des Bouches-du-Rhône, Aix-en-Provence, January 10–April 7, 2002

*Victor Hugo: L'homme océan*, Bibliothèque nationale de France, Paris, March 21–June 23, 2002

*Aubes: Rêveries au bord de Victor Hugo*, Maison de Victor Hugo, Paris, October 19, 2002–January 19, 2003

*Victor Hugo (1802–1885): Photographies et dessins gravés*, Salle des Voûtes Poyennes, Bordeaux, November 4–December 14, 2002

**2005**

*"Cet immense rêve de l'océan": Paysages de mer et autres sujets marins par Victor Hugo*, Maison de Victor Hugo, Paris, December 2, 2005–March 5, 2006

**2007**

*Turner—Hugo—Moreau: Entdeckung der Abstraktion*, Schirn Kunsthalle, Frankfurt, October 6, 2007–January 6, 2008

*L'esprit de la lettre*, Maison de Victor Hugo, Paris, October 26, 2007–February 3, 2008

**2008**

*Victor Hugo: Dessins visionnaires*, Fondation de l'Hermitage, Lausanne, February 1–May 18, 2008

*Victor Hugo: Visionen eines Schriftstellers*, Schiller-Museum Klassik Stiftung Weimar, May 16–July 27, 2008

**2010**

*Les Orientales*, Maison de Victor Hugo, Paris, March 26–July 4, 2010

**2011**

*Arnulf Rainer, Victor Hugo: Surpeintures*, Maison de Victor Hugo, Paris, October 6, 2011–January 15, 2012

**2012**

*Les arcs-en-ciel du noir: Invitation à Annie Le Brun*, Maison de Victor Hugo, Paris, March 15–August 19, 2012

*Entrée des médiums: Spiritisme et art de Hugo à Breton*, Maison de Victor Hugo, Paris, October 18, 2012–January 20, 2013

**2013**

*La cime du rêve: Les surréalistes et Victor Hugo*, Maison de Victor Hugo, Paris, October 17, 2013–February 16, 2014

**2014**

*Victor Hugo: Du côté du gothique*, Musée départemental Victor Hugo, Maison Vacquerie, Villequier, April 12–July 6, 2014

*Victor Hugo: Les Misérables; From Page to Stage,* State Library of Victoria, Melbourne, July 18–November 9, 2014

**2015**

*Louis Soutter, Victor Hugo: Dessins parallèles*, Maison de Victor Hugo, Paris, April 30–August 30, 2015

**2017**

*Victor Hugo: Der schwarze Romantiker / The Dark Romanticist*, Leopold Museum, Vienna, November 17, 2017–January 15, 2018

## LENDERS TO THE EXHIBITION

The Art Institute of Chicago
Frances Beatty and Allen Adler
Bibliothèque nationale de France
Fundación Almine y Bernard Ruiz-Picasso para el Arte
David Lachenmann
Maisons de Victor Hugo, Paris / Guernesey
Maison Vacquerie–Musée Victor Hugo, Villequier
The Metropolitan Museum of Art, New York
The Morgan Library & Museum, New York
Musée des Beaux-Arts de Dijon
Musée d'Orsay, Paris
Nationalmuseum Stockholm
Véronique and Louis-Antoine Prat
Gordon VeneKlasen
Yale University Art Gallery
And private lenders who wish to remain anonymous

## CONTRIBUTORS

**Cynthia Burlingham** is deputy director of curatorial affairs at the Hammer Museum. She is also director of the Grunwald Center for the Graphic Arts, Hammer Museum.

**Allegra Pesenti** is associate director and senior curator of the Grunwald Center for the Graphic Arts, Hammer Museum.

**Florian Rodari** is an independent scholar and curator.

**Matthieu Vahanian** is a curatorial assistant at the Grunwald Center for the Graphic Arts, Hammer Museum.

## HAMMER MUSEUM

## ILLUSTRATION CREDITS

Front and back covers: *Taches* (Stains), ca. 1875(?) (detail; see pp. 182–83).

Front endpapers: Charles Hugo (French, 1826–1871). *Victor Hugo au Dicq, Jersey* (Victor Hugo at the Dicq, Jersey), ca. 1853 (detail; see p. 129).

Back endpapers: *Brise-lames à Jersey* (A breakwater in Jersey), ca. 1854–55 (detail; see p. 128).

Page 2: *Silhouette de château illuminé par un orage* (Silhouette of a castle illuminated by lightning), ca. 1854–57(?) (detail; see p. 85).

Page 4: *Planète-œil* (Planet-eye), ca. 1854–55 (detail; see p. 143).

Page 8: *Taches avec empreintes de doigts* (Abstract composition with fingerprints), ca. 1864–65 (detail; see p. 163).

Pages 68–69: *Les Needles, île de Wight* (The Needles, Isle of Wight), 1865 (detail; see p. 125).

Page 70: *Souvenir de Suisse* (Souvenir of Switzerland), ca. 1854–55 (detail; see p. 97).

Page 120: *Marine avec bateau à voile et figure monstrueuse dans le ciel* (Seascape with sailboat and a monstrous figure in the sky), pasted in *Les travailleurs de la mer*, vol. 2 of *Œuvres complètes* (Paris: Hetzel, 1880–83), ca. 1874–78 (detail; see p. 133).

Page 140: *Planète* (Planet), ca. 1854 (detail; see p. 151).

Page 152: *Justitia* (Justice), 1857 (detail; see p. 159).

Page 160: *Tête de diable* (Head of a devil), ca. 1864–69 (detail; see p. 181).

Page 190: *Taches* (Stains), ca. 1875(?) (detail; see p. 167).

Page 196: *Souvenir d'un burg des Vosges* (Souvenir of a castle in the Vosges), 1857 (detail; see p. 86).

## REPRODUCTION CREDITS

© The Art Institute of Chicago / image source, Art Resource, NY: 55 (right), 75

© Bibliothèque nationale de France: 2, 4, 8, 24, 25, 26, 30, 32, 33, 36, 41 (left) 42, 43, 48, 58, 68–69, 78–79, 80, 81, 85, 89, 92–93, 99, 102 (left), 111, 113, 125, 135, 137, 143, 163, 166, 167, 168, 182–83, 190

© Camerart / Alister Alexander: 77

© CNAC / MNAM / Dist. RMN–Grand Palais / Art Resource, NY; photo Philippe Migeat: 56, 57

© FABA; photo Hugard & Vanoverschelde: 160, 181

© Christophe Fouin: 103, 147, 149, 172, 177

Digital image courtesy Getty Open Content Program: 64, 65

© Hammer Museum, Los Angeles: 63 (left), 123

© Maisons de Victor Hugo, Paris / Guernesey / Roger-Viollet: 17, 19, 20, 22, 23, 35, 38, 39, 41 (right), 49 (bottom), 50, 53, 55 (left), 70, 74, 83, 97, 100, 102 (right), 107, 109, 110, 115, 116, 117, 119, 124, 127, 128, 131, 134, 136, 139, 152, 154, 155, 156, 157, 159, 165, 169, 171, 174, 179

© Maison Vacquerie–Musée Victor Hugo, Villequier-Dépt. 76: 14, 175

The Metropolitan Museum of Art / CC0 1.0 Universal (CC0 1.0) Public Domain Dedication: 61

© The Metropolitan Museum of Art / image source, Art Resource, NY: 86, 196

© Musée des Beaux-Arts de Dijon; photo François Jay: 173

Nationalmuseum Stockholm: 178 (photo Cecilia Heisser); 46, 144, 145 (photo Hans Thorwid)

New York University Archives: 62

Photo by Allegra Pesenti: 49 (top)

© The Pierpont Morgan Library, New York: 120, 133

Photo by Adam Reich: 82, 105

© RMN-Grand Palais / Art Resource, NY: 51 (photo Gérard Blot); 91, 95, 98, 101, 129 (photo Hervé Lewandowski); 184 (photo Patrice Schmidt)

Universitätsbibliothek Heidelberg: 63 (right)

Yale University Art Gallery: 73

# INDEX

Page numbers in *italics* refer to captions for figures and plates. The abbreviation *VH* refers to Victor Hugo.

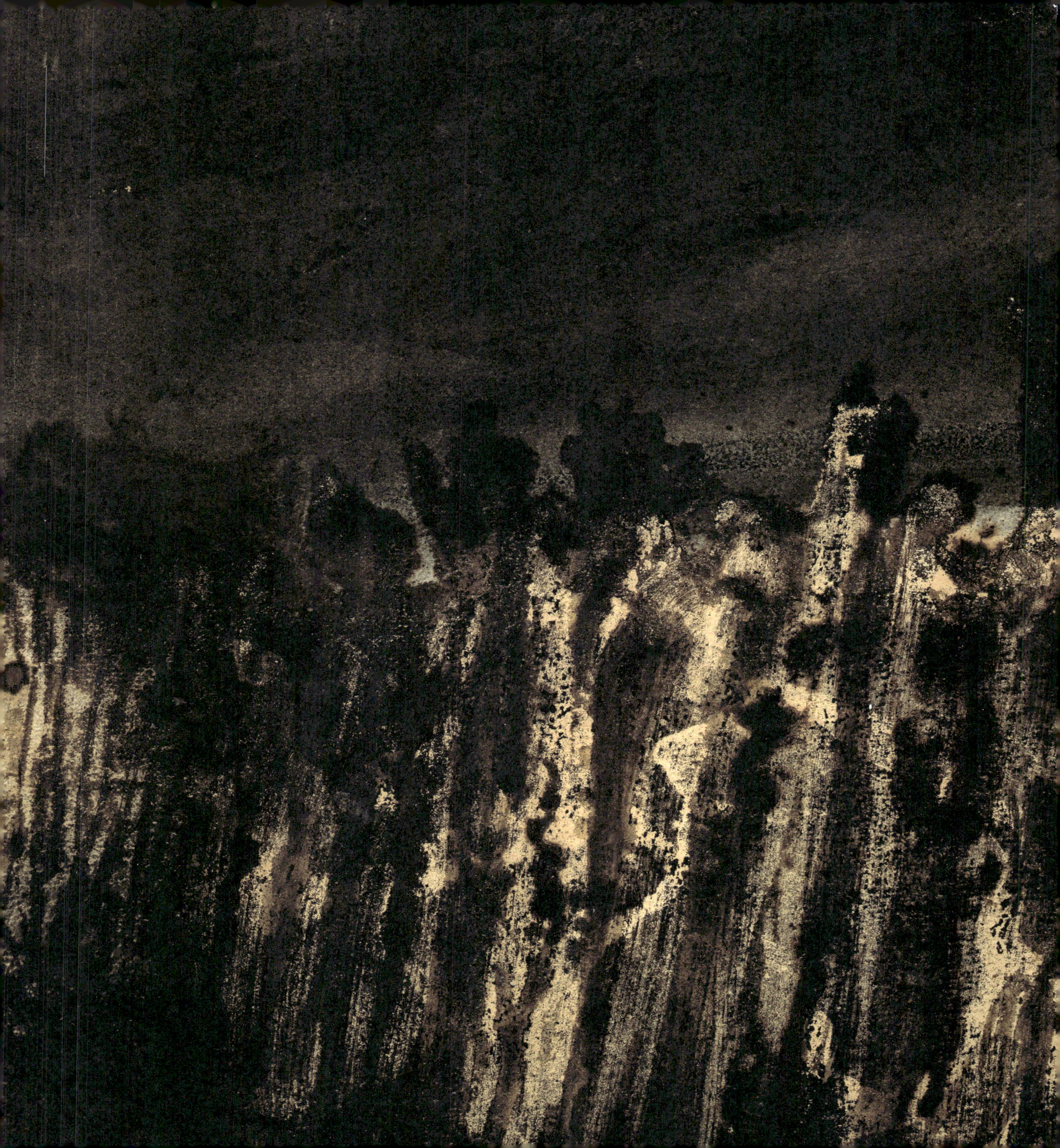